ANNUAL EDITIONS

Psychology

Thirty-seventh Edition

S0-BJJ-408

07/08

EDITOR

Karen G. Duffy

SUNY at Geneseo (Emerita)

Karen G. Duffy holds a doctorate in psychology from Michigan State University, and she is an emerita Distinguished Service Professor of State University of New York at Geneseo. Dr. Duffy continues to work on her books and research, and she is also involved in several community service projects both in the United States and Russia.

Contemporary Learning Series

2460 Kerper Blvd., Dubuque, IA 52001

Visit us on the Internet
http://www.mhcls.com

Credits

1. **The Science of Psychology**
   Unit photo—Chad Baker/Getty Images
2. **Biological Bases of Behavior**
   Unit photo—Royalty-Free/CORBIS
3. **Perceptual Processes**
   Unit photo—Thinkstock Images/Jupiter Images
4. **Learning and Remembering**
   Unit photo—Getty Images
5. **Cognitive Processes**
   Unit photo—Image 100 Ltd.
6. **Emotion and Motivation**
   Unit photo—Goodshoot/PictureQuest
7. **Development**
   Unit photo—Photodisc
8. **Personality Processes**
   Unit photo—Library of Congress (LC-USZ62-72266)
9. **Social Processes**
   Unit photo—Getty Images
10. **Psychological Disorders**
    Unit photo—U.S. Army photo by Master Sgt. Johancharles Van Boers
11. **Psychological Treatments**
    Unit photo—Royalty-Free/CORBIS

Copyright

Cataloging in Publication Data
Main entry under title: Annual Editions: Psychology. 2007/2008.
1. Psychology—Periodicals. I. Duffy, Karen G., *comp.* II. Title: Psychology.
ISBN-13: 978–0–07–351629–5   ISBN-10: 0–07–351629–5   658'.05   ISSN 0272–3794

Thirty-seventh Edition

Cover image © Photos.com
Printed in the United States of America   1234567890QPDQPD9876   Printed on Recycled Paper

Editors/Advisory Board

Members of the Advisory Board are instrumental in the final selection of articles for each edition of ANNUAL EDITIONS. Their review of articles for content, level, currentness, and appropriateness provides critical direction to the editor and staff. We think that you will find their careful consideration well reflected in this volume.

EDITOR

Karen G. Duffy
SUNY at Geneseo (Emerita)

ADVISORY BOARD

Staff

Preface

In publishing ANNUAL EDITIONS we recognize the enormous role played by the magazines, newspapers, and journals of the public press in providing current, first-rate educational information in a broad spectrum of interest areas. Many of these articles are appropriate for students, researchers, and professionals seeking accurate, current material to help bridge the gap between principles and theories and the real world. These articles, however, become more useful for study when those of lasting value are carefully collected, organized, indexed, and reproduced in a low-cost format, which provides easy and permanent access when the material is needed. That is the role played by ANNUAL EDITIONS.

Ronnie's parents couldn't understand why he didn't want to be picked up and cuddled as did his older sister when she was a baby. As an infant, Ronnie did not respond to his parents' smiles, words, or attempts to amuse him. By the age of two, Ronnie's parents knew that he was not like other children. He spoke no English, was very temperamental, and often rocked himself for hours. Ronnie is autistic. His parents feel that some of Ronnie's behavior may be their fault. As young professionals, they both work long hours and leave both of their children with an older woman during the work week. Ronnie's pediatrician assures his parents that their reasoning does not hold merit, because the causes of autism are little understood and are likely to be biological rather than parental. What can we do about children like Ronnie? From where does autism come? Can autism be treated or reversed? Can autism be prevented?

Psychologists attempt to answer these and other complex questions with scientific methods. Researchers, using carefully planned research designs, try to discover the causes of complex human behavior—normal or not. The scientific results of psychological research typically are published in professional journals, and therefore may be difficult for the lay person to understand.

Annual Editions: Psychology 07/08 is designed to meet the needs of lay people and introductory level students who are curious about psychology. This Annual Edition provides a vast selection of readable and informative articles primarily from popular magazines and newspapers. These articles are typically written by journalists, but a few are written by psychologists with writing styles that are clear yet retain the excitement of the discovery of scientific knowledge.

The particular articles selected for this volume were chosen to be representative of the most current work in psychology. They were selected because they provide examples of the types of psychological research and issues discussed in most introductory psychology classes. As in any science, some of the topics discussed in this collection are startling, while others confirm what we already know. Some articles invite speculation about social and personal issues; others encourage careful thought about potential misuse of research findings. You are expected to make the investment of effort and critical reasoning necessary to answer such questions and concerns.

I assume that you will find this collection of articles readable and useful. I suggest that you look at the organization of this book and compare it to the organization of your textbook and course syllabus. By examining the topic guide provided after the table of contents, you can identify those articles most appropriate for any particular unit of study in your course. Your instructor may provide some help in this effort or assign articles to supplement the text. As you read the articles, try to connect their contents with the principles you are learning from your text and classroom lectures. Some of the articles will help you better understand a specific area of psychology, while others are designed to help you connect and integrate information from diverse research areas. Both of these strategies are important in learning about psychology or any other science; it is only through intensive investigation and subsequent integration of the findings from many studies that we are able to discover and apply new knowledge.

Please take time to provide us with some feedback to guide the annual revision of this anthology by completing and returning the article rating form in the back of the book. With your help, this collection will be even better next year. Thank you.

Karen Grover Duffy

Karen Grover Duffy
Editor

Contents

Preface   iv

Topic Guide   xi

Internet References   xiii

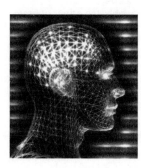

UNIT 1
The Science of Psychology

Unit Overview   xvi

1. **Why Study Psychology?,** Linda M. Bartoshuk et al., *APS Observer,* May 2004

   Four well-known *psychologists* describe why they studied psychology and how they are currently using their training. Each psychologist works in a different but important *subfield of psychology*.   3

2. **Does Psychology Make a Significant Difference in Our Lives?,** Philip G. Zimbardo, *American Psychologist,* July/August 2004

   Noted psychologist Philip Zimbardo argues that *psychology* indeed does make a difference in our lives. Psychologists, however, need to continue to "give psychology away" to the public. Zimbardo highlights psychology's achievements in the fields of *testing, behavior change, therapy, life-span development, parenting, stress, the unconscious, work, and prejudice*. He also highlights areas where psychology can make notable differences in the future, for example preventing the spread of *AIDS*.   6

3. **The 10 Commandments of Helping Students Distinguish Science from Pseudoscience in Psychology,** Scott O. Lilienfield, *APS Observer,* September 2005

   Author Scott Lilienfield contends that beginning psychology students believe that the term "psychology" is synonymous with popular psychology, a discipline not firmly grounded in science. Lilienfield continues that students should learn to be skeptical about *popular psychology* and to learn to discriminate *good science and sound psychology* from *pseudoscience* and psychology as presented in the mass media.   19

4. **Causes and Correlations,** Massimo Pigliucci, *Skeptical Inquirer,* January/February 2003

   This article reminds the reader to *think critically about science*. Too many phenomena, such as ESP (extra-sensory perception), are explained post hoc. Few lay people understand the difference between *correlation* and *causation*. The author reviews these two concepts and also explains *control, experimentation, and statistical inference*.   24

UNIT 2
Biological Bases of Behavior

Unit Overview   26

5. **The Amazing Brain: Is Neuroscience the Key to What Makes Us Human?,** Richard Restak, *The Washington Times,* September 5, 2004

   Neuroscience is helping psychologists and other scientists understand *the brain* and its functions. Important discoveries are helping researchers and practitioners make sense out of seemingly incomprehensible *neurological syndromes* now that we know more about *neural pathways* in the brain.   28

The concepts in bold italics are developed in the article. For further expansion, please refer to the Topic Guide and the Index.

6. **Genetic Influence on Human Psychological Traits,** Thomas J. Bouchard, Jr., *Current Directions in Psychological Science,* August 2004
A large body of evidence supports the conclusion that *individual differences* in many psychological characteristics, normal or not, are influenced by *genetic factors*. Bouchard reviews why the study of genetics is important to psychology and then proved estimates of the magnitude of genetic influence on various traits such as *intelligence, interests, mental health, personality, and social attitudes.*   **30**

7. **The Structure of the Human Brain,** John S. Allen, Joel Bruss, and Hanna Damasio, *American Scientist,* May/June 2004
Various *brain-imaging technologies* have now made possible *the study of brain structure and function*. Studies are revealing information about *brain development, differences and similarities between the sexes*, and other matters related to *the size and shape of the brain.*   **35**

UNIT 3
Perceptual Processes

Unit Overview   **40**

8. **Sensational Tune-ups,** Sid Kirchheimer, *AARP Magazine,* September/October 2005
There are a myriad of ways to *protect and improve many of our senses*, such as *sight, audition, olfaction, and taste*. Simple strategies such as loosening one's necktie, taking vitamins, wearing ear plugs, and exercising regularly help keep our senses sharp and thus make our lives richer.   **43**

9. **Eye Wise: Seeing Into the Future,** Bonnie Liebman, *Nutrition Action Health Letter,* November 2004
Vision loss is not inevitable, although some loss occurs with age. Mounting evidence indicates that proper care and nutrition can help to maintain healthy vision. This article covers *eye problems* such as *cataracts and macular degeneration*. First, the article explains what these maladies are, then covers the causes for them, and finally reviews how such problems might be prevented.   **45**

10. **A Matter of Taste,** Mary Beckman, *Smithsonian,* August 2004
The author reviews the research of psychologist Linda Bartoshuk who studies *taste*. She has discovered "*supertasters*", individuals who have many taste buds (papillae on their tongues) and whose taste experiences are intense. Bartoshuck also discovered that *taste sensitivity* can affect *health* via the foods people prefer.   **50**

11. **Extreme States,** Steven Kotler, *Discover,* July 2005
Out-of-body and near-death experiences are part of the parcel of the *parapsychological phenomena* that have fascinated people for centuries. Psychologists armed with new *brain imaging techniques* are just beginning to understand how and why these experiences occur.   **52**

UNIT 4
Learning and Remembering

Unit Overview   **56**

12. **Teaching for Understanding,** Tom Sherman and Barbara Kurshan, *Learning & Leading with Technology,* December 2004
The authors review several important *principles of learning* and then explore how teachers can and should implement the principles. These same principles can be employed even when *technology* is used in the classroom. The important concept of *metacognition* is also considered.   **59**

The concepts in bold italics are developed in the article. For further expansion, please refer to the Topic Guide and the Index.

13. **Memory Flexibility,** Sadie F. Dingfelder, *Monitor on Psychology,* September 2005

Working memory is that part of memory that can be accessed and of which we are aware at any given moment. It affects *how much information we can manage or process* at any given moment. Researchers are studying *how to improve working memory*, which would benefit everyone from chess masters to learning-disabled children.   **63**

14. **Theory of Multiple Intelligences: Is It a Scientific Theory?,** Jie-Qi Chen, *Teachers College Record,* January 2004

This valuable article reviews what a *theory* is, *the purpose of a theory, how a theory is validated*, as well as the theory of *multiple intelligences* and whether it is a credible contribution to psychology and education.   **72**

UNIT 5
Cognitive Processes

Unit Overview   **76**

15. **Shouldn't There Be a Word...?,** Barbara Wallraff, *The American Scholar,* Spring 2006

With a practiced eye, Wallraff looks at *the development of various worldwide languages*. From Shakespeare to lay people, individuals are busy adding new words to their native tongues. The addition of such words might just reveal something about our *inner lives*.   **78**

16. **What Was I Thinking?,** Eric Jaffe, *APS Observer,* May 2004

Nobel Laureate and psychologist Daniel Kahneman's remarks at the National Institute of Health are reviewed by Eric Jaffe. Kahneman purposely flawed his talk to demonstrate that flawed thinking plays no favorites, even with Nobel Laureates. Kahneman's studies of *expert intuitions* have found that under certain conditions, such as being overly confident, even experts are subject to *cognitive mistakes*.   **85**

17. **Mysteries of the Mind,** Marianne Szegedy-Maszak, *U.S. News & World Report,* February 28, 2005

According to this article, our inner lives are rich and interesting but often inaccessible. As *Freud* suggested, much of our everyday behavior is not *conscious or volitionally controlled*. Brain imaging and other forms of innovative research are leading the way toward understanding what may occur in *the unconscious*.   **88**

UNIT 6
Emotion and Motivation

Unit Overview   **92**

18. **Unconscious Emotion,** Piotr Winkielman and Kent C. Berridge, *Current Directions in Psychological Science,* 2004

Traditionally, psychologists believed that *emotions* are consciously experienced and thus provide awareness of each emotion. Research in *evolutionary psychology, subliminal stimulation, and neuroscience* now indicates that *emotions can be unconscious* and therefore remain inaccessible to introspection.   **95**

19. **Feeling Smart: The Science of Emotional Intelligence,** Daisy Grewal and Peter Salovey, *American Scientist,* July/August 2005

The study of *emotional intelligence* (EQ) has come of age in that there is a substantial amount of research on the concept. Not only can emotional intelligence be defined and *measured*, EQ has *practical implications* for everyday life.   **99**

The concepts in bold italics are developed in the article. For further expansion, please refer to the Topic Guide and the Index.

20. **The Value of Positive Emotions,** Barbara L. Fredrickson, *American Scientist,* July/August 2003

Positive psychology has taken root in mainstream psychology. Psychologists are being urged to study human *resilience* and *well-being* instead of typical and mostly negative human elements of past interest. The author of this article examines the history of the study of negativity and illuminates the reader about what positive psychology has to offer by way of science.   **106**

21. **Ambition: Why Some People Are Most Likely to Succeed,** Jeffrey Kluger, *Time,* November 14, 2005

Ambition or achievement motivation, as psychologists label it, varies by the individual and the culture. Some aspects of it appear to be *learned* but other aspects may be *inherited*. Nonetheless, it is what gives us the drive to succeed.   **112**

22. **Obesity—An Epidemic of the Twenty-First Century: An Update for Psychiatrists,** Richard I.G. Holt, *Journal of Psychopharmacology,* 2005

Written in a readable fashion, a physician leads readers through an introduction to the *causes of and problems related to obesity*. Causes range from *environmental changes to personality dimensions to biological syndromes*. The author also examines why obesity is an important problem to be reckoned with in contemporary society.   **118**

UNIT 7
Development

Unit Overview   **128**

23. **Why Newborns Cause Acrimony and Alimony,** Dolores Puterbaugh, *USA Today Magazine,* May 2005

While couples look forward to their *first child*, social scientists are finding that newborns cause increased *distress for new parents*. Why this is so is revealed in this enlightening article.   **130**

24. **The Methuselah Report,** Wayne Curtis, *AARP Bulletin,* July/August 2004

Scientists are finding ways to help us *live longer*. But is such a goal desirable? The important questions are, "Will we extend the number of days we live or actually extend the usefulness of our lives?" Author Wayne Curtis replies that the answer is complex; when we live longer, our *patterns of housing, work, interpersonal relationships, and other factors must also change*.   **134**

25. **A Peaceful Adolescence,** Barbara Kantrowitz and Karen Springen, *Newsweek,* April 25, 2005

Adolescence need not be a time of high drama or *conflict between parents and children*. Research shows that many teens escape their adolescence without getting into trouble. Several factors such as *confidence* and *competence* predict who will and will not fare well.   **137**

26. **Ageless Aging: The Next Era of Retirement,** Ken Dychtwald, *The Futurist,* July/August 2005

The *baby boomers* are expected to live longer than any previous generation. Because of their sheer size and *longevity* of their cohort group they are going to rewrite how Americans retire, rehire, stay well, and find sufficient income to live on.   **139**

27. **The Borders of Healing,** Marianne Szegedy-Maszak, *U.S. News & World Report,* January 17, 2005

Each culture has its own way of *coping with grief*. Major differences are thought to exist between *Eastern (interdependent) and Western (independent) cultures* in how *mourning* occurs. This interesting article provides a close look at attendant *cultural differences*, for example in *how people communicate and whether they seek social support* in times of loss.   **144**

The concepts in bold italics are developed in the article. For further expansion, please refer to the Topic Guide and the Index.

UNIT 8
Personality Processes

Unit Overview   **146**

28. **Freud in Our Midst,** Jerry Adler, *Newsweek,* March 27, 2006
    Jerry Adler reviews the criticism of as well as the advancements provided by
    Freudian (psychoanalytic) theory. The article also provides an excellent "family
    tree" for several *other psychological theories* as well as a glossary of terms
    that trace back to Freud but which are found in common parlance today.   **148**

29. **Exploding the Self-Esteem Myth,** Roy F. Baumeister, Jennifer D.
    Campbell, Joachim I. Krueger, and Kathleen D. Vohs, *Scientific Amer-
    ican,* January 2005
    High self-esteem is a good thing according to humanistic psychologists and ed-
    ucators who try to instill it in America's children. "But is it necessarily good?"
    question the authors of this article. Baumeister and his colleagues sort through
    the *scientific literature* on high self-esteem and its effect on various behaviors
    such as *teen sexuality, bullying, and school performance* and conclude that
    its influence is mixed at best.   **151**

30. **The Testing of America,** Caroline Hsu, *U.S. News & World Report,*
    September 20, 2004
    All of us have been administered *psychological tests* whether we know it or not.
    Personality tests, although among the most debated of tests, are popular screen-
    ing devices for personnel managers and other seeking shortcuts to understanding
    another individual. Controversy swirls not just around the quality and *standard-
    ization of the tests* but also around *the interpretation of test results*.   **154**

UNIT 9
Social Processes

Unit Overview   **156**

31. **To Err Is Human,** Bruce Bower, *Science News,* August 14, 2004
    Classic studies in social psychology are still causing a stir. *Milgram's obedi-
    ence to authority research, Zimbardo's prison study, and Latane and Darley's
    bystander apathy studies*, among others, all point to human flaws and foibles.
    Criticism of these studies and their conclusions have spawned further re-
    search with quite different results and interpretations.   **158**

32. **Deception Detection,** Carrie Lock, *Science News,* July 31, 2004
    The average person thinks he or she knows exactly how to detect whether another
    person is *lying*—through gaze aversion. *Social psychologists* have discovered,
    however, that this technique is based on myth. Research on *deception detection*
    is now revealing what liars really do to give themselves away.   **161**

33. **Mirror, Mirror: Seeing Yourself As Others See You,** Carlin Flora,
    Psychology Today, May/June 2005
    This essay discloses how *self-concept* develops and how we incorporate *reflect-
    ed appraisal* from significant others into our self-concept. Additionally, information
    about related concepts such as *shyness, the role of the environment (or con-
    text), and self-awareness* are discussed in this article.   **164**

34. **Young and Restless,** Afshin Molavi, *Smithsonian,* April 2006
    Molavi reviews some of the historic *demographic and social changes* that have
    occurred in *Saudi Arabia*, including *women's rights, education, burgeoning
    use of the Internet, the influence of rock music*, and *the new worldview of
    Islam*. Molavi also addresses whether these changes are for the better and if
    they are received warmly by several generations.   **168**

The concepts in bold italics are developed in the article. For further expansion, please refer to the Topic Guide and the Index.

UNIT 10
Psychological Disorders

Unit Overview   172

35. **The Age of Depression,** Allan V. Horwitz and Jerome C. Wakefield, *Public Interest,* Winter 2005

The authors review the history of **the study of depression**. They claim that what used to be normal sadness has now become a **psychiatric disorder** named depression. The implications for society of these historic changes are also discussed in detail.   175

36. **Soldier Support,** Christopher Munsey, *Monitor on Psychology,* April 2006

The Iraqi war is predicted to cause more **psychological casualties** than any **war** in our history. Soldiers face the **stress of leaving their families and friends** behind after deployment as well as intense **combat stress** once inside Iraq. Psychologists are helping to fashion **treatment programs** for the soldiers as well as all-important **follow-up care**.   182

UNIT 11
Psychological Treatments

Unit Overview   184

37. **The Quandary Over Mental Illness,** Richard E. Vatz, *USA Today Magazine,* November 2004

Debates continue to churn within and outside of **psychiatry and psychology** with regard to **mental disorders**. What mental disorder is, whether indeed the term "disorder" is appropriate, which **medications**, if any, are effective, and how **the talking cure** work are just some of the issues under scrutiny.   187

38. **The Discover Interview: Nobel Laureate Eric Kandel,** Susan Kruglinski, *Discover,* April 2006

An interview with a recent Nobel Laureate **neurobiologist** reveals much about the **relationship between psychology and biology**. Besides describing what a **psychotherapist** needs to know about biology, Eric Kandel, the Nobel Laureate, also elaborates upon his research on **happiness, memory, and consciousness**.   191

39. **Offering Hope to the Emotionally Depressed,** Norbert R. Myslinski, *The World & I,* April 2004

Depression is among the most common mental disorders; thus, scientists have rushed to find better treatments. Advances in **brain research** and in understanding the brain's responses to **stress** are paving the way for the development of promising **interventions**.   194

40. **Computer- and Internet-Based Psychotherapy Interventions,** C. Barr Taylor and Kristine H. Luce, *Current Directions in Psychological Science,* February 2003

The **Internet** offers great promise as an alternative to **face-to-face testing, diagnosis, and therapy.** One of the main problems, however, is that there is little actual **science** demonstrating that the Internet is a safe and effective place for people to find the psychological assistance they need.   198

Index   203

Test Your Knowledge Form   206

Article Rating Form   207

The concepts in bold italics are developed in the article. For further expansion, please refer to the Topic Guide and the Index.

Topic Guide

This topic guide suggests how the selections in this book relate to the subjects covered in your course. You may want to use the topics listed on these pages to search the Web more easily.

On the following pages a number of Web sites have been gathered specifically for this book. They are arranged to reflect the units of this *Annual Edition*. You can link to these sites by going to the student online support site at *http://www.mhcls.com/online/.*

ALL THE ARTICLES THAT RELATE TO EACH TOPIC ARE LISTED BELOW THE BOLD-FACED TERM.

Adolescence
25. A Peaceful Adolescence

Aging
24. The Methuselah Report
26. Ageless Aging: The Next Era of Retirement
27. The Borders of Healing

Assessment
30. The Testing of America

Biological issues
5. The Amazing Brain: Is Neuroscience the Key to What Makes Us Human?
6. Genetic Influence on Human Psychological Traits
7. The Structure of the Human Brain
38. The Discover Interview: Nobel Laureate Eric Kandel
39. Offering Hope to the Emotionally Depressed

Brain
5. The Amazing Brain: Is Neuroscience the Key to What Makes Us Human?
7. The Structure of the Human Brain
39. Offering Hope to the Emotionally Depressed

Business
30. The Testing of America

Children
12. Teaching for Understanding
23. Why Newborns Cause Acrimony and Alimony
25. A Peaceful Adolescence

Cognition
16. What Was I Thinking?
17. Mysteries of the Mind

Critiques of Psychology
20. The Value of Positive Emotions

Critiques of psychology
1. Why Study Psychology?
2. Does Psychology Make a Significant Difference in Our Lives?
3. The 10 Commandments of Helping Students Distinguish Science from Pseudoscience in Psychology

Culture
27. The Borders of Healing
34. Young and Restless

Death
11. Extreme States
27. The Borders of Healing

Deception
31. To Err Is Human

Depression
35. The Age of Depression
39. Offering Hope to the Emotionally Depressed

Development
23. Why Newborns Cause Acrimony and Alimony
24. The Methuselah Report

25. A Peaceful Adolescence
26. Ageless Aging: The Next Era of Retirement

Diagnosis
30. The Testing of America

Drugs and drug treatment
37. The Quandary Over Mental Illness
39. Offering Hope to the Emotionally Depressed

Emotional intelligence
19. Feeling Smart: The Science of Emotional Intelligence

Emotions
18. Unconscious Emotion
19. Feeling Smart: The Science of Emotional Intelligence
20. The Value of Positive Emotions

Environment
6. Genetic Influence on Human Psychological Traits
22. Obesity—An Epidemic of the Twenty-First Century: An Update for Psychiatrists
33. Mirror, Mirror: Seeing Yourself As Others See You

Forgetting
13. Memory Flexibility

Freud
17. Mysteries of the Mind
18. Unconscious Emotion
28. Freud in Our Midst

Goals
21. Ambition: Why Some People Are Most Likely to Succeed

Happiness
20. The Value of Positive Emotions

History of psychology
20. The Value of Positive Emotions
28. Freud in Our Midst

Infants and infancy
23. Why Newborns Cause Acrimony and Alimony

Intelligence
14. Theory of Multiple Intelligences: Is It a Scientific Theory?

Internet
34. Young and Restless
40. Computer- and Internet-Based Psychotherapy Interventions

Interpersonal relations
32. Deception Detection
33. Mirror, Mirror: Seeing Yourself As Others See You

Intuition
16. What Was I Thinking?

Language
15. Shouldn't There Be a Word...?

Learning
12. Teaching for Understanding

Longevity
24. The Methuselah Report
26. Ageless Aging: The Next Era of Retirement

Marriage
23. Why Newborns Cause Acrimony and Alimony

Memory
13. Memory Flexibility

Mental disorder
39. Offering Hope to the Emotionally Depressed

Mental disorders
35. The Age of Depression
36. Soldier Support
37. The Quandary Over Mental Illness

Mind
16. What Was I Thinking?
17. Mysteries of the Mind

Motivation
21. Ambition: Why Some People Are Most Likely to Succeed

Nature and nurture
6. Genetic Influence on Human Psychological Traits

Nervous system
5. The Amazing Brain: Is Neuroscience the Key to What Makes Us Human?
7. The Structure of the Human Brain

Neuroscience
5. The Amazing Brain: Is Neuroscience the Key to What Makes Us Human?
7. The Structure of the Human Brain
18. Unconscious Emotion

Obesity
22. Obesity—An Epidemic of the Twenty-First Century: An Update for Psychiatrists

Parapsychology
11. Extreme States

Parents and parenting
23. Why Newborns Cause Acrimony and Alimony
25. A Peaceful Adolescence

Personality and personality tests
28. Freud in Our Midst
29. Exploding the Self-Esteem Myth
30. The Testing of America

Psychology
1. Why Study Psychology?
2. Does Psychology Make a Significant Difference in Our Lives?
3. The 10 Commandments of Helping Students Distinguish Science from Pseudoscience in Psychology

Psychotherapy
36. Soldier Support
37. The Quandary Over Mental Illness
38. The Discover Interview: Nobel Laureate Eric Kandel
40. Computer- and Internet-Based Psychotherapy Interventions

Research issues
3. The 10 Commandments of Helping Students Distinguish Science from Pseudoscience in Psychology
4. Causes and Correlations
31. To Err Is Human

Schools
12. Teaching for Understanding

Scientific methods
3. The 10 Commandments of Helping Students Distinguish Science from Pseudoscience in Psychology
4. Causes and Correlations
7. The Structure of the Human Brain
31. To Err Is Human

Self and self-esteem
29. Exploding the Self-Esteem Myth
33. Mirror, Mirror: Seeing Yourself As Others See You

Sensation
8. Sensational Tune-ups
9. Eye Wise: Seeing Into the Future
10. A Matter of Taste

Social behavior
31. To Err Is Human
32. Deception Detection
33. Mirror, Mirror: Seeing Yourself As Others See You
34. Young and Restless

Social change
34. Young and Restless

Taste
8. Sensational Tune-ups
10. A Matter of Taste

Technology
12. Teaching for Understanding

Testing
30. The Testing of America

Theories
14. Theory of Multiple Intelligences: Is It a Scientific Theory?
17. Mysteries of the Mind
28. Freud in Our Midst

Trauma
36. Soldier Support

Unconscious
17. Mysteries of the Mind
18. Unconscious Emotion

Vision
8. Sensational Tune-ups
9. Eye Wise: Seeing Into the Future

Weight and weight loss
22. Obesity—An Epidemic of the Twenty-First Century: An Update for Psychiatrists

Internet References

The following internet sites have been carefully researched and selected to support the articles found in this reader. The easiest way to access these selected sites is to go to our student online support site at *http://www.mhcls.com/online/*.

AE: Psychology 07/08

The following sites were available at the time of publication. Visit our Web site—we update our student online support site regularly to reflect any changes.

General Sources

APA Resources for the Public
http://www.apa.org/psychnet/

Use the site map or search engine to access *APA Monitor,* the American Psychological Association newspaper, APA books on a wide range of topics, PsychINFO, an electronic database of abstracts on scholarly journals, and the HelpCenter.

Health Information Resources
http://www.health.gov/nhic/Pubs/tollfree.htm

Here is a long list of toll-free numbers that provide health-related information. None offer diagnosis and treatment, but some do offer recorded information; others provide personalized counseling, referrals, and/or written materials.

Mental Help Net
http://mentalhelp.net

This comprehensive guide to mental health online features more than 6,300 individual resources. Information on mental disorders and professional resources in psychology, psychiatry, and social work is presented.

Psychology: Online Resource Central
http://www.psych-central.com

Thousands of psychology resources are currently indexed at this site. Psychology disciplines, conditions and disorders, and self-development are among the most useful.

School Psychology Resources Online
http://www.schoolpsychology.net

Numerous sites on special conditions, disorders, and disabilities, as well as other data ranging from assessment/evaluation to research, are available on this resource page for psychologists, parents, and educators.

Social Psychology Network
http://www.socialpsychology.org

The Social Psychology Network is the most comprehensive source of social psychology information on the Internet, including resources, programs, and research.

UNIT 1: The Science of Psychology

Abraham A. Brill Library
http://plaza.interport.net/nypsan/service.html

Containing data on over 40,000 books, periodicals, and reprints in psychoanalysis and related fields, the Abraham A. Brill Library has holdings that span the literature of psychoanalysis from its beginning to the present day.

American Psychological Society (APS)
http://www.psychologicalscience.org/about/links.html

The APS is dedicated to advancing the best of scientific psychology in research, application, and the improvement of human conditions. Links to teaching, research, and graduate studies resources are available.

Psychological Research on the Net
http://psych.hanover.edu/Research/exponnet.html

This Net site provides psychologically related experiments. Biological psychology/neuropsychology, clinical psychology, cognition, developmental psychology, emotions, health psychology, personality, sensation/perception, and social psychology are some of the areas covered.

UNIT 2: Biological Bases of Behavior

Institute for Behavioral Genetics
http://ibgwww.colorado.edu/index.html

Dedicated to conducting and facilitating research on the genetic and environmental bases of individual differences in behavior, this organized research unit at the University of Colorado leads to genetic sites, statistical sites, and the Biology Meta Index, as well as to search engines.

Serendip
http://serendip.brynmawr.edu/serendip/

Serendip, which is organized into five subject areas (brain and behavior, complex systems, genes and behavior, science and culture, and science education), contains interactive exhibits, articles, links to other resources, and a forum area.

UNIT 3: Perceptual Processes

Five Senses Home Page
http://www.sedl.org/scimath/pasopartners/senses/welcome.html

This elementary lesson examines the five senses and gives a list of references that may be useful.

Psychology Tutorials and Demonstrations
http://psych.hanover.edu/Krantz/tutor.html

Interactive tutorials and simulations, primarily in the area of sensation and perception, are available here.

UNIT 4: Learning and Remembering

Mind Tools
http://www.psychwww.com/mtsite/

Useful information on stress management can be found at this Web site.

The Opportunity of Adolescence

http://www.winternet.com/~webpage/adolescencepaper.html

According to this paper, adolescence is the turning point, after which the future is redirected and confirmed. The opportunities and problems of this period are presented with quotations from Erik Erikson, Jean Piaget, and others.

Project Zero

http://pzweb.harvard.edu

The Harvard Project Zero has investigated the development of learning processes in children and adults for 30 years. Today, Project Zero's mission is to understand and enhance learning, thinking, and creativity in the arts and other disciplines for individuals and institutions.

UNIT 5: Cognitive Processes

American Association for Artificial Intelligence (AAAI)

http://www.aaai.org/AITopics/index.html

This AAAI site provides a good starting point to learn about artificial intelligence (AI)--what artificial intelligence is and what AI scientists do.

Chess: Kasparov v. Deep Blue: The Rematch

http://www.chess.ibm.com/home/html/b.html

Clips from the chess rematch between Garry Kasparov and IBM's supercomputer, Deep Blue, are presented here along with commentaries on chess, computers, artificial intelligence, and what it all means.

UNIT 6: Emotion and Motivation

Emotional Intelligence Discovery

http://www.cwrl.utexas.edu/~bump/Hu305/3/3/3/

This site has been set up by students to talk about and expand on Daniel Goleman's book, *Emotional Intelligence*. There are links to many other EI sites.

John Suler's Teaching Clinical Psychology Site

http://www.rider.edu/users/suler/tcp.html

This page contains Internet resources for clinical and abnormal psychology, behavioral medicine, and mental health.

Nature vs. Nurture: Gergen Dialogue with Winifred Gallagher

http://www.pbs.org/newshour/gergen/gallagher_5-14.html

Experience modifies temperament, according to this TV interview. The author of *I.D.: How Heredity and Experience Make You Who You Are* explains a current theory about temperament.

UNIT 7: Development

American Association for Child and Adolescent Psychiatry

http://www.aacap.org

This site is designed to aid in the understanding and treatment of the developmental, behavioral, and mental disorders that could affect children and adolescents. There is a specific link just for families about common childhood problems that may or may not require professional intervention.

Behavioral Genetics

http://www.ornl.gov/hgmis/elsi/behavior.html

This government-backed Web site includes helpful information on behavioral genetics.

UNIT 8: Personality Processes

The Personality Project

http://personality-project.org/personality.html

This Personality Project (by William Revelle) is meant to guide those interested in personality theory and research to the current personality research literature.

UNIT 9: Social Processes

National Clearinghouse for Alcohol and Drug Information

http://www.health.org

Information on drug and alcohol facts that might relate to adolescence and the issues of peer pressure and youth culture is presented here. Resources, referrals, research and statistics, databases, and related Net links are available.

Nonverbal Behavior and Nonverbal Communication

http://www3.usal.es/~nonverbal/

This Web site has a detailed listing of nonverbal behavior and nonverbal communication sites, including the work of historical and current researchers.

UNIT 10: Psychological Disorders

American Association of Suicidology

http://www.suicidology.org

The American Association of Suicidology is a nonprofit organization dedicated to the understanding and prevention of suicide. This site is designed as a resource to anyone concerned about suicide.

Anxiety Disorders

http://www.adaa.org/mediaroom/index.cfm

Anxiety Disorders Association of America (ADAA) reviews anxiety disorders in children, adolescents, and adults here. A detailed glossary is available.

Ask NOAH About: Mental Health

http://www.noah-health.org/en/mental/

Information about child and adolescent family problems, mental conditions and disorders, suicide prevention, and much more is available here.

Mental Health Net Disorders and Treatments

http://www.mentalhelp.net/

Presented on this site are hotlinks to psychological disorders pages, which include anxiety, panic, phobic disorders, schizophrenia, and violent/self-destructive behaviors.

Mental Health Net: Eating Disorder Resources

http://www.mentalhelp.net/poc/center_index.php/id/46

This mental health Net site provides a complete list of Web references on eating disorders, including anorexia, bulimia, and obesity.

www.mhcls.com/online/

National Women's Health Resource Center (NWHRC)
http://www.healthywomen.org
   NWHRC's site contains links to resources related to women's substance abuse and mental illnesses.

UNIT 11: Psychological Treatments

The C.G. Jung Page
http://www.cgjungpage.org
   Dedicated to the work of Carl Jung, this is a comprehensive resource, with links to Jungian psychology, news and opinions, reference materials, graduate programs, dreams, multilingual sites, and related Jungian themes.

Knowledge Exchange Network (KEN)
http://www.mentalhealth.org
   Information about mental health (prevention, treatment, and rehabilitation services) is available via toll-free telephone services, an electronic bulletin board, and publications.

NetPsychology
http://netpsych.com/index.htm
   This site explores the uses of the Internet to deliver mental health services. This is a basic cybertherapy resource site.

Sigmund Freud and the Freud Archives
http://plaza.interport.net/nypsan/freudarc.html
   Internet resources related to Sigmund Freud, which include a collection of libraries, museums, and biographical materials, as well as the Brill Library archives, can be found here.

We highly recommend that you review our Web site for expanded information and our other product lines. We are continually updating and adding links to our Web site in order to offer you the most usable and useful information that will support and expand the value of your Annual Editions. You can reach us at: *http://www.mhcls.com/annualeditions/.*

UNIT 1
The Science of Psychology

Unit Selections

1. **Why Study Psychology?**, Linda M. Bartoshuk et al.
2. **Does Psychology Make a Significant Difference in Our Lives?**, Philip G. Zimbardo
3. **The 10 Commandments of Helping Students Distinguish Science from Pseudoscience in Psychology**, Scott O. Lilienfield
4. **Causes and Correlations**, Massimo Pigliucci

Key Points to Consider

- What are the various subfields within psychology? In each subfield, what is the main work of the psychologists? Which area of psychology (e.g. biological psychology, social psychology, human development, etc.) do you think is the most valuable and why?

- Many people are aware of clinical psychology by virtue of having watched films and television where psychotherapists are depicted. Is this the most valuable area of the discipline? About which other areas of psychology do you think the public is most informed? What other areas ought the public be informed about? Why? What do you hope to learn about psychology in your class? Why?

- Do you think psychology relates well to other scientific disciplines, such as sociology, biology, and human medicine? Are there non-science disciplines to which psychology might be related, for example, philosophy, religion, and mathematics? How so? What contributions has psychology made to scientific endeavors? How has psychology improved your life?

- How and why should psychologists give psychology away, that is, make the general public aware of the discipline? Do you think the general public has stereotypes or misconceptions about psychology and psychologists? Does the public confuse psychiatry and psychology? Does the general public have enough knowledge of relevant issues, research, and data analysis to understand the intricacies of scientific findings? Do you think the average person can discriminate science from pseudoscience and scientific psychology from pop psychology?

- Why is research important to psychology? What kinds of information can be gleaned from psychological research? What types of research methods do psychologists utilize? Why do psychologists employ a variety of research methods?

- What research methods do psychologists utilize? Why? What is the difference between experimentation and correlation? What does a psychologist mean by the word "control"? Why does a psychologist make a statistical inference or use inferential statistics?

- Do you think editors of psychological journals should publish results "as is" or should they exclude certain types of research or results from their journals? For example, would a study showing no differences between men and women be as a valuable as one that does demonstrate sex differences? If you excluded a study, what factors would make you, as an editor, exclude it?

Student Website
www.mhcls.com/online

Internet References
Further information regarding these websites may be found in this book's preface or online.

Abraham A. Brill Library
http://plaza.interport.net/nypsan/service.html
American Psychological Society (APS)
http://www.psychologicalscience.org/about/links.html
Psychological Research on the Net
http://psych.hanover.edu/Research/exponnet.html

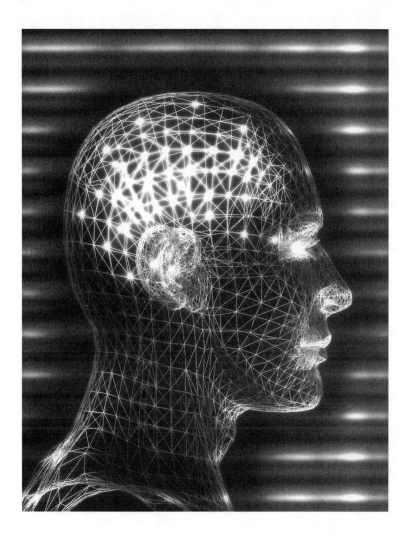

Little did Wilhelm Wundt realize his monumental contribution to science when in 1879 in Germany, he opened the first psychological laboratory to examine consciousness. Wundt would barely recognize modern psychology compared to the way he practiced it.

Contemporary psychology is defined *as the science of individual mental activity and behavior*. This definition reflects the two parent disciplines from which psychology emerged: philosophy and biology. Compared to its parents, psychology is very much a new discipline. Some aspects of modern psychology are particularly biological, such as neuroscience, perception, psychophysics, and behavioral genetics. Other aspects are more philosophical, such as the study of personality, while other areas within psychology approximate sociology, as does social psychology.

Today's psychologists work in a variety of settings. Many psychologists are academics, teaching and researching psychology on university campuses. Others work in applied settings such as hospitals, mental health clinics, industry, and schools. Most psychologists specialize in psychology only after graduate training. Industrial psychologists specialize in human performance in organizational settings, while clinical psychologists are concerned about the assessment, diagnosis, and treatment of individuals with a variety of mental disorders. Each specialty typically requires a graduate education and sometimes requires a license to practice.

Since its establishment, the field has expanded to many different areas. As mentioned above, some areas are very practical. Other areas appear to emphasize theory and research. Growing pains in the field resulted in conflict over what the agenda of the first national psychological association, the American Psychological Association, should be. Because academics perceived this association as mainly serving practitioners, academics and researchers established their own competing association, the American Psychological Society that recently changed its name to the Association for Psychological Science. Despite its varied nature and sporadic development, psychology remains a viable and exciting field. The first unit of the book is designed to introduce you to the study and history of psychology.

An excellent question and article begin this anthology. The first article addresses "Why Study Psychology?" Four renowned psychologists from various areas of the discipline reveal why they became psychologists and how they currently use their

1

knowledge of the field. Perhaps their revelations will inspire you pursue psychology, too.

The second article addresses another cogent question, "Does Psychology Make a Significant Difference in Our Lives?" Noted psychologist Philip Zimbardo answers the question in a resoundingly affirmative fashion. He suggests that we should "give away" psychology so that the general public knows more about important issues such as how to prevent AIDS and how to become better parents.

The third article by Scott O. Lilienfield explicates the differences between science and pseudoscience and between psychology and popular psychology (as often found in the mass media). Although the article was written for professors, it is highly readable and important to beginning students of psychology because of its emphasis on what dimensions produce high quality science.

Why Study Psychology?

Why did psychology's leading researchers take that first course?
Was it the compelling advice of a master? Perhaps a sudden [epiphany]?
Why Did You Study Psychology?
There probably are as many reasons as there are people in the field.
In this series, leading psychology researchers talk about getting into science.

DEVELOPING A SUPERTASTE

Linda M. Bartoshuk
Yale University School of Medicine
PhD 1965 from Brown University

AS A KID growing up in Aberdeen, South Dakota, I read science fiction and dreamed of astronomy. Junior high had a career day; students got to interview members of the profession to which they aspired. I asked for a scientist, but was assigned to interview a secretary.

In high school, when I signed up for math and science, my guidance counselor suggested these were unrealistic choices, but relented when I agreed to take bookkeeping and typing. Fifty-four words a minute later (not bad in the world before word processors) I still preferred trigonometry.

When it came time for college, I came in second in a math contest and won a slide rule (for anyone who has never used one, they are amazing little devices). I headed to Rapid City to tour the South Dakota School of Mines and Technology. Women were welcomed but few went, and I was not attracted to the prospect. Carleton College had a telescope and an astronomy major. The cost was daunting but a National Merit Scholarship came to my aid and I was off. Again, few women turned up in math and science, but we were treated well by our instructors.

Not so in the real world. I learned that some observatories banned women from using the telescopes; those big, complex machines were too much for us. I had had it. I remember the night my roommate and I sat with the Carleton course book and discovered that a psychology major would give me credit for all the math and science I had taken. Wow! As a junior I signed up for introductory psychology taught by John Bare, the new department chair. The class scintillated. When we got to psychophysics, I knew I was home. Astronomy had taught me that measurement of the perceived brightness of stars played a role in measuring the size of the universe. The farther away the star, the dimmer it appears from earth. If we only knew how bright it was at the source, we could calculate the distance.

Discovering that some supertasters live in neon taste worlds has brought me full circle.

One of the few women in astronomy provided the missing link; some stars pulse and we can see their brightness wax and wane. Theory related the periodicity of the pulsation to the absolute brightness of the star. We had the size of the universe! John Bare sent me to Brown University to study taste with his mentor, Carl Pfaffmann. Discovering that some supertasters live in neon taste worlds compared to non tasters (like me) who live in pastel taste worlds has brought me full circle. We cannot share experiences, so how could we discover that taste is more vivid to some? The missing link was a standard. If we could find some sensation that was not correlated with taste, everyone could express taste intensities relative to that standard. Assuming any variability in perception of the standard to be roughly equal across groups, we could compare tastes across groups. To my delight, one of the best standards we have tested is the brightness of the sun.

An APS Fellow and Charter Member, Bartoshuk has served on the APS Board of Directors. She will give the Bring the Family Address at the 16th Annual Convention.

THE CHILDREN COME FIRST

Patrice Marie Miller
Salem State College
EdD 1988 from Harvard University

IT IS HARD to choose a major or a career when you have never really been exposed to it. Thinking back, though, it seems as if the issues that I am involved in as a developmental psychologist started as early as ninth grade. At that time, I was living in Rio de Janeiro, Brazil. Rio, then as now, was a city full of natural beauty and poverty. In the ninth grade I worked on a project started by my history professor, in which we visited one of the *favelas* (the hillside slums) on Saturdays and engaged in games and crafts activities with the children. The idea was to try and have a positive impact on their development by giving them something constructive to do and some contact with other models for doing things.

Based on that experience, I decided that I wanted to do something that would have a positive impact on the lives of children, especially poor children. In high school and the early years of college, I tried different ways of having an impact on the lives of children, such as tutoring in East Harlem and working as a teacher's assistant. I enjoyed these experiences in many ways, but I felt as if we did not know enough about how children developed to know how best to help them.

> **I decided that I wanted to do something that would have a positive impact on the lives of children, especially poor children.**

My senior year at New York University, I was still wondering what to do. I thought I might teach for a few years—perhaps back in Rio—while I figured out my future. The August before senior year, while at a psychological meeting with my mother, a school psychologist, I met a professor teaching behavior analysis at NYU. Second semester of that year, I worked with him on a research project involving autistic children. This experience pushed me into thinking of a different kind of career, one as an academic psychologist. I enjoy the problem solving involved in planning, carrying out, analyzing and writing up research. Thinking out issues and having things work out the way you had hoped is a special kind of thrill that I only experienced when I began to do research.

When I finished my BA, I still was not ready to forge ahead. First, I had to go back and learn some of the mathematics I had managed to duck. During this time, I worked on several research projects, along with my psychologist husband (surely, also, a reinforcing influence in all this). When we moved to Cambridge, Massachusetts, I obtained my doctorate in human development from Harvard's Graduate School of Education. My dissertation on very young infants' reactions to be being taken care of by a stranger versus their mother was an attempt to look at whether and in what ways young infants differentiated between their mothers and other caregivers. It was the first of several projects I have been engaged in since on early social and emotional development of children. Teaching, which I also do, allows me to communicate some of my passions to newer students.

The way I think about it now is that my work ideally combines intellectual activities that I greatly enjoy, with an opportunity to work on issues in a field that, as a whole, I believe makes a difference in the lives of children.

Miller is a developmental psychologist specializing in social and emotional development.

CLINICAL COGNITION
Teresa A. Treat
Yale University
PhD 2000 from Indiana University

THROUGHOUT MY undergraduate and graduate years at Indiana University, I was inspired by Dick McFall's vision of an integrative psychological science. Dick spoke eloquently about a new generation of clinical scientists who were fully trained in both clinical and cognitive science, or in clinical and neural science, such that they were viewed as legitimate in both fields. And he wondered whether such hybrid scholars would view psychopathology from a novel vantage that might help to move forward our understanding, assessment, and treatment of psychological problems. I tested the waters by taking a mathematical psychology course with Jim Townsend during my first year in the clinical-science program. The course damn near killed me—granted, this is not an uncommon experience in a Townsend course—but Jim was unfailing in his support and encouragement, and I emerged with numerous ill-formed notions about the potential utility of formal mathematical modeling of clinically relevant cognitive processing.

In the meantime, McFall, Rick Viken, and I had begun developing photo stimulus sets that would allow us to use cognitive science models and methods to investigate men's perceptions of women's sexual interest (with implications for our understanding of acquaintance-initiated sexual aggression), as well as women's perceptions of other women's shape- and weight-related information (with implications for our understanding of eating disorders). The resulting photo stimulus sets were a far cry from the simpler, well-controlled stimuli that cognitive scientists typically used to investigate normative cognitive processes. Thus, it was unclear whether the principles and paradigms developed in this more highly controlled context would generalize to the messiness of investigations of clinically relevant individual differences in complex social perception.

As the work progressed, I became accustomed to hearing cognitive scientists insist that "those are the most uncontrolled stimuli I've ever seen!" In contrast, of course, many clinical scientists claimed that they were "the most over-controlled stimuli" they'd ever seen. Fortunately Rob Nosofsky, John Kruschke, and David MacKay—as well as two extremely gifted graduate students at the time, Tom Palmeri and Mike Erickson—worked with us every step of the way on these two lines of research and spent countless hours training me in the rudiments of multidimensional scaling, formal models of categorization and learning, and computational modeling.

Eventually, I had completed all the coursework necessary for a joint degree in clinical and cognitive science, but I had yet to declare my additional major. It felt presumptuous to call myself a clinical-cognitive scientist, because that implied that I was a "real" cognitive scientist as well as a "real" clinical scientist. The latter had been a central piece of my academic identity for years, but I had yet to recognize the former. Three years of working side by side with cognitive students in Kruschke's lab finally changed this. And then one day, when I was musing out loud in the lab about whether to declare the joint degree, one of my lab mates challenged me by saying, "What's wrong with you? You're as much a cognitive scientist as the rest of us." Soon thereafter, I remember nervously marching upstairs to the cognitive-science office to officially declare the joint major and choose a career as a clinical-cognitive scientist—long after I already was living and loving a career in McFall's "integrative psychological science."

Treat is a clinical and counseling psychologist who specializes in cognitive science.

REDEFINING A CAREER
Milton D. Hakel
Bowling Green State University
PhD 1966 from the University of Minnesota

IT WASN'T PRETTY. It wasn't easy. But especially in the perspective offered by the passage of over 40 years, choosing a major, then choosing to pursue graduate study, and then deciding study for the PhD was a chaotic, sometimes frantic, and always exciting process.

As a teen, I knew I wanted to go to college, but I had no clear direction in mind. When I was a high school junior, I wanted to go anyplace but the University of Minnesota. After investigating the costs, and considering my grades (which made me a weak competitor for scholarships), dissonance reduction worked its magic and I applied only to the University of Minnesota. It was a fortunate application (and acceptance), and I have always appreciated the excellent and challenging education I received there.

As an undergraduate beginning in 1959, I ran through a succession of 12 declared and undeclared majors, hoping to find something that could suit me for the long run. Some majors lasted as little as three weeks, until I got the results of a mid-term or final that I interpreted as a signal to apply my efforts elsewhere. Other majors lasted much longer, and I graduated with a double major in philosophy and psychology. But by my senior year I knew I wanted to pursue graduate study in psychology. Many small but significant events led to that career direction.

As a third-quarter freshman, I talked my way into a limited-enrollment honors section of an introductory laboratory course (my grades put me just below the formal cut score). The course offered hands-on experience in research. In trios we collected data to replicate a one trial learning experiment originally published by William K. Estes, and individually we analyzed and reported the findings. I concluded that I could learn how to design and conduct research. All three of us in my group eventually earned PhDs, and it was a special pleasure many years later to actually meet Estes, when he became the editor of *Psychological Science* (I was part of the original APS Publication Committee that invited him to be the founding editor).

As a junior I quit commuting and moved on campus, meeting that first day a delightful and spirited woman who became my

wife within a year. I took two courses in individual differences; in retrospect, they are the most important courses I ever had—thank you Jim Jenkins and Marv Dunnette. The issues I first studied there continue to animate scientific discourse and public policy: testing and learning, heritability, group differences. I also took a course in vocational guidance, and heard about "varch" as an attribute of a career, variety, and change. I knew this was what I wanted, and guessed that a career in research would offer it.

In defining my career I redefined a few key words: chaos, frantic, excitement.

I hung out in the psychology building, getting to know graduate students and some faculty. When an opening occurred for an undergraduate teaching assistant (they needed someone to sharpen mark-sense pencils and do other tasks too menial for graduate students), I applied and got the job, and my exposure to psychology and psychologists expanded.

As a senior in 1962–63 I did a voluntary research project under Dunnette's guidance. The work I did in that "job sample" was sufficient as a demonstration of capability to get me into graduate school. I applied to only one, but my grades and scores were borderline, so I was admitted on probation (the US Air Force was my other "employment" option, and one could already see that the Vietnam War was getting ugly). The senior project eventually became my first publication.

In graduate school to pursue a master's, I found it considerably surprising when I was invited at the end of my first year to bypass the MA and work directly toward the doctorate. I became interested in how people form impressions of others and use those impressions to make consequential decisions, such as who to hire. The topic was partly a consequence of having been interviewed by about 50 different potential employers (and being rejected by 40 of them) while looking for summer jobs. I completed the degree, and research that Dunnette and I proposed was supported by the National Science Foundation in 1966. I stayed at Minnesota for two years as a postdoc, and then moved to Ohio State, Houston, and Bowling Green.

My experiences sensitized me to the fallibility of predictors and the need to devise effective and equitable systems for 1) selecting employees/admitting students, and 2) enabling people to develop their capabilities fully. These continue to be engaging issues.

So in defining my career I redefined a few key words. Chaos—going from no direction through 12 majors to one. Frantic—marrying while still an undergraduate, having two children while in graduate school, and worrying about employment and the draft raised occasional anxieties. Excitement—enough for a lifetime, and that was just the beginning.

Hankel is an APS Fellow and Charter Member and has served on the APS Board of Directors. He is an industrial/organizational psychologist.

Does Psychology Make a Significant Difference in Our Lives?

PHILIP G. ZIMBARDO
Stanford University

The intellectual tension between the virtues of basic versus applied research that characterized an earlier era of psychology is being replaced by an appreciation of creative applications of all research essential to improving the quality of human life. Psychologists are positioned to "give psychology away" to all those who can benefit from our wisdom. Psychologists were not there 35 years ago when American Psychological Association (APA) President George Miller first encouraged us to share our knowledge with the public. The author argues that psychology is indeed making a significant difference in people's lives; this article provides a sampling of evidence demonstrating how and why psychology matters, both in pervasive ways and specific applications. Readers are referred to a newly developed APA Web site that documents current operational uses of psychological research, theory, and methodology (its creation has been the author's primary presidential initiative): www.psychologymatters.org.

oes psychology matter? Does what we do, and have done for a hundred years or more, really make a significant difference in the lives of individuals or in the functioning of communities and nations? Can we demonstrate that our theories, our research, our professional practice, our methodologies, our way of thinking about mind, brain, and behavior make life better in any measurable way? Has what we have to show for our discipline been applied in the real world beyond academia and practitioners' offices to improve health, education, welfare, safety, organizational effectiveness, and more?

Such questions, and finding their answers, have always been my major personal and professional concern. First, as an introductory psychology teacher for nearly six decades, I have always worked to prove relevance as well as essence of psychology to my students. Next, as an author of the now classic basic text, *Psychology and Life* (Ruch & Zimbardo, 1971), which claimed to wed psychology to life applications, I constantly sought to put more psychology in our lives and more life in our psychology (Gerrig & Zimbardo, 2004; Zimbardo, 1992). To reach an even broader student audience, I have coauthored *Core Concepts in Psychology* (Zimbardo, Weber, & Johnson, 2002) that strives to bring the excitement of scientific and applied psychology to students in state and community colleges.

In order to further expand the audience for what is best in psychology, I accepted an invitation to help create, be scientific advisor for, and narrator of the 26-program PBS TV series, *Discovering Psychology* (1990/2001). For this general public audience, we have provided answers—as viewable instances—to their "so what?" questions. This award-winning series is shown both nationally and internationally (in at least 10 nations) and has been the foundation for the most popular telecourse among all the Annenberg CPB Foundation's many academic programs (see www.learner.org). Finally, as the 2002 president of the American Psychological Association, my major initiative became developing a compendium of exemplars of how psychology has made a significant difference in our lives. This Web-based summary of "psychology in applied action" has been designed as a continually modifiable and updateable repository of demonstrable evidence of psychological knowledge in meaningful applications. In a later section of this article, the compendium will be described more fully and some of its examples highlighted.

I was fortunate in my graduate training at Yale University (1954-1960) to be inspired by three exceptional mentors, each of whom modeled a different aspect of the relevance and applicability of basic psychology to vital issues facing individuals and our society. Carl Hovland developed the Yale Communication and Attitude Change Program after coming out of his military assignment in World War II of analyzing the effectiveness of propaganda and training programs (Hovland, Lumsdaine, & Sheffield, 1949). He went on to transform what was at that time a complex, global, and vague study of communication and persuasion into identifiable processes, discrete variables, and integrative hypotheses that made possible both experimental research and applications (Hovland, Janis, & Kelley, 1953). Neal Miller always straddled the fence between basic and applied research, despite being known for his classic experimental and theoretical formulations of motivation and reward in learning and conditioning. His World War II experience of training pilots to overcome fears so that they could return to combat was an applied precursor of his later role in developing biofeedback through his laboratory investigations of conditioning autonomic nervous system responses (N. E. Miller, 1978, 1985, 1992). The last of my Yale mentors, Seymour Sarason, moved out from his research program on test anxiety in children into the community as one of the founders of Community Psychology (Sarason, 1974). It was a daring move at that time in a field that honored only the scientific study of *individual* behavior.

Psychology of the 50s was also a field that honored basic research well above applied research, which was typically accorded second-class status, if not denigrated by the "experimentalists," a popular brand name in that era. Psychology at many major universities aspired to be "soft physics," as in the heady days of our Germanic forebears, Wundt, Fechner, Ebbinghaus, Titchner, and others (see Green, Shore, & Teo, 2001). Anything applied was seen at best as crude social engineering by tinkerers, not real thinkers. Moreover, behaviorism was still rampant, with animal models that stripped away from learning what nonsense syllable memory researchers had deleted from memory—merely the context, the content, the human meaning, and the culture of behavior. The most prominent psychologist from the 50s through the 80s, B.F. Skinner, was an anomaly in this regard. Half of him remained a Watsonian radical behaviorist who refused to admit the existence of either motivation or cognition into his psychology (Skinner, 1938, 1966, 1974). Meanwhile, the other Skinner side applied operant conditioning principles to train pigeons for military duties and outlined a behaviorist Utopia in *Walden Two* (Skinner, 1948).

Giving Psychology Away: The Call for Societal Accountability

And then along came George Miller whose American Psychological Association (APA) presidential address in 1969 stunned the psychological establishment because one of its own firstborn sons committed the heresy of exhorting them to go public, get real, get down, give it up, and be relevant. Well, that is the way I think I heard it back then when George Miller (1969) told his audience that it was time to begin "to give psychology away to the public." It was time to stop talking only to other psychologists. It was time to stop writing only for professional journals hidden away in library stacks. It was time to go beyond the endless quest for experimental rigor in the perfectly designed study to test a theoretically derived hypothesis. Maybe it was time to begin finding answers to the kinds of questions your mother asked about why people acted the way they did. Perhaps it was acceptable to start considering how best to translate what we knew into a language that most ordinary citizens could understand and even come to appreciate.

I for one applauded George Miller's stirring call to action for all these reasons. It was heady for me because I believed that coming from such a distinguished serious theorist and re-

searcher—not some do-gooder, liberal communitarian whom the establishment could readily dismiss—his' message would have a big impact in our field Sadly, the banner raised by Miller's inspirational speech, did not fly very high over most psychology departments for many years to come. Why not? I think for four reasons: Excessive modesty about *what* psychology really had of value to offer the public, ignorance about *who* was "the public," cluelessness about *how* to go about the mission of giving psychology away, and lack of sufficient concern about *why* psychology needed to be accountable to the public.

How shall we counterargue against such reasoning? First, scanning the breadth and depth of our field makes apparent that there is no need for such professional modesty. Rather, the time has come to be overtly proud of our past and current accomplishments, as I will try to demonstrate here. We have much to be proud of in our heritage and in our current accomplishments. Second, the public starts with our students, our clients, and our patients and extends to our funding agencies, national and local politicians, all nonpsychologists, and the media. And it also means your mother whose "bubba psychology" sometimes needs reality checks based on solid evidence we have gathered. Third, it is essential to recognize that the media are the gatekeepers between the best, relevant psychology we want to give away and that elusive public we hope will value what we have to offer. We need to learn how best to utilize the different kinds of media that are most appropriate for delivering specific messages to particular target audiences that we want to reach. Psychologists need to learn how to write effective brief press releases, timely op-ed newspaper essays, interesting articles for popular magazines, valuable trade books based on empirical evidence, and how best to give radio, TV, and print interviews. Simple awareness of media needs makes evident, for example, that TV requires visual images, therefore, we should be able to provide video records of research, our interventions, or other aspects of the research or therapeutic process that will form a story's core.

"Media smarts" also means realizing that to reach adolescents with a helpful message (that is empirically validated), a brief public service announcement on MTV or an article in a teen magazine will have a broader impact than detailed journal articles or even popular books on the subject.[1] Thus, it becomes essential to our mission of making the public wiser consumers of psychological knowledge to learn how to communicate effectively to the media and to work with the media.

Finally, we can challenge the fourth consideration regarding societal accountability with the awareness that taxpayers fund much of our research as well as some of the education of our graduate students. It is imperative that we convey the sense to the citizens of our states and nation that we are responsive to society's needs and, further, that we feel responsible for finding solutions to some of its problems (Zimbardo, 1975). It has become standard operating procedure for most granting agencies now to require a statement about the potential societal value of any proposed research. That does not mean that all research must be applied to dealing with current social or individual problems because there is considerable evidence that research that originally seemed esoterically "basic" has in time found valuable applications (see Swazey, 1974). It does mean that although some of our colleagues begin with a focus on a problem in an applied domain, the others who start with an eye on theory testing or understanding some basic phenomena should feel obligated to stretch their imaginations by considering potential applications of their knowledge. I believe we have much worthy applicable psychology, basic research, theory, and methodology that is awaiting creative transformations to become valuable applied psychology.

The Profound and Pervasive Impact of Past Psychological Knowledge

Before I outline some recent, specific instances of how psychological research, theory, and methodology have been applied in various settings, I will first highlight some of the fundamental contributions psychology has already made in our lives. Many of them have become so pervasive and their impact so unobtrusively profound that they are taken for granted. They have come to be incorporated into the way we think about certain domains, have influenced our attitudes and values, and so changed the way individuals and agencies behave that they now seem like the natural, obvious way the world should be run. Psychology often gets little or no credit for these contributions—when we should be deservedly proud of them.

Psychological Testing and Assessment

One of psychology's major achievements has been the development and the extensive reliance on objective, quantifiable means of assessing human talents, abilities, strengths, and weaknesses. In the 100 years since Alfred Binet first measured intellectual performance, systematic assessment has replaced the subjective, often biased judgments of teachers, employers, clinicians, and others in positions of authority by objective, valid, reliable, quantifiable, and normed tests (Binet, 1911; Binet & Simon, 1915). It is hard to imagine a test-free world. Modern testing stretches from assessments of intelligence, achievement, personality, and pathology to domains of vocational and values assessment, personnel selection, and more. Vocational interest measures are the backbone of guidance counseling and career advising. The largest single application of classified testing in the world is the Armed Services Vocational Aptitude Battery that is given to as many as 2 million enlisted personnel annually. Personnel selection testing has over 90 years of validity research and proven utility.

We are more familiar with the SAT and GRE standardized testing, currently being revised in response to various critiques, but they are still the yardstick for admission to many colleges and universities (Sternberg, 2000). Workplace job skills assessment and training involves huge numbers of workers and managers in many countries around the world (DuBois, 1970). Little wonder, then, that such pervasive use of assessments has spawned a multibillion dollar industry. (Because I am serving here in this article in the capacity as cheerleader for our discipline, I will not raise questions about the political misuse or overuse of testing nor indeed be critical of some of the other contributions that follow; see Cronbach, 1975.)

Positive Reinforcement

The earlier emphasis in schools and in child rearing on punishment for errors and inappropriate behavior has been gradually displaced by a fundamentally divergent focus on the utility of positive reinforcement for correct, appropriate responding (Straus & Kantor, 1994). Punishing the "undesirable person" has been replaced by punishing only "undesirable behavioral acts." Time-outs for negative behavior have proven remarkably effective as a behavior-modification strategy (Wolfe, Risley, & Mees, 1965). It has become so effective that it has become a favorite technique for managing child behavior by parents in the United States. "Half the parents and teachers in the United States use this nonviolent practice and call it 'time-out,' which makes it a social intervention unmatched in modern psychology," according to the American Academy of Pediatrics' (1998) publication.

Animal training has benefited enormously from procedures of shaping complex behavioral repertoires and the use of conditioned reinforcers (such as clickers' soundings paired with food rewards). An unexpected value of such training, as reported by animal caregivers, is that they enhance the mental health of many animal species through the stimulation provided by learning new behaviors (San Francisco Chronicle, 2003). Skinner and his behaviorist colleagues deserve the credit for this transformation in how we think about and go about changing behavior by means of response-contingent reinforcement. Their contributions have moved out of animal laboratories into schools, sports, clinics, and hospitals (see Axelrod & Apsche, 1983; Druckman & Bjork, 1991; Kazdin, 1994; Skinner, 1974).

Psychological Therapies

The mission of our psychological practitioners of relieving the suffering of those with various forms of mental illness by means of appropriately delivered types of psychological therapy has proven successful. Since Freud's (1896/1923, 1900/1965) early cases documenting the efficacy of "talk therapy" for neurotic disorders, psychotherapy has taken many forms. Cognitive behavior modification, systematic desensitization, and exposure therapies have proven especially effective in treating phobias, anxiety disorders, and panic attacks, thanks to the application of Pavlovian principles of classical conditioning (Pavlov, 1897/1902, 1897/1927), first developed by Joseph Wolpe (1958). Even clinical depression is best treated with a combination of psychotherapy and medication, and psychotherapy has been shown to be as effective as the drugs alone (Hollon, Thase, & Markowitz, 2002). At a more general level, psychology has helped to demystify "madness," to bring humanity into the treatment of those with emotional and behavioral disorders, and to give people hope that such disorders can be changed (Beck, 1976). Our practitioners and clinical theorists have also developed a range of treatments designed especially for couples, families, groups, for those in rehabilitation from drugs or physical disabilities, as well as for many specific types of problems such as, addictions, divorce, or shyness.

Self-Directed Change

The shelves of most bookstores in the United States are now as likely to be filled with "self-help" books as they are with cooking and dieting books. Although many of them can be dismissed as bad forms of "pop psych" that offer guidance and salvation without any solid empirical footing to back their claims, others provide a valuable service to the general public. At best, they empower people to engage in self-directed change processes for optimal personal adjustment (see Maas, 1998; Myers, 1993; Zimbardo, 1977). In part, their success comes from providing wise advice and counsel based on a combination of extensive expert experience and relevant research packaged in narratives that ordinary people find personally meaningful.

Dynamic Development Across the Life Span

Earlier conceptions of children as small adults, as property, and later as valuable property were changed in part by the theories and research of developmental psychologists (see McCoy, 1988; Pappas, 1983). In recent times, the emerging status of "the child as person" has afforded children legal rights, due process, and self-determination, along with the recognition that they should be regarded as competent persons worthy of considerable freedom (Horowitz, 1984). Psychology has been a human service profession whose knowledge base has been translated into support for a positive ideology of children (Hart, 1991). The human organism is continually changing, ever modifying itself to engage its environments more effectively, from birth through old age. This fundamental conception has made evident that babies need stimulation of many kinds for optimal development, just as do their grandparents. There is now widespread psychological recognition that infants do experience pain; learning often depends on critical age-related developmental periods; nature and nurture typically interact in synergistic ways to influence our intelligence and many attributes; mental growth follows orderly progressions, as does language acquisition and production; and that the elderly do not lose their mental agility and competence if they continue to exercise their cognitive skills throughout life (see Baltes & Staudinger 2000; Bee, 1994; Erikson, 1963; Piaget, 1954; Pinker, 1994; Plomin & McClearn, 1993; Scarr, 1998). These are but a few of the fundamental contributions of psychology to the way our society now thinks about human development over the course of a lifetime because of decades of research by our developmentalist colleagues.

Parenting

Advice by psychologists on best parental practices has varied in quality and value over time. However, there now seems to be agreement that children need to develop secure attachments to parents or caregivers and that the most beneficial parenting style for generating an effective child-parent bond is authoritative. Authoritative parents make age-appropriate demands on children while being responsive to their needs, autonomy, and freedom (see Baumrind, 1973; Collins, Maccoby, Steinberg, Hetherington, & Bornstein, 2000; Darling & Steinberg, 1993; Maccoby, 1980, 1992, 2000).

Psychological Stress

Is there any day in our modern lives that stress does not seem to be omnipresent? We are stressed by time pressures on us, by our jobs (Maslach, 1982), by our marriages, by our friends or by our lack of them. Back when I was a graduate student, stress was such a novel concept that it was surprising when our professor Irving Janis (1958) wrote one of the first books on the subject of psychological stress. The concept of psychological stress was virtually unrecognized in medical care in the 50s and 60s. Psychosomatic disorders baffled physicians who never recognized stress as a causal factor in illness and disease. Since then, psychological research and theorizing has helped to move the notion of stress to the center of the bio-psychosocial health model that is revolutionizing medical treatments (Ader & Cohen, 1993; Cohen & Herbert, 1996). Psychologists have shown that our appraisals of stress and our lifestyle habits have a major impact on many of the major causes of illness and death (see Lazarus, 1993; Lazarus & Folkman, 1984). We have made commonplace the ideas of coping with stress, reducing lifestyle risk factors, and building social support networks to enable people to live healthier and longer lives (see Coe, 1999; Cohen & Syme, 1985; Taylor & Clark, 1986).

Unconscious Motivation

Psychology brought into the public mind, as did dramatists such as William Albee, Arthur Miller, and Tennessee Williams, that what we think and do is not always based on conscious decisions. Rather, human behavior may be triggered by unconscious motivations of which we have no awareness. Another nod of thanks goes out to the wisdom of Sigmund Freud and of Carl Jung (1936/1959) for helping to illuminate this previously hidden side of human nature. In a similar vein, slips of the tongue and pen are now generally interpreted as potentially meaningful symptoms of suppressed intentions. It is relatively common in many levels of U.S. society for people to believe that accidents may not be accidental but motivated, that dreams might convey important messages, and also that we use various defense mechanisms, such as projection, to protect fragile egos from awareness of negative information.

Prejudice and Discrimination

Racial prejudice motivates a range of emotions and behaviors among both those targeted and those who are its agents of hatred. Discrimination is the overt behavioral sequeala of prejudiced beliefs. It enforces inequalities and injustices based on categorical assignments to presumed racial groups. Stereotypes embody a biased conception of the attributes people presumably possess or lack. The 1954 decision by the Supreme Court of the United States (*Brown v. Board of Education of*

Topeka, KS) that formally desegregated public schools was based on some critical social psychological research. The body of empirical research by Kenneth and Mamie Clark (1939a, 1939b, 1940, 1950) effectively demonstrated for the Court that the segregated educational conditions of that era had a negative impact on the sense of self-worth of Negro (the then-preferred term) school children. The Court, and the thoughtful public since then, accepted the psychological premise that segregated education, which separates the races, can never be really equal for those being stigmatized by that system of discrimination. Imposed segregation not only is the consequence of prejudice, it contributes further to maintaining and intensifying prejudice, negative stereotypes, and discrimination. In the classic analysis of the psychology of prejudice by Gordon Allport (1954), the importance of equal status contact between the races was advanced as a dynamic hypothesis that has since been widely validated in a host of different contexts (Pettigrew, 1997).

Humanizing Factory Work

Dehumanizing factory assembly lines in which workers were forced to do the same repetitive, mindless task, as if they were robots, initially gave Detroit automakers a production advantage. However, Japanese automakers replaced such routinized assembly lines with harmonious, small work teams operating under conditions of participatory management and in-group democratic principles. The remarkable success of the Japanese automakers in overtaking their American counterparts in a relatively short time is due in part to their adaptation of the principles of group dynamics developed by Kurt Lewin, his colleagues and students at the Massachusetts Institute of Technology, and the University of Michigan (Lewin, 1947a, 1947b, 1948). Paradoxically, U.S. auto manufacturers are now incorporating this Japanese work model into their factories, decades after they should have done so. This is one way in which psychological theory can be credited with a humanizing impact on industrial work. But psychologists working in the industrial/organizational framework have done even more to help businesses appreciate and promote the importance of goal setting, worker-job fit, job satisfaction, and personnel selection and training.

Political Polling

It is hard to imagine elections without systematic polling of various segments of the electorate using sampling techniques as predictors of election outcomes. Polling for many other purposes by Gallup, Roper, and other opinion polling agencies has become big business. Readers might be surprised to learn that psychologist Hadley Cantril (1991) pioneered in conducting research into the methodology of polling in the 1940s. Throughout World War II, Cantril provided President Roosevelt with valuable information on American public opinion. He also established the Office of Public Opinion Research, which became a central archive for polling data.

How and Why Psychology Matters in Our Lives

I am proud to be a psychologist. As the 2002 APA president, one of my goals was to spread that pride far and wide among my colleagues as well as among all students of psychology. For starters, we can all be proud of the many contributions we have made collectively to enrich the way people think about the human condition, a bit of which was outlined above. I am also proud of the fact that our scientific approach to understanding the behavior of individuals has guided some policy and improved some operating procedures in our society. We have always been one of the most vigilant and outspoken proponents of the use of the scientific method for bringing reliable evidence to bear on a range of issues (Campbell, 1969). Given any intervention or new policy, psychologists insist on raising the question, "but does it really work?" and utilizing evaluative methodologies and meta-analyses to help make that decision. Psychologists have modeled the approach to reducing errors in advancing behavior-based conclusions through random assignment, double-blind tests, and sensitivity to the many biases present in uncontrolled observations and research procedures. Many of us have also been leaders in advancing a variety of innovations in education through our awareness of principles of attention, learning, memory, individual differences, and classroom dynamics. In addition, I am proud of our discipline's dedication to relieving all forms of human suffering through effective therapeutic interventions along with promoting prevention strategies and appropriate environmental change. As psychologists, we should also be pleased by discovering that our theories, research, and methodologies are serving to influence individual and societal actions, as will be shown next.

Psychologymatters.org

The scaffolding for such pride in psychology might best be manifest in a newly developed compendium, which shows society what we have done and are doing to improve the quality of life. I wanted to have available in one easily accessible and indexed source a listing of the research and theories that have been translated into practice. Such a resource would indicate how each item is being applied in various settings, such as schools, clinics, hospitals, businesses, community services, and legal and governmental agencies. It would establish the fact that psychology makes a significant difference in our lives by means of these concrete exemplars of its relevant applications. Ideally, this compendium would indicate how psychological contributions have saved lives, reduced or prevented suffering, saved money, made money, enhanced educational goals, improved security and safety, promoted justice and fairness, made organizations operate more effectively, and more. By designing this compendium as a Web-based open file, it can be continually updated, modified, and expanded as promising research meets the criterion of acceptability as having made a practically significant difference.

This effort to devise a compendium began with the help of APA's Science Directorate, by issuing a call for submissions to many e-mail lists serving APA members and through re-

10

quests in APA's *Monitor on Psychology* and on the www.apa.org Web site. The initial set of items was vetted independently by Len Mitnick (formerly of the National Institute of Mental Health) and me. A "blue-ribbon" task force of journal editors, textbook authors, and senior scientists was formed to further vet these final items, help revise them, and then to work at expanding our base.[2]

Because this compendium offers the opportunity to portray an attractive, intelligent face of psychology to the public, final drafts have been edited or rewritten by science writers in APA's Public Communication's office, ably directed by Rhea Farberman. Ideally, the submissions appear in a jargon-free, readable style appealing to the nonpsychologist public, as well as to our professional colleagues. In addition to having the individual items categorized into many general topical domains, readily searchable by key words or phrases, we have expanded the value of this site by adding an extensive glossary of psychological terms, a historical timeline of major psychological events and contributors, and basic information on "how to be a wiser consumer of research." We will include other extensions as appropriate based on feedback from colleagues and the public we are serving.

The criteria for inclusion are that each submission be presented (a) in sufficient detail to allow an independent assessment; (b) with evidence of significant statistical effects obtained within the study; (c) with reported application or extension of the submitted research, methodology, or theory in some specific domain of relevance; and (d) with evidence of where and how it has made a significant difference, such as citation of a new law, policy, standardized procedure, or operating system that was based on the submitted item. Items with *promise* of such applicability in the future (because they were too new to have been subject to any evaluation of outcome effectiveness) are being held in a "wait-and-check-back-later" file. I should mention in passing that many submitted items described research that was interesting, including some classic studies, but they have never met the test of societal applicability.

I welcome the feedback of *American Psychologist* readers on this first phase of our efforts, while also issuing a cordial invitation to add your voice to this compendium with additional worthy submissions. The reach of these initial efforts will hopefully be extended by having this compendium serve as a model to the psychological associations of countries around the world, adding to psychology's global relevance.

Please visit us at www.psychologymatters.org. But please wait a moment before booting up your computer, until you finish reading the next section of this article, which highlights a sampling of what you will find there.

Highlights of Psychology's Real World Relevance

I want to conclude with a dozen or so examples taken from our compendium that illustrate a range of its different topics and domains of applicability. This presentation will end with one ex-

tended instance of what I consider a model collaboration of theory, research, media applicability, and global dissemination of psychological knowledge conveyed in a unique format—soap operas! It is the ingenious application of the theory of social modeling by Albert Bandura (1965, 1977) in the design of scenarios used in soap operas to encourage literacy, birth control, the education of woman, environmental sustainability, and more.

Human Factors

Traffic safety has been improved by researchers in the area of human factors and ergonomics through a better understanding of visual perception. We now know that changing the standard color of red emergency trucks to a lime-green color reduces accidents because that greenish hue is better perceived in dim light. Similarly, changing traffic sign fonts to increase their recognition at night is another safety improvement resulting from psychological research by Allen (1970), Solomon and King (1985), and Garvey, Pietrucha, and Meeker (1997).

Scott Geller's (2001, 2003) research program applies Skinnerian behavior analysis to increase safe behaviors, reduce at-risk behaviors, and prevent unintentional injuries at work and on the road. Such unintentional injury is the leading cause of death to people ages 44 years and under. The behavior-based safety (BBS) approach for increasing safety identifies critical behaviors that are targeted for change, establishes baselines, applies change interventions, and evaluates workers' change away from specific risky behaviors to more beneficial directions. This approach has been applied in thousands of organizations with great success, such as in having people wear seat belts and in occupational safety programs. The rate of reported injuries after five years of implementation of this behavioral approach decreased by as much as an average 72% across a number of organizations (for a summary of the evidence for the extent of injury reduction, see the report by Beth Sulzer-Azaroff & John Austin, 2000). One indicator of the social significance of applying behavior analysis is apparent in the *Clinical Practice Guidelines* of New York States' (1999) Department of Health, Early Intervention Program: "It is recommended that principles of applied behavior analysis (ABA) and behavior intervention strategies be included as important elements in any intervention program for young children with autism" (p. 13).

Navigational aids for the blind and visually impaired people have been developed by psychologists Roberta Klatsky and Jack Loomis, working with geographer Reginald Golledge (Loomis, Klatsky, & Golledge, 2001) over several decades. They utilize principles of spatial cognition along with those of space and auditory perception to guide locomotion. Their new technology is now in development funded by the National Institute for Disability and Rehabilitation Research.

Criminal Justice

Cognitive and social psychologists have shown that eyewitness testimony is surprisingly unreliable. Their research reveals the ease with which recall of criminal events is biased by external influences in interrogations and police line-ups. The seminal work of Beth Loftus (1975, 1979, 1992) and Gary Wells (Wells

& Olson, 2003), among others, has been recognized by the U.S. Attorney General's office in drawing up national guidelines for the collection of accurate and unbiased eyewitness identification (see Malpass & Devine, 1981; Stebley, 1997).

The Stanford Prison Experiment has become a classic demonstration of the power of social situational forces to negatively impact the behavior of normal, healthy participants who began to act in pathological or evil ways in a matter of a few days (Zimbardo, Haney, Banks, & Jaffe, 1973). It added a new awareness of institutional power to the authority power of Stanley Milgram's (1974) blind obedience studies (see Blass, 1999; Zimbardo, Maslach, & Haney, 1999). The lessons of this research have gone well beyond the classroom. In part as a consequence of my testimony before a Senate judiciary committee on crime and prisons (Zimbardo, 1974), its committee chair, Senator Birch Bayh, prepared a new law for federal prisons requiring juveniles in pretrial detention to be housed separately from adult inmates (to prevent their being abused). Our participants were juveniles in the pretrial detention facility of the Stanford jail. A video documentary of the study, "Quiet Rage: The Stanford Prison Experiment," has been used extensively by many agencies within the civilian and military criminal justice system as well as in shelters for abused women. I recently discovered that it is even used to educate role-playing military interrogators in the Navy SEAR (survival, evasion, and resistance) program about the dangers of abusing their power against others role-playing pretend spies and terrorists (Annapolis Naval College psychology staff, personal communication, September 18, 2003). The Web site for the Stanford Prison Experiment gets more than 500 visitors daily and has had more than 13 million unique page views in the past four years (www .prisonexp.org). Those surprising figures should be telling us that we must focus more effort on utilizing the power of the Web as a major new medium for disseminating psychology's messages directly to a worldwide audience.

Education

Among the many examples of psychology at work in the field of education, two of my favorites naturally have a social psychological twist. Elliot Aronson and his research team in Austin, Texas, dealt with the negative consequences of desegregated schools by creating "jigsaw classrooms." Prejudice against minority children was rampant, those children were not performing well, and elementary school classes were marked by high degrees of tension. But when all students were taught to share a set of materials in small learning teams where each child has one set of information indispensable to the rest of the team, and on which tests and grades depend, remarkable things happened. All kids started to listen to the other kids, especially minority kids who they used to ignore or disparage, because such attention and cooperation is essential to getting a good grade. Not only did the self-esteem of the minority children escalate, but so did their academic performance, as prejudice and discrimination went down. The techniques of the jigsaw classroom are inexpensive for teachers to learn and to operationalize, so it is no wonder that Aronson's simple concept is now being incor-

porated into the curricula of hundreds of schools in many states, with similarly impressive results (Aronson, 1990; Aronson, Blaney, Stephan, Sikes, & Snapp, 1978; Aronson & Gonzalez, 1988; Aronson & Patnoe, 1997).

Teaching young children interpersonal cognitive problem solving skills, known as ICPS, reduces physical and verbal aggression, increases coping with frustrations, and promotes positive peer relationships. This research program developed by Myrna Shure and George Spivak (1982) over the past several decades is a major violence prevention approach being applied in schools and family agencies in programs called "Raising a Thinking Child" and by the U.S. Department of Education's "I Can Problem Solve" program.

Health

Environmental health is threatened by a host of toxic substances, such as lead, mercury, solvents, and pesticides. Experimental psychologists, behavioral analysts, and psychometricians have helped create the field of behavioral toxicology that recognizes the nervous system as the target for many toxins, with defects in behavior and mental processes as the symptomatic consequences. Pioneering work by psychologist Bernard Weiss (1992,1999) and others has had a significant impact on writing behavioral tests into federal legislation, thereby better regulating the use of a wide range of neurotoxins in our environment. That research documents the vulnerability of children's developing brains to chemicals in the environment.

Among the many negative consequences of America's involvement in the Vietnam War was the explosion of the phenomenon of posttraumatic stress disorder (PTSD). Many veterans were experiencing this debilitating disorder that was uncovered during their psychotherapy treatments. The more we discovered about this delayed, persistent, intense stress reaction to violence and trauma, the more we realized that veterans of earlier wars had also experienced PTSD, but it was unlabeled. That was also the case with many civilian victims of trauma, among them rape victims and those who had experienced child abuse. PTSD has become a well-recognized and publicly acknowledged phenomenon today because it was one of the mental health consequences of the monumental trauma from the terrorist attacks on September 11, 2001, in New York City and Washington, DC. Credit for the early recognition, identification, measurement, and treatment of PTSD goes to the programs of research funded by the Veteran's Administration, which was pioneered by the research team of clinical psychologist Terry Keane (Keane, Malloy, & Fairbank, 1984; Weathers, Keane, & Davidson, 2001).

The Magic of Touch

One of the consequences of a host of amazing medical advances is saving the lives of many premature infants who would have died even just a decade ago. With modern intensive care, preemies weighing only a few pounds now survive, but the essential hospital costs are staggering, up to $10,000 a day for weeks or months! One simple solution for sending them home sooner depends on accelerating their growth by means of touch therapy.

Psychologist Field extended earlier research she had done with biologist Saul Shanberg (Field, 1998; Field & Schanberg, 1990; Field et al., 1986) on massaging infant rat pups that were motherless. Just as the infant rats rapidly grew in response to that vigorous touch, so did the human preemies. Massaging them several times a day for only 15 minutes was sufficient to stimulate growth hormones. On average, such massaged infants are able to go home six days sooner than comparison preemies treated in the conventional way. Given 470,000 premature infants are born each year in the United States alone, it is evident that billions of dollars in health care costs could be saved if this simple, inexpensive treatment was made standard procedure in more hospital intensive care units (see also Meltz, 2000).

To establish the societal value of any intervention designed to save lives or enhance health and well-being, one must systematically evaluate its cost-effectiveness. That means establishing a ratio of the benefits compared with various cost estimates of putting the intervention into operation and sustaining it over time. Such a ratio was developed for dollar costs per year of life saved and applied to more than 500 life-saving interventions (Tengs et al., 1995). Across all of these interventions, the median cost was $42,000 per year of life saved. Although some programs save more resources than they cost, others cost millions of dollars for each year of life they save and thus become of questionable social value. Using this standard measure, we discover that new neonatal intensive care for low-birth-weight infants (preemies) costs a whooping $270,000 for each year of their lives saved. By that yardstick, the inexpensive touch therapy intervention would dramatically reduce that cost-effectiveness ratio.

The puzzling issue then is why such a simple procedure is not now standard operating procedure in every such intensive care unit in the nation or the world? One goal of our compendium development team is also to investigate why some potentially useful interventions have not been applied in the venues where they could make a significant difference. For instance, social psychologists have shown convincingly that elderly patients in a home for the aged who were given a sense of control and responsibility over even minor events became healthier and lived significantly longer than comparison patients (Langer & Rodin, 1976; Rodin & Langer, 1977). Amazingly, this simple, powerful intervention has not ever been utilized—even in the institution where the research was conducted.

Undoing Dyslexia via Video Games

Treatment for dyslexia by speech therapists and counselors is a slow, long, expensive, and frustrating experience for professionals, parents, and children. Cognitive neuroscientist, Paula Tallal, is using new functional magnetic resonance imaging techniques to identify the source of reading dyslexia in brain regions that do not adequately process fast appearing sound-sight phonemic combinations. She then worked with a computer-programming agency to develop special video games that systematically shape these children's ever-faster responses to various sights and sounds in the games. With this new technology, children treat themselves in an atmosphere of entertainment and ad-

venture, rely only on intrinsic motivation of game playing, get personalized feedback, and need minimal supervision by highly skilled professionals.

The special computerized video game is called "Fast ForWord." It provides intensive, highly individualized adaptive training across a large number of cognitive, linguistic, and reading skills that are vital for academic success. By adapting trial by trial to each child's performance, progress in aural and written language skills of children with dyslexia is reduced to but a few weeks from what had been typically years of intervention efforts. Approximately 375,000 individuals have completed such training across 2,200 public schools nationwide, and over 2,000 private practice professionals use Fast ForWord programs in their clinics (for more information, visit www.scientificlearning.com and www.brainconnection.com).

This sensitive application of psychological knowledge and new methods blended with high technology has resulted in enhanced quality of life for these children as well as their families and teachers, not to mention much money and resources saved (see Holly Fitch & Tallal, 2003; Tallal & Benasich, 2002; Tallal, Galaburda, Llinas, & Von Euler, 1993).

An Idealized Example of Psychology Applied Globally

The use of intrinsically interesting media, such as video games and Tele-Health dynamic systems, enables adults as well as children to play central roles in individualized health-management programs. The power of the media also has been extended to television as a far-reaching medium to convey vital persuasive messages about behavior changes that are essential to cope with many of the social, economic, political, and health problems facing individuals around the globe. Can psychology contribute to effectively dealing with the population explosion in many countries, increase the status and education of women, and minimize or prevent AIDS? A tall order, for sure. However, it is now happening through a remarkable collaboration of a wise TV producer, a brilliant psychologist, and an international agency that distributes their unusual messages worldwide (Bandura, 2002; Smith, 2002).

Promoting Family Planning

The explosion in population around the world is one of our most urgent global problems. Ecologically sustainable development and growth is being challenged by a variety of entwined phenomena, such as high fertility rates in many countries coupled with suboptimal birth rates in others, dramatically increased longevity in some nations along with the spread of deadly communicable diseases in others. One means of population control in overpopulated countries involves women and men actively engaged in their own family planning. However, the question is how to do so effectively and efficiently because most previous efforts have met with minimal success?

A TV producer in Mexico, Miguel Sabido, created soap operas that were serialized daily dramas, with prosocial messages about practicing family planning and also others that promote literacy and education of women. Woven into the narrative of his commercial dramas were elements taken from Albert Bandura's sociocognitive theory of the importance of social models in shaping desired behaviors (Bandura, 1965, 1977, 1986). In many Spanish-speaking countries, most family members watch soap operas fervently each day as their plots unfold over many weeks or months. Viewers identify with attractive, desirable models and dis-identify with those whose actions seem repulsive or create unwanted problems for the "good" guys. In some scenarios, there are also actors who represent "transitional models," starting off engaging in high-risk or undesirable behaviors but then changing in socially appropriate directions. After some programs, there is informational or community support for the cause being projected, by celebrities, government officials, or members of the clergy. This secondary influence path for behavior change adds the key element of making connections to the viewers' personal social networks and community settings in addition to the direct path from the media message to desired changes in target behaviors.

Does it really work? After watching the Mexican programs promoting family planning, many women enrolled in family planning clinics. The 32% increase of woman starting to use this service was similar to the increase in contraceptive users. This was true even though there was never an explicit message about contraception for family planning (in deference to the negative position on this birth control issue by the Catholic Church). Another key result was that the greater the level of media exposure to these family-oriented TV soap operas, the greater was the percentage of women using contraceptives and also discussing family planning with spouses "many times" (Bandura, 2002).

Preventing the Spread of AIDS

These dramas were shown in one region of Tanzania, Africa, and their effects compared with a control region where TV viewers were not exposed to the dramas (later on they got to see the same soap operas). One of the many prosocial effects was an increase in new family planning adopters following the viewing of these dramatic serials compared with no change in the control region. Seventeen segments were included in dramas in Tanzania to prevent the spread of the AIDS virus, a special problem among truck drivers who have unprotected sex with hundreds of prostitutes working at truck stop hubs. Actors portrayed positive models who adopt safe sex practices or negative ones who do not—and then they die of AIDS! Condom distribution soared following viewing this series, whereas it remained low in the control, no soap opera region. Along with this critical change in behavior were also reports of reduced number of sexual partners, more talk about HIV infection, and changed beliefs in personal risk of HIV infection from unprotected sex. Such attitudinal and behavioral changes are vital to slowing the spread of AIDS, which is estimated to make orphans of up to 25 million children worldwide in the next half dozen years (Naik, 2002; The Straits Times, 2002).

Female Literacy

Education of women is one of the most powerful prophylaxes for limiting population growth, so these soap opera programs in many countries show stories that endorse women continuing with their education as one way of liberating young women from male and matriarchal dominance. In one village in India, there was an immediate 30% increase in women going to school after the airing of these soap operas.

A Potent Blending of Talents, Wisdom, and Resources for Social Good

So here we have the unique case of a wise person in the media borrowing ideas from a psychologist and then extending the scope of influence by pairing up with a nonprofit agency, Population Communications International (PCI) to disseminate these dramas worldwide. PCI's "mission is to work creatively with the media and other organizations to motivate individuals and communities to make choices that influence population trends encouraging development and environmental protection" (PCI, 2002). PCI's efforts at social diffusion span more than 17 countries worldwide with radio and TV serial dramas, comic books, and videos for classroom use. Finally, there is a fourth essential component: systematic evaluation of outcomes by an independent organization of all of these entertainment-educational change programs (see www.population.org).

It is evident that these serial dramatizations use the power of narrative story telling over an extended time, which the public views voluntarily, to motivate specific behavior change in directions guided by the information conveyed in the drama, which in turn has its origins in sound psychological theory and research. What also becomes evident is that when psychologists want to give psychology away to the public, we need to collaborate with those who understand best *how* to reach the public, namely those intimately involved with the mass media. They are our gatekeepers to the audiences we want to reach and influence. We have to find ways of inviting and intriguing media with the utility of psychological knowledge for crafting entertaining stories that can make a significant difference in the quality of lives of individuals and society.

Accentuating Psychology's Positive Messages

The collaboration between psychologist Albert Bandura, media master Miguel Sabido, and the resourcefulness of the PCI agency is an ideal model for us to emulate and extend in spreading more of our positive messages. Among those new messages are the two exciting directions that psychology can be expected to take in the next decade. The emergence of Martin Seligman's (2002) revolutionary "Positive Psychology" enterprise is creating a new vital force for recognizing and enriching the talents, strengths, and virtues of even ordinary people (see Diener, 2000; Myers, 2002; Snyder & Lopez, 2002). It is shifting attention away from deficits, disabilities, and disorders toward a focus on what is special about human nature like our resilience in the face of trauma, our joys, our sense of wonder and curiosity, and our capacity for goodness and love.

The fertile field of "behavioral economics" integrates psychology with economics and neuroscience to understand the economically irrational human element in judgments under uncertainty (see Kahneman & Tversky, 1979; Simon, 1955; Tversky & Kahneman, 1974, 1986). We can anticipate that Daniel Kahneman's winning the 2003 Nobel Prize in economics has made him a role model for the next generation of professional psychologists to emulate and to enter this exciting domain of relevant inquiry.

In conclusion, I repeat the questions that got me to this point and the simple answer that I now feel is justified—and I hope readers of this article agree with its positive bias.

Does psychology matter? Can psychological research, theory, methods, and practice make a significant difference in the lives of individuals, communities, and nations? Do we psychologists have a legacy of which we can be proud? Can we do more and better research that has significant applicable effects in the real world? Are we ready now "to give psychology away to the public" in useful, accessible ways? And finally, can we learn how better to collaborate with the media, with technology experts, with community leaders, and with other medical and behavioral scientists for psychology to make an even more significant difference in the coming decade?

My final answer is simply YES, YES indeed! May the positive forces of psychology be with you, and with our society.

Editor's note. Philip G. Zimbardo was president of APA in 2002. This article is based on his presidential address, delivered in Toronto, Canada, at APA's 111th Annual Convention on August 9, 2003. Award addresses and other archival materials, including presidential addresses, are peer reviewed but have a higher chance of publication than do unsolicited submissions. Presidential addresses are expected to be expressions of the authors' reflections on the field and on their terms as president. Both this address and that of Robert J. Sternberg, the 2003 APA president, were presented at this convention to catch up on the year lag that had developed in the last decade of giving presidential addresses.

Author's note. Correspondence concerning this article should be addressed to Philip G. Zimbardo, Department of Psychology, Stanford University Building 430, Mail Code 380, Stanford, CA 94305. E-mail: zim@stanford.edu

NOTES

1. Recognizing the importance of bringing psychology's understanding that violence is a learned behavior to the public, APA has joined with the National Association for the Education of Young Children and the Advertising Council to create a national multimedia public service advertising campaign designed to remind adults of the role they play in teaching children to use or avoid violence and then empower these adults to model and teach the right lessons. The campaign, first launched in 2000, has reached over 50 million households. At the community level, the campaign includes collaborations with local groups in a train-the-

trainer model to bring early childhood violence prevention awareness and know-how to parents, teachers, and other caregivers.

2. The task force selected to identify and evaluate the research, theory, and methodology in psychology that qualified for inclusion in the Psychology Matters compendium has been ably cochaired by David Myers and Robert Bjork. Other members have included Alan Boneau. Gordon Bower, Nancy Eisenberg, Sam Glucksberg, Philip Kendall, Kevin Murphy, Scott Pious, Peter Salovey, Alana Conner-Snibbe, Beth Sulzer-Azaroff, Chris Wickens, and Alice Young. They have been assisted by the addition of Brett Pelham and David Partenheimer. Rhea Farberman and her staff in APA's Office of Public Communications have played a vital role in the development and continuing evolution of this project. The staff of the Science Directorate aided in the early development of the survey that was circulated to initiate electronic input of candidate items from APA constituent groups.

REFERENCES

Ader, R., & Cohen, N. (1993). Psychoneuroimmunology: Conditioning and stress. *Annual Review of Psychology, 44,* 53–85.

Alien, M. J. (1970). *Vision and highway safety.* Philadelphia: Chilton.

Allport, G. (1954). *The nature of prejudice.* Reading, MA: Addison-Wesley.

American Academy of Pediatrics, Committee on Psychosocial Aspect of Child and Family Health. (1998). Guidance for effective discipline. *Pediatrics, 101,* 723–728.

Aronson, E. (1990). Applying social psychology to desegregation and energy conservation. *Personality and Social Psychology Bulletin, 16,* 118–132.

Aronson, E., Blaney, N., Stephan, C., Sikes, J.. & Snapp, M. (1978). *The jigsaw classroom.* Beverly Hills, CA: Sage.

Aronson, E., & Gonzalez, A. (1988). Desegregation jigsaw, and the Mexican-American experience. In P. A. Katz & D. Taylor (Eds.), *Eliminating racism: Profiles in controversy* (pp. 301–314). New York: Plenum Press.

Aronson, E., & Patnoe, S. (1997). *The jigsaw classroom: Building cooperation in the classroom* (2nd ed.). New York: Addison Wesley Longman.

Axelrod, S., & Apsche, H. (1983). *Effects of punishment on human behavior.* New York: Academic Press.

Baltes, P. B., & Staudinger, U. M. (2000). Wisdom: A metaheuristic (pragmatic) to orchestrate mind and virtue toward excellence. *American Psychologist, 55,* 122–136.

Bandura, A. (1965). Influence of models' reinforcement contingencies on the acquisition of imitated responses. *Journal of Personality and Social Psychology. 1,* 589–595.

Bandura, A. (1977). *Social learning theory.* Englewood Cliffs, NJ: Prentice Hall.

Bandura, A. (1986). *Social foundations of thought and action: A social cognitive theory.* Englewood Cliffs, NJ: Prentice Hall.

Bandura, A. (2002). Environmental sustainability by sociocognitive deceleration of population growth. In P. Schmuck & W. Schultz (Eds.), *The psychology of sustainable development* (pp. 209–238). Dordrecht, the Netherlands: Kluwer.

Baumrind, D. (1973). The development of instrumental competence through socialization. In A. Pick (Ed.), *Minnesota Symposium on Child Development* (Vol. 6, pp. 3–46). Minneapolis: University of Minnesota Press.

Beck, A. T. (1976). *Cognitive therapy and emotional disorders.* New York: International Universities Press.

Bee, H. (1994). *Lifespan development.* New York: HarperCollins.

Binet, A. (1911). *Les idé es modernes sur les enfants* [Modern ideas about children]. Paris: Flammarion.

Binet, A., & Simon. T. (1915). *A method of measuring the development of intelligence of young children*. Chicago: Chicago Medical Books.

Blass, T. (Ed.). (1999). *Obedience to authority: Current perspectives on the Milgram Paradigm* (pp. 193–237). Mahwah, NJ: Erlbaum.

Campbell. D. T. (1969). Reforms as experiments. *American Psychologist, 24*, 409–429.

Cantril, A. H. (1991). *The opinion connection: Polling, politics, and the press*. Washington, DC: CQ Press.

Clark, K. B., & Clark, M. K. (1939a). The development of consciousness of self and the emergence of racial identification in negro preschool children. *Journal of Social Psychology, 10*, 591–599.

Clark, K. B., & Clark, M. K. (1939b). Segregation as a factor in the racial identification of negro preschool children: A preliminary report. *Journal of Experimental Education, 8*, 161–163.

Clark, K. B., & Clark, M. K. (1940). Skin color as a factor in racial identification of negro preschool children. *The Journal of Social Psychology, II*, 159–169.

Clark, K. B., & Clark, M. K. (1950). Emotional factors in racial identification and preference in negro children. *Journal of Negro Education, 19*, 341–350.

Coe, C. L. (1999). Psychosocial factors and psychoneuroimmunology within a lifespan perspective. In D. P. Keating & C. Hertzman (Eds.), *Developmental health and the wealth of nations: Social, biological, and educational dynamics* (pp. 201–219). New York: Guilford Press.

Cohen, S., & Herbert, T. B. (1996). Health psychology: Psychological factors and physical disease from the perspective of human psychoneuroimmunology. *Annual Review of Psychology, 47*, 113—142.

Cohen, S., & Syme, S. L. (Eds.). (1985). *Social support and health*. Orlando. FL: Academic Press.

Collins, W. A., Maccoby, E. E., Steinberg, L., Hetherington, E. M., & Bornstein, M. H. (2000). Contemporary research on parenting: The case for nature and nurture. *American Psychologist, 55*, 218–232.

Cronbach, L. J. (1975). Five decades of public controversy over mental testing. *American Psychologist, 30*, 1–14.

Darling, N., & Steinberg, L. (1993). Parenting style as context: An integrative model. *Psychological Bulletin, 113*, 487–496.

Diener, E. (2000). Subjective well-being: The science of happiness and a proposal for a national index. *American Psychologist, 55*, 34–43.

Discovering psychology [Television series]. (1990; updated 2001). Boston: WGBH, with the American Psychological Association. (Funded and distributed by the Annenberg CPB Foundation, Washington, DC)

Druckman. D., & Bjork, R. A. (1991). *In the mind's eye: Enhancing human performance*. Washington, DC: National Academy Press.

DuBois, P. H. (1970). *A history of psychological testing*. Boston: Allyn & Bacon.

Erikson, E. H. (1963). *Childhood and society* (2nd ed.). New York: Norton.

Field, T. (1998). Massage therapy effects. *American Psychologist, 53*, 1270–1281.

Field, T., & Schanberg, S. M. (1990). Massage alters growth and catecholamine production in preterm newborns. In N. Gunzenhauser (Ed.), *Advances in touch* (pp. 96–104). Skillman, NJ: Johnson & Johnson.

Field, T., Schanberg, S. M., Scafidi, F., Bauer, C. R., Vega-Lahr, N., Garcia, R., et al. (1986). Tactile/kinesthetic stimulation effects on preform neonates. *Pediatrics, 77*, 654–658.

Freud, S. (1923). *Introductory lectures on psycho-analysis* (J. Riviera, Trans.). London: Allen & Unwin. (Original work published 1896)

Freud, S. (1965). *The interpretation of dreams*. New York: Avon. (Original work published 1900)

Garvey, P. M., Pietrucha, M. T., & Meeker, D. (1997). Effects of font and capitalization on legibility of guide signs. *Transportation Research Record No. 1605*, 73–79.

Geller, E. S. (2001). *The psychology of safety handbook*. Boca Raton, FL: CRC Press.

Geller, E. S. (2003). Behavior-based safety in industry: Realizing the large-scale potential of behavior analysis to promote human welfare. *Applied & Preventive Psychology, 10*, 87–105.

Gerrig, R., & Zimbardo, P. G. (2004). *Psychology and life* (17th ed.). Boston: Allyn & Bacon.

Green, C. D., Shore, M., & Teo, T. (2001). *The transformation of psychology: Influences of 19th century philosophy, technology, and natural science*. Washington, DC: American Psychological Association.

Hart, S. N. (1991). From property to person status: Historical perspective on children's rights. *American Psychologist, 46*, 53–59.

Hollon, S. D., Thase, M. E., & Markowitz, J. C. (2002). Treatment and prevention of depression. *Psychological Science in the Public Interest, 3*, 39–77.

Holly Fitch, R., & Tallal, P. (2003). Neural mechanisms of language-based learning impairments: Insights from human populations and animal models. *Behavior and Cognitive Neuroscience Reviews, 2*, 155–178.

Horowitz, R. M. (1984). Children's rights: A look backward and a glance ahead. In R. M. Horowitz & J. B. Lazar (Eds.), *Legal rights of children* (pp. 1–9). New York: McGraw-Hill.

Hovland, C. I., Janis, I. L., & Kelley, H. H. (1953). *Communication and persuasion*. New Haven, CT: Yale University Press.

Hovland, C. I., Lumsdaine, A. A., & Sheffield, F. D. (1949). *Experiments on mass communication*. Princeton, NJ: Princeton University Press.

Janis, I. L. (1958). *Psychological stress: Psychoanalytical and behavioral studies of surgical patients*. New York: Wiley.

Jung, C. G. (1959). The concept of the collective unconscious. In *The archetypes and the collective unconscious, collected works* (Vol. 9, Part 1, pp. 54–74). Princeton, NJ: Princeton University Press. (Original work published 1936)

Kahneman, D.. & Tversky, A. (1979). Prospect theory: An analysis of decision under risk. *Econometrica, 47*, 263–291.

Kazdin, A. E. (1994). *Behavior modification in applied settings* (5th ed.). Pacific Grove, CA: Brooks/Cole.

Keane, T. M., Malloy, P. F., & Fairbank, J. A. (1984). Empirical development of an MMPI subscale for the assessment of PTSD. *Journal of Consulting and Clinical Psychology, 52*, 138–140.

Langer, E. F., & Rodin, J. (1976). The effects of choice and enhanced personal responsibility for the aged: A field experiment in an institutionalized setting. *Journal of Personality and Social Psychology, 34*, 191–198.

Lazarus, R. S. (1993). From psychological stress to the emotions: A history of changing outlooks. *Annual Review of Psychology, 44*, 1–21.

Lazarus, R. S., & Folkman, S. (1984). *Stress, appraisal, and coping*. New York: Springer.

Lewin, K. (1947a). Frontiers in group dynamics: Concept, method and reality in social science; social equilibria and social change. *Human Relations, 1*, 5–41.

Lewin, K. (1947b). Frontiers in group dynamics: II. Channels of group life; social planning and action research. *Human Relations, 1,* 143–153.

Lewin, K. (1948). *Resolving social conflicts.* New York: Harper.

Loftus, E. F. (1975). Leading questions and the eyewitness report. *Cognitive Psychology, 7,* 560–572.

Loftus, E. F. (1979). Eyewitness testimony. Cambridge, MA: Harvard University Press. Loftus, E. F. (1992). When a lie becomes memory's truth: Memory distortion after exposure to misinformation. *Current Directions in Psychological Science, 1,* 121–123.

Loomis, J. M., Klatsky, R. L., & Golledge, R. G. (2001). Navigating without vision: Basic and applied research. *Optometry and Vision Science, 78,* 282–289.

Maas, J. (1998). *Power sleep: The revolutionary program that prepares your mind for peak performance.* New York: Villard.

Maccoby, E. E. (1980). *Social development: Psychological growth and the parent-child relationship.* San Diego, CA: Harcourt Brace Jovanovich.

Maccoby, E. E. (1992). The role of parents in the socialization of children: An historical overview. *Developmental Psychology, 28,* 1006–1017.

Maccoby, E. E. (2000). Parenting and its effects on children: On reading and misreading behavior genetics. *Annual Review of Psychology, 51,* 1–27.

Malpass, R. S., & Devine, P. G. (1981). Eyewitness identification: Lineup instructions and the absence of the offender. *Journal of Applied Psychology, 66,* 482–489.

Maslach, C. (1982). *Burnout: The cost of caring.* Englewood Cliffs, NJ: Prentice Hall.

McCoy, E. (1988). Childhood through the ages. In K. Finsterbush (Ed.), *Sociology 88/89* (pp. 44–47). Guilford, CT: Duskin.

Meltz, B. F. (2000, November 2). Do you touch your baby enough? *Boston Globe,* p. H1.

Milgram, S. (1974). *Obedience to authority.* New York: Harper & Row.

Miller, G. (1969). Psychology as a means of promoting human welfare. *American Psychologist, 24,* 1063–1075.

Miller, N. E. (1978). Biofeedback and visceral learning. *Annual Review of Psychology, 29,* 373–404.

Miller, N. E. (1985). The value of behavioral research on animals. *American Psychologist, 40,* 423–440.

Miller, N. E. (1992). Introducing and teaching much-needed understanding of the scientific process. *American Psychologist, 47,* 848–850.

Myers, D. G. (1993). *The pursuit of happiness.* New York: Avon.

Myers, D. G. (2002). *Intuition: Its powers and perils.* New Haven, CT: Yale University Press.

Naik, G. (2002, July 5). Uganda AIDS study suggests education stems spread of HIV. *Wall Street Journal,* p. A14.

New York State. (1999). *Clinical practice guidelines.* New York: Department of Health, Early Intervention Program, Autism.

Pappas. A. M. (1983). Introduction. In A. M. Pappas (Ed.), *Law and the status of the child* (pp. xxvii–lv). New York: United Nations Institute for Training and Research.

Pavlov, I. P. (1902). *The work of the digestive glands* (W. H. Thompson, Trans.) London: Griffin. (Original work published in 1897)

Pavlov, I. P. (1927). *Conditioned reflexes* (G. V. Anrep, Trans.). London: Oxford University Press. (Original work published 1897)

Pettigrew, T. F. (1997). Generalized intergroup contact effects on prejudice. *Personality and Social Psychology Bulletin, 23,* 173–185.

Piaget, J. (1954). *The construction of reality in the child.* New York: Basic Books.

Pinker, S. (1994). *The language instinct: How the mind creates language.* New York: Morrow.

Plomin, R., & McClearn, G. E. (1993). *Nature, nurture, and psychology.* Washington, DC: American Psychological Association.

Population Communications International. (2002). *15th anniversary: Keeping pace with change.* New York: Author.

Rodin, J., & Langer, E. F. (1977). Long-term effects of a control-relevant intervention with the institutionalized aged. *Journal of Personality and Social Psychology. 35,* 897–902.

Ruch, F. L., & Zimbardo, P. G. (1971). *Psychology and life* (8th ed.). Glenview, IL: Scott, Foresman.

Sarason, S. B. (1974). *The psychological sense of community: Prospects for a community psychology.* Oxford, England: Jossey-Bass.

Scarr, S. (1998). American child care today. *American Psychologist, 53,* 95–108.

Seligman, M. (2002). *Authentic happiness: Using the new positive psychology to realize your potential for lasting fulfillment.* New York: Free Press.

Shure, M. B., & Spivak, G. (1982). Interpersonal problem solving in children: A cognitive approach to prevention. *American Journal of Community Psychology, 10,* 341–356.

Simon, H. (1955). A behavioral model of rational choice. *Quarterly Journal of Economics, 69,* 99–118.

Skinner, B. F. (1938). *The behavior of organisms: An experimental analysis.* New York: Appleton-Century.

Skinner, B. F. (1948). *Walden two.* New York: Macmillan.

Skinner, B. F. (1966). What is the experimental analysis of behavior? *Journal of the Experimental Analysis of Behavior, 9,* 213–218.

Skinner, B, F. (1974). *About behaviorism.* New York: Knopf.

Smith, D. (2002). The theory heard "round the world." *Monitor on Psychology, 33,* 30–32.

Snyder, C. R., & Lopez, S. J. (2002). *Handbook of positive psychology.* New York: Oxford University Press.

Solomon, S. S., & King, J. G. (1985). Influence of color on fire vehicle accidents. *Journal of Safety Research, 26,* 47.

Stebley, N. M. (1997). Social influence in eyewitness recall: A meta-analytic review of line-up instruction effects. *Law and Human Behavior, 21,* 283–298.

Sternberg, R. J. (Ed.). (2000). *Handbook of intelligence.* Cambridge, England: Cambridge University Press.

The Straits Times. (2002, July 12). *The HIV orphan mega-crises.* Hong Kong: 14th International AIDS Conference.

Straus, M. A., & Kantor, G. K. (1994). Corporal punishment of adolescents by parents: A risk factor in the epidemiology of depression, suicide, alcohol abuse, child abuse, and wife beating. *Adolescence, 29,* 543–561.

Sulzer-Azaroff, B., & Austin, J. (2000, July). Does BBS work? Behavior-based safety and injury reduction: A survey of the evidence. *Professional Safety,* 19–24.

Swazey, J. P. (1974). *Chlorpromazine in psychiatry: A study of therapeutic innovation.* Cambridge, MA: MIT Press.

Tallal, P., & Benasich, A. A. (2002). Developmental language learning impairments. *Development and Psychopathology, 14,* 559–579.

Tallal, P., Galaburda, A. M., Llinas, R. R., & Von Euler, C. (Eds.). (1993). *Temporal information processing in the nervous system: Special reference to dyslexia and dysphasia* (Vol. 682). New York: New York Academy of Sciences

Taylor, S. E., & Clark, L. F. (1986). Does information improve adjustments to noxious events? In M. J. Saks & L. Saxe (Eds.), *Advances in applied social psychology* (Vol. 3, pp. 1–28). Hillsdale, NJ: Erlbaum.

Tengs, T, O., Adams, M. E., Pliskin, J. S., Safan, D. G., Siegel, J. E., Weinstein, M. C., & Graham, J. D, (1995). Five-hundred life-saving interventions and their cost effectiveness. *Risk Analysis, 15,* 369–390.

Tversky, A., & Kahneman, D. (1974). Judgment under uncertainty: Heuristics and biases. *Science, 185,* 1124–1131.

Tversky, A., & Kahneman, D. (1986). The framing of decisions and the psychology of choice. *Science, 211,* 453–458.

Weathers, F. W., Keane, T. M., & Davidson, J. R. T. (2001). Clinicians' administered PTSD scale: A review of the first ten years of research. *Depression & Anxiety, 13,* 132–156.

Weiss, B. (1992). Behavioral toxicology: A new agenda for assessing the risks of environmental pollution. In J. Grabowski & G. VandenBos (Eds.), *Psychopharmacology: Basic mechanisms and applied interventions. Master lectures in psychology* (pp. 167–207). Washington, DC: American Psychological Association.

Weiss, B. (1999, May). *The vulnerability of the developing brain to chemicals in the environment.* Paper presented at the New York Academy of Medicine conference on Environmental Toxins and Neurological Disorders, New York.

Wells, G. L., & Olson, E. A. (2003). Eyewitness testimony. *Annual Review of Psychology, 54,* 277–295.

Wolfe, M. M., Risely, T. R., & Mees, H. L. (1965). Application of operant conditioning procedures to behavior problems of an autistic child. *Research and Therapy, 1,* 302–312.

Wolpe, J. (1958). *Psychotherapy by reciprocal inhibition.* Stanford, CA: Stanford University Press.

Zimbardo, P. G. (1974). *The detention and jailing of juveniles* (pp. 141–161) [Hearings before U. S. Senate Committee on the Judiciary Subcommittee to Investigate Juvenile Delinquency, September 10, 11, 17, 1973], Washington, DC: U.S. Government Printing Office.

Zimbardo, P. G. (1975). On transforming experimental research into advocacy for social change. In M. Deulsch & H. Hornstein (Eds.), *Applying social psychology: Implications for research, practice and training* (pp. 33–66). Hillsdale, NJ: Erlbaum.

Zimbardo, P. G. (1977). *Shyness: What it is, what to do about it.* Reading, MA: Addison-Wesley.

Zimbardo, P. G. (1992). *Psychology and life* (13th ed.). New York: HarperCollins.

Zimbardo, P. G., Haney, C., Banks, W. C., & Jaffe, D. (1973, April 8). The mind is a formidable jailer: A Pirandellian prison. *The New York Times Magazine,* Section 6, pp. 38–46.

Zimbardo, P. G., Maslach, C., & Haney, C. (1999). Reflections on the Stanford prison experiment: Genesis, transformations, consequences. In T. Blass (Ed.), *Obedience to authority: Current perspectives on the Milgram Paradigm* (pp. 193–237). Mahwah, NJ: Erlbaum.

Zimbardo, P. G., Weber, A. L., & Johnson, R. L. (2002). *Psychology: Core concepts* (4th ed.). Boston, MA: Allyn & Bacon.

From *American Psychologist,* Vol. 59, No. 5, July/August 2004, pp. 339-351. Copyright © 2004 by the American Psychological Association. Reprinted by permission.

The 10 Commandments of Helping Students Distinguish Science from Pseudoscience in Psychology

SCOTT O. LILIENFIELD

"Professor Schlockenmeister, I know that we have to learn about visual perception in your course, but aren't we going to learn anything about extrasensory perception? My high school psychology teacher told us that there was really good scientific evidence for it."

"Dr. Glopelstein, you've taught us a lot about intelligence in your course. But when are you going to discuss the research showing that playing Mozart to infants increases their I.Q. scores?"

"Mr. Fleikenzugle, you keep talking about schools of psychotherapy, like psychoanalysis, behavior therapy, and client-centered therapy. But how come you've never said a word about sensory-motor integration therapy? My mother, who's an occupational therapist, tells me that it's a miracle cure for attention-deficit disorder."

The Psuedoscience of Popular Psychology

If you're like most introductory psychology instructors, these sorts of questions probably sound awfully familiar. There's a good reason: much of the popular psychology "knowledge" that our students bring to their classes consists of scant more than pseudoscience. Moreover, our students are often fascinated by dubious claims on the fringes of scientific knowledge: extrasensory perception, psychokinesis, channeling, out-of-body experiences, subliminal persuasion, astrology, biorhythms, "truth serum," the lunar lunacy effect, hypnotic age regression, multiple personality disorder, alien abduction reports, handwriting analysis, rebirthing therapy, and untested herbal remedies for depression, to name but a few. Of course, because some of these claims may eventually be shown to contain a core of truth, we should not dismiss them out of hand. Nevertheless, what is troubling about these claims is the glaring discrepancy between many individuals' beliefs in them and the meager scientific evidence on their behalf.

Yet many introductory psychology instructors accord minimal attention to potentially pseudoscientific topics in their courses, perhaps because they believe that these topics are of, at best, marginal relevance to psychological science. Moreover, many introductory psychology textbooks barely mention these topics. After all, there is already more than enough to cover in psychology courses, so why tack on material of doubtful scientific status? Furthermore, some instructors may fear that by devoting attention to questionable claims they will end up sending students the unintended message that these claims are scientifically credible.

Benefits of Teaching Students to Distinguish Science from Psuedoscience

So why should we teach psychology students to distinguish science from pseudoscience? As personality theorist George Kelly (1955) noted, an effective understanding of a construct requires an appreciation of both of its poles. For example, we cannot grasp fully the concept of "cold" unless we have experienced heat. Similarly, students may not grasp fully the concept of scientific thinking without an understanding of pseudoscientific beliefs, namely those that at first blush appear scientific but are not.

Moreover, by addressing these topics, instructors can capitalize on a valuable opportunity to impart critical thinking skills, such as distinguishing correlation from causation and recognizing the need for control groups, by challenging students' misconceptions regarding popular psychology. Although many students find these skills to be "dry" or even deadly dull when presented in the abstract, they often enjoy acquiring these skills in the context of lively and controversial topics (e.g., extrasensory perception) that stimulate their interest. Students often learn about such topics from various popular psychology sources that they seek out in everyday life, such as magazine articles, Internet sites, and television programs.

Indeed, for many beginning students, "psychology" is virtually synonymous with popular psychology. Yet because so much of popular psychology consists of myths and urban legends, such as most people use only 10 percent of their brains, expressing anger is usually better than holding it in, opposites attract in interpersonal relationships, high self-esteem is necessary for psychological health, people with schizophrenia have more than one personality, among a plethora of others, many students probably emerge from psychology courses with the same misconceptions with which they entered. As a consequence, they often depart college incapable of distinguishing the wheat from the chaff in popular psychology.

Teaching students to distinguish science from pseudoscience can prove immensely rewarding. Foremost among these rewards is producing discerning consumers of the popular psychology literature. Indeed, research evidence supports the efficacy of teaching psychology courses on pseudoscience and the paranormal. For example, Morier and Keeports (1994) reported that undergraduates enrolled in a "Science and Pseudoscience" seminar demonstrated a statistically significant reduction in paranormal beliefs relative to a quasi-control group of students enrolled in a psychology and law class over the same time period (see also Dougherty, 2004). They replicated this effect over a 2-year period with two sections of the course. Wesp and Montgomery (1998) found that a course on the objective examination of paranormal claims resulted in a statistically significant improvement in the evaluation of reasoning flaws in scientific articles. Specifically, students in this course were better able to identify logical errors in articles and provide rival explanations for research findings.

The 10 Commandments

Nevertheless, teaching students to distinguish science from pseudoscience brings more than its share of challenges and potential pitfalls. In my introductory psychology course (in which I emphasize strongly the distinction between science and pseudoscience in psychology) and in my advanced undergraduate seminar, "Science and Pseudoscience in Psychology," I have learned a number of valuable lessons (by first making just about every mistake about which I'll warn you).

In the following section, I summarize these teaching tips, which I refer to as the "10 Commandments" of teaching psychology students to distinguish science from pseudoscience. To avoid being accused of failing to separate Church from State, I have worded all of these injunctions in the positive rather than the negative to distinguish them from the (only slightly better known) biblical 10 Commandments. I urge readers of this column to inscribe these commandments on impressive stone tablets to be mounted outside of all psychology departments.

First Commandment

Thou shalt delineate the features that distinguish science from pseudoscience. It's important to communicate to students that the differences between science and pseudoscience, although not absolute or clear-cut, are neither arbitrary nor subjective. In-stead, philosophers of science (e.g., Bunge, 1984) have identified a constellation of features or "warning signs" that characterize most pseudoscientific disciplines. Among these warning signs are:

- A tendency to invoke ad hoc hypotheses, which can be thought of as "escape hatches" or loopholes, as a means of immunizing claims from falsification.
- An absence of self-correction and an accompanying intellectual stagnation.
- An emphasis on confirmation rather than refutation.
- A tendency to place the burden of proof on skeptics, not proponents, of claims.
- Excessive reliance on anecdotal and testimonial evidence to substantiate claims.
- Evasion of the scrutiny afforded by peer review.
- Absence of "connectivity" (Stanovich, 1997), that is, a failure to build on existing scientific knowledge.
- Use of impressive-sounding jargon whose primary purpose is to lend claims a facade of scientific respectability.
- An absence of boundary conditions (Hines, 2003), that is, a failure to specify the settings under which claims do not hold.

Teachers should explain to students that none of these warning signs is by itself sufficient to indicate that a discipline is pseudoscientific. Nevertheless, the more of these warning signs a discipline exhibits, the more suspect it should become.

Second Commandment

Thou shalt distinguish skepticism from cynicism. One danger of teaching students to distinguish science from pseudoscience is that we can inadvertently produce stude reflexively dismissive of any claim that appears implausible. Skepticism, which is the proper mental set of the scientist, implies two seemingly contradictory attitudes (Sagan, 1995): an openness to claims combined with a willingness to subject these claims to incisive scrutiny. As space engineer James Oberg (see Sagan, 1995) reminded us, we must keep our minds open but not so open that our brains fall out. In contrast, cynicism implies close-mindedness. I recall being chastised by a prominent skeptic for encouraging researchers to keep an open mind regarding the efficacy of a novel psychotherapy whose rationale struck him as farfetched. However, if we foreclose the possibility that our preexisting beliefs are erroneous, we are behaving unscientifically. Skepticism entails a willingness to entertain novel claims; cynicism does not.

Third Commandment

Thou shalt distinguish methodological skepticism from philosophical skepticism. When encouraging students to think critically, we must distinguish between two forms of skepticism: (1) an approach that subjects all knowledge claims to scrutiny with the goal of sorting out true from false claims, namely methodological (scientific) skepticism, and (2) an approach that denies the possibility of knowledge, namely philosophical skepticism. When explaining to students that scientific knowledge is inherently tentative and open to revision, some students may mistakenly conclude that genuine knowledge is impossible. This view, which is popular in certain postmodernist circles, neglects to distinguish knowledge claims that are more certain from those that are less certain. Although absolute certainly is probably unattainable in science, some scientific claims, such as Darwin's theory of natural selection, have been extremely well corroborated, whereas others, such as the theory underpinning astrological horoscopes, have been convincingly refuted. Still others, such as cognitive dissonance theory, are scientifically controversial. Hence, there is a continuum of confidence in scientific claims; some have acquired virtual factual status whereas others have been resoundingly falsified. The fact that methodological skepticism does not yield completely certain answers to scientific questions and that such answers could in principle be overturned by new evidence does not imply that knowledge is impossible, only that this knowledge is provisional. Nor does it imply that the answers generated by controlled scientific investigation are no better than other answers, such as those generated by intuition (see Myers, 2002).

Fourth Commandment

Thou shalt distinguish pseudoscientific claims from claims that are merely false. All scientists, even the best ones, make mistakes. Sir Isaac Newton, for example, flirted with bizarre alchemical hypotheses throughout much of his otherwise distinguished scientific career (Gleick, 2003). Students need to understand that the key difference between science and pseudoscience lies not in their content (i.e., whether claims are factually correct or incorrect) but in their approach to evidence. Science, at least when it operates properly, seeks out contradictory information and—assuming that this evidence is replicable and of high quality—eventually incorporates such information into its corpus of knowledge. In contrast, pseudoscience tends to avoid contradictory information (or manages to find a way to reinterpret this information as consistent with its claims) and thereby fails to foster the self-correction that is essential to scientific progress. For example, astrology has changed remarkably little over the past 2,500 years despite overwhelmingly negative evidence (Hines, 2003).

Fifth Commandment

Thou shalt distinguish science from scientists. Although the scientific method is a prescription for avoiding confirmatory bias (Lilienfeld, 2002), this point does not imply that scientists are free of biases. Nor does it imply that all or even most scientists are open to evidence that challenges their cherished beliefs. Scientists can be just as pigheaded and dogmatic in their beliefs as anyone else. Instead, this point implies that good scientists strive to become aware of their biases and to counteract them as much as possible by implementing safeguards against error (e.g., double-blind control groups) imposed by the scientific

method. Students need to understand that the scientific method is a toolbox of skills that scientist have developed to prevent themselves from confirming their own biases.

Sixth Commandment

Thou shalt explain the cognitive underpinnings of pseudoscientific beliefs. Instructors should emphasize that we are all prone to cognitive illusions (Piatelli-Palmarini, 1994), and that such illusions can be subjectively compelling and difficult to resist. For example, class demonstrations illustrating that many or most of us can fall prey to false memories (e.g., Roediger & McDermott, 1995) can help students to see that the psychological processes that lead to erroneous beliefs are pervasive. Moreover, it is important to point out to students that the heuristics (mental shortcuts) that can produce false beliefs, such as representativeness, availability, and anchoring (Tversky & Kahneman, 1974), are basically adaptive and help us to make sense of a complex and confusing world. Hence, most pseudoscientific beliefs are cut from the same cloth as accurate beliefs. By underscoring these points, instructors can minimize the odds that students who embrace pseudoscientific beliefs will feel foolish when confronted with evidence that contradicts their beliefs.

Seventh Commandment

Thou shalt remember that pseudoscientific beliefs serve important motivational functions. Many paranormal claims, such as those concerning extrasensory perception, out-of-body experiences, and astrology, appeal to believers' deep-seated needs for hope and wonder, as well as their needs for a sense of control over the often uncontrollable realities of life and death. Most believers in the paranormal are searching for answers to profound existential questions, such as "Is there a soul?" and "Is there life after death?" As psychologist Barry Beyerstein (1999) noted (in a play on P.T. Barnum's famous quip), "there's a seeker born every minute" (p. 60). Therefore, in presenting students with scientific evidence that challenges their paranormal beliefs, we should not be surprised when many of them become defensive. In turn, defensiveness can engender an unwillingness to consider contrary evidence.

One of the two best means of lessening this defensiveness (the second is the Eighth Commandment) is to gently challenge students' beliefs with sympathy and compassion, and with the understanding that students who are emotionally committed to paranormal beliefs will find these beliefs difficult to question, let alone relinquish. Ridiculing these beliefs can produce reactance (Brehm, 1966) and reinforce students' stereotypes of science teachers as close-minded and dismissive. In some cases, teachers who have an exceptionally good rapport with their class can make headway by challenging students' beliefs with good-natured humor (e.g., "I'd like to ask all of you who believe in psychokinesis to please raise my hand"). However, teachers must ensure that such humor is not perceived as demeaning or condescending.

Eigth Commandment

Thou shalt expose students to examples of good science as well as to examples of pseudoscience. In our classes, it is critical not merely to debunk inaccurate claims but to expose students to accurate claims. We must be careful not merely to take away student's questionable knowledge, but to give them legitimate knowledge in return. In doing so, we can make it easier for students to swallow the bitter pill of surrendering their cherished beliefs in the paranormal. Students need to understand that many genuine scientific findings are at least as fascinating as are many scientifically dubious paranormal claims. In my own teaching, I have found it useful to intersperse pseudoscientific information with information that is equally remarkable but true, such as lucid dreaming, eidetic imagery, subliminal perception (as opposed to subliminal persuasion, which is far more scientifically dubious), extraordinary feats of human memory (Neisser & Hyman, 2000), and appropriate clinical uses of hypnosis (as opposed to the scientifically unsupported use of hypnosis for memory recovery; see Lynn, Lock, Myers, & Payne, 1997). In addition, we should bear in mind the late paleontologist Stephen Jay Gould's (1996) point that exposing a falsehood necessarily affirms a truth. As a consequence, it is essential not only to point out false information to students, but also to direct them to true information. For example, when explaining why claims regarding biorhythms are baseless (see Hines, 2003), it is helpful to introduce students to claims regarding circadian rhythms, which, although often confused with biorhythms, are supported by rigorous scientific research.

Ninth Commandment

Thou shalt be consistent in one's intellectual standards. One error that I have sometimes observed among skeptics, including psychology instructors who teach critical thinking courses, is to adopt two sets of intellectual standards: one for claims that they find plausible and a second for claims that they do not. The late psychologist Paul Meehl (1973) pointed out that this inconsistency amounts to "shifting the standards of evidential rigor depending on whose ox is being gored" (p. 264). For example, I know one educator who is a vocal proponent of the movement to develop lists of empirically supported therapies, that is, psychological treatments that have been shown to be efficacious in controlled studies. In this domain, he is careful to draw on the research literature to buttress his assertions regarding which psychotherapies are efficacious and which are not. Yet he is dismissive of the research evidence for the efficacy of electroconvulsive therapy (ECT) for depression, even though this evidence derives from controlled studies that are every bit as rigorous as those conducted for the psychotherapies that he espouses. When I pointed out this inconsistency to him, he denied emphatically that he was adhering to a double standard. It eventually became apparent to me that he was casting aside the evidence for ECT's efficacy merely because this treatment struck him as grossly implausible. Why on earth, he probably wondered, should inducing an epileptoid seizure by administering electricity

to the brain alleviate depression? But because surface plausibility is a highly fallible barometer of the validity of truth claims, we must remain open to evidence that challenges our intuitive preconceptions and encourage our students to do so as well.

Tenth Commandment

Thou shalt distinguish pseudoscientific claims from purely metaphysical religious claims. My final commandment is likely to be the most controversial, especially for skeptics who maintain that both pseudoscientific and religious beliefs are irrational. To appreciate the difference between these two sets of beliefs, we must distinguish pseudoscience from metaphysics. Unlike pseudoscientific claims, metaphysical claims (Popper, 1959) cannot be tested empirically and therefore lie outside the boundaries of science. In the domain of religion, these include claims regarding the existence of God, the soul, and the afterlife, none of which can be refuted by any conceivable body of scientific evidence. Nevertheless, certain religious or quasi-religious beliefs, such as those involving "intelligent design" theory, which is the newest incarnation of creationism (see Miller, 2000), the Shroud of Turin, and weeping statues of Mother Mary, are indeed testable and hence suitable for critical analysis alongside of other questionable naturalistic beliefs. By conflating pseudoscientific beliefs with religious beliefs that are strictly metaphysical, instructors risk (a) needlessly alienating a sizeable proportion of their students, many of whom may be profoundly religious; and (b) (paradoxically) undermining students' critical thinking skills, which require a clear understanding of the difference between testable and untestable claims.

Conclusion

Adherence to the Ten Commandments can allow psychology educators to assist students with the crucial goal of distinguishing science from pseudoscience. If approached with care, sensitivity, and a clear understanding of the differences between skepticism and cynicism, methodological and philosophical skepticism, the scientific method and the scientists who use it, and pseudoscience and metaphysics, incorporating pseudoscience and fringe science into psychology courses can be richly rewarding for teachers and students alike. In a world in which the media, self-help industry, and Internet are disseminating psychological pseudoscience at an ever-increasing pace, the critical thinking skills needed to distinguish science from pseudoscience should be considered mandatory for all psychology students.

References

Beyerstein, B. L. (1999). Pseudoscience and the brain: Tuners and tonics for aspiring superhumans. In S. D. Sala (Ed.), *Mind myths: Exploring popular assumptions about the mind and brain* (pp. 59–82). Chichester, England: John Wiley.

Brehm, J. (1966). *A theory of psychological reactance.* New York: Academic Press.

Bunge, M. (1984, Fall). What is pseudoscience? *Skeptical Inquirer, 9,* 36–46.

Dougherty, M. J. (2004). Educating believers: Research demonstrates that courses in skepticism can effectively decrease belief in the paranormal. *Skeptic, 10*(4), 31–35.

Gilovich, T. (1991). How we know what isn't so: *The fallibility of human reason in everyday life.* New York: Free Press.

Gleick, J. (2003). *Isaac Newton.* New York: Pantheon Books.

Gould, S. J. (1996, May). Keynote address, *"Science in the age of (mis)information."* Talk presented at the Convention of the Committee for the Scientific Investigation of Claims of the Paranormal, Buffalo, New York.

Hines, T. (2003). Pseudoscience and the paranormal: A critical examination of the evidence. Buffalo, NY: Prometheus.

Kelly, G. A. (1955). *The psychology of personal constructs, Vols. 1 and 2.* New York:Norton.

Lilienfeld, S. O. (2002). When worlds collide: Social science, politics, and the Rind et al. child sexual abuse meta-analysis. *American Psychologist, 57,* 176–88.

Lilienfeld, S. O., Lohr, M., & Morier, D. (2001). The teaching of courses in the science and pseudoscience of psychology. *Teaching of Psychology, 28,* 182–191.

Lilienfeld, S. O., Lynn, S. J., & Lohr, J. M. (2003). *Science and pseudoscience in clinical psychology.* New York: Guilford.

Lynn, S. J., Lock, T. G., Myers, B., & Payne, D. G. (1997). Recalling the unrecallable: Should hypnosis be used to recover memories in psychotherapy? *Current Directions in Psychological Science, 6,* 79–83.

Meehl, P. E. (1973). Psychodiagnosis: Selected papers. Minneapolis, MN: University of Minnesota Press.

Miller, K. (2000). *Finding Darwin's God: A scientist's search for common ground between God and evolution.* New York: Cliff Street Books.

Morier, D., & Keeports, D. (1994). Normal science and the paranormal: The effect of a scientific method course on students' beliefs in the paranormal. *Research in Higher Education, 35,* 443–453.

Myers, D. G. (2002). *Intuition: Its powers and perils.* New Haven: Yale University Press.

Neisser, U., & Hyman, I. E. (2000). *Memory observed: Remembering in natural contexts.* New York: Worth Publishers.

Piatelli-Palmarini, M. (1994). *Inevitable illusions: How mistakes of reason rule our minds.* New York: John Wiley & Sons.

Popper, K. R. (1959). *The logic of scientific discovery.* New York: Basic Books.

Roediger, H. L., & McDermott, K. B. (1995). Creating false memories: Remembering words not presented in lists. *Journal of Experimental Psychology: Learning, Memory, and Cognition, 21,* 803–814.

Ruscio, J. (2002). *Clear thinking with psychology: Separating sense from nonsense.* Pacific Grove, CA: Wadsworth.

Sagan, C. (1995). *The demon-haunted world: Science as a candle in the dark.* New York: Random House.

Shermer, M. (2002). *Why people believe weird things: Pseudoscience, superstition, and other confusions of our time.* New York: Owl Books.

Stanovich, K. (1997). *How to think straight about psychology* (4th ed.). New York: HarperCollins.

Tversky, A., & Kahneman, D. (1974). Judgment under uncertainty: Heuristics and biases. *Science, 185,* 1124–1131.

Wesp, R., & Montgomery, K. (1998). Developing critical thinking through the study of paranormal phenomena. *Teaching of Psychology, 25,* 275–278.

THINKING ABOUT SCIENCE

Causes and Correlations

MASSIMO PIGLIUCCI

One of the most common fallacies committed by believers in the paranormal is what in philosophy is known by the Latin name of *post hoc, ergo propter hoc*, which loosely translates to "after this, therefore because of this." Surely you have heard some version of it: "I dreamed of my brother the other night, and the following morning he called me, though he rarely does." The implication here is that there is some causal connection between the dream and the phone call, that one happened because of the other. We all know what is wrong with this argument: a correlation between two events does not constitute good enough evidence of a causal connection between them. In the case of the dream as precognition, we probably dream of our relatives often enough, and most often the dream is not followed by their call; yet, because of an innate tendency of the human brain to remember hits and forget misses, we pay attention to the exceptions and charge them with special meaning.

But the good skeptic could go further and ask herself what exactly we mean by causation to begin with. If a correlation is not the hallmark of a causal relationship, what is? The modern study of causation started with the Italian physicist Galileo Galilei, who viewed causes as a set of necessary and sufficient conditions for a given effect. According to Galileo, the dream can be considered a cause of

the call only if every time the subject dreams of his brother, the following morning the brother actually does call. The problem with this idea is that it is too restrictive: many phenomena have multiple causes, a subset of which may be sufficient to generate the effect. The brother could call for other reasons than the dream, notwithstanding a true causal connection between dreaming and calling. Or, the dream may be causing the brother to have the impulse to call, but he can't do it because he is at a vacation spot where there are no phones in sight (as hard as this may seem to believe).

Scottish skeptic philosopher David Hume made the next important contribution to our understanding of causality, one that many philosophers (and a few scientists) are still grappling with. Hume argued that we never actually have any evidence that causal connections are real, we only have perceptions of the likely association between what we call a cause and an effect. Here Hume was being a good empiricist, something that a skeptic ought to appreciate. For him, talk of "causes" sounded as strange as talking of action at a distance, which in pre-Newtonian times was an exercise for mystics, not scientists. So Hume decided to settle on a very pragmatic concept of causality. He suggested that we are justified in talking about causes and effects if three conditions hold: 1) the first event (say, the dream) precedes the second one

(say, your brother's call); 2) the two events are contiguous in time, i.e., your brother called the morning after the dream, not a month or a year later; 3) there is a constant conjunction between the two events, i.e., every time you dream of your brother, he will call. As the reader will have noticed, however, the latter clause is very similar to Galileo's idea of necessary and sufficient condition, and will not actually help the scientist in real situations.

John Stuart Mill, well known as a utilitarian, proposed a concept of causation that is at the basis of much modern experimental science and, hence, of skeptical investigations. Mill argued that causality simply cannot be demonstrated without experimentation. Essentially, Mill said that in order to establish a causal connection between two phenomena, we have to be able to do experiments that allow us to manipulate the conditions so that only one factor at a time is allowed to change. A series of these experiments will eventually pinpoint the cause(s) of certain effects.

While Mill's idea has been of fundamental importance for modern science, the problem with it is that it imposes on the investigators logistic requirements that are often too restrictive. What if it is not possible to control all variables but one during an inquiry? Carefully controlled manipulative experiments are possible only in certain fields and under very taxing conditions. Should we then give up the concept of causality for the much larger number of instances in which such manipulations are not possible, unethical, or simply too expensive? That would be problematic because, for example, we could nor conclude that smoking causes cancer. It is simply not possible to do the right experiment, especially with human beings: there are too many variables, nor to mention deep ethical issues.

What then? One of the most modern conceptions of causality is the so-called probabilistic one. According to probabilistic causality we can reasonably infer that, say, cancer is caused by smoking if the probability of getting cancer is measurably higher when the subjects smoke than when they don't. Other factors here are taken into consideration statistically, not necessarily by experimental manipulation. That is, one carries out the investigation taking care of sampling individuals with different socioeconomic backgrounds, diets, exercise habits, and genetic constitution. If, when these other variables are kept in check statistically, we still detect an increase in the likelihood of getting cancer in the smokers compared to the nonsmokers, we are justified in tentatively accepting a causal connection.

Notice, however, that while the probabilistic account of causality is indeed very powerful in practice, conceptually it brings us back toward Hume: the only reason we are talking about causality is because we perceive a series of regularities, not because we know that actual causes are at play. So, in science as in skeptical investigations, we might have to admit that the most we can get is a certain probability of being right. Definitive truth is a chimera tha[t] science after all.

Further

David Hume (1739–1740). *A Treatise of Human Nature.*

Author **Massimo Pigliucci** is an associate professor in the Departments of Botany and Ecology & Evolutionary Biology at the University of Tennessee at Knoxville and author of the new book *Denying Evolution: Creationism, Scientism, and the Nature of Science* (Sinauer 2002). His earlier SKEPTICAL INQUIRER articles include "Hypothesis Testing and the Nature of Skeptical Investigations" (November/ December 2002), "Design Yes, Intelligent No" (September/October 2001), and "Where Do We Come From? A Humbling Look at the Biology of Life's Origins" (September/October 1999). His Web site is www.rationallyspeaking.org

Biological Bases of Behavior

Unit Selections

5. **The Amazing Brain: Is Neuroscience the Key to What Makes Us Human?**, Richard Restak
6. **Genetic Influence on Human Psychological Traits**, Thomas J. Bouchard, Jr.
7. **The Structure of the Human Brain**, John S. Allen, Joel Bruss, and Hanna Damasio

Key Points to Consider

- What is genetic research and how is it conducted? Why carry out genetic research? How much of human behavior is influenced by genes? Do you agree that evolution or genetics account for most of our "humanness"? Can you give some examples of the influence of genes on human behavior? Can you provide some examples of how human behavior differs from animal behavior?

- What are individual differences? What most accounts for such differences? Can you provide some examples of behaviors or traits where individual differences manifest themselves, such as intelligence?

- How does brain imaging research help experts in psychology and medicine predict and treat various disorders? Do you think such information could be or has been misused? How? When? Why? What environmental factors affect genetic expression? Or do they?

- Why do psychologists study the human brain? Do you know the names and functions of parts of the brain? Of other parts of the nervous system? What parts of the brain control which aspects of our behavior? That is, how does the brain influence human behavior and psychological characteristics?

- What is neuroscience? How are psychology and neuroscience related? Are there some realms of psychology that are not related to neuroscience? If yes, which ones? Are there areas of neuroscience that are not related to psychology?

Student Website

www.mhcls.com/online

Internet References

Further information regarding these websites may be found in this book's preface or online.

Institute for Behavioral Genetics
http://ibgwww.colorado.edu/index.html
Serendip
http://serendip.brynmawr.edu/serendip/

As a child, Angelina vowed she did not want to turn out like either of her parents. Angelina's mother was very passive and acquiescent about her father's drinking. When Dad was drunk, Mom always called his boss to report that Dad was "sick" and then acted as if there was nothing wrong at home. Angelina's childhood was a nightmare. Her father's behavior was erratic and unpredictable. If he drank just a little bit, most often he was happy. If he drank a lot, which was usually the case, he frequently but not always became belligerent.

Despite vowing not to become her father, as an adult Angelina found herself in the alcohol rehabilitation unit of a large hospital. Angelina's employer could no longer tolerate her on-the-job mistakes or her unexplained absences from work. Angelina's supervisor therefore referred her to the clinic for help. As Angelina pondered her fate, she wondered whether her genes preordained her to follow in her father's inebriated footsteps or whether the stress of her childhood had brought her to this point in her life. After all, being the child of an alcoholic is not easy.

Just as Angelina is, psychologists also are concerned with discovering the causes of human behavior. Once the cause is known, treatments for problematic behaviors can be developed. In fact, certain behaviors might even be prevented when the cause is known. But for Angelina, prevention was too late.

One of the paths to understanding humans is to understand the biological underpinnings of their behavior. Genes and chromosomes, the body's chemistry (as found in hormones, neurotransmitters, and enzymes), and the nervous system comprised of the brain, spinal cord, nerve cells, and other parts are all implicated in human behavior. All represent the biological aspects of behavior and ought, therefore, to be worthy of study by psychologists.

Physiological psychologists and psychobiologists are often the ones who examine the role of biology in behavior. The neuroscientist is especially interested in brain functioning; the psychopharmacologist is interested in the effects of various pharmacological agents or psychoactive drugs on behavior.

These psychologists often utilize one of three techniques to understand the biology-behavior connection. Animal studies involving manipulation, stimulation, or destruction of certain parts of the brain offer one method of study; these studies remain controversial with animal rights activists. There is also a second available technique that includes the examination of unfortunate individuals whose brains are malfunctioning at birth or damaged later by accidents or disease.

We can also use animal models to understand genetics; with animal models we can control reproduction as well as manipulate and develop various strains of animals if necessary. Such tactics with humans would be considered extremely unethical and are often disdained by animal rights activists. Also, by studying an individual's behavior in comparison to both natural and adoptive parents or by studying identical twins reared together or apart, we can begin to understand the role of genetics versus environment in human behavior.

The articles in this unit are designed to familiarize you with the knowledge psychologists have gleaned by using these and other techniques to study physiological processes and other underlying mechanisms in human behavior. Each article should interest you and make you more curious about the role of biology in human actions.

The article, "Genetic Influence on Human Psychological Traits," by Thomas Bouchard, is also about the nature-nurture dispute, but he falls heavily on the side of nurture. He explains what genetics is, why it is important, and how much it impacts various psychological characteristics, such as intelligence and mental health.

The last article in this section discusses the nervous system. "The Structure of the Human Brain" discusses what neuroscience is, how it pertains to understanding the brain and its functions, and how brain imaging techniques are helping scientists understand various principles of size and structure of the brain.

The Amazing Brain

Is Neuroscience the Key to What Makes Us Human?

Richard Restak, a review of *A Brief Tour of Human Consciousness* by V. S. Ramachandran

While in medical school, V. S. Ramachandran, director of the Center for Brain and Cognition at the University of California at San Diego, encountered a patient given to episodes of alternately weeping and laughing uncontrollably. This display of emotional mercuriality struck Ramachandran as a replay of the human condition. "Were these just mirthless joy and crocodile tears, I wondered? Or was he actually feeling alternately happy and sad, the same way a manic-depressive might, but on a compressed scale?"

During his professional career as a neurologist and researcher, Ramachandran has retained his curiosity and formulated about his patients the "kinds of very simple questions that a schoolboy might ask but are embarrassingly hard for experts to answer."

For example, "Why does this patient display these curious symptoms? What do the symptoms tell us about the working of the normal brain?" In the process, Ramachandran has learned that many patients with damage in a localized part of the brain often suffer a highly selective loss of one specific function with other functions remaining unaffected—an indication that the damaged area is normally involved somehow in mediating the impaired function. Further, some of these selective impairments can be both fascinating and informative.

Consider David, a patient of Ramachandran's who emerged from a coma mentally intact, with the exception of the bizarre delusion that his mother had been replaced by an impostor.

Further evaluation revealed an important distinction: Although David couldn't recognize his mother when encountering her face to face, he had no trouble identifying her when talking to her on the telephone. What could account for such an anomaly?

It turns out that separate pathways lead from the auditory and visual regions of the brain to the amygdala, an important component of the brain's emotional circuitry. In David's case, the fibers connecting the visual center to the amygdala were no longer functioning normally. As a result, whenever he looked at his mother he no longer got that warm feeling of recognition that

normally accompanies seeing one's parent. He therefore accused her of being an impostor.

The auditory fibers in David's brain, in contrast, retained their normal connections with the amygdala. Consequently, the emotional linkage of voice and person remained intact and David recognized his mother's voice.

"This is a lovely example… of neuroscience in action; of how you can take a bizarre, seemingly incomprehensible neurological syndrome … and then come up with a simple explanation in terms of the known neural pathways in the brain," writes Ramachandran.

Other bizarre but informative disorders taken up in this wide-ranging book include phantom limb (the sensation that an amputated arm or leg is still present); synesthesia (a condition in which the senses are mingled so that the affected person tastes a shape, or sees a color in a sound or a number); and achromotopsia (seeing the world in shades of gray, like a black-and-white film).

"By studying neurological syndromes which have been largely ignored as curiosities or mere anomalies, we can sometimes acquire novel insights into the functions of the normal brain," the author writes. Moreover, he suggests, "the study of patients with neurological disorders has implications for the humanities, for philosophy, maybe even for aesthetics and art."

While all this sounds reasonable, Ramachandran sometimes comes across like the proverbial carpenter who approaches all issues as resolvable via the use of hammer and nail. Specifically, he claims that neuroscience can answer (or soon will) "some lofty questions that have preoccupied philosophers since the dawn of history: What is free will? What is body image? What is art? What is the self? Who am I?"

At times, his reductionism pushes the envelope a bit: "We recognize that life is a word loosely applied to a collection of processes—DNA replication and transcription, Krebs cycle, Lactic acid cycle, etc., etc." At another point, after naming several brain structures he asserts, "Know how they perform their individual operations, how they interact, and you will know what it means to be a conscious human being."

Despite such extravagant and hubristic statements, no one so far has been able to perform the alchemical conversion whereby "To be or not to be" can be understood in terms of neurotransmitters and brain structures. Nor is such a conversion ever likely since, as philosopher Gilbert Ryle pointed out, it would invoke the category mistake: intermingling separate and distinct orders of discourse.

For example (Ryle's own example, incidentally), the university that I attended cannot be equated except associatively with the buildings comprising it. True, the buildings when considered together may loosely be referred to as "the university"; but the entity defined by that word is far more nuanced than just real estate.

Likewise, can the mind be explained totally in terms of the brain? Ramachandran thinks so and while, on the whole, I tend to agree with him, I also have to admit to a trace of agnosticism on the question.

Not surprisingly, when discussing mental illness, Ramachandran is strictly in the neuropsychiatric camp: Neurology and psychiatry are so interpenetrated that future treatments and cures can only come about via increased knowledge about the brain. As a neurologist and neuropsychiatrist myself, I certainly don't disagree with that claim. Many psychiatrists, however, may find Ramachandran's phrasing of the matter a bit off-putting ("it is only a matter of time before psychiatry becomes just another branch of neurology").

But his heart is in the right place. Freudianism and other guru-driven "isms" are dead, replaced by an emphasis on the brain. Indeed, so much has been learned about mental illness in the past two decades as a result of brain research that it's difficult to imagine any alternative approach.

My principal criticism of this book concerns its odd arrangement: 112 pages of text accompanied by 44 pages of endnotes. As he mentions in his introduction, Ramachandran holds a rather quirky notion about endnotes ("the real book is in the endnotes"). Perhaps that's true, but the delegation of large parts of the narrative to the endnotes presents several difficulties.

For one, this text-endnote dichotomy makes it too easy for both author and editor to forsake their most important duty: organizing the material into a free-flowing narrative. Second, on occasion—such as his description of the more exotic forms of synesthesia—the endnotes prove even more interesting than the main text.

Finally, material in the text is sometimes repeated in the endnotes, such as Ramachandran's explanation of the origin of the ear. And given this emphasis on the endnotes, why are the notes corresponding to the last two citations in the final chapter missing?

Admittedly, these are minor quibbles that detract not at all from a perfectly marvelous book. Overall, reading Ramachandran in *A Brief Tour of Human Consciousness* is like listening to a John Coltrane solo: The man is here, there, and everywhere; he's inventive, inspired, wildly speculative, and yet disciplined by the demands of his craft. Give him a fact about the brain and he'll link it with a quote from Shakespeare; a nanosecond later he'll suggest an experiment that you can carry out in your living room to learn more about the fact.

To Ramachandran, the brain is more than an enchanted loom, and wider than the sky; it's an endless source for manic excitement, intriguing questions, profound reflections and a zany humor ("our brains ... if raised in a culture-free environment like Texas would barely be human"). And like Coltrane, Ramachandran leaves you marveling at how he does it; wondering how he's learned all that he knows; and spinning like a top from the effort of trying to absorb all the wonderful things that he's telling you.

A Brief Tour of Human Consciousness is well worth the effort. You'll be entertained, provoked, amused and—most important of all—eager to learn more.

RICHARD RESTAK, a neurologist and neuropsychiatrist, is the author of *Poe's Heart and the Mountain Climber: Exploring the Effects of Anxiety on Our Brains and Our Culture,* to be published in November 2004.

Article 6

Genetic Influence on Human Psychological Traits

A Survey

THOMAS J. BOUCHARD, JR.

There is now a large body of evidence that supports the conclusion that individual differences in most, if not all, reliably measured psychological traits, normal and abnormal, are substantively influenced by genetic factors. This fact has important implications for research and theory building in psychology, as evidence of genetic influence unleashes a cascade of questions regarding the sources of variance in such traits. A brief list of those questions is provided, and representative findings regarding genetic and environmental influences are presented for the domains of personality, intelligence, psychological interests, psychiatric illnesses, and social attitudes. These findings are consistent with those reported for the traits of other species and for many human physical traits, suggesting that they may represent a general biological phenomenon.

Among knowledgeable researchers, discussions regarding genetic influences on psychological traits are not about whether there is genetic influence, but rather about how much influence there is, and how genes work to shape the mind. As Rutter (2002) noted, "Any dispassionate reading of the evidence leads to the inescapable conclusion that genetic factors play a substantial role in the origins of individual differences with respect to all psychological traits, both normal and abnormal" (p. 2). Put concisely, all psychological traits are heritable. Heritability (h^2) is a descriptive statistic that indexes the degree of population variation in a trait that is due to genetic differences. The complement of heritability $(1 - h^2)$ indexes variation contributed by the environment (plus error of measurement) to population variation in the trait. Studies of human twins and adoptees, often called behavior genetic studies, allow us to estimate the heritability of various traits. The name behavior genetic studies is an unfortunate misnomer, however, as such studies are neutral regarding both environmental and genetic influences. That they repeatedly and reliably reveal significant heritability for psychological traits is an empirical fact and one not unique to humans. Lynch and Walsh (1998) pointed out that genetic influence on most traits, as indexed by estimates of heritability, is found for all species and observed that "the interesting questions remaining are, How does the magnitude of h^2" differ among characters and species and why?" (p. 175).

WHY STUDY GENETIC INFLUENCES ON HUMAN BEHAVIORAL TRAITS?

A simple answer to the question of why scientists study genetic influences on human behavior is that they want a better understanding of how things work, that is, better theories. Not too many years ago, Meehl (1978) argued that "most so-called 'theories' in the soft areas of psychology (clinical, counseling, social, personality, community, and school psychology) are scientifically unimpressive and technologically worthless" (p. 806). He listed 20 fundamental difficulties faced by researchers in the social sciences. Two are relevant to the current discussion: heritability and nuisance variables. The two are closely related. Nuisance variables are variables assumed to be causes of group or individual differences irrelevant to the theory of an investigator. Investigators seldom provide a full theoretical rationale in support of their choice of nuisance variables to control. As Meehl pointed out, removing the influence of parental socioeconomic status (SES; i.e., treating it as a nuisance variable) on children's IQ, when studying the causes of individual differences in IQ, makes the assumption that parental SES is exclusively a source of environmental variance, as opposed to being confounded with genetic influence. Meehl argued that this example "is perhaps the most dramatic one but other less emotion-laden examples can be found on all sides in the behavioral sciences" (p. 810). His point was that knowledge of how genetic factors influence any given measure (e.g., SES) or trait (e.g., IQ) will allow scientists to develop more scientifically impressive and worthwhile theories about the sources of individual differences in psychological traits.

Evidence of genetic influence on a psychological trait raises a series of new questions regarding the sources of population variance for that trait. All the questions addressed in quantitative genetics (Lynch & Walsh, 1998) and genetic epidemiology (Khoury, 1998) become relevant. What kind of gene action is involved? Is it a simple additive influence, with the effects of genes simply adding up so that more genes cause greater expression of the trait, or is the mode of action more complex? Are the effects of genes for a particular trait more pronounced in men or women? Are there interactions between genes and the environment? For example, it has been known for a long time that stressful life events lead to depression in some people but not others. There is now evidence for an interaction. Individuals who carry a specific genetic variant are more susceptible to depression when exposed to stressful life events than individuals who do not carry the genetic variant (Caspi et al., 2003). Are there gene-environment correlations? That is, do individuals with certain genetic constitutions seek out specific environments? People who score high on measures of sensation seeking certainly, on average, tend to find themselves in more dangerous environments than people who score low for this trait. McGue and I have provided an extended list of such questions (Bouchard & McGue, 2003).

ESTIMATES OF THE MAGNITUDE OF GENETIC INFLUENCE ON PSYCHOLOGICAL TRAITS

Table 1 reports typical behavior genetic findings drawn from studies of broad and relatively representative samples from affluent Western societies. In most, but not all, of these studies, estimates of genetic and environmental influences were obtained from studies of twins. Because the studies probably undersampled people who live in the most deprived segment of Western societies, the findings should not be considered as generalizable to such populations. (Documentation for most of the findings can be found in Bouchard & McGue, 2003.)

Personality

Psychologists have developed two major schemes for organizing specific personality traits into a higher-order structure, the Big Five and the Big Three. As Table 1 shows, the findings using the two schemes are much the same. Genetic influence is in the range of 40 to 50%, and heritability is approximately the same for different traits. There is evidence of nonadditive genetic variance. That is, genes for personality, in addition to simply adding or subtracting from the expression of a trait, work in a more complex manner, the expression of a relevant

gene depending to some extent on the gene with which it is paired on a chromosome or on genes located on other chromosomes. Research has yielded little evidence for significant shared environmental influence, that is, similarity due to having trait-relevant environmental influences in common. Some large studies have investigated whether the genes that influence personality traits differ in the two sexes (sex limitation). The answer is no. However, sometimes there are sex differences in heritability.

Mental Ability

Early in life, shared environmental factors are the dominant influence on IQ, but gradually genetic influence increases, with the effects of shared environment dropping to near zero (see the twin studies in Table 1). Although not reported here, adoption studies of (a) unrelated individuals reared together and (b) adoptive parents and their adopted offspring have reported similar results—increasing genetic influence on IQ with age and decreasing shared environmental influence. Results from two twin studies of IQ in old age (over 75) are reported in Table 1. Both studies found a substantial level of genetic influence and little shared environmental influence. The results do, however, suggest some decline in heritability when compared with results for earlier ages. There is no evidence for sex differences in heritability for IQ at any age.

Psychological Interests

Heritabilities for psychological interests, also called vocational or occupational interests, are also reported in Table 1. These heritabilities were estimated using data gathered in a single large study that made use of a variety of samples (twins, siblings, parents and their children, etc.) gathered over many years. All respondents completed one form or another of a standard vocational interest questionnaire. There is little variation in heritability for the six scales, with an average of .36. As with personality traits, there is evidence for nonadditive genetic influence. Unlike personality, psychological interests show evidence for shared environmental influence, although this influence is modest, about 10% for each trait.

Psychiatric Illnesses

Schizophrenia is the most extensively studied psychiatric illness, and the findings consistently suggest a very high degree of genetic influence (heritability of about .80), mostly additive genetic influence, with no shared environmental influence. There do not appear to be gender differences in the heritability of schizophrenia. Major depression is less heritable (about .40) than schizophrenia. Men and women share most, but not all, genetic influences for depression. Panic disorder, generalized anxiety disorder, and phobias are moderately heritable, and the effect is largely additive, with few if any sex differences. The heritability of alcoholism is in the range of .50 to .60. mostly because of additive genetic effects. Findings regarding the possibility of sex differences in the heritability of alcoholism are mixed.

TABLE 1
Estimates of Broad Heritability and Shared Environmental Influence and Indications of Nonadditive Genetic Effects and Sex Differences in Heritability for Representative Psychological Traits

Trait	Heritability	Nonadditive genetic effect	Shared environmental effect	Sex differences in heritabilily
Personality (adult samples)				
Big Five				
Extraversion	.54	Yes	No	Perhaps
Agreeableness (aggression)	.42	Yes	No	Probably not
Conscientiousness	.49	Yes	No	Probably not
Neuroticism	.48	Yes	No	No
Openness	.57	Yes	No	Probably not
Big Three				
Positive emotionality	.50	Yes	No	No
Negative emotionality	.44	Yes	No	No
Constraint	.52	Yes	No	No
Intelligence				
By age in Dutch cross-sectional twin data				
Age 5	.22	No	.54	No
Age 7	.40	No	.29	No
Age 10	.54	No	.26	No
Age 12	.85	No	No	No
Age 16	.62	No	No	No
Age 18	.82	No	No	No
Age 26	.88	No	No	No
Age 50	.85	No	No	No
In old age (> 75 years old)	.54-.62	Not tested	No	No
Psychological interests				
Realistic	.36	Yes	.12	NA
Investigative	.36	Yes	.10	NA
Artistic	.39	Yes	.12	NA
Social	.37	Yes	.08	NA
Enterprising	.31	Yes	.11	NA
Conventional	.38	Yes	.11	NA
Psychiatric illnesses (liability estimates)				
Schizophrenia	.80	No	No	No
Major depression	.37	No	No	Mixed findings
Panic disorder	.30-.40	No	No	No
Generalized anxiety disorder	.30	No	Small female only	No
Phobias	.20-.40	No	No	No
Alcoholism	.50-.60	No	Yes	Mixed findings
Antisocial behavior				
Children	.46	No	.20	No
Adolescents	.43	No	.16	No
Adults	.41	No	.09	No
Social attitudes				
Conservatism				
Under age 20 years	.00	NR	Yes	NR
Over age 20 years	.45-.65	Yes	Yes in females	Yes
Right-wing authoritarianism (adults)	.50-.64	No	.00-.16	NA
Religiousness				
16-year-olds	.11-.22	No	.45-.60	Yes
Adults	.30-.45	No	.20-.40	Not clear
Specific religion	Near zero	NR	NA	NR

Note. NA = not available: NR = not relevant.

Antisocial behavior has long been thought to be more heritable in adulthood than childhood. The results of a recent analysis do not support that conclusion. The genetic influence is additive and in the range of .41 to .46. Shared environmental influences decrease from childhood to adulthood, but do not entirely disappear in adulthood. There are no sex differences in heritability.

Social Attitudes

Twin studies reveal only environmental influence on conservatism up to age 19; only after this age do genetic influences manifest themselves. A large study (30,000 adults, including twins and most of their first-degree relatives) yielded heritabilities of .65 for males and .45 for females. Some of the genetic influence on conservatism is nonadditive. Recent work with twins reared apart has independently replicated these heritability findings. Conservatism correlates highly, about .72, with right-wing authoritarianism, and that trait is also moderately heritable.

Religiousness is only slightly heritable in 16-year-olds (.11 for girls and .22 for boys in a large Finnish twin study) and strongly influenced by shared environment (.60 in girls and .45 in boys). Religiousness is moderately heritable in adults (.30 to .45) and also shows some shared environmental influence. Good data on sex differences in heritability of religiousness in adults are not available. Membership in a specific religious denomination is largely due to environmental factors.

A Note on Multivariate Genetic Analysis

In this review, I have addressed only the behavior genetic analysis of traits taken one at a time (univariate analysis). It is important to recognize that it is possible to carry out complex genetic analyses of the correlations among traits and compute genetic correlations. These correlations tell us the degree to which genetic effects on one score (trait measure) are correlated with genetic effects on a second score, at one or at many points in time. The genetic correlation between two traits can be quite high regardless of whether the heritability of either trait is high or low, or whether the correlation between the traits is high or low. Consider the well-known positive correlation between tests of mental ability, the evidentiary base for the general intelligence factor. This value is typically about .30. The genetic correlation between such tests is, however, much higher, typically closer to .80. Co-occurrence of two disorders, a common finding in psychiatric research, is often due to common genes. The genetic correlation between anxiety and depression, for example, is estimated to be very high. Multivariate genetic analysis of behavioral traits is a very active domain of research.

CONCLUDING REMARKS

One unspoken assumption among early behavior geneticists, an assumption that was shared by most for many years, was that some psychological traits were likely to be significantly influenced by genetic factors, whereas others were likely to be primarily influenced by shared environmental influences. Most behavior geneticists assumed that social attitudes, for example, were influenced entirely by shared environmental influences, and

so social attitudes remained largely unstudied until relatively recently. The evidence now shows how wrong these assumptions were. Nearly every reliably measured psychological phenotype (normal and abnormal) is significantly influenced by genetic factors. Heritabilities also differ far less from trait to trait than anyone initially imagined. Shared environmental influences are often, but not always, of less importance than genetic factors, and often decrease to near zero after adolescence. Genetic influence on psychological traits is ubiquitous, and psychological researchers must incorporate this fact into their research programs else their theories will be "scientifically unimpressive and technologically worthless," to quote Meehl again.

At a fundamental level, a scientifically impressive theory must describe the specific molecular mechanism that explicates how genes transact with the environment to produce behavior. The rudiments of such theories are in place. Circadian behavior in humans is under genetic influence (Hur, Bouchard, & Lykken, 1998), and some of the molecular mechanisms in mammals are now being revealed (Lowrey & Takahashi, 2000). Riclley (2003) and Marcus (2004) have provided additional examples of molecular mechanisms that help shape behavior. Nevertheless, the examples are few, the details are sparse, and major mysteries remain. For example, many behavioral traits are influenced by nonadditive genetic processes. These processes remain a puzzle for geneticists and evolutionists, as well as psychologists, because simple additive effects are thought to be the norm (Wolf, Brodie, & Wade, 2000). We also do not understand why most psychological traits are moderately heritable, rather than, as some psychologists expected, variable in heritability, with some traits being highly heritable and others being largely under the influence of the environment. It seems reasonable to suspect that moderate heritability may be a general biological phenomenon rather than one specific to human psychological traits, as the profile of genetic and environmental influences on psychological traits is not that different from the profile of these influences on similarly complex physical traits (Boomsma, Busjahn, & Peltonen, 2002) and similar findings apply to most organisms.

Recommended Reading

Bouchard, T.J., Jr., & McGue. M. (2003). (See References)

Carey, G. (2003). *Human genetics for the social sciences*. Thousand Oaks, CA: Sage.

Plomin, R., DeFries, J.C.. Craig, I.W., & McGuffin, P. (Eds.). (2003). *Behavioral genetics in the post genomic era*. Washington, DC: American Psychological Association.

Rutter, M., Pickels, A., Murray, R., & Eaves, L.J. (2001). Testing hypotheses on specific environmental causal effects on behavior. *Psychological bulletin, 127,* 291-324.

Note

1. See Evans (2004, Fig. 1) for a recent commission of this error.

REFERENCES

Boomsma, D. I., Busjahn, A., & Peltonen, L. (2002). Classical twin studies and beyond. *Nature Reviews: Genetics, 3,* 872–882.

Bouchard, T. J., Jr., & McGue, M. (2003). Genetic and environmental influences on human psychological differences. *Journal of Neurobiology, 54,* 4–45.

Caspi, A., Sugden, K., Moffitt, T. E., Taylor. A., Craig, I. W., Harrington, H., McClay, J., Mill, J., Martin, J., Braiwaite. A., & Poulton, R. (2003). Influence of life stress on depression: Moderation by a polymorphism in the 5-HTT gene. *Science, 301,* 386–389.

Evans, G. W. (2004). The environment of childhood poverty. *American Psychologist, 59,* 77–92.

Hur, Y.- M., Bouchard, T. J., Jr., & Lykken. D. T. (1998). Genetic and environmental influence on morningness-eveningness. *Personality and Individual Differences, 25,* 917–925.

Khoury, M. J. (1998). Genetic epidemiology. In K. J. Rothman & S. Greenland (Eds.), *Modem epidemiology* (pp. 609–622). Philadelphia: Lippincott-Raven.

Lowrey, P. L., & Takahashi, J. S. (2000). Genetics of the mammalian circadian system: Photic entrainment, circadian pacemaker mechanisms, and postranslational regulation. *Annual Review of Genetics, 34,* 533–562.

Lynch, M., & Walsh, B. (1998). *Genetics and analysis of quantitative traits.* Sunderland. MA: Sinauer.

Marcus, G. (2004). *The birth of the mind: How a tiny number of genes creates the complexities of human thought.* New York: Basic Books.

Meehl, P. E. (1978). Theoretical risks and tabular asterisks: Sir Karl, Sir Ronald, and the slow progress of soft psychology. *Journal of Consulting and Clinical Psychology, 46,* 806–834.

Ridley, M. (2003). *Nature via nurture: Genes, experience and what makes us human.* New York: HarperCollins.

Rutter, M. (2002). Nature, nurture, and development: From evangelism through science toward policy and practice. *Child Development, 73,* 1–21.

Wolf, J. B., Brodie. E. D. I., & Wade. M. J. (Eds.), (2000). *Epistasis and the evolutionary process.* New York: Oxford University Press.

The Structure of the Human Brain

Precise studies of the size and shape of the brain have yielded fresh insights into neural development, differences between the sexes and human evolution

JOHN S. ALLEN, JOEL BRUSS, AND HANNA DAMASIO

If you lived in the 19th century, your entire character—attributes such as ambition, tenderness, wit and valor—might have been judged by the size and shape of your skull, this practice, called phrenology, was developed by Franz Joseph Gall and Johann Spurzheim in Vienna during the early 1800s. Adherents claimed different mental "faculties" were localized to different parts of the brain, and these regions would be bigger if you possessed the traits in abundance. Phrenologists also believed the brain determined the shape of the skull, so they reasoned an external examination of the cranium would detect regional brain development. This led to the popular (arid not inaccurate) characterization of phrenology as the "science" of bumps on the head.

We are right to be skeptical of these early explorations of brain size and its functional correlates. However, there was a nugget of truth in the phrenological view of world: Brain structure is a fundamental aspect of neuroscience because brain functions take place in specific combinations of brain regions. In complex animals, the size and shape of the brain reflect a host of evolutionary, developmental, genetic, pathological and functional processes that interact to produce an individual organism.

Because many factors influence neural structures, the study of brain volume, or volumetrics, has the potential to offer insights from many perspectives. In an evolutionary context, studies of brain volume across species can link anatomical, behavioral and ecological data. Species that have unpredictably large or small brains are useful for studying the forces of evolution that influence brain size. For example, Katharine Milton at the University of California, Berkeley has suggested that fruit-eating primates have a higher brain-to-body mass ratio than leaf-eating primates because locating widely dispersed, seasonally available fruit makes greater cognitive demands than finding more convenient foods, such as leaves. Volumetrics can also illuminate developmental patterns within and across species, which in turn suggest how evolution might be constrained by implicit rules of neurological growth. The study of neurological diseases also depends on a systematic analysis of brain size and shape. For instance, some children with autism have atypically large brains, and Alzheimer's disease causes progressive brain atrophy. In both cases, the pathological processes that underlie these conditions manifest as changes in brain volume. So volumetric studies are both a means to understanding brain function and an end in themselves.

Tools of the Trade

Neuroanatomy has undergone a resolution in the past 30 years. The leap became possible with the introduction of new imaging technologies such as x-ray computed tomography (CT, also called CAT scanning), magnetic resonance imaging (MRI) and positron emission tomography (PET). With these tools, scientists can view the structure and activity of the living human brain in unprecedented detail. For the structural and volumetric study of the brain, CT and MRI have been of critical importance.

Computed tomography is the older technology. It uses the variable absorption of x-rays by different brain components to visualize structures inside the skulls of living subjects. A single CT image is the product of thousands of individual measurements, which are made as the x-ray source swivels in a full circle around the head.

Unlike CT, MRI does not use x rays, relying instead on powerful magnets to momentarily align the nuclei of hydrogen atoms in body tissues, most of which are within water molecules. When the magnet is turned off, the infinitesimal spinning (or resonating) nuclei fall back to a normal state, releasing energy in the form of radio waves. The frequency of these waves provides a measure of local hydrogen concentration, which varies according to tissue type, such as bone or fat. This produces a very fine-grained map—often as good as a postmortem analysis. The technique clearly distinguishes gray matter (mostly neuronal cell bodies), white matter (mostly nerve fibers insulated by fatty myelin, plus supporting cells) and cerebrospinal fluid or CSF (the liquid that fills the spaces within and around the brain). In addition, individual MR scans can be stacked to form a virtual three-dimensional model, then resliced along any plane or angle.

Draw the Line

The process of dividing the brain into different regions is known *as parcellation,* and there are many ways to do it depending on the goals of the investigators and the methods available. MRI parcellation uses visible anatomical landmarks, such as the sulci (folds) and gyri (bulges) on the surface of the brain to create "regions of interest" or ROIs. They can include broad structural divisions—for example, the temporal, parietal and occipital lobes—as well as smaller structures such as the hippocampus or corpus callosum. The locations of specific brain activities, when they are known, can also guide anatomical parcellation.

A three-dimensional MR scan is made from a series of separate, contiguous images. A typical high-resolution analysis might have a slice thickness of 1.5 millimeters, meaning that an average brain would be compiled from more than 100 sections. Specialized image-processing software can then "extract" the brain from the skull and visualize it as a solid object. It can be sliced in any plane, rotated or resized to match a standard model. At this point, ROIs can be defined by marking the boundary limits of the structure on the surface of the brain. These marks are then transferred to "coronal" slices (parallel to the plane of a person's face) to define the region on each image. The ROI volume (area multiplied by slice thickness) from each section is summed to give an overall value. The studies mentioned in this article, like others in the field, were done through a laborious process of manually tracing ROIs onto each image. Several methods are currently being developed to automate this painstaking process, but to date none exists that can match the precision of hand tracing with expert knowledge of anatomy.

One of the most useful aspects of an MR scan for imaging neural structures is that it sharply defines gray matter, white matter and cerebrospinal fluid. Many research groups are studying the relative gray:white composition of various structures, aided by automated methods (which do work well for this purpose) for segmenting; MRIs into these categories.

Genes and Brains

Genetic processes underlie the development and evolution of the brain, and several research teams are studying the genetics of human brain volume and structure. One strategy is to use MRI to look at the brain volumes of identical and fraternal twins. The studies indicate that human cranial capacity is a strongly inherited trait, and most of the variation in total or hemispheric volume can be explained by genetic factors. In one report, by William Baaré and his colleagues at the University Medical Center of Utrecht in the Netherlands, genes accounted for the large majority of brain volume differences: 90 percent for the brain as a whole, 82 percent for gray matter and 88 percent for white-matter.

However, two major neuroanatomical features appear to be free of strong getietic control. In the same paper, Baaré stated that the lateral ventricles—CSF-filled cavities inside the brain—were only mildly influenced by heredity. A separate study by Alycia Bartley and her colleagues at the National In-stitute of Mental Health explained how patterns of sulci and gyri were more similar in monozygotic (identical) twins than in dizygotic (fraternal) twins. Interestingly, siblings from both groups were still very different from each other, especially in the smaller sulci. Thus, while overall volumes of major brain sectors are under strong genetic control, smaller regions may be more responsive to environmental influence. These insights into the relative contributions of genes and environments to this phenotype are useful in framing another area of volumetrics research—the evolution of the modern human brain.

Lobe Row over Low Brows

Scientists have debated for decades the hypothesis that frontal lobe expansion accelerated during hominid evolution. When we compare our own high foreheads to the low brows of our closest living kin (the chimpanzee) and extinct cousins (the Neandertals), the idea seems obvious. In terms of brain functions in which parts of the frontal lobe play a critical role, language, prediction and judgment represent important cognitive differences between us and other animals. So the idea that the frontal lobe expanded disproportionately during hominid evolution makes intuitive sense.

The equation of a big frontal lobe with intelligence is also embedded in the popular imagination. The 1955 science-fiction movie This Island Earth featured three intelligent species: humans, Metalunan aliens (similar to humans but more advanced, with unnervingly large foreheads) and the menacing but highly advanced Zagons. The mutant alien brains of the Zagons had apparently become so large that they literally burst through their foreheads. The implicit notion in this hierarchy is that brain size is linked with mental acuity. More specifically, the increasing size of the foreheads (especially in the humanlike Metalunans) highlights a belief that cognitive ability is tied to the frontal regions. But is this assumption true?

Several recent studies have turned the tools of neuroimaging to the issue of relative frontal lobe expansion during hominid evolution. Our colleague Katerina Semendeferi, now at the University of California, San Diego, used MRI to compare the proportional size of the frontal lobe in people and other primates. She found that the frontal cortex (gray matter) and the entire frontal lobe (including gray and white matter) had very similar relative proportions in humans, orangutans, gorillas and chimpanzees. In these four species the frontal lobe as a whole comprised between 33 and 36 percent of the total volume of the cerebrum, and the frontal cortex made up 36 to 39 percent of the cerebral gray matter. Although the human brain is approximately three times larger than the brains of the great apes, regression analyses of the data indicated that the proportion of the frontal lobe is not greater than expected for an ape with our size brain. By contrast, our brain proportions are different than those of a "lesser ape" (the small-bodied gibbon) and two monkey species (rhesus macaque and cebus monkey), which have significantly smaller frontal lobes.

Semendeferi suggests the evolution of a proportionally larger frontal lobe happened after the human and great ape lineage split off from the other anthropoid primates (20 to 25 million years ago), but before the divergence of hominids during the late Miocene (5 to 10 million years ago). Therefore, frontal lobe expansion is not a recent development in humans. She offers several hypotheses about the evolutionary origins of brain enlargement and cognitive change In the hominid line. These traits may have arisen from cortical reorganization within small subsectors of the lobe, enriched connectivity between selected regions, regional changes in cytoarchitecture or some combination of these features. The evidence from comparative anatomy supports all three possibilities.

Lobal Forming

Our most recent work on proportionate volume also relates to the debate over frontal lobe expansion. We found that variation in total brain size is much greater than variation in the proportions of the major lobes. In other words, people vary more in brain size than in how the major regions of the brain are apportioned. This is strikingly evident when we compare men and women. Although men have larger brains, the proportions of the major lobes are similar. In both sexes, the frontal lobe comprises about 38 percent of the hemisphere (ranging from 36 to 43 percent), the temporal lobe 22 percent (ranging from 19 to 24 percent), the parietal lobe 25 percent (ranging from 21 to 28 percent), and the occipital lobe 9 percent (ranging from 7 to 12 percent). (Note that these values differ slightly from those of Semendeferi because of a parcellation scheme in this study that includes more of the white matter core.)

Comparing frontal- and parietal-lobe volumes has added another twist to the story, As we expected, people with large frontal lobes also have large parietal lobes, since they both reflect large overall brain size. However, after controlling for overall dimensions, we found that there was a highly significant, negative correlation between frontal and parietal lobe volume: People with larger frontal lobes had smaller parietal lobes and vice versa. We concluded that this inverse relation probably reflects genetic rather than environmental factors, because the boundary between these lobes, the central sulcus, appears early in the developing brain, and its course and position are strongly influenced by inheritance.

The negative correlation indicates that frontal lobe expansion during hominid evolution likely would have come at the cost of a smaller parietal lobe. And the contraction of the parietal lobe makes little sense from a cognitive standpoint. After all, association cortices in the parietal lobe serve many important language functions, and tool use, a hallmark of hominid cognitive evolution, depends on the connections between parietal and frontal lobes. Thus if is possible that there could have been selection *against* relative frontal lobe expansion if it compromised the functions of the parietal lobe. In light of this evidence, the frontal lobe probably grew at the same time as other major regions of the cerebrum during the past 2 million years.

A third perspective on frontal lobe evolution comes from a CT study of the skulls of several hominid fossils from the past half-million years. Fred Bookstein at the University of Michigan and his colleagues compared the skulls of our extinct hominid cousins with those of modern human beings. Archaic members of genus *Homo* are characterized by cranial capacities that equal or exceed those of modern *Homo sapiens sapiens*. However, the bones of the cranium and face are very thick and strong, and most specimens have large brow ridges and some degree of mid-facial prognathism (protruding nose), which together give the impression of a low, sloping forehead. But despite these external differences, Bookstein et al. showed that the inside of the cranial vault was identical by using a statistical method known as Procrustes analysis. This strategy uses a series of floating intervals between fixed anatomical landmarks to standardize the measurement of size, position, orientation and, ultimately, shape. (Procrustes was the highwayman of Greek mythology who forced each victim to fit the same terrible bed—stretching or axing the unfortunates as necessary.) The authors determined that the interior shape of the frontal bone (and presumably the shape of the frontal lobe itself) had not changed over the past 500,000 years—despite substantial changes in the external morphology of the face.

Sex in the Brain

Postmortem and MRI studies show that on average, men's brains are larger than women's brains, even after correcting for body size. This dimorphism is unlikely to be a recently evolved trait, as other primates brain similar patterns. But size is not the only difference. It turns out that women tend to have a higher proportion of gray matter than men.

We recently published a pair of papers that examined differences in brain structures of men and women. On average, male brains (mean 1,241 cubic centimeters) were about 12 percent larger than female brains (mean 1,100 cubic centimeters), although there was significant overlap between the two groups. This dissimilarity did not seem to involve sex-specific differences in hemispheric volume, as the majority of men and women had larger right hemispheres. In general, sex differences for each of the major lobes of the brain reflected those of the brain as a whole. However, the occipital lobe, which processes visual information, was less sexually dimorphic than other regions.

Our segmentation of the brain into gray and white matter revealed that women have a mean gray:white ratio of 1.35 compared with 1.26 for men. This higher ratio in women appears to be caused by less white matter rather than more gray matter. Men had, on average, 9.3 percent more gray matter than women, but the increase in white matter volume was almost twice as big— 17.4 percent. When we analyzed the covariance in this data set, the ratio difference disappeared with white matter volume normalized. This analysis indicated that the variability in white-matter volume had the most influence on sex differences.

Of all brain structures, the corpus callosum has probably drawn the most attention over the years for putative differences between the sexes. This large band of white matter connects the right and left hemispheres, and early research suggested that it might be larger in women than men. However, the current generation of studies has found the opposite to be true—it is actually larger in men, reflecting the greater overall size of male brains. In our ongoing studies, we observe that the corpus callosum is about 10 percent larger in men; however, it constitutes a significantly greater percentage of the total white matter in women (2.4 percent versus 2.2 percent).

This detail suggests an explanation for why men have a greater proportion of white matter. In MR images, most white matter includes myelinated axon fibers, glial cells and blood vessels. By contrast, the white matter of the corpus callosum is mostly just fiber tracts. Therefore, if the callosum is an index of the axonal fraction of white matter, then men may have more non-axonal components (glia, blood vessels) in the overall makeup of their white matter. In other words, the "excess" white matter in men (underlying the lower gray:white ratio) probably doesn't represent a big step up in the connectivity of male brains.

Dispelling an Old Cliché

What do these differences in brain volume tell us about the way that male and female brains actually work? When the sexually dimorphic corpus callosum was first suggested in the early 1980s, many scientists speculated that the "larger" band in women meant they had a greater degree of communication between the two hemispheres. This idea seemed to support the cliché that in women, the "emotional" "analytical" left side were more "in touch" with each other. Of course, we now know that women do not have larger corpus callosa than men. This fact doesn't preclude greater functional connectivity between the hemispheres (as the stereotype would have it), but there is no anatomical evidence for the claim.

On average, the brains of men and women differ by more than 100 cubic centimeters, or about two and a half golf balls. Should we expect this difference to have direct cognitive effects? Not necessarily, for several important reasons. First, although the sex difference in brain volume is present after correction for body size, some of the variation can be attributed to a person's physical dimensions. In a careful MRI study (in which equal attention was paid to both brain and body size parameters), Michael Peters of the University of Guelph and his colleagues found that the difference in brain volume between the sexes dropped by two-thirds after height was included as a covariate.

Next, volume differences between the sexes are distributed fairly evenly throughout the major lobes of the brain; there is no "sex-specific" region that accounts for an undue share of the difference in total brain volume. This diffuse pattern indicates that it will be difficult to find a functional sex difference that correlates with differences in total brain volume. Furthermore, a similar pattern of sexual dimorphism is seen in several other primate species: the human sex difference in brain volume evolved before the profound changes in brain size and cognition that occurred during hominid evolution.

Although we have argued against a strong functional explanation for sexual dimorphism in total brain volume—indeed, if may reflect primate ancestry rather than cognitive adaptations—we do not suggest that there are no structural-functional differences in brain anatomy between men and women. Rather, we would expect the changes to exist in more subtle ways—particular regions or networks of the brain that are associated with specific behaviors (for example, visual-spatial tasks) that exhibit sexual dimorphism.

The Mark of Silence

Heschl's gyrus (HG) is a small structure on the top of the temporal lobe, buried within the Sylvian fissure. It is important because it marks the approximate position of the primary auditory cortex—the place in the brain where sound is initially processed. But how would HG develop in people who had never heard sounds in their lives?

The examination of HG in deaf individuals is related to a series of now classic animal studies that proved the requirement for sensory information during critical periods of neural development. When the animal's sensory input was blocked (by covering one eye, for example), the brain structures that normally received those projections failed to develop. Obviously, such experiments cannot be conducted in people, so we have little direct information on sensory deprivation and the development of the human brain. With this in mind, we collaborated with Karen Emmorey at the Salk Institute to record gray and white matter volumes of HG in hearing and congenitally deaf individuals using high-resolution MRI.

We measured the volume of HG and other regions in the brains of 25 congenitally deaf individuals and 25 age and sex-matched controls. One of these areas, the planum temporale, borders HG and is involved with secondary processing of sound. This structure is one of the most reliably asymmetric parts of the human brain, being larger in the left hemisphere than the right. In fact, many scientists once thought that the asymmetry might have evolved with spoken language. However, a similar pattern also exists in chimpanzees, so hemispheric language functions must have developed within the context of preexisting lateralization (at least in this area).

The planum temporale proved to be the same in deaf and hearing subjects, indicating that the structure of this region is not critically influenced by sensory input. However, HG did change: The gray:white ratio was significantly higher in deaf subjects compared to hearing controls. This increase was caused by a reduction in white matter volume, as the amount of gray matter (after normalization) varied little between deaf and hearing subjects. We speculated that the auditory deprivation from birth might have led to a combination of less myelination, fewer connections with the auditory cortex and the gradual decay of unused axonal fibers. This part of the brain is not dead—it responds to nonauditory stimuli, according to functional imaging studies. But our results do indicate that exposure to sound may influence the anatomical development of this primary sensory region.

Mind the Gap

Given the complexity of the subject matter and the number of issues that need to be addressed, the volumetric study of the human brain is still in its infancy We have not yet ascertained the full scope of human-brain variability, and more normative research is necessary. And despite the fact that MKI has been used in hundreds of studies of schizophrenia, Alzheimer's disease and autism, quantitative volumetric data is not yet a standard component of clinical diagnoses. We anticipate the next generation of higher-resolution MRI studies will add even more analytical power to further elucidate the links between brain structure and function.

Bibliography

Allen, J. S., H. Damasio and T. J. Crabowski. 2002. Normal neuroanatomical variation in the human brain: An MRI-volumetric study. *American Journal of Physical Anthropology* 118:341–358.

Allen, J. S., H. Damasio, T. J. Grabowski, J. Bruss and W. Zhang. 2003. Sexual dimorphism and asymmetries in the gray-white composition of the human cerebrum. *NenroImage* 18:880-894.

Baaré, W. F. C., H. E. Hulshoff Pol, D. I. Boomsma, D. Posthuma, E. J. C. de Geus, H. G. Schnack, N. E. M. van Haren, C. J. van Oel and R. S. Kahn. 2001. Quantitative genetic modeling of variation in human brain morphology. *Cerebral Cortex* 11:816–824.

Bartley, A. J., D. W. Jones and D. R. Weinberger. 1997. Genetic variability of human brain size and cortical gyral patterns. *Brain* 120:257–269.

Bookstein, F., K. Schäfer, H. Prossinger, H. Seid-ler, M. Eieder, C. Stringer, G. W. Weber, J.-L. Arsuaga, D. E. Slice, E. J- Rohlf, W. Recheis, A. J. Mariam and L. F. Marcus. 1999. Comparing frontal cranial profiles in archaic and modern *Homo* by morphometric analysis. *Anatomical Record (New Anatomist)* 257:217–224.

Emniorey, K., J. S. Allen, J. Bruss, N. Schenker and H. Damasio. 2003. A morphometric analysis of auditory brain regions in congenitally deaf adults. *Proceedings of the National Academy of Sciences of the U.S.A.* 100:10049–10054.

Grabowski, T. J., R. J. Frank, N. R. Szumski, C. K. Brown and H. Damasio. 2000. Validation of partial tissue segmentation of single-channel magnetic resonance images of the brain. *NeuroImage* 12:640–636.

Holloway, R. L. 1980. Within-species brain-body weight variability: A reexamination of the Danish data and other primate species. *American Journal of Physical Anthropology* 53:109–121.

Milton, K. 1981. Distribution patterns of tropical plant foods as an evolutionary stimulus to primate mental development. *American Anthropologist* S8:534–548.

Peters, M., L. Jancke, J. E Staiger, G. Schlaug, Y. Huang and H. Steinmetz. 1998. Unsolved problems in comparing brain sizes in *Homo sapiens*. *Brain and Cognition* 37:254–285.

Semendeferi, K. and H. Damasio. 2000. The brain and its main anatomical subdivisions in living hominoids using magnetic resonance imaging, *Journal of Human Evolution* 38:317–332.

Semendeferi, K., A. Lu, N. Schenker and H. Damasio. 2002. Humans and great apes share a large frontal cortex. *Nature Neuroscience* 5:272–276.

JOHN S. ALLEN is a biological anthropologist who received his Ph.D. from the University of California, Berkeley in 1989. He is a research scientist and adjunct associate professor in the Department of Neurology, University of Iowa College of Medicine. **Joel Bruss** is a research assistant in the Human Neuroanatomy and Neuroimaging Laboratory at the University of Iowa College of Medicine. **Hanna Damasio** received her M.D. from the University of Lisbon School of Medicine. She is the University of Iowa Foundation Distinguished Professor of Neurology, and director of the human Neuroanatomy and Neuorimaging laboratory. Address for Allen: Department of Neurology, 2 RCP, University of Iowa Hospitals and Clinics, 200 Hawkins Drive, Iowa City, IA 52242. Internet: john-s-allen@uiowa.edu

---

UNIT 3
Perceptual Processes

Unit Selections

8. **Sensational Tune-ups**, Sid Kirchheimer
9. **Eye Wise: Seeing Into the Future**, Bonnie Liebman
10. **A Matter of Taste**, Mary Beckman
11. **Extreme States**, Steven Kotler

Key Points to Consider

- Why would psychologists be interested in studying sensations and perceptions? Can you differentiate the two terms? Isn't sensation the domain of biologists and physicians (e.g. ophthalmologists)? Can you rank-order the senses, that is, place them in a hierarchy of importance? Can you justify your rankings?

- What role does the brain play in sensation and perception? Can you give specific information about the role of the brain for each sense? Are some senses "distant" senses (e.g. the stimulus can be far away) and some "near" senses (e.g. we have to come in direct contact with the stimulus), despite whether the stimulus is physical or social? Can you think of other ways to categorize the various senses?

- What are some of the ways to keep your senses sharp? Do some of the strategies surprise you due to their simplicity? Do you think vision is the most important human sense? Is it the dominant sense in all other animals? How is the brain involved in vision? What are some of the various eye disorders and their causes? Can such disorders be prevented? What behaviors can you change so as to ensure good vision?

- Why is taste important? Do other organisms possess a sense of taste? What role does taste play in survival? How do sensation and perception interact to determine our food preferences? What is a supertaster? How is health related to the ability to taste foods?

- What is an out-of-body experience? Is this a common experience? Why do scientists think such experiences occur? What is a near-death experience? Is this a common experience? Why do scientists think such experiences occur? Do you know people who have had these types of experiences? How did their experiences differ, if at all, from those reported in this book? How would you feel if you had such an experience?

Student Website
www.mhcls.com/online

Internet References
Further information regarding these websites may be found in this book's preface or online.

Five Senses Home Page
  http://www.sedl.org/scimath/pasopartners/senses/welcome.html
Psychology Tutorials and Demonstrations
  http://psych.hanover.edu/Krantz/tutor.html

Marina and her roommate have been friends since freshmen year. Because they share so much in common, they decided to become roommates in their sophomore year. They both want to travel abroad one day. Both date men from the same college, are education majors, and want to work with young children after graduation from college. Today they are at the local art museum. As they walk around the galleries, Marina is astonished at her roommate's taste in art. Whatever her roommate likes, Marina hates. The paintings and sculptures that Marina admires are the very ones to which her roommate turns up her nose. "How can our tastes in art be so different when we share so much in common?" Marina wonders.

What Marina and her roommate are experiencing is a difference in perception or the interpretation of the sensory stimulation provided by the artwork. Perception and its sister area of psychology, sensation, are the focus of this unit.

For many years, it was popular for psychologists to consider sensation and perception as two distinct processes. Sensation was defined in passive terms as the simple event of some stimulus energy (i.e. a sound wave) impinging on the body or on a specific sense organ that then reflexively transmitted appropriate information to the central nervous system. With regard to the concept of sensation, in the past both passivity and simple reflexes were stressed. Perception, on the other hand, was defined as an integrative and interpretive process that the higher

centers of the brain supposedly accomplish based on sensory information and available memories for similar events.

The Gestalt psychologists, early German researchers, were convinced that perception was a higher order function compared to sensation. The Gestalt psychologists believed that the whole stimulus was more than the sum of its individual sensory parts; Gestalt psychologists believed this statement was made true by the process of perception.

For example, some of you listen to a song and hear the words, the loudness, and the harmony as well as the main melody. However, you do not really hear each of these units; what you hear is the whole song. If the song is pleasant to you, you proclaim that you like the song and even buy the CD or download it to your MP3 player. If the song is raucous to you, you may perceive that you do not like it and hope it ends soon. However, even the songs you first hear and do not like may become likeable after repeated exposure to those songs. Hence perception, according to these early Gestalt psychologists, was a more advanced and complicated process than sensation.

The strict dichotomy of sensation and perception is no longer widely accepted by today's psychologists. The revolution came in the mid-1960s when a psychologist published a then-radical treatise in which he reasoned that perceptual processes included *all* sensory events that he believed were directed by an actively searching central nervous system. Also, this view provided that certain perceptual patterns, such as recognition of a piece of artwork, may be species-specific. That is, all humans, independent of learning history, should share some of the same perceptual repertoires. This unit on perceptual processes is designed to further your understanding of these complex and interesting processes.

The first article is entitled "Sensational Tune-Up" and discusses the importance of the senses as well as ways that we can damage our sense organs if we are not cautious. The article also shares simple strategies we can use to keep our senses sharp. You would be well served to heed the advice in this article.

"Eye Wise: Seeing into the Future" by Bonnie Liebman is, of course, about vision. Vision is usually considered the dominant sense in humans. Vision is a complicated process, and various things we do, such as consume nutritious foods or stare too long at a computer, can enhance or hurt our vision. In this important article, Liebman discusses several different eye problems, such as macular degeneration, and describes how these maladies might be avoided by altering our behaviors.

The article that follows pertains to another sensation—taste. Humans can often be particular about how things taste and what food they will eat. Their pickiness might have survival value or, on the other hand, might be learned. The author showcases work on supertasters—individuals who have ultra-sensitive tastes buds. Supertasters may eat or refuse foods that affect their long-term health; thus, it is important to understand the sense of taste. This topic also provides good insight into how sensation and perception typically operate in tandem.

The final selection of this unit concerns altered states of perception or altered states of consciousness (a state outside of normal sensation and perception or awareness). This last article is about two unique perceptual experiences—near-death and out-of-body experiences. Scientists are attempting to take the mystery out of each of these by studying them in targeted individuals, individuals who have experienced them. Scientists soon hope to understand how and why such occurrences happen.

Sensational Tune-ups

Fifteen ways to improve your vision, hearing, taste, and sense of smell

SID KIRCHHEIMER

Are people around you mumbling more often these days? Does food seem to need an extra splash of Tabasco to please the palate? Would the newspaper be easier to read if your arms were just a few feet longer and the print a bit bigger?

Welcome to the club. By the time we hit middle age, most of us suffer from some decline of the senses. But don't despair. There are ways to protect—and even improve—your ability to see, hear, smell, and taste all of life's offerings. Experts we consulted recommend the following senses-sharpening strategies:

Sight

Only reading glasses or other special eyewear can foil the common cause of weakened vision: presbyopia, the so-called aging eyes that result when the lens of the eye loses its flexibility, making it harder to focus clearly on close objects. But you can take measures to stave off some of the leading causes of age-related blindness. See if these work for you:

Pop five a day A National Eye Institute study shows that one of the best ways to arrest macular degeneration is by following a simple five-pill supplement regimen: daily doses of 500 mg of vitamin C, 400 international units of vitamin E, 15 mg of beta carotene, 80 mg of zinc oxide, and 2 mg of cupric oxide. "You really need to take these in supplement form because there is no way you could get these amounts from food alone," says National Eye Institute researcher Emily Chew, M.D.

Loosen up A study in the *British Journal of Ophthalmology* finds that a tight necktie may increase risk of glaucoma by constricting neck veins, boosting fluid pressure inside the eyes to dangerous levels. "No one says you have to strangle yourself," says study author Robert Ritch, M.D., of the New York Eye and Ear Infirmary. "If you can't get your finger in between your neck and your collar easily, it's too tight."

Keep your specs on The mainstay material in prescription eyewear—polycarbonate lenses—helps block harmful ultraviolet light, a key cause of cataracts, says ophthalmologist William Lloyd, M.D., of UC Davis Medical Center. So keep your glasses on whenever you're outdoors (or don prescription sunglasses). And if you're 20/20, look for nonprescription sun-glasses at the drugstore or mall that are labeled to protect against both UVA and UVB rays.

Plow into power plants Some of the disease-protecting chemicals naturally found in fruits and vegetables also shield these plants from UV rays and other environmental pollutants that can damage your vision. While most types of produce are beneficial, peas, peppers, and green leafy vegetables such as kale, romaine lettuce, and spinach stand out because they're rich in lutein and other key vision-protecting nutrients.

Get an early start Eye-harming environmental pollutants—smog, in plain English—are at their lowest levels early in the day. To limit your exposure to toxins in the air, Lloyd suggests doing yard work, exercise, and other outdoor activities early in the morning.

Hearing

While illness, injury, overuse of certain drugs, and genetics can all lead to hearing loss, the primary reason most aging Americans go deaf is their past exposure to noise. With every noise that is loud or long enough, some of the 16,000 or so tiny hairs inside each ear that allow sound waves to be heard are permanently damaged, causing a gradual hearing loss that becomes noticeable in middle age and beyond. Some sound advice:

Plug 'em Wearing ear protection is the obvious way to protect these sensitive hair cells, but you don't have to look like an airport baggage handler while doing it. Small foam plugs that discreetly fit in your ear may actually be better than the bulky, padded earmuff types, says David Nielsen, M.D., of the American Academy of Otolaryngology–Head and Neck Surgery. These plugs reduce noise by about 20 decibels compared with the 15-decibel protection you get from more expensive padded earmuffs. "Plus, the plugs are cooler," he points out.

Work out in silence Regular exercise keeps hearing sharp by improving or maintaining good blood flow to the inner ear. But during exercise, when more blood is feeding muscles, less may get to nerves that control hearing, making them more vulnerable to noise-caused damage. Some studies indicate that loud music or noise heard during exercise may be more damaging than noise heard at the same volumes when you're sedentary. Researchers are not unanimous about this, "but unless you need to listen to loud music while you exercise, you probably shouldn't," says Nielsen.

Spark Your "Sixth" Sense

Just for fun, we asked leading experts what can be done to maintain or enhance the "sixth sense"—abilities such as ESP, telepathy, and clairvoyance. It turns out psychic abilities may actually benefit from aging. "Conditions that are more conducive for psychic experiences seem to occur more readily in older people than in younger ones," says researcher Emily Williams Kelly, Ph.D., of the University of Virginia's division of personality studies, which studies psychic phenomena. How better to get in touch with the "other side"? Consider the following:

- **Use the quiet** When the house is absent of yelling kids, blaring music, and other immediate distractions, you're more likely to be able to focus on the beyond. "These events seem to occur more readily in those who have them with quiet, solitude, and meditation," says Kelly.
- **Watch for signs** "People who are extroverted and open to the idea of having these experiences are more likely to show ESP abilities," says Kelly. And their "glass is half full" attitude includes taking clues from everyday events. "Signs are everywhere," adds Lisa Nash, a clairvoyant and online psychic reader at Global Psychic, Inc. "Pay attention to what you see while you are driving. It may be an indication of what's in your life's path. A dead deer on the side of the road might indicate that you are neglecting your inner power that comes from gentleness."
- **Eat for illumination** Nash says many psychics eat healthfully, avoiding alcohol and drugs as well as caffeine, sugar, and processed foods in order to maintain mental focus and clarity. Meanwhile, recent research shows that one of the omega-3 fatty acids found in heart-healthy fish such as salmon and mackerel can prevent age-related damage to a part of the brain where cells responsible for learning and memory communicate with one another.   —S.K.

Don't be a blowhard Strenuous nose blowing can cause temporary or permanent hearing loss by rupturing the delicate structures inside the eardrum. To relieve nasal congestion, advises Nielsen, gently blow one nostril at a time.

Get screened If you have diabetes, you're more likely to suffer earlier and faster hearing loss, probably because of impeded blood flow to nerves that control hearing. "If you have diabetes in particular, you really should consider getting a yearly hearing test, just as you get annual tests for vision, kidney function, and other possible diabetes complications," says Nancy Vaughan, Ph.D., a researcher at the National Center for Rehabilitative Auditory Research in Portland, Oregon, who has investigated the diabetes-early-hearing-loss link. Those with high blood pressure or high cholesterol could also benefit from regular hearing screenings, she adds.

Watch your aspirin Aspirin is among the 200 or so medications that can cause hearing loss by damaging hearing hair cells and nerves that carry sounds to the brain. This is not to say you should ditch your daily aspirin therapy. But it does mean you should be diligent about following the typical recommended dosages for heart health and pain—and not take much higher doses. You'll know you're taking too much aspirin if your ears "ring" but the ringing stops when you stop taking aspirin.

Smell and Taste

When smell is impaired, an inability to taste usually follows. This not only makes eating less pleasurable; it can also lead to other problems. "Smell and taste get the digestive process rolling by triggering saliva and gastric juices to help digest food," says Marcia Levin Pelchat, Ph.D., a scientist at Monell Chemical Senses Center in Philadelphia, the nation's leading institute for smell and taste research. "Before food is even eaten, these senses allow the body to anticipate food and make absorption more efficient." And when you can't smell or taste food, you're less likely to eat it, risking malnutrition. Chew over the following strategies for preserving the flavor in your life:

Breathe in If you're sitting down for a hot meal, says Alan Hirsch, M.D., director of the Smell and Taste Treatment and Research Foundation in Chicago, take advantage of the cool fact that "it's good to sniff food before you eat because heat aerates odor molecules that you'll perceive as taste."

Hit the showers A less practical but equally effective variation on the above principle: "The heat and humidity of a warm shower clears sinuses and helps dissolve molecules that facilitate the ability to smell," says Hirsch. Plus, you'll be nice and clean for dinner.

Manage your sniffles People with recurrent colds or allergy problems are more vulnerable to smell and taste impairment because they often develop nasal polyps that block the sense receptors inside the top of the nose, Hirsch adds. "It's most noticeable while they have a cold or allergies, but frequent nasal or sinus problems can lead to chronic problems in the ability to smell."

...But rethink that cold remedy A zinc deficiency is one suspected cause of smell problems, but that doesn't mean cold remedies containing this nutrient are a cure-all. "Zinc lozenges such as Cold-Eeze and zinc nose sprays that you can buy over the counter actually cause a temporary distortion in smell and taste, especially in sweet sensations," says Pelchat. "When you stop using them, your normal senses of smell and taste usually return."

Buckle up The single most common cause of a complete smell impairment? "Head injury, like that sustained in a car accident," says Hirsch. "Perhaps the easiest thing you can do to protect your senses of smell and taste is to always wear a seat belt while driving."

Sid Kirchheimer last wrote for *AARP The Magazine* about scams ("Rip-off Alert," July–August 2004). He is also the author of a forthcoming action guide that collects hundreds of tips on how to avoid consumer rip-offs (AARP Books/Sterling, spring 2006).

Eye Wise: Seeing into the Future

Bonnie Liebman

Eventually, your eyes wear out. First your focus starts to falter. Even middle-aged people who used to have 20/20 vision need glasses to read the fine print.

But that's just the beginning. Cataracts blur the vision of 20 percent of people in their 60s, more than 40 percent of people in their 70s, and nearly 70 percent of those in their 80s.

Worse yet, by age 75, more than one out of four people shows signs of damage to the retina. Degeneration of the macula, the center of the retina, is the leading cause of irreversible blindness in the U.S.

But vision loss isn't inevitable. The right foods, vitamins, and exercise may keep your eyes younger as you age.

Spinach salad or Caesar? Grilled salmon or roast chicken? Nuts or chips? An apple or a doughnut?

It's no surprise that what you eat can inflate your waistline, clog your arteries, and raise your blood pressure. But few people think of their eyes as they scan a menu or pack a snack.

Yet a growing body of evidence suggests that certain vegetables, fruits, fish, nuts, and other foods can protect your vision, while certain fats and baked sweets like cakes, cookies, and pies may blur it. And some supplements may stave off eye damage while others are useless.

The catch is that vision rarely deteriorates in the blink of an eye. To keep seeing clearly, you've got to start early.

Cataracts

At first, it seems like you've got dirty glasses. Colors seem dimmer. Bright lights have a glare. By the time you have a ready-to-be-extracted, or "ripe," cataract, it's almost as though you're looking through a waterfall. (That's what the word "cataract" means.)

What causes the lens to become opaque in places? Researchers aren't sure, but they believe that fibers in the lens play a role.

"The lens continues to lay down new fibers throughout life," says Frederick Ferris III, director of clinical research at the National Eye Institute. "But it can't grow in size because it's stuck inside the eye, so the fibers become more densely packed."

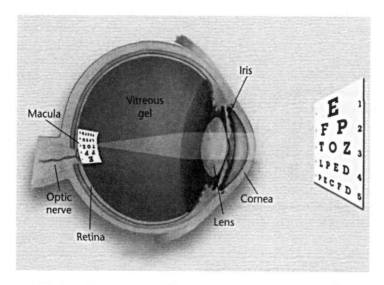

The lens, which focuses light rays onto the retina, is supposed to be translucent. Opaque areas, called cataracts, scatter light and blur vision. When the macula—the center of the retina—degenerates, it blurs the sharp, detailed vision you need to read, drive, sew, etc.

Illustration: adapted from National Eye Institute.

Got a Cataract?

These symptoms of a cataract may also signal other eye problems. Check with your doctor to find out.

- Cloudy or blurry vision
- Colors seem faded
- Glare (headlights, lamps, or sunlight may appear too bright or a halo may appear around lights)
- Poor night vision
- Double vision or multiple images in one eye (this symptom may clear as the cataract gets larger)
- Frequent prescription changes in your eyeglasses or contact lenses

Playing the Lutein

If you're looking for lutein-rich vegetables and fruit, here's where to start.

Vegetables and Fruits (1/2 cup cooked vegetable, unless noted)	Lutein + Zeaxanthin (milligrams)
Kale	11.9
Spinach	10.2
Swiss chard	9.6
Collard greens	7.3
Spinach (1 cup raw)	3.7
Peas, frozen	1.9
Broccoli	1.2
Romaine lettuce (1 cup raw)	1.1
Brussels sprouts	1.0
Zucchini	1.0
Asparagus	0.7
Corn	0.6
Green beans	0.4
Iceberg lettuce (1 cup raw)	0.2
Nectarine (1)	0.2
Orange (1)	0.2

That's one reason people lose the ability to see things that are near as they age, he explains. "The lens loses flexibility so it can't focus up close."

Proteins in the lens are also at fault. "Normally, molecules in the lens keep the proteins separate, in a pattern that allows light through," says Ferris. "But the balance that keeps the lens clear may tip in the direction of proteins clumping together."

The solution: surgery. Out goes the clouded lens; in goes a clear plastic replacement.

Doctors remove more than 1.5 million cataracts each year in the U.S., at a cost that accounts for more than 12 percent of the Medicare budget.

"Delaying cataracts by 10 years could reduce the number of extractions by half," says Julie Mares, a professor in the department of ophthalmology and visual sciences at the University of Wisconsin Medical School in Madison.

But how? Here's what we know so far.

•**Antioxidant vitamins.** "We have pretty consistent evidence that people who take multivitamins have lower rates of cataract," says Mares.

Researchers believe that oxidation promotes cataracts by damaging the proteins in the lens. "Oxidative stress is high in the eye due to the intense light exposure," explains Mares. And antioxidants seem to protect the lens in animal studies.

But the evidence in humans isn't airtight. In several studies, people who took multivitamins were less likely to get cataracts.[1,2] But in one study, the risk was lower only in people who took vitamin C, not other antioxidants. And the longer they took it, the better.[3]

"You don't seem to get the benefit until you've taken supplements for at least five years, and we see the greatest benefit in people who've taken them for at least 10 years," says Paul Jacques of the Jean Mayer U.S. Department of Agriculture Human Nutrition Research Center on Aging at Tufts University in Boston.

But that doesn't mean that more is better. While women who got 240 mg to 360 mg a day of vitamin C had the lowest risk, higher doses didn't cut the risk further.

"That's consistent with our observation that human eye tissues are saturated at intakes of 200 to 300 mg of vitamin C a day," says Jacques.

Still, researchers aren't convinced that vitamin C is a magic bullet. "It's too early to narrow it down to vitamin C," says Mares. "We don't have enough data."

One reason: so far, most evidence that vitamins of any kind keep cataracts at bay comes from studies of people who choose to take supplements on their own.

"We're not sure if people who take multivitamins also eat better and do more physical activity," says Mares, though studies try to account for those and other factors.

To get stronger evidence, researchers have to randomly assign people to take vitamins or a placebo and wait five or 10 years. So far, five out of six of those trials found no benefit from high doses of vitamins.[2]

For example, in the Age-Related Eye Disease Study (AREDS), which followed more than 4,600 people for more than seven years, cataracts were no less common in people who were given high daily doses of beta-carotene (15 mg, or 25,000 IU), vitamin C (500 mg), and vitamin E (400 IU) than in those who got a placebo.[4]

"But both groups were well-nourished," says Jacques. "Two-thirds of the controls were taking Centrum like supplements provided by the investigators." Were the lower doses in an ordinary multi enough to protect their eyes?

Two trials in China suggest that a multivitamin might be enough for people who are undernourished. "In a nutritionally deprived region in China, multivitamins lowered the prevalence of cataract," says Mares. "A supplement containing 120 milligrams of vitamin C and molybdenum did not."

Whose macula is at risk?

Macular degeneration causes no pain. Age is by far the greatest risk factor. Others include:
- Caucasian race
- Family history
- Female gender
- Obesity
- Smoking

A clearer answer for Americans may come in a nine-year trial testing ordinary multivitamins against a placebo on 1,000 people in Italy, says Mares. "So far, the literature doesn't suggest that taking anything more than a regular multivitamin would be useful."

• **Lutein.** Lutein and its close cousin, zeaxanthin, are pigments found mostly in fruits and vegetables, especially leafy greens like spinach, collards, and kale. (The two are so close that when we say "lutein," we generally mean both.)

In studies that ask people what they're eating and wait to see who gets which disease, lutein seems to help ward off cataracts. "The data from observational studies on cataracts and lutein is quite consistent," says Mares.

In three large studies, people who got the most lutein from their food had a 20 to 50 percent lower risk of getting a cataract or having cataract surgery than people who got the least lutein.[5,6] But exactly how lutein might protect the lens is still fuzzy.

"Lutein and zeaxanthin absorb blue light," says Mares, "but as far as we know, only ultraviolet light is damaging to the lens." So it's too early to say that light at the blue end of the spectrum matters.

"Until we know more, we have to assume that lutein works as an antioxidant," says Jacques.

How much lutein is enough? In studies of more than 36,000 men and 77,000 women, researchers found the lowest risks of cataract surgery in those who consumed about six milligrams (6,000 micrograms) or more a day. "That's well within the range you can get in the diet," says Mares.

For example, men who ate broccoli or raw spinach more than twice a week were about 25 percent less likely to have cataract surgery than men who ate those vegetables less than once a month.[6] Men who ate cooked spinach at least twice a week had about half the risk of surgery, probably because there's more lutein in a typical serving of cooked than raw greens (see "Playing the Lutein").

Corn is rich in zeaxanthin, but it wasn't linked to a lower risk.

• **Overweight.** Most cataracts are either in the inner (nuclear) or outer (cortical) section of the lens. But a cataract at the back of the lens (posterior subcapsular) is the worst.

"Posterior subcapsular cataracts are the least common but the most important because they lead to surgery more frequently than other cataracts," explains Jacques.

Seeing AREDS

Do you have macular degeneration that's either intermediate or advanced (not early)?

If so, talk to your doctor about whether to take the high-dose daily supplements used in AREDS—the Age-Related Eye Disease Study: vitamin C (500 mg), vitamin E (400 IU), beta-carotene (15 mg, or 25,000 IU), zinc (80 mg), and copper (2 mg).

Make sure you take *zinc oxide*, because *zinc gluconate* could lead to higher blood levels of zinc. Researchers added the copper because high doses of zinc may interfere with copper absorption.

At high doses, zinc may raise the risk of prostate cancer, lower HDL ("good") cholesterol, and impair immunity. High doses of beta-carotene may increase the risk of lung cancer in smokers. But if your vision is in danger, the benefits to your eyes may outweigh those potential risks.

Clouding in the back of the lens is most likely to blur vision because that's where light rays are focused into a narrow beam. They're the cataracts that typically cause glare and halos, and they're linked to your waistline.

"Individuals who are overweight tend to have a higher risk of posterior subcapsular cataracts" says Jacques. A supersized belly puts you in greatest jeopardy. Posterior cataracts are roughly twice as common in women with a waist larger than 35 inches than in women with a waist smaller than 31 inches.[7]

"People with diabetes are also more likely to get posterior subcapsular cataracts" says Jacques. What's the link? In both diabetes and obesity, "high blood sugar levels may damage the protein in that part of the lens."

Macular Degeneration

Think of your retina as the film in your (old-fashioned, non-digital) camera. Rods (which handle peripheral and night vision) and cones (responsible for color and sharp vision) convert the image into electrical impulses, which travel to your brain via the optic nerve.

The most sensitive part of the retina is the macula. There, millions of cones are tightly packed to create a high resolution image. It's the macula that can deteriorate with age.

"The cells in your retina—which are there from birth—work very hard," explains Ferris. "They're among the most metabolically active cells in the body."

And time takes its toll. "The cells accumulate debris over the years, and eventually it catches up with them and they stop functioning properly."

The macula decays in one of two ways. "In dry macular degeneration, cells essentially give up the ghost and die," Ferris explains. "In wet macular degeneration, the cells are sick and crying for help."

The body pitches in by building new blood vessels to nourish the cells. "But this call for blood vessels messes up the job," says

Ferris, "because the blood vessels are abnormal and fragile. They can bleed and leak fluid and that causes rapid vision loss."

Doctors can treat the wet type by destroying the new blood vessels with lasers. There is no treatment for the dry type, which accounts for 90 percent of cases. That's why scientists are so eager to prevent or slow the disease. Some of what they're looking at:

• Zinc & antioxidant vitamins. You win some, you lose some. High doses of antioxidant vitamins (C, E, and beta-carotene) didn't prevent cataracts in the Age-Related Eye Disease Study, but they did slow macular degeneration (see "Seeing AREDS," p. 3)." So did a high dose (80 mg a day) of zinc.

"Either antioxidants or zinc made a difference, but the combination worked better than either one alone," says Ferris. Taking both supplements cut the odds that macular degeneration got worse by about 25 percent, but only in people who were at high risk for advanced macular degeneration when the study began.

That's no small potatoes. An estimated eight million people in the U.S. fall into that group.

"If they all took the AREDS supplements, it would prevent more than 300,000 cases of advanced macular degeneration during the next five years," says Ferris. "But that leaves over a million cases still in progress, so we have a long way to go."

How zinc might protect the retina isn't clear, but researchers have some clues. "The epithelial cells that lie under the retina and nourish it have the highest concentration of zinc of any tissue of the body, with the possible exception of the prostate gland," explains Ferris. "And zinc is tied up in many enzymes that may be important in the eye," a number of which act as antioxidants.

But some experts worry that healthy people will start taking high doses of antioxidants and zinc to *prevent* the disease.

"When I talk to people with macular degeneration, they proudly announce that they've told their sons and daughters to take these supplements," says Mares. "So some people may be taking boatloads of antioxidants and zinc for decades."

She worries that high doses of antioxidants could interfere with statin drugs like Lipitor and Zocor, and that beta-carotene could raise the risk of lung cancer in smokers.

What's more, she adds, "the long-term use of zinc has been linked with prostate cancer, and AREDS found more urinary tract problems in people who took zinc."

Most of those problems were benign prostatic hypertrophy (enlarged prostate) and urinary tract infections, with only a few prostate cancers—and there were no more cancers in the zinc takers than in placebo takers, says Ferris. So far, only one study has found a higher risk of advanced prostate cancer in people who took zinc for at least 10 years.

Until we know more, says Mares, only people with intermediate or advanced macular degeneration should take high-dose supplements. "We don't know if they're effective in people in the early stages of the disease," she says. (AREDS wasn't large enough to tell.) "And it's unknown whether half of the AREDS doses would be equally effective."

• Lutein. It's no surprise that lutein is a prime candidate for chief macula defender. "Lutein is deposited in the retina and concentrated in the macula," says Ferris. In contrast, beta-carotene is nowhere to be found.

The Bottom Line

To lower your risk of cataracts and/or macular degeneration:
- Don't smoke.
- Eat leafy green vegetables like spinach and broccoli at least twice a week.
- Eat fish at least once a week.
- Take a multivitamin for insurance.
- Lose excess weight.
- Snack on fruits, vegetables, or nuts instead of cookies, cakes, pies, or chips.
- Have a doctor check your eyes after dilating them at least once in your 20s, twice in your 30s, every two to four years between ages 40 and 64, and every one or two years at age 65 or older.
- If you have Intermediate or advanced macular degeneration, talk to your doctor about taking antioxidants or zinc.

And researchers have theories to explain why lutein may help. "Lutein absorbs blue light and it's in front of the cells that develop macular degeneration, so it may lessen the potential for light to cause oxidative or photochemical damage," suggests Mares. "Lutein is also found in the membranes of cells that die in macular degeneration, so it may have an antioxidant role there." Studies show that taking a lutein supplement raises lutein levels in the macula. But so far, they haven't consistently found a lower risk of macular degeneration in people who happen to eat more lutein-rich foods.

"Some studies show a link and some don't," says Mares, possibly because many studies have looked at well nourished populations like nurses, most of whom get sufficient lutein.

The answer may come in a large trial that the National Eye Institute is now planning. "We're still working on the dose," says Ferris, "but it will probably be between six and 15 mg a day."

It's easier to get there with leafy greens than with most supplements. Six milligrams is 24 times more than the 250 micrograms (0.25 mg) you would get in a multivitamin like Centrum Silver.

"Lutein is expensive," says Jacques, "so most supplements have incredibly low amounts compared to what you would get in the diet."

• Fish, nuts, sweets. The National Eye Institute's lutein trial will also test DHA (docosahexaenoic acid), one of the two major omega-3 fish oils.

"In AREDS, people who ate fish at least twice a week had a 50 percent lower risk of advanced macular degeneration compared to people who ate no fish," says Ferris.

Results from other studies are similar. For example, when Harvard researchers tracked more than 42,000 women and 29,000 men for 10 to 12 years, those who ate fish one to four times a week had a 23 percent lower risk of macular degeneration than those who ate fish three times a month or less.[9] People who ate fish (mostly canned tuna) more than four times a week had a 35 percent lower risk.

Why single out DHA? "We know that DHA is a very important lipid in rods and cones," says Ferris. "It's also important in the brain, and the eye is really an outcropping of the brain."

Only one other food seemed to keep macular degeneration from getting worse. Harvard researchers found that patients who ate nuts at least once a week had a 40 percent lower risk of advanced disease than those who never ate them.

In contrast, those who ate baked sweets—like store-bought cakes, cookies, pies and potato chips at least two or three times a day had more than double the risk of people who ate those foods only once every two weeks or so.[10]

Trans fats in the sweets and chips may be to blame, says Harvard researcher Johanna Seddon. But since anyone with eyes also has a heart, they should already be avoiding trans-heavy foods.

• **Obesity.** Can the battle of the bulge turn into a battle for your eyesight? Only a few studies have looked.

Researchers who studied more than 21,000 men in the Physicians Health Study found that obese men had more than double the risk of macular degeneration of men of normal weight.[11]

How fat affects the eyes isn't clear. "It could be an increase in inflammation or an increase in oxidative stress," explains Debra Schaumberg, director of ophthalmic epidemiology at Brigham and Women's Hospital in Boston. Her study found a smaller elevated risk in people who were leaner than in people of normal weight, "but we've had a hard time coming up with a plausible explanation for that."

Extra pounds—especially around the waist—also seem to speed up damage to the macula. In a study of roughly 260 people who already had early or intermediate macular degeneration, the risk of progressing to advanced disease was double in those who were overweight or obese.[12]

Physical activity appeared to slow the disease's progress, but the study wasn't large enough to say for sure.

Eye Opener

As scientists try to nail down the foods or pills that can protect your eyes, don't forget to bring your blinkers in for a check-up every once in a while.

"Of the four leading causes of blindness—cataracts, diabetic retinopathy, glaucoma, and macular degeneration—all but cataracts can progress without your knowing it," warns Ferris. "The sad part is that by the time you can tell you have them, it's often too late to make a difference."

Anyone older than 60 should have a dilated eye exam. Just getting a new prescription for glasses isn't enough. "You can have good vision and these processes could be rampant," Ferris explains. "Only by looking at dilated eyes can the doctor tell."

Notes

1. *Arch. Ophthalmol. 118:* 1556, 2000.
2. *Nutr. Rev. 62:* 28, 2004,
3. *Arch. Ophthalmol. 119:* 1009, 2001,
4. *Arch. Ophthalmol. 119:* 1439, 2001.
5. *Amer. J. Epidemiol. 149:* 810, 1999,
6. *Amer. J. Gin. Nutr. 70:* 509, S1 7, 1999.
7. *Amer. J. Clin. Nutr. 78:* 400, 2003.
8. *Arch. Ophthalmol. 119:* 1417, 2001
9. *Amer. J. Clin. Nutr. 73:* 209, 2001.
10. *Arch. Ophthalmol. 121:* 1728, 2003.
11. *Arch. Ophthalmol. 119:* 1259, 2001.
12. *Arch. Ophthalmol. 121:* 785, 2003.

From *Nutrition Action Healthletter,* November 2004, pp. 3-7. Copyright © 2004 by Nutrition Action Healthletter. Reprinted by permission via the Copyright Clearance Center.

A Matter of Taste

Are you a supertaster? Just stick out your tongue and say "yuck"

MARY BECKMAN

THERE'S GOOD TASTE, and according to scientists, there's supertaste. Blue food coloring is going to tell me where I lie on the continuum. Armed with a bottle of blue dye No. 1 and a Q-tip, I paint my tongue cobalt, swish some water in my mouth and spit into the bathroom sink. In the mirror I see a smattering of pink bumps—each hiding as many as 15 taste buds apiece—against the lurid blue background. Now I'm supposed to count how many of those bumps, called fungiform papillae, appear inside a circle a quarter-inch in diameter, but I don't need to do that. Obviously, I have fewer than the 30 that would qualify me as having an extraordinary palate. I am not a supertaster. Thank goodness.

Normally, people prize highly acute senses. We brag about twenty-twenty vision or the ability to eavesdrop on whispers from across the room. But taste is not so simple: supertaste may be too much of a good thing, causing those who have it to avoid bitter compounds and find some spicy foods too hot to handle. This unusual corner of perception science has been explored by Linda Bartoshuk of Yale University, who first stumbled upon supertasting about 15 years ago while studying saccharin. While most people found the sugar substitute sweet and palatable, others sensed a bitter aftertaste. She went on to test hundreds of volunteers with a host of chemicals found in food. About one in four, she discovered, qualified as supertasters, a name she coined.

To find what made them special, Bartoshuk zeroed in on the tongue's anatomy. She found that people have different numbers of fungiform papillae, with tongue topography ranging from, say, sparse cactus-pocked deserts to lush lawns. To qualify for supertasterdom, which is a genetically inherited trait, a person has to have wall-to-wall papillae on his or her tongue and also have an ability to readily taste PROP, a bitter synthetic compound also known as 6-*n*-propylthiouracil, which is used as a thyroid medication.

As it happens, Bartoshuk is a non-taster—she's among another one in four who can't detect PROP at all—and likes it that way. "I prefer the dumb, happy life I lead," she says. "'Super' connotes superiority, but supertaste often means sensory unpleasantness." In the course of her research she has relied on volunteers and colleagues to perceive what she cannot, such as the difference in creaminess between skim and 2 percent milk.

"PROP tastes like quinine," says Laurie Lucchina, a supertaster who made this discovery about ten years ago when she worked with Bartoshuk. Another person in the lab, Valerie Duffy, now at the University of Connecticut, is a medium taster. Bartoshuk routinely tested "the junk food of the month," sent to the lab through a food subscription service, on the two women. "Once she brought in a cookie that she thought was very bland. But to me, it tasted just right," recalls Lucchina.

"Mother's milk reflects the culture into which babies are born."

Perhaps not surprisingly, supersensitive taste influences what people eat. Bartoshuk and other researchers found that supertasters tend to shun or restrict strong-flavored foods and drinks—coffee, frosted cake, greasy barbequed ribs, hoppy hand-crafted ales. Also, supertasters tend to crave neither fats nor sugars, which probably helps explain why researchers have found that supertasters also tend to be slimmer than people without the sensitivity. When it comes to rich desserts, Lucchina says, "I usually eat just a bite or two and then I'm done."

Taste sensitivity may also affect health. According to recent studies, supertasters have better cholesterol profiles than the norm, helping reduce their risk of heart disease. Yet supertasting may also have a downside. Some scientists have speculated that supertasters don't eat enough bitter vegetables, which are believed to protect against various types of cancer. And in a still-preliminary study of 250 men by Bartoshuk and co-workers, nontasters had fewer colon polyps, a risk factor for colon cancer, than did medium tasters or supertasters. To be sure, not everyone is convinced that supertasters put themselves in harm's way by skimping on vegetables. Adam Drewnowski, a nutrition scientist at the University of Washington, says a dollop of butter or maybe a splash of cheese sauce may be all a supertaster needs to find spinach or broccoli palatable. Still, the new data intrigue medical researchers, who don't usually consider taste an inherited factor in disease risk.

Of course, there's more to satisfaction than meets the tongue. Flavors are a combination of taste and odors, which float up through the back of our mouths to activate a suite of smell receptors in the nose. (Hold your nose while tasting a jellybean. You can tell it's sweet but not what flavor it is. Then unplug your nose. See?) Each smell tingles a different constellation of neurons in the brain, and with experience we learn what these different patterns mean—it's bacon sizzling in the kitchen, not liver. Nature may dictate whether or not we're supertasters, but it's nurture that shapes most of our food preferences.

And taste training starts earlier than one might think—during breast-feeding or even in the womb, according to biopsychologist Julie Mennella of the Monell Chemical Senses Center in Philadelphia. She asked pregnant women and breast-feeding mothers to drink carrot juice for three weeks. In both cases, when it came time to switch to solid food, babies of these mothers liked carrots better than babies whose mothers never drank the stuff. "These are the first ways they learn what foods are safe," Mennella says. "Mother's milk reflects the culture into which babies are born."

Learning can even trump innate good sense, according to a study Mennella reported this past April. She found that 7-month-old babies normally disliked bitter and sour flavors, and when given a bottle with a slightly bitter, sour formula, they pushed it away and wrinkled their angelic faces in disgust. But 7-month-olds who had been introduced to the bitter formula months earlier happily drank it again. In another study of babies who'd never been fed carrots, she found that those who'd been exposed to a variety of other vegetables clearly enjoyed carrots more than did babies who'd dined on a more monotonous diet. She suggests that early exposure to a diversity of flavors enables babies to trust new foods later in life. "Clearly experience is a factor in developing food habits," says Mennella. "But we don't know how that interacts with genetics."

Beyond genes and even learning lies a more ineffable aspect of taste: its emotional content. Certain foods can bring back unpleasant experiences; it may take only one rotten hot dog to put you off franks for life. Other tastes unlock happy memories. To an extent that researchers are still trying to understand, learning which foods are safe to eat while in the security of mother's arms may be the source of some of our most enduring desires. This learning process could be, Mennella says, "one of the foundations of how we define what is a comfort food."

MARY BECKMAN, *a freelance writer in Idaho, specializes in the life sciences.*

Extreme States

Out-of-body experiences? Near-death experiences? Researchers are beginning to understand how they occur and how they may alter the brain

STEVEN KOTLER

I WAS 17 YEARS OLD AND TERRIFIED. The whole "let's go jump out of an airplane" concept had been dreamed up at a Friday night party, but now I was Saturday-morning sober and somehow still going skydiving. To make matters worse, this was in 1984, and while tandem skydiving was invented in 1977, the concept had yet to make its way to the airfield in mid-Ohio where I had wound up. So my first jump wasn't done with an instructor tethered to my back handling any difficulties we might encounter. Instead, I jumped alone 2,000 feet, my only safety net an unwieldy old Army parachute, dubbed a "round."

Thankfully, nobody expected me to pull my own rip cord. A static line, nothing fancier than a short rope, had been fixed between my rip cord and the floor of the airplane. If everything went according to plan, 15 feet from the plane, when I reached the end of my rope, it would tug open the chute. *Getting* to this point was more complicated.

As the plane flew along at 100 miles per hour, I had to clamber out a side door, ignore the vertiginous view, step onto a small metal rung, hold onto the plane's wing with both hands, and lift one leg behind me, so that my body formed a giant T. From this position, when my instructor gave the order, I was to jump. If all this wasn't bad enough, when I finally leaped out of the plane, I also leaped out of my body.

It happened the second I let go of the wing. My body started falling through space, but my consciousness was hovering about 20 feet away, watching me descend. During training, the instructor had explained that rounds opened, closed, and opened again in the first milliseconds of deployment. He had also mentioned that it happened too fast for the human eye to see and that we shouldn't worry about it. Yet in the instant I began falling, I was worried. I was also watching the chute's open-close-open routine, despite knowing that what I was watching was technically impossible to see.

My body began to tip over, tilting into an awkward position that would produce quite a jerk when the chute caught. In what might best be described as a moment of extracorporeal clarity, I told myself to relax rather than risk whiplash. In the next instant, my chute caught with a jerk. The jerk snapped my consciousness back into my body, and everything returned to normal.

OUT-OF-BODY EXPERIENCES BELONG TO A SUBSET OF not-so-garden-variety phenomena broadly called the paranormal, although the dictionary defines that word as "beyond the range of normal experience or scientific explanation," and out-of-body experiences are neither. This type of experience has been reported in almost every country in the world for centuries. Mystics of nearly every faith, including all five of the world's major religions, have long told tales of astral projection. But this phenomenon is not reserved for only the religious. The annals of action sports are packed with accounts of motorcyclists who recall floating above their bikes, watching themselves ride, and pilots who occasionally find themselves floating outside their airplane, struggling to get back inside. However, most out-of-body tales do not take place within the confines of an extreme environment. They transpire as part of normal lives.

The out-of-body experience is much like the near-death experience, and any exploration of one must include the other. While out-of-body experiences are defined by a perceptual shift in consciousness, no more and no less, near-death experiences start with this shift and then proceed along a characteristic trajectory. People report entering a dark tunnel, heading into light, and feeling an all-encompassing sense of peace, warmth, love, and welcome. They recall being reassured along the way by dead friends, relatives, and a gamut of religious figures. Occasionally, there's a life review, followed by a decision of the "should I stay or should I go?" variety. A 1990 Gallup poll of American adults found that almost 12 percent of Americans, roughly 30 million individuals, said they have had some sort of near-death experience.

Both phenomena have had a serious credibility problem. Much of it stems from the scientists who did the earliest investigations. Charles Tart, a psychologist at the University of California at Davis, who did the first major study of out-of-body experiences in 1969, and Raymond Moody, a psychiatrist recently retired from the University of Nevada at Las Vegas who did the same for near-death experiences in the early 1970s, designed experiments of questionable rigor and made matters worse by ignoring the peer-review process and publishing their results in best-selling books. Both Tart and Moody later wrote follow-up books partially debunking and partially recanting their previous ones.

Unfortunately, many researchers studying these extreme states of consciousness are unaware of these follow-up books and still point to the original work as evidence that none of this should be taken seriously. Simultaneously, many skeptics are unaware of much of the research done since then. But forget for the moment this troubled history and concentrate on more recent work. And there is plenty.

In 1982, while a children's brain cancer researcher and finishing his residency in pediatrics at Children's Hospital in Seattle, Melvin Morse was also moonlighting for a helicopter-assisted EMT service. One afternoon he was flown to Pocatello, Idaho, to perform CPR on 8-year-old Crystal Merzlock, who had apparently drowned in the deep end of a community swimming pool. When Morse arrived on the scene, the child had been without a heartbeat for 19 minutes; her pupils were already fixed and dilated. Morse got her heart restarted, climbed into the chopper, and went home. Three days later Crystal regained consciousness.

A few weeks passed. Morse was back at the hospital where Crystal was being treated, and they bumped into each other in the hallway. Crystal pointed at Morse, turned to her mother, and said, "That's the guy who put the tube in my nose at the swimming pool." Morse was stunned. "I didn't know what to do. I had never heard of OBEs [out-of-body experiences] or NDEs [near-death experiences]. I stood there thinking: How was this possible? When I put that tube in her nose, she was brain dead. How could she even have this memory?"

Morse decided to make a case study of Crystal's experience, which he published in the *American Journal of Diseases of Children*. He labeled the event a fascinoma, which is both medical slang for an abnormal pathology and a decent summary of the state of our knowledge at the time. He was the first to publish a description of a child's near-death experience.

He started by reviewing the literature, discovering that the classic explanation—delusion—had been recently upgraded to a hallucination provoked by a number of different factors, including fear, drugs, and a shortage of oxygen to the brain. But it was drugs that caught Morse's eye. He knew that ketamine, used as an anesthetic during the Vietnam War, frequently produced out-of-body experiences and that other drugs were suspected of being triggers as well. Morse decided to study halothane, another commonly used anesthetic, believing his study might help explain the many reports of near-death experiences trickling out of emergency rooms. "It's funny to think of it now," he says, "but really, at the time, I set out to do a long-term, large-scale debunking study."

Morse's 1994 report, commonly referred to as the Seattle study and published in *Current Problems in Pediatrics*, spanned a decade. During that period, he interviewed 160 children in the intensive care unit at Children's Hospital in Seattle who had been revived from apparent death. Every one of these children had been without a pulse or sign of breathing longer than 30 seconds. Some had been in that state for as long as 45 minutes; the average apparent death lasted between 10 and 15 minutes. For a control group, he used hundreds of other children also in intensive care, also on the brink of death, but whose pulse and breathing hadn't been interrupted for more than 30 seconds. That was the only difference. In other dimensions—age, sex, drugs administered, diseases suffered, and setting—the groups were the same. In setting, Morse not only included the intensive care unit itself but also scary procedures such as insertion of a breathing tube and mechanical ventilation. These are important additions because fear has long been considered a trigger for a near-death experience (and might have been the trigger responsible for what happened when I skydived).

Morse graded his subjects' experiences according to the Greyson scale, a 16-point questionnaire designed by University of Virginia psychiatrist Bruce Greyson that remains the benchmark for determining whether or not an anomalous experience should be considered a near-death experience. Using this test, Morse found that 23 out of 26 children who experienced apparent death—the cessation of heartbeat and breathing—reported a classic near-death experience, while none of the other 131 children in his control group reported anything of the kind.

Morse later videotaped the children recalling their experiences, which included such standard fare as long tunnels, giant rainbows, dead relatives, and deities of all sorts. But many descriptions—augmented by crayon drawings—included memories of the medical procedures performed and details about doctors and nurses whose only contact with the child occurred while the child was apparently dead.

Other scientists have duplicated Morse's findings. Most recently, cardiologist Pim van Lommel, a researcher at Rijnstate Hospital in Arnhem, the Netherlands, conducted an eight-year study involving 344 cardiac-arrest patients who seemed to have died and were later revived. Out of that total, 282 had no memories, while 62 reported a classic near-death experience. Just as in Morse's study, van Lommel examined the patients' records for any factors traditionally used to explain near-death experiences—such as setting, drugs, or illness—and found no evidence of their influence. Apparent death was the only factor linked to near-death experiences. He also found that one person in his study had difficult-to-explain memories of events that happened in the hospital while he was presumed dead.

Possible clues to the biological basis of these unusual states turned up in studies conducted in the late 1970s, when the Navy and the Air Force introduced a new generation of high-performance fighter planes that underwent extreme acceleration. Those speeds generated tremendous g-forces, which pulled too much blood out of the pilots' brains, causing them to black out. The problem, known as G-LOC, for g-force-induced loss of consciousness, was serious, and James Whinnery, a specialist in aerospace medicine, was in charge of solving it.

Over a 16-year period, working with a massive centrifuge at the Naval Air Warfare Center in Warminster, Pennsylvania, Whinnery spun fighter pilots into G-LOC. He wanted to determine at what force tunnel vision occurred. More than 500 pilots accidentally blacked out during the study, and from them Whinnery learned how long it took pilots to lose consciousness under acceleration and how long they remained unconscious after the acceleration ceased. By studying this subset he also learned how long they could be unconscious before brain damage started.

He found that G-LOC could be induced in 5.67 seconds, that the average blackout lasted 12 to 24 seconds, and that at least 40 of the pilots reported some sort of out-of-body experience while they were unconscious. Not knowing anything about out-of-body experiences, Whinnery called these episodes dreamlets, kept detailed records of their contents, and began examining the literature on anomalous unconscious experiences. "I was reading about sudden-death episodes in cardiology," Whinnery says, "and it led me right into near-death experiences. I realized that a smaller percentage of my pilots' dreamlets, about 10 to 15 percent, were much closer in content to a classic NDE."

When Whinnery reviewed his data, he noted a correlation: The longer his pilots were knocked out, the closer they got to brain death. And the closer they got to brain death, the more likely it was that an out-of-body experience would turn into a near-death experience. This was the first hard evidence for what had been long suspected—that the two states are not two divergent phenomena, but two points on a continuum.

Whinnery found that G-LOC, when gradually induced, produced tunnel vision. "The progression went first to grayout (loss of peripheral vision) and then to blackout," he explains, and the blindness occurred just before a person went unconscious. "This makes a lot of sense. We know that the occipital lobe (the portion of the brain that controls vision) is a well-protected structure. Perhaps it continued to function when signals from the eyes were failing due to compromised blood flow. The transition from grayout to unconsciousness resembles floating peacefully within a dark tunnel, which is much like some of the defining characteristics of a near-death experience. The pilots also recalled a feeling of peace and serenity as they regained consciousness.

The simplest conclusion to draw from these studies is that, give or take some inexplicable memories, these phenomena are simply normal physical processes that occur during unusual circumstances. After all, once scientists set aside the traditional diagnosis of delusion as a source of these unusual mental states and began looking for biological correlates, there were plenty of possibilities. Compression of the optic nerve could produce tunnel vision; neurochemicals such as serotonin, endorphins, and enkephalins could help explain the euphoria; and psychotropics like LSD and mescaline often produce vibrant hallucinations of past events. But no one has directly tested these hypotheses.

What researchers have studied is the effect of a near-death experience. Van Lommel conducted lengthy interviews and administered a battery of standard psychological tests to his study group of cardiac-arrest patients. The subset that had had a near-death experience reported more self-awareness, more social awareness, and more religious feelings than the others.

Van Lommel then repeated this process after a two-year interval and found the group with near-death experience still had complete memories of the event, while others' recollections were strikingly less vivid. He found that the near-death experience group also had an increased belief in an afterlife and a decreased fear of death compared with the others. After eight years he again repeated the whole process and found those two-year effects significantly more pronounced. The near-death experience group was much more empathetic, emotionally vulnerable, and often showed evidence of increased intuitive awareness. They still showed no fear of death and held a strong belief in an afterlife.

Morse, too, did follow-up studies long after his original research. He also did a separate study involving elderly people who had a near-death experience in early childhood. "The results were the same for both groups," says Morse. "Nearly all of the people who had had a near-death experience—no matter if it was 10 years ago or 50—were still absolutely convinced their lives had meaning and that there was a universal, unifying thread of love which provided that meaning. Matched against a control group, they scored much higher on life-attitude tests, significantly lower on fear-of-death tests, gave more money to charity, and took fewer medications. There's no other way to look at the data. These people were just transformed by the experience."

Morse has gone on to write three popular books about near-death experiences and the questions they raise about the nature of consciousness. His research caught the attention of Willoughby Britton, a doctoral candidate in clinical psychology at the University of Arizona who was interested in post-traumatic stress disorder. Britton knew that most people who have a close brush with death tend to have some form of post-traumatic stress disorder, while people who get that close and have a near-death experience have none. In other words, people who have a near-death experience have an atypical response to life-threatening trauma. No one knows why.

B
ritton also knew about work done by legendary neurosurgeon and epilepsy expert Wilder Penfield in the 1950s. Penfield, one of the giants of modern neuroscience, discovered that stimulating the brain's right temporal lobe—located just above the ear—with a mild electric current produced out-of-body experiences, heavenly music, vivid hallucinations, and the kind of panoramic memories associated with the life review part of the near-death experience. This helped explain why right temporal lobe epilepsy was a condition long defined by its most prominent symptom: excessive religiosity characterized by an intense feeling of spirituality, mystical visions, and auditory hallucinations of the voice-of-God variety. And given what Whinnery has found, it is possible that his pilots' near-death-like dreamlets were related to brief episodes of compromised blood flow in the temporal lobe.

Britton hypothesized that people who have undergone a near-death experience might show the same altered brain firing patterns as people with temporal lobe epilepsy. The easiest way to determine if someone has temporal lobe epilepsy is to monitor the brain waves during sleep, when there is an increased likelihood of activity indicative of epilepsy. Britton recruited 23 people who had a near-death experience and 23 who had undergone neither a near-death experience nor a life-threatening traumatic event. Then, working at a sleep lab, she hooked up her subjects to electrodes that measured EEG activity all over the brain—including the temporal lobes—and recorded everything that happened while they slept.

She then asked a University of Arizona epilepsy specialist who knew nothing about the experiment to analyze the EEGs. Two features distinguished the group with near-death experience from the controls: They needed far less sleep, and they went into REM (rapid eye movement) sleep far later in the sleep cycle than normal people. "The point at which someone goes into REM sleep is a fantastic indicator of depressive tendencies," says Britton. "We've gotten very good at this kind of research. If you took 100 people and did a sleep study, we can look at the data and know, by looking at the time they entered REM, who's going to become depressed in the next year and who isn't."

Normal people enter REM at 90 minutes. Depressed people enter at 60 minutes or sooner. Britton found that the vast majority of her group with near-death experience entered REM sleep at 110 minutes. With that finding, she identified the first objective neurophysiological difference in people who have had a near-death experience.

Britton thinks near-death experience somehow rewires the brain, and she has found some support for her hypothesis regarding altered activity in the temporal lobe: Twenty-two percent of the group with near-death experience showed synchrony in the temporal lobe, the same kind of firing pattern associated with temporal lobe epilepsy. "Twenty-two percent may not sound like a lot of anything," says Britton, "but it's actually incredibly abnormal, so much so that it's beyond the realm of chance."

She also found something that didn't fit with her hypothesis. The temporal lobe synchrony wasn't happening on the right side of the brain, the site that had been linked in Penfield's studies to religious feeling in temporal lobe epilepsy. Instead she found it on the left side of the brain. That finding made some people uncomfortable because it echoed studies that pinpointed, in far more detail than Penfield achieved, the exact locations in the brain that were most active and most inactive during periods of profound religious experience.

Over the past 10 years a number of different scientists, including neurologist James Austin from the University of Colorado, neuroscientist Andrew Newberg, and the late anthropologist and psychiatrist Eugene D'Aquili from the University of Pennsylvania, have done SPECT (single photon emission computed tomography) scans of the brains of Buddhists during meditation and of Franciscan nuns during prayer. They found a marked decrease in activity in the parietal lobes, an area in the upper rear of the brain. This region helps us orient ourselves in space; it allows us to judge angles and curves and distances and to know where the self ends and the rest of the world begins. People who suffer injuries in this area have great difficulties navigating life's simplest landscapes. Sitting down on a couch, for example, becomes a task of Herculean impossibility because they are unsure where their own legs end and the sofa begins. The SPECT scans indicated that meditation temporarily blocks the processing of sensory information within both parietal lobes.

When that happens, as Newberg and D'Aquili point out in their book *Why God Won't Go Away*, "the brain would have no choice but to perceive that the self is endless and intimately interwoven with everyone and everything the mind senses. And this perception would feel utterly and unquestionably real." They use the brain-scan findings to explain the interconnected cosmic unity that the Buddhists experienced, but the results could also explain what Morse calls the "universal, unifying thread of love" that people with near-death experience consistently reported.

These brain scans show that when the parietal lobes go quiet, portions of the right temporal lobe—some of the same portions that Penfield showed produced feelings of excessive religiosity, out-of-body experiences, and vivid hallucinations—become more active. Newberg and D'Aquili also argue that activities often found in religious rituals—like repetitive chanting—activate (and deactivate) similar areas in the brain, a finding that helps explain some of the more puzzling out-of-body experience reports, like those of the airplane pilots suddenly floating outside their planes. Those pilots were as intensely focused on their instrumentation as meditators focused on mantras. Meanwhile, the sound of the engine's spinning produces a repetitive, rhythmic drone much like tribal drumming. If conditions were right, says Newberg, these two things should be enough to produce the same temporal lobe activity to trigger an out-of-body experience.

Neuropsychologist Michael Persinger of Laurentian University in Sudbury, Ontario, has conducted other studies that explore the generation of altered mental states. Persinger built a helmet that produces weak, directed electromagnetic fields. He then asked over 900 volunteers, mostly college students, to wear the helmets while he monitored their brain activity and generated variations in the electromagnetic field. When he directed these fields toward the temporal lobes, Persinger's helmet induced the sort of mystical, free-of-the-body experiences common to right temporal lobe epileptics, meditators, and people who have had near-death experiences.

None of this work is without controversy, but an increasing number of scientists now think that our brains are wired for mystical experiences. The studies confirm that these experiences are as real as any others, because our involvement with the rest of the universe is mediated by our brains. Whether these experiences are simply right temporal lobe activity, as many suspect, or, as Britton's work hints and Morse believes, a whole brain effect, remains an open question. But Persinger thinks there is a simple explanation for why people with near-death experience have memories of things that occurred while they were apparently dead. The memory-forming structures lie deep within the brain, he says, and they probably remain active for a few minutes after brain activity in the outer cortex has stopped. Still, Crystal Merzlock remembered events that occurred more than *19 minutes* after her heart stopped. Nobody has a full explanation for this phenomenon, and we are left in that very familiar mystical state: the one where we still don't have all the answers.

UNIT 4
Learning and Remembering

Unit Selections

12. **Teaching for Understanding**, Tom Sherman and Barbara Kurshan
13. **Memory Flexibility**, Sadie F. Dingfelder
14. **Theory of Multiple Intelligences: Is It a Scientific Theory?**, Jie-Qi Chen

Key Points to Consider

- What is learning? What is a metacognition? What are some of the important principles of learning? How can teachers incorporate principles of learning into their classrooms? Is learning via technology done the same way as without technology? How do you incorporate technology into your learning experiences?

- What is memory? What is working memory? What is forgetting? Why is memory important? Why do psychologists want to learn about the various mechanisms that underlie good memory? To what use can we put scientific information on memory? Why do we forget?

- How are learning and remembering linked? Are they necessarily always linked to each other? Why is human memory so bad sometimes? That is, why do we forget what we want to remember? How can we improve memory and learning?

- What methods could you use to improve your memory? What types of memory lapses are normal? What memory mistakes signal problems such as Alzheimer's disease?

- How do you define intelligence? How do scientists define intelligence? Can you think of people whom you would call "bright" by standards other than the traditional definitions of intelligence? Is the concept of intelligence unitary or are there subcomponents of intelligence? Why is the concept of intelligence so criticized?

- Do you think intelligence tests are accurate or are they subject to the vagaries of a person's current situation? Given your answer, should intelligence tests be used in schools, employment, and armed services to place people in certain positions?

- What are some of the myths Americans hold about intelligence? Are these myths true? Why use science to investigate these myths if they seem so commonsensical? What does science say about intelligence and our commonly held beliefs? Is the theory of multiple intelligences up to par in terms of its being a valid scientific theory? Can you think of any other forms of intelligence not included in this theory?

Student Website

www.mhcls.com/online

Internet References

Further information regarding these websites may be found in this book's preface or online.

Mind Tools
   http://www.psychwww.com/mtsite/
The Opportunity of Adolescence
   http://www.winternet.com/~webpage/adolescencepaper.html
Project Zero
   http://pzweb.harvard.edu

Do you remember your first week of classes at college? There were so many new buildings and so many people's names to remember. And you had to recall accurately where all your classes were as well as your professors' names. Just remembering your class schedule was problematic enough. For those of you who lived in residence halls, the difficulties multiplied. You had to remember where your residence was, recall the names of individuals living on your floor, and learn how to navigate from your room to other places on campus, such as the dining halls and library. Then came examination time. Did you ever think you would survive college exams? The material, in terms of difficulty level and amount, was perhaps more than you thought you could manage.

What a stressful time you experienced when you first came to campus! Much of what created the stress was the strain on your learning and memory systems, two complicated processes unto themselves. Indeed, most of you survived just fine and with your memories, learning strategies, and mental health intact.

Two of the processes you depended on when you first came to college are the processes of learning and memorizing, some of the oldest psychological processes studied by psychologists. Today, with their sophisticated experimental techniques, psychologists have distinguished several types of memory pro-

cesses and have discovered what makes learning more complete so that subsequent memory is more accurate. We also have discovered that humans aren't the only organisms capable of these processes. All types of animals can learn, even if the organism is as simple as an earthworm or amoeba.

Psychologists know, too, that rote learning and practice are not the only forms of learning. For instance, at this point in time in your introductory psychology class, you might be studying operant and classical conditioning, two very simple but nonetheless important forms of learning of which both humans and simple organisms are capable. Both types of conditioning can occur without our awareness or active participation in them. The articles in this unit examine the processes of learning and remembering (or its reciprocal, forgetting) in some detail.

What might underpin learning and memory abilities is intelligence, another all-important but controversial concept in psychology. With regard to intelligence, one persistent problem has been the difficulty of defining just what intelligence is. David Wechsler, author of several of the most popular intelligence tests in current clinical use, defines intelligence as the global capacity of the individual to act purposefully, to think rationally, and to deal effectively with the environment. Other psychologists have proposed more alternative or more complex definitions.

The definitional problem arises when we try to develop tests that validly and reliably measure such abstract, intangible concepts. A valid test is one that measures what it purports to measure. A reliable test yields the same score for the same individual over and over again. Because defining and assessing intelligence has been so controversial and so difficult, historian Edward Boring once suggested that we define intelligence as whatever it is that an intelligence test measures!

In the first article of this unit, "Teaching for Understanding," David Premack reviews some of the principles of learning. For example, he discusses the concept of metacognition (which essentially is thinking about thinking) and its relationship to learning. Premack suggests that certain universal principles of learning can be applied to most learning situations, for instance, when technology is introduced into a classroom.

In "A Workout for Working Memory," Sadie Dingfelder of the American Psychological Association presents information on that part of memory which is active at any given moment, other-wise known as working memory. Working memory affects what we can process or how much information we can manage at any point in time. Knowing how to improve working memory would help you in your studies as well as help a myriad of other groups who rely on remembering or whose disability prevents them from otherwise remembering well.

The final selection of this unit is about an important concept pertinent to learning and memory—the concept of intelligence. As mentioned above, psychologists have long bickered about how to define intelligence as well as what it means to be intelligent. One theory of intelligence is that of multiple intelligences; in other words, the idea that intelligence is not a unitary construct but rather that people possess several forms of intelligence, such as artistic or athletic intelligence. In "Theory of Multiple Intelligences: Is It a Scientific Theory," the author assesses whether the concept of multiple intelligences is robust enough to withstand its classification as a *bona fide* scientific theory.

Teaching for Understanding

TOM SHERMAN AND BARBARA KURSHAN

Wiggins' view of understanding requires students to integrate facts, information, knowledge, and applications to develop understanding. Understanding, from this perspective, is an extensive web of interrelated ideas, experiences, and beliefs that transforms information from simple, memorized facts into knowledge that can be the basis for action. Recent research and theory have provided a relatively clear picture of how technologies can support classroom teaching and learning that leads to this genuine understanding. Moreover, teaching for understanding appears to result in students passing or scoring higher on high stakes tests.

Over the past 8–10 years scientists, teachers, and behavioral investigators have synthesized research and practice to explain how to develop the intellectual tools and learning strategies needed to acquire the knowledge that allows people to think productively. These scientists believe that learners construct their knowledge from their experiences, a perspective that generates many implications for how to teach students to understand.

Psychologist John Bransford and his colleagues propose three strongly supported findings that capture the essence of this evidence for teaching and learning:

1. Preconceptions influence all learning.
2. Understanding comes from knowing facts and principles.
3. Metacognition is essential for understanding.

Teachers and learners can use technology in many ways to support these findings on human learning. Technology can help teachers discover students' preconceptions and provide a broad range of instructional options to meet diverse learner needs. Technology is a tool for teachers to more effectively and accurately create profiles of each learner's experiences and background and how students learn and then develop technology-based instruction consistent with each student's needs. For learners, technologies can open alternatives to mastering ideas, concepts, processes, and outcomes. Learners can employ technology to expose misconceptions, simulate solution applications, test facts, and respond to problem-solving challenges. Integrating technology into instructional practices often improves student achievement; presents relevant, timely, and appropriate remediation; and provides content that can be crafted to meet different learning styles. We examine specific ways that technologies can contribute to meeting the findings of modern learning psychology.

Preconceptions Influence All Learning

Students come to school with well-formed ideas about how the world works. Called preconceptions, existing ideas that children hold are central to constructing new learning. Humans begin learning right from birth, and even very young children form ideas about their worlds based on observations and experiences. These preconceptions have powerful and enduring effects on how children learn new information as well as how they will remember and use new knowledge.

A main challenge for teachers is to use these preconceptions as the foundation for helping learners expand or modify their existing understandings. Another challenge is to correct misconceptions. Until recently, the impact of misconceptions has not been well understood, and they were generally thought to be easily corrected. However, most misconceptions are relatively firmly held beliefs based on observations of natural events and have practical explanatory power or are effective in limited applications.

For example, a flat earth theory is intuitive because the earth looks flat and we have no experience that contradicts the idea of a flat earth. And, a flat earth conception works very well with most experiences we have, for instance, building a small house. However, flat earth thinking becomes problematic for long-range navigation, as well as understanding geography and other sciences. It is not unusual for people to operate cognitively from a flat earth theory even though they know intellectually that the earth is not flat.

Classroom instruction is rarely designed to correct students' incorrect assumptions. Generally, the instructional approach is to teach the correct answer and problem-solving strategy. Misconceptions cannot be ignored because new and accurate information inconsistent with these misconceptions is likely to be learned superficially, recalled only for tests, and then forgotten.

Perhaps practicing teachers' most frequent question about students' prior knowledge is, "How is it possible to assess every student's prior knowledge?" One answer is to use technology to assist with this critical task by allowing students to reveal their preconceptions on well-designed assessments that focus on commonly held misconceptions. Technology tools provide teachers the ability to assess students' misconceptions. Recent applications on handhelds and PCs can be used to aggregate class responses, test knowledge, and provide feedback to the class. Discourse, published by ETS (Educational Testing Service), lets teachers know instantly if each and every student in the class is following the lesson. (Editor's note: For company contact information, see Resources on p. 11.) With instant feedback, instruction can be modified as it occurs for every student. Similarly, Classroom Performance System from eInstruction Corporation provides a nonthreatening environment allowing all students to participate and teachers to give immediate feedback and aggregate results.

Technologies also offer great potential to integrate preconceptions with new knowledge by providing learners with many examples of concepts to be taught from which students can choose the most salient for them. Concept mapping tools enable students to visually see their misconceptions and correct them, leading to increased understanding and retention of content. CTOOLS, from Michigan State University and developed through an NSF grant, provides a Web-based problem-solving environment for exploring concepts in science. WebLearn, developed by the computer science department of RMIT University in Australia, focuses on identifying students' misconceptions in learning college mathematics. If an answer specified is incorrect, commonly occurring misconceptions are checked for and appropriate feedback is provided to the student.

Students benefit because they have the option of choosing examples that are most consistent with their personal backgrounds and knowledge. In addition, an array of examples allows students to test applications of their understandings in different and unfamiliar situations. When students engage their understanding through these examples, they can examine the relationships between their beliefs and outcomes. Students and teachers can develop a stronger sense of the intellectual strategies that may be helpful in developing more extensive and accurate understandings.

Finally, technology-assisted learning tools can provide simulated intellectual challenges through which students can confront the inconsistencies between the knowledge they have and the new knowledge in a lesson. For example, students who misunderstand a concept such as retrograde motion of stars is a product of distance and the earth's rotation rather than the varying speeds of stars can manipulate models of the solar system to see the consequences of varying speed. Students who hold views such as welfare mothers never get off the dole can explore databases with accurate statistical information as well as primary sources. By creating this disequilibrium, teachers can motivate students to learn and focus their attention on critical features of the concept being taught.

Understanding Comes from Knowing Facts and Principles

Understanding evolves from a combination of learning factual knowledge and general principles. Learning factual information is essential, because without facts students have nothing to understand. However, isolated facts are difficult to learn and unlikely to be recalled. Although this may appear obvious, the ways that facts should be connected is often not well understood. The relation between facts, concepts, and principles requires multiple interactions between the learners existing and new facts and more general or higher-level conceptualization that provides a framework for making these facts meaningful.

Students must develop extensive conceptual frameworks to organized facts into knowledge in their memories much like a well organized file cabinet makes facts easy to retrieve. When knowledge is extensively connected with other concepts and well organized, it is much more accessible and more accurately used. Organization facilitates applying knowledge in different situations and on novel problems, a process called transfer.

To present the facts and guide students to develop the broad frameworks to organize the facts, teachers must have a strong mastery of the material they are teaching and recognize how students typically learn that material.

Computer-based programs can provide students with a menu of choices from which they can develop experience with varying applications of ideas drawn from examples embedded in multiple contexts. For example, if the goal of instruction was to teach students how the concept of transportation can explain the formation of population centers, students can search maps looking for potential sites based on geographical features. Once sites are selected, the map can reveal where cities actually formed. Students will be challenged to ex-plain both their accurate and inaccurate choices. The SimCity program published by Electronic Arts is one example of software that can leverage the power of technology to facilitate thinking about the accuracy of held beliefs.

A variety of experiences coupled with collaborative discussions enables students to use and organize facts. In addition, as they build experience, students can develop broader conceptions. Finally, technology-based concept maps can show students other ways to organize their understandings and allow them to compare their concept structures. Software that helps learners to brainstorm, organize, plan, and create is valuable for supporting development of concepts. Products, such as Inspiration (Inspiration Software Inc.) and MindMapper (The Bosley Group) graphically present these skills and promote the development of visual learning strategies.

Metacognition Is Essential for Understanding

Students must be aware of and control their thinking. Metacognition describes the personal awareness of individuals to choose, monitor, and adjust the thinking strategies they use to learn and solve problems. In other words, students select and control their mental processes so that they can think efficiently and effectively. It is well known that successful learners have more thinking skills and use their intellectual abilities differently than less successful learners.

Genuine understanding is most likely when students are cognitively managing the interaction between what they know and what they are learning. Because learning begins with learners' existing conceptions, growth comes from changing and expanding their existing beliefs. Teachers help students learn to monitor their understanding by using cognitive skills such as reflection and summarizing. In this way, students master the material and the thinking strategies needed to understand. We have developed a site called Study Smart that illustrates how online programs can teach the metacognitive intellectual tools, skills, strategies, and attitudes that are characteristic of successful learners. Many programs integrate these kinds of thinking strategies and provide the opportunity to summarize and reflect on knowledge. Two that effectively engage learners while teaching these skills are the Zoombinis series developed by TERC (distributed by Riverdeep) and BrainCogs developed by Fablevison.

Although metacognition may seem intuitive, developing good metacognitive strategies is difficult for most learners. The most effective ways to teach these cognitive management skills is to provide many models and continuous opportunities. Teachers are one good source of models, but technologies can also encourage students to address the disequilibrium created by the differences between current and new information.

Simulations and dramatizations of events and situations as well as strategies to solve problems let learners compare, contrast, and experiment with new and old ways of thinking in a variety of settings. For example, in science, a common misconception is that a ball thrown in the air has energy that propels it upward. Using technologies, students can manipulate the variables acting on the ball and compare the outcomes with their predictions. Computer simulations and animations can clearly depict and simulate learning situations and also provide the tools for exploring the concepts through "what if" strategies. The Logal Science Explore Series, published by Riverdeep, includes computer simulations that help students more effectively discover and understand scientific concepts. With the simulations, students develop problem-solving skills as they form hypotheses, manipulate variables, generate and collect data, analyze relationships, and draw conclusions.

Another example that promotes higherorder thinking skills and lasting conceptual understanding is the series of research-based interactive math and science simulations called Gizmos from Explore-learning. These knowledge interactions help students to build stronger understandings and to identify ways to manipulate their cognitive actions to stimulate more active thinking.

Summary

These three findings summarize the basic premise that human learning is a complex interaction between existing understandings and new knowledge. Changing beliefs is often difficult because our inclination is to fit new ideas into existing conceptual frameworks. Information, whether observed or presented by a teacher, that does not fit existing frameworks is usually forgotten because it is either irrelevant or incorrect.

Successfully modifying existing beliefs comes from discovering that a current belief is inadequate to explain new information or as a result of a purposeful quest to expand or to challenge an existing conceptual framework. Although teachers can devise these events for students, it is essential for students to engage personally to change their understandings. And, students who are aware of thinking strategies and are open to new ideas are much more likely to understand in new ways. One of the appeals of technologies is to entice learners to think differently and more expansively.

Technologies can be used to present new knowledge in carefully crafted learning environments that stimulate students to examine their beliefs and revise what and how they think based on new facts and expanded conceptual frameworks.

Because technology is powerful and responsive, it can be used to assess students' existing knowledge so teachers have a clear picture of student needs. In addition, technology-based programs can present students with situations that are inconsistent with their existing conceptions, allowing multiple opportunities to confront misconceptions and to identify and experiment with alternative conceptions.

From a pedagogical perspective, teaching involves creating situations in which students can confront their misconceptions, enhance their incomplete knowledge, improve their intellectual abilities, and construct ever more accurate representations of ideas and processes. As they mature as knowers, learners not only build more extensive and accurate understandings but also develop more sophisticated learning skills and strategies. Thus, the twofold general goals of teaching are for students to master content and to develop the skills, strategies, and attitudes characteristic of successful learners. There are many technologies that can be among teachers' pedagogical tools to meet both goals.

Consider your teaching and how you can integrate technology to better teach for understanding. We suggest you begin by considering your beliefs about teaching and learning. Current thinking about learning indicates that there are substantial differences in the ways we teach if we want the majority of students to learn beyond only recalling facts. Understanding requires a more significant and intense interaction between learners and content so that new ideas are processed deeply and extensively connected to existing and new knowledge. One practical advantage of a well developed and evidence-based theory such as constructivism is that you can make purposeful decisions about using technology in teaching. This is in marked contrast, for example, to using technologies merely because it is possible to expose students to a program or Web site. The benefits of exposure increase markedly when the technology application fits with a purpose consistent with how people learn. Here we have suggested a variety of technology-based applications that are consistent with well developed theoretical propositions to transform classrooms to be more consistent with the conditions that promote learning. In addition, it appears that technologies can be valuable resources for teachers to respond to the increasing demands for students to get passing marks on high stakes tests. Although certainly not magic, technologies can be an important pedagogical tool that increases the ability for teachers to successfully teach all students to learn with understanding.

Thomas M. Sherman is a professor of education in the College of Liberal Arts and Human Sciences at Virginia Tech. He teaches courses in educational psychology, evaluation, and instructional design and has written more than 100 articles for professional publications. Tom works regularly with practicing teachers and students in the areas of learning improvement and teaching strategies. He is also active in civic affairs, serving on local and state committees.

Dr. Barbara Kurshan is the president of Educorp Consulting Corporation. She has a doctorate in education with an emphasis on computer-based applications. She has written numerous articles and texts and has designed software and networks to meet the needs of learners. She works with investment banking firms and venture groups on companies related to educational technology. She serves on the boards of Fablevision, Headsprout, and Medalis, and is currently on the advisory boards of Pixel, WorldSage, and Tegrity.

Memory Flexibility

A Workout for Working Memory

New research suggests that mental exercises might enhance one of the brain's central components for reasoning and problem-solving.

SADIE F. DINGFELDER

People may be able to remember a nearly infinite number of facts, but only a handful of items—held in working memory—can be accessed and considered at any given moment. It's the reason why a person might forget to buy an item or two on a mental grocery list, or why most people have difficulty adding together large numbers. In fact, working memory could be the basis for general intelligence and reasoning: Those who can hold many items in their mind may be well equipped to consider different angles of a complex problem simultaneously.

If psychologists could help people expand their working-memory capacity or make it function more efficiently, everyone could benefit, from chess masters to learning-disabled children, says Torkel Klingberg, MD, PhD, an assistant cognitive neuroscience professor at the Karolinska Institute in Sweden. Children with attention-deficit hyperactivity disorder (ADHD), for example, might especially benefit from working-memory training, says Rosemary Tannock, PhD, a psychologist and psychiatry professor at The Hospital for Sick Children in Toronto.

"It could be that working-memory problems give rise to observable behavioral symptoms of ADHD: distractibility and also poor academic achievement," she says. Working-memory deficits might also underpin some reading disabilities, as it controls the ability to recall words read earlier in a sentence, says Tannock.

But how—or even if—working memory can be expanded through training remains a topic of hot contention among psychologists. Some argue that working memory has a set limit of about four items, and that individual differences in working memory arise from the ability to group small bits of information into larger chunks. However, new research suggests that working-memory capacity could expand with practice—a finding that could shed new light on this central part of the mind's ar-chitecture, as well as potentially lead to treatments for ADHD or other learning disabilities.

Functional Limitations

One such study—by researchers at Syracuse University—hit upon the potential trainability while attempting to resolve a debate in the literature on the limits of working memory.

Since the 1950s, psychologists have found one aspect of working memory—sometimes referred to as the focus of attention—to have severe limitations. For example, George Miller, PhD—a founder of cognitive psychology and a psychology professor at Princeton University—established that people generally can't recall lists of numbers more than seven digits long. Those who exceeded that limit tended to make smaller groups of numbers into larger ones, using a process called "chunking." For example, people familiar with U.S. intelligence agencies would see the letter group "FBICIA" as two chunks, rather the six letters, and that set of letters would only occupy two slots in a person's memory, rather than six.

> **If psychologists could help people expand their working-memory capacity or make it function more efficiently, everyone could benefit, from chess masters to learning-disabled children.**

In recent years, however, evidence is mounting that the limitation of working memory is somewhere between one and four information chunks. The downward revision results from new techniques to keep people from chunking information, which can create the illusion of greater fundamental storage capacity, says Nelson Cowan, PhD, a psychology professor at the University of Missouri–Columbia. In one common chunking-prevention method, participants repeat meaningless phrases over and over while performing working memory tasks such as memorizing lists of numbers.

A recent literature review by Cowan, published in *Behavioral and Brain Sciences* (Vol. 24, No. 1, pages 87–185), makes the case that a variety of working-memory measures all converge on a set limit of four items.

Other researchers have suggested that working-memory capacity is limited even further—to just a single item. In a study by Brian McElree, PhD, a psychology professor at New York University, participants underwent a test of working memory called "n-back." In the task, the participants read a series of numbers, presented one at a time on a computer screen. In the easiest version of the task, the computer presents a new digit, and then prompts participants to recall what number immediately preceded the current one. More difficult versions might ask participants to recall what number appeared two, three or four digits ago.

McElree found that participants recalled the immediately preceding numbers in a fraction of the time it took them to recall numbers presented more than one number ago—a finding published in the *Journal of Experimental Psychology: Learning, Memory and Cognition* (Vol. 27, No. 1, pages 817–835.)

"There is clear and compelling evidence of one unit being maintained in focal attention and no direct evidence for more than one item of information extended over time," says McElree.

In an attempt to reconcile the two theories, psychology professor Paul Verhaeghen, PhD, and his colleagues at Syracuse University replicated McElree's experiment, but tracked participants' response times as they practiced at the task for 10 hours over five days.

"We found that by the end of day five ... their working memory [capacity] had expanded from one to four items, but not to five," says Verhaeghen. "It seems that both theories are correct."

The focus of attention might expand as other working-memory processes become automated, Verhaeghen says. Perhaps practice improves the process of attaching a position to a number, freeing up the mind to recall up to four numbers, he notes.

Some researchers believe the practice effect uncovered by Verhaeghen reflects more efficient information encoding rather than expanded working-memory capacity. According to McElree, the response time measures used by Verhaeghen do not provide pure measures of memory-retrieval speed, and the changes in response time with practice could indicate that participants in his study simply became more practiced at encoding numbers vividly, he says.

If Verhaeghen's findings can be replicated using other tasks, it could change how scientists conceptualize working-memory limitations. Rather than there being a set limitation, working-memory capacity could improve through practice—suggesting that those with working-memory problems could improve their capacities through repetition. However, practice would need to occur on a task-by-task basis, says Verhaeghen, and, as he points out, "It is doubtful that practice on n-back generalizes to anything in real life."

Stretching the Limits

New research on children with ADHD, however, might show tasks such as n-back can improve working memory in general, and could help children with the condition.

People with ADHD tend to have difficulty with working-memory capacity, and that deficit could be responsible for their tendency to be distracted and resulting problems at school, says Tannock.

Seeking to alleviate such difficulties with his research, Klingberg ran a randomized controlled trial of 53 children with ADHD in which half of the participants practiced working-memory tasks that gradually increased in difficulty. The other half completed tasks that did not get harder as the children became better at them. Both groups of children—who were 7 to 12 years old—practiced tasks such as recalling lists of numbers for 40 minutes a day over five weeks.

The children who practiced with increasingly difficult memory tasks performed better on two working memory tests—which were different than the practice tasks—than the control group, reported Klingberg in the *Journal of the American Academy of Child & Adolescent Psychiatry* (Vol. 44, No. 2, pages 177–186.) In addition, the parents of children with memory training reported a reduction in their children's hyperactivity and inattention three months after the intervention, while the parents of the control group participants did not.

Subsequent, yet-unpublished experiments build on those results, Klingberg says.

"We have looked at other groups too: adults with stroke, young adults without ADHD, children with ... traumatic brain injuries," he says." A general pattern [we've found] is as long as you have working-memory problems and you have the ability to train, you can improve your abilities."

Some researchers suggest that memory training may have more of an effect on motivation than working memory.

"It seems to me that children in the training group may have learned to have a better attitude toward the testing situation, whereas children in the control group—who repeated easy problems—may have learned that the testing situation was boring and uninteresting," says Cowan. "The differences that emerged on a variety of tasks could be the result of better motivation and attitude rather than a basic improvement in working memory."

Or, says Klaus Oberauer, PhD, a psychology professor and memory researcher at the University of Bristol in England, the practice effect in both Klingberg's studies might result from people learning to use their limited working-memory capacity more efficiently—perhaps by grouping information into larger chunks or by enlisting long-term memory.

"I think the practice effect [they found] basically is just an ordinary practice effect, in that everything gets faster" he says.

So, even if working memory can't be expanded, adults with grocery lists and children with ADHD may be able to make better use of what little space is available by practicing the task itself or repeating tests of general working memory. And, in the end, the milk gets bought and the reading assignment finished.

Two Web sites offer free programs for working out working memory: **www.memorise.org/memoryGym.htm** and **www.easysurf.us/menu.htm.**

Further Reading

Cowan, N. (2005). Working-memory capacity limits in a theoretical context. In C. Izawa & N. Ohta (Eds.), *Human learning and memory: Advances in theory and application: The 4th Tsukuba International Conference on Memory*. (pp. 155–175). Mahwah, NJ: Erlbaum.

Klingberg, T., Fernell, E., Olesen, P.J., Johnson, M., Gustafsson, P., Dahlstrom, K., et al. (2005). Computerized training of working memory in children with ADHD—A randomized, controlled trial. *Journal of the American Academy of Child & Adolescent Psychiatry, 44*(2), 177–186.

Martinussen, R., Hayden J., Hogg-Johnson, S., & Tannock, R. (2005). A meta-analysis of working memory components in children with Attention-Deficit/Hyperactivity Disorder. *Journal of the American Academy of Child & Adolescent Psychiatry, 44*(4), 377–384.

McElree, B. (2001). Working memory and focal attention. *Journal of Experimental Psychology: Learning, Memory, & Cognition, 27*(3), 817–835.

Pernille, J.O., Westerberg, H., & Klingberg, T. (2004). Increased prefrontal and parietal activity after training in working memory. *Nature Neuroscience, 7*(1), 75–79.

Verhaeghen, P., Cerella, J., & Basak, C. (2004). A working memory workout: How to expand the focus of serial attention from one to four items in 10 hours or less. *Journal of Experimental Psychology: Learning, Memory, & Cognition, 30*(6), 1322–1337.

Can You Force Yourself to Forget?

One psychologist says he's discovered a mechanism that could explain how people suppress unwanted memories; others disagree.

LEA WINERMAN
Monitor Staff

All of us have memories we'd prefer to forget. That foot-in-the-mouth moment at a party last summer, that embarrassing performance in our high-school talent show...

When memories like those come unwittingly to mind—prompted, say, by a run-in with someone who witnessed the moment—we might try to push the thought quickly away. But could such repeated suppressions actually make us less likely to remember the event years later?

Yes, quashing memories could impede our recall, suggests a recent series of studies by University of Oregon psychologist Michael Anderson, PhD, and his colleagues. Anderson says that his laboratory model—which taps the executive control processes that people use to concentrate and overcome interference during memory tasks—could in principle explain how people, over time, suppress distracting, unwanted or even traumatic memories.

His work could possibly help explain post-traumatic stress disorder and even, controversially, repressed memories of childhood trauma. But some researchers remain unconvinced and question whether his lab-based results will translate to real-world memory.

The Experiments

Psychologists have been debating the existence of repressed memories—first suggested by Sigmund Freud—for years. And Anderson hasn't shied away from the controversial implications of his work. In his very first paper on the topic, published in 2001 in the journal *Nature* (Vol. 410, No. 6826, pages 366–369), he begins the abstract by acknowledging that "Freud proposed that unwanted memories can be forgotten by pushing them into the unconscious, a process called repression. The existence of repression has remained controversial for more than a century."

At the end of the paper, he writes that his study bolsters the evidence that suppression is real: "These findings thus support a suppression mechanism that pushes unwanted memories out of awareness, as posited by Freud."

In the study, which used what Anderson has termed the "think/no-think" paradigm, he asked 32 college student participants to memorize pairs of unrelated words, like "ordeal, roach." Then he showed the participants the first word in each pair and asked them to either think of the second word or to consciously try to avoid thinking of it.

Finally, in the recall phase of the study, Anderson showed the participants the first words again and asked them to recall the second words. He found that participants were nearly 20 percent more likely to remember words that they had been asked to think about than words they'd been asked to avoid thinking about.

"Obviously this research is proof of principle," Anderson says. "In the past, people have said that there's no mechanism for memory suppression ... and here's a mechanism."

Anderson also wanted to make sure that the participants had actually forgotten the target words and were not simply continuing to come up with diverting thoughts when they saw the cue word. So in a second experiment, he showed them related clues (like "insect R___" for roach) and asked them to recall the target word that best fit that clue. Again, participants were less likely to remember the words that they had been instructed to avoid thinking about.

Curious about the neural underpinnings of the phenomenon, Anderson and his colleagues decided to repeat the experiment while examining participants using functional magnetic resonance imaging. In the resulting study, published in 2004 in *Science* (Vol. 303, No. 5655, pages 232–235), he found that the hippocampus—which is generally active when people retrieve memories—was not active when participants were trying to suppress thoughts of the target word. On the other hand, the dorsolateral prefrontal cortex—an area that helps inhibit motor activity—was more active than usual. This suggests that people may be using the prefrontal cortex to overcome memory processes in the hippocampus, Anderson says.

Of course, in the real world people rarely try to suppress a thought as simple as a single word. Given this, other researchers have picked up and are extending Anderson's work. University of Colorado at Boulder psychologist Marie Banich, PhD, for example, is investigating whether Anderson's think/no-think paradigm will work for nonverbal as well as verbal stimuli, and for emotional stimuli. In a study in press at *Psychological Science*, she and her colleagues used the same research design that Anderson did, but instead paired pictures of faces with pictures of different scenes—some neutral, like a hippo in a lake, and some emotional, like the aftermath of a car crash.

As in Anderson's study, Banich had her participants memorize the face/scene pairs, then showed them the faces and asked them to either think about or avoid thinking about the associated scene.

She found two things: First, the think/no-think paradigm worked—participants recalled the scenes they'd been asked to think about better than the scenes they'd been asked not to think about. Second, it actually worked *better* for scenes with emotional content than for scenes with nonemotional content.

This result makes sense, Banich says: "Emotional regulation requires us to have cognitive control over things that are difficult for us to think about."

"Obviously this research is proof of principle," Anderson says. **"In the past people have said that there's no mechanism for memory suppression ... and here's a mechanism."**

Michael Anderson
University of Oregon

The Controversy

Despite these results, some researchers remain skeptical of Anderson's work. In an upcoming issue of the journal *Memory & Cognition*, Washington University psychologist Henry L. Roediger III, PhD, and graduate student John Bulevich will report that they haven't been able to replicate Anderson's results.

Bulevich says that he began the studies—part of his master's thesis—intending to replicate Anderson's study and then expand it to implicit memory tests. However, his project stalled when he failed to replicate the original results.

"Inhibitory paradigms are notoriously fragile," he says. "I'm still interested in this, but I have nothing planned right now, until Anderson or his colleagues can pin down what makes this paradigm difficult to deal with."

Anderson—who helped Bulevich and Roediger with their study—says he's unconcerned with the team's failure to replicate his results. There are, he says, many variables that can go awry if not carefully controlled. For example, in the real world, we don't need to be reminded not to think about the things we don't want to think about. But, Anderson says, in the experiment it's crucial to ensure that the participants really are trying their hardest to avoid thoughts of the suppressed target words. And, he says, he has conducted a meta-analysis of the more than 1,000 participants he's tested in all his think/no-think studies, and he's found a strongly significant effect.

"I think that Roediger's paper will be useful in the long run," he says, "and it does remind us that there are factors here that are yet to be understood."

Other psychologists question whether Anderson's results, even if replicable, really mean what he thinks they mean.

In a letter to the journal *Trends in Cognitive Sciences* (Vol. 6, No. 12, page 502) and in an upcoming book chapter, University of California, Berkeley, psychologist John Kihlstrom, PhD, argues that Anderson's mechanism involves *conscious* suppression, while Freud's theories posited *unconscious* repression.

And, of course, the debate about whether repressed memories of childhood trauma are credible has raged for more than a decade—and those who believe they aren't find Anderson's work hard to take.

"There is no evidence that traumatized people repress memories of traumatic events," Kihlstrom says.

Anderson acknowledges that his studies are only the beginning of what will need to be many more years of research—but he says he thinks that such work will be worthwhile. "Whether or not what I've found could be scaled up to explain intense emotional memories is an empirical question that should be researched," he says. "But it's premature to conclude that it's not relevant—we just don't know enough yet."

Feelings' sway over memory

New research suggests that emotions can strengthen and shape memory.

SADIE F. DINGFELDER

Where were you during the terrorist attacks of 9/11? For most, recalling this information is easier than remembering, for example, the details of Wednesday morning last week. This phenomenon—along with more than two decades of experimental evidence—has led many psychologists to posit that emotions can enhance memory and recall. (See May *Monitor*, page 10.)

However, new research suggests a more complicated picture, says Daniel Reisberg, PhD, a psychology professor at Reed College in Oregon. Some psychologists are finding that the stress associated with an emotion may affect how deeply an event is etched into memory, he notes.

Additionally, the type of emotion felt may determine what details people recall from an event, says University of California, Irvine, psychology professor Linda Levine, PhD.

"People don't just feel 'emotional.' They feel sad, scared, angry, happy," says Levine. "Those emotions have different functions, and they influence information processing and memory in different ways."

For example, people generally feel anger when something is keeping them from reaching their goals, she notes. As a result, angry people tend to focus on what they perceive to be the obstacle and may retain obstacle-related information particularly well, Levine says. In contrast, happiness signals that all is well, and happy people will perceive—and recall—a scene broadly without focusing in on particular details, found Levine and Susan Bluck, PhD, a University of Florida psychology professor, in a recent study in *Cognition and Emotion* (Vol. 18, No. 4, pages 559–574.)

In addition to adding to psychologists' understanding of the inner workings of memory, such research may also help judges and juries evaluate the testimony of eyewitnesses—who typically experience high levels of emotion when watching a crime, says Reisberg.

Tunnel Memory

People who witness an armed robbery often demonstrate how negative emotion can narrow attention and memory, says Reisberg. Such witnesses tend to recall the gun in great detail, but not the particulars of the perpetrator's appearance.

"You focus your attention on the weapon because, quite obviously, whether or not it is pointing at you is very important," says Reisberg.

Even when not in immediate peril, people experiencing negative emotions tend to focus in on specific details, while happy people take in a situation more broadly, found Levine and Bluck in their 2004 study.

To test their hypothesis, the researchers took advantage of an unusual situation: the televised announcement of the 1995 O.J. Simpson murder trial verdict. The event offered a unique opportunity to study the effect of different emotions on memory because a large number of people witnessed the same footage, says Levine. Moreover, many people experienced strong positive or negative emotions, depending on whether they deemed the defendant guilty or innocent, she says.

Seven days after the verdict, the researchers asked 156 undergraduate students how they felt about the trial's result. About half of the students were angry or sad about the verdict, a quarter were happy and a quarter did not care. Fourteen months after the verdict, the researchers tested the participants' memory of the announcement by asking them which items on a list of events occurred during the announcement. Half of the events listed actually happened—such as Simpson mouthing the words "thank you" to the jury. The other half were made up by the researchers—such as the defendant giving a "thumbs up" to his lawyer.

As the researchers expected, the students who felt happy about the verdict tended to recall the entire scene better than the sad, angry or neutral students. However, the happy students also tended to make more errors of commission—saying that events happened that did not. Students flooded with negative emotions tended to recall less about the verdict announcement overall, but they also made fewer errors in which they recalled details that did not happen.

> ## "Emotions have different functions, and they influence information processing and memory in different ways."
> Linda Levine
> University of California, Irvine

"The happy people and the people who felt negative made opposite types of errors, so there was no overall difference in accuracy," says Levine. However, the happier or angrier the person felt about the event, the more vivid their memory of it, she says.

The results suggest that happiness works like a broad-tipped highlighter, illuminating an event in memory and capturing many details, says Levine. However, unlike a highlighter, happy memories also can include events that did not occur but seem plausible, Levine says. Negative emotions tended to act like a narrow highlighter, accentuating particular details at the expense of others, she notes.

Memory Illusions

Other researchers, such as David Rubin, PhD, have found that intensity of emotion matters more than an emotion's kind. In one study, published in *Memory & Cognition* (Vol. 32, No. 1, pages 1,118–1,132), Rubin—a psychology professor at Duke University in North Carolinia—and his collaborators found that when recalling episodes in their own lives, people tended to recall emotional memories equally vividly regardless of whether they were happy, sad, angry or fearful at the time. However, he notes, the detailed nature of such memories could be illusory.

"After an important event, you tell a story about it, and you eventually come to believe your own story," he says.

For example, many people talked for days or months after 9/11 about where they were and how they felt at the time of the attacks. As people fill in missing details, it can lead to a false sense of accuracy about a memory, notes Rubin.

However, if future studies support Levine's theory that strong emotions—happiness in particular—can lead to broadly remembered events, people may be able to harness their emotions to aid memory, says Bluck. However, such practices could go against memory's primary function, she says.

"People in the classroom and the courtroom are of course concerned with complete accuracy, but it is not clear that the memory system has accuracy as its primary goal in everyday life," she notes.

Specifically, memory helps people use their experiences to inform their future actions, says Bluck. By highlighting important information or even including things that did not happen, emotion-bound memory may allow us to make better decisions than a picture-accurate memory would, she notes.

The Culture of Memory

Researchers are discovering that our culture helps shape how we remember our past—and how far back our memory stretches.

LEA WINERMAN

Ask an American his or her earliest memory, and you'll probably hear something like this: "My cousin's wedding, I was 3." Or perhaps: "Sitting on the beach, making a sandcastle with my brother. I was almost 4."

Any earlier than about 3.5 years is, for most of us, a blank slate. We all have what Freud first called "childhood amnesia"—an inability to remember our earliest childhood.

Ask a Maori New Zealander about his or her earliest memory, though, and you might find that the childhood amnesia ended a bit sooner. A Maori's first memory might be of attending a relative's funeral at 2.5 years old. A Korean adult, on the other hand, might not remember anything before age 4.

Of course, memory varies widely from person to person. But over the past decade, researchers have also found that the average age of first memories varies up to two years between different cultures

"We think that this is a function of the meaning of memory within a particular cultural system," says Michelle Leichtman, PhD, a psychologist at the University of New Hampshire who studies childhood memory. In other words, the way parents and other adults discuss—or don't discuss—the events in children's lives influences the way the children will later remember those events.

People who grow up in societies that focus on individual personal history, like the United States, or ones that focus on personal family history, like the Maori, will have different—and often earlier—childhood memories than people who grow up in cultures that, like many Asian cultures, value interdependence rather than personal autonomy, says Leichtman.

Now, she and other researchers are working to understand the nuances of these differences and the particular factors that shape memory in different cultures.

How Old Were You?

In 1994, psychologist Mary Mullen, PhD, published the first research comparing the ages of first memories across cultures. In a study in the journal *Cognition* (Vol. 52, No. 1, pages 55–79), she asked more than 700 Caucasian and Asian or Asian-American undergraduates to describe their earliest memories. Mullen—a Harvard University graduate student at the time—found that on average the Asian and Asian-American students' memories happened six months later than the Caucasian students' memories.

The next year Mullen repeated the study with Caucasian Americans and native Koreans, and she found an even bigger difference: Nearly 16 months separated the two, according to the study published in *Cognitive Development* (Vol. 10, No. 3, pages 407–419).

"Those papers were really the springboard from which we began," says Harlene Hayne, PhD, a psychologist who studies culture and memory at the University of Otago in Dunedin, New Zealand.

Hayne has looked at earliest memories among Caucasian, Asian and Maori New Zealanders. In a 2000 study in the journal *Memory* (Vol. 8, No. 6, pages 365–376), she found that on average, as in Mullen's studies, Asian adults' first memories were later than Caucasians' (57 months as compared with 42 months). But she also found that Maori adults' memories reached even further back, to 32 months on average.

These differences can be explained by the social-interaction model developed by Katherine Nelson, PhD, a psychologist at the City University of New York, says Leichtman. According to this model, our autobiographical memories don't develop in a vacuum; instead, as children, we encode our memories of events as we talk over those events with the adults in our life. The more those adults encourage us to spin an elaborate narrative tale, the more likely we are to remember details about the event later.

This model applies within as well as between cultures, Leichtman says. She and colleague David Pillemer, EdD, have examined the effect that "high-elaborative" versus "low-elaborative" mothers have on their children. High-elaborative mothers spend a lot of time talking to their children about past events and encourage their children to give them detailed stories about daily life. Low-elaborative mothers, on the other hand, talk less about past events and tend to ask closed rather than open-ended questions.

In a 2000 study in *Cognitive Development* (Vol. 15, No. 1, pages 99–114), Leichtman arranged for a preschool teacher who'd been on maternity leave to come back and visit her class. The next day, Leichtman and her colleagues observed the mothers of the students talk to their children about the visit and coded the degree to which the mothers used a high-elaborative or low-elaborative style of speaking. Three weeks later, the researchers asked the children what they remembered about the visit—and the children with high-elaborative mothers remembered more details.

In general, Leichtman says, parents in Asian cultures have a more low-elaborative style than parents in the United States. In contrast, Maori culture is even more focused on personal history and stories than American culture, Hayne says.

"In Maori culture there's a very strong emphasis on the past—both the personal past and the family's past," she explains. "They look backward with an eye to the future." And hence they remember more of their own past as well.

> **"In Maori culture there's a very strong emphasis on the past—both the personal past and the family's past. They look backward with an eye to the future."**
>
> Herlene Haryne
> University of Otago

We Remember What We Need

Leichtman and the other researchers emphasize that their studies do not imply that Caucasians or Maoris have "better" memories than Asians. Instead, Leichtman explains, people have the types of memories that they need to get along well in the world they inhabit. In the United States, she says, it's adaptive to have detailed narratives of childhood to relate.

"That's the way we bond with each other, by telling stories of our personal past," she says. "It's consistent with our independently oriented culture, where the emphasis is on standing out and being special and unique. In more interdependently oriented cultures, the focus is more on interpersonal harmony and making the group work, and the way in which people connect to each other is less often through sharing memories of personal events."

In other cultures, she says, the attitude is different: "They might think 'If both of you were at an event, then what would be the purpose of rehashing it between you?'"

To many Americans, she says, this lack of interest in ones own or others' personal pasts violates what we think of as a truism—that the fundamental thing that makes us who we are is our personal memories. But in some cultures she's examined, personal memory isn't nearly as important as it is to Americans. In an unpublished study of adults in rural India, for example, she found that, during a scripted interview, only 12 percent of the participants identified a specific memory from childhood. A specific memory might be "the day my father fell down a well," as opposed to a general memory like "I went to school," Leichtman explains. In comparison, 69 percent of American participants related a specific memory.

Future Directions

That there are cultural differences in memory is by now fairly well established, says Leichtman, and researchers are beginning to untangle the nuances of what causes those differences.

For example, Cornell University psychologist Qi Wang, PhD, is studying Chinese-American immigrants to see how their early childhood memories compare with those of native Chinese and native Americans. Leichtman is examining the differences between rural and urban Indians to see whether patterns of how people discuss the past, and thus early memory, are changing in that culture.

Pillemer, of the University of New Hampshire, is taking a slightly different tack on early-memory research. In a recent study in press at the journal *Memory*, he and graduate student Kate Fiske asked Caucasian and Asian participants about their earliest memories of a dream.

"Dreams are private, so the only way someone else would know about it is if you talked to them about it," he says, "so it's an interesting test of the social-interaction model." The researchers found that, as they had hypothesized, Caucasians' average age for their first remembered dream was almost one year younger than that of Asians—5.6 years old compared with 6.4 years.

Overall, Leichtman says, "It's not yet an old idea" that culture influences memory. "Right now we're really refining it and working out the wide variety of mechanisms that cause it."

Mending Memory

Psychologists are exploring memory enhancers that exploit the latest research in brain function.

RACHEL ADELSON

B rain injury, such as that from an accident or stroke, or a memory-draining disease such as Alzheimer's, can leave people struggling with everything from cooking dinner to knowing their own children. What's more, as the number of older adults in America grows, so will the number with age-related dementia, boosting the prevalence of this frustrating and usually invisible disability.

As the need for intervention grows, U.K. neuropsychologist Barbara Wilson, PhD, an authority on memory rehabilitation at the Medical Research Council's Cognition and Brain Sciences Unit in Cambridge and the Oliver Zangwill Centre for Neuropsychological Rehabilitation in Ely, says that due to lack of specialists and insurance barriers, few are being shown how best to keep their handicap from hurting everyday functioning. Yet much more is possible. "We can help people adapt to, understand, bypass and compensate for their memory difficulties," Wilson says.

Thanks to new scientific insights, the field of memory rehabilitation made remarkable strides in its first 25 years, says Allen Heinemann, PhD, president of APA's Div. 22 (Rehabilitation) and a rehabilitation psychologist with Northwestern University and the Rehabilitation Institute of Chicago. Now, says Heinemann, "the challenge is to apply what modern imaging techniques have shown about localization of memory function."

Accordingly, psychologists are studying everything from memory-related brain-activation patterns to mobile Internet devices, searching for ways to support independent living and even help the brain repair itself.

Heinemann expects the next decade to bring more clinical trials of various behavioral interventions, a growing cadre of investigators and a greater number of high-quality outpatient services and inpatient facilities providing cognitive rehab. "Our research investment will start to bear fruit," he predicts.

From Finding Keys to Greeting Friends

Although most people think that good memory means good retrieval, good memory is actually good learning—forming a strong association when acquiring new information, say rehab experts. That's why they often advise memory-impaired people to systematically take note of things. For example, they can learn to habitually take a mental snapshot when they put down their keys—say, next to the fruit bowl on the kitchen table.

Thus, Keith Cicerone, PhD, clinical director of cognitive rehabilitation at the JFK-Johnson Rehabilitation Institute in Edison, N.J., and his clinical team teach people with early-stage dementia and similar forms of memory loss—who are still capable of learning—to pay attention to routine, actively process information, avoid being distracted and write notes.

Using a similar approach is neuropsychologist Linda Clare, PhD, of University College London and the Dementia Services Development Centre Wales. Clare and her associates help patients with early-stage dementia to set goals that are relevant to daily life, for them and their families. Sample goals include:

- Learning names of familiar people they meet socially so that they do not feel awkward when they go out.
- Using a memory aid such as a calendar or memory board instead of asking family members the same question over and over again.
- Remembering family information so that it is easier to join in conversations at home.
- Identifying different types of coins to make it easier to pay for things.

In a 2002 study reported in APA's *Neuropsychology* (Vol. 16, No. 4, pages 538–547), Clare found that patients with mild Alzheimer's benefit in a lasting way from simple, systematic memory training that may enlist the still-intact neocortex. Participants were able to learn people's names by using mnemonic devices, "vanishing cues" (filling in more and more letters in a name until recall kicks in) and "expanding rehearsal" (testing themselves in spaced intervals over time). This kind of training doesn't rely on faulty parts of the brain, such as the hippocampus. Clare speculated at the time that, "If other brain areas can take over some of the functions of damaged areas, then this opens up new directions for rehabilitation."

When providing rehab services, memory experts employ a powerful approach called "errorless learning," which minimizes mistakes during training. Wilson and Clare have demonstrated in, among other journals, the *Journal of Clinical and Experimental Neuropsychology* (Vol. 22, No. 1, pages 132–146) that people with severe deficits learn better with confidence-boosting errorless training. Fostering awareness of memory loss also appears to aid therapy.

Cognitive support is central, but living with memory loss involves the whole person, says Suzanne Corkin, PhD, a neuroscientist with the Massachusetts Institute of Technology's brain and cognitive sciences department.

"Rehabilitation [also] teaches ways to keep people's mood up by taking the memory-impaired person out for lunch, to museums, for walks, by giving them a healthy level of mental stimulation," she says.

Memory Technologies

For people with mild to moderate memory loss, assistive technologies essentially take what was lost or compromised about memory on the inside and put it on the outside—in the form of everything from digital watches to computerized schedules, pagers programmed with streams of reminders and wireless personal digital assistants (PDAs), which take patients step-by-step through complex tasks.

In a controlled study published in 2001 in the *Journal of Neurology, Neurosurgery and Psychiatry* (Vol. 70, No. 4, pages 477–482), Barbara Wilson and her colleagues found that a paging system helped patients become significantly more successful in carrying out everyday activities. As if they were asking for a wake-up call, patients picked the messages and listed routine appointment dates and times in advance.

Things get more futuristic at the University of Michigan Health Systems in Ann Arbor, where rehabilitation psychologist Ned Kirsch, PhD, director of adult neurorehabilitation programs, is using PDAs and laptop computers with wireless Internet connections to help with complex functional tasks. For example, in one study, published in *Rehabilitation Psychology* (Vol. 49, No. 3, pages 200–212), Kirsch's team used a wireless PDA to help one patient who could not remember the way from one room to another in the treatment center to follow large colored circles on the walls. In this special treasure hunt, he taps the screen each time he finds a circle; progressive instructions guide him to the next one and enable him to navigate independently through his therapy day. Kirsch adds that once a home has broadband, it's cheap and easy to set up a wireless node. This type of technological approach to treatment will also become increasingly available in the community as city-wide wireless Internet installations spread, Kirsch notes.

"We can help people adapt to, understand, bypass and compensate for their memory difficulties."

Barbara Wilson
U.K. Medical Research Council

Assistive technology has limits: For example, people with weak memories may have problems learning to use these devices, or they may lose them. And, notes Cicerone, "You have to remember to use it." People who never liked technology probably still won't; "early adopters" may be more proficient. Better interfaces should help, he notes.

Some may grow out of research projects under way at the Rehabilitation Engineering and Research Center for Advancing Cognitive Technologies, a new program established in 2004 by the National Institute on Disability and Rehabilitation Research and housed at the University of Colorado.

Cicerone says that some private companies have developed proprietary devices specifically for neurological support, but the evidence of their effectiveness is anecdotal only. There's also limited evidence that so-called memory-building software works: "People get good at playing that particular game, but it doesn't transfer," he adds.

The Future of Memory

Meanwhile, even though drug companies are pouring resources into memory drugs because of the huge market, pharmaceutical options for improving memory are meager. First-generation antidementia drugs called cholinesterase inhibitors haven't been shown to support significant improvement in everyday life; they may help a subset of patients in a limited way. Still, Corkin is intrigued by drugs under development that are directed at toxic forms of the amyloid protein and could limit the proliferation of amyloid plaques, which are a neuropathological hallmark of Alzheimer's disease.

On the imaging front, at the University of Illinois Medical School in Chicago, psychologist Linda Laatsch, PhD, and her colleagues in neurology and rehabilitation are using functional magnetic resonance imaging (fMRI) to gather information on normal brain-activation patterns during simple memory tasks. Conceivably, fMRI could help differentiate patients whose brains respond to cognitive rehab from those who should stick with external cues, and help follow progress via changes in brain activation. She says, "If we could reach for the stars, we'd give feedback on activation patterns during imaging"—the ultimate in biofeedback.

Theory of Multiple Intelligences:

Is It a Scientific Theory?

This essay discusses the status of multiple intelligences (MI) theory as a scientific theory by addressing three issues: the empirical evidence Gardner used to establish MI theory, the methodology he employed to validate MI theory, and the purpose or function of MI theory.

JIE-QI CHEN
Erikson Institute

How Is The Credibility Of A Scientific Theory Established?

Of critical importance to the scientific establishment of a theory is the methodology by which the theory is created and developed (Kuhn, 1962). This principle became clearer as the fields of the history and philosophy of science matured. Before the mid-20th century, philosophers of science such as Karl Popper (1959) attempted to define an objective and universally applicable methodology for all sciences. Such an attempt inevitably failed because it did not recognize the necessary interconnection between methodologies and the objects of study. By the 1960s, scholars in the history and philosophy of science agreed that the methodologies of science both shape and are shaped by the subjects they are applied to. Thus, the absolute objectivity of any methodology is illusionary (Kuhn, 1962). The history of this debate about methodology parallels the debate regarding the scientific credibility of MI theory.

Since the inception of MI theory, some scholars in the field of cognitive psychology have questioned its status as a scientific theory. Specific criticisms of the theory include the following: "This looks like pop psychology"; "There has been no empirical data to validate the theory"; and "The independence of multiple intelligences has not been tested empirically". In the process of developing MI theory, Gardner (1993a) considered the range of adult end-states that are valued in diverse cultures around the world. To identify the abilities that support these end-states, he examined empirical data from disciplines that had not been considered previously for the purpose of defining human intelligence. The results of Gardner's analyses consistently supported his emerging notion of specific and relatively independent sets of cognitive abilities. His examination of these data sets also yielded eight criteria for identifying an intelligence. To

be defined as an intelligence, an ability has to be tested in terms of the following eight criteria:

- An intelligence should be isolable in cases of brain damage and there should be evidence for its plausibility and autonomy in evolutionary history. These two criteria were derived from biology.
- Two criteria came from developmental psychology: An intelligence has to have a distinct developmental history with a definable set of expert end-state performances and it must exist within special populations such as idiot savants and prodigies.
- Two criteria emerged from traditional psychology: An intelligence needs to demonstrate relatively independent operation through the results of specific skill training and also through low correlation to other intelligences in psychometric studies.
- Two criteria were derived from logical analysis: An intelligence must have its own identifiable core operation or set of operations and must be susceptible to encoding in a symbol system such as language, numbers, graphics, or musical notations.

Although Gardner (1993a) did not base his theory on testing of children and statistical analyses of the results, the primary method used by psychometricians to establish the credibility of the construct of IQ, he did ground the theory on analysis of empirical data. The eight criteria used to identify intelligences are not the reverie of a giant mind. Rather they are derived from Gardner's comprehensive, thorough, and systematic review of empirical data from studies in biology, neuropsychology, developmental psychology, and cultural anthropology.

Because MI theory is based on the conception of human cognitive functioning in diverse real-life situations, its scientific establishment is grounded in empirical data that describe the functioning of multiple abilities in diverse situations. For example, MI theory better accounts for data that describe the cognitive functions of special population than intelligence defined as IQ does. Exhibiting differentiated profiles of specific abilities, these populations include those who have suffered brain injury as well as prodigies and savants. MI theory also better describes various learning profiles that teachers and educators encounter on a daily basis. Finally, MI theory better explains the diverse abilities required to succeed in different professions.

Clearly, the scientific evidence used to support the psychometric notion of intelligence as IQ and the evidence used to establish MI theory are radically different. Referring back to lessons learned from the history of science, there can and should be more than one way to study human intelligence. If we limit studies by relying on a single standard for the acceptable measurement of intelligence, our understanding of this most central capacity of human beings will be significantly restrained.

What Methods Are Used To Validate A Theory?

In the field of psychology, a theory of intelligence is typically validated by establishing two psychometric properties of tests based on the theory: validity and reliability. *Validity* refers to the degree to which a test measures its intended attributes or desired outcomes. Although there are many kinds of validity, the most commonly reported in the manual of standardized intelligence tests is concurrent validity. It is usually established by comparing scores on one test with scores of other standardized tests of the same nature. *Reliability* refers to the consistency of a test's result over time and is usually determined by using one or more of the following methods: test-retest, equivalent-form, and split-half. Correlation is the statistical technique that almost all standardized intelligence tests use to report the degree of validity and reliability.

Validity and reliability are useful measures for testing the theoretical construct that human intelligence is a general ability that remains stable over time. If human intelligence is a general ability, different measures of the ability should be positively correlated (validity). Since the general ability is stable, measures of it at different times should be correlated as well (reliability). Defining and measuring intelligence using IQ tests makes it possible to rank order individuals based on a single numerical score that is expected to remain constant. Scores on IQ tests can also be used to categorize individuals based on the amount of intelligence they possess.

The means used to validate a theory are shaped by the constructs and uses of the theory. Gardner (1993a) argues that human intelligence is not a general ability. Rather, it is a biopsychological potential with an emergent, responsive, and pluralistic nature. To validate this theoretical construct, one has to develop means radically different from intelligence tests. As Vygotsky (1978) argued, "Any fundamentally new approach to a scientific problem inevitably leads to new methods of investigation and analysis. The invention of new methods that are ad-

equate to the new ways in which problems are posed requires far more than a simple modification of previously accepted methods" (p. 58).

If we were developing a psychological assessment to test multiple intelligences what would its critical features be? For one, accurate assessment of multiple intelligences demands a range of measures that tap the different facets of each intellectual capacity. Also, intelligence-fair instruments are needed to assess the unique faculties of each intelligence. Intelligence-fair instruments engage the key components of particular intelligences, allowing one to look directly at the functioning of each intellectual capacity. Further, the assessment must be an ongoing process based on multiple samples of an individual's abilities over time in different contexts, taking into consideration the child's educational and cultural experiences. Finally, assessments of multiple intelligences are designed to identify and build on individuals' strengths by creating rich educational environments with learning opportunities that match children's specific abilities and interests (Chen & Gardner, 1997). Needless to say, the development of such assessments requires concerted efforts over a long period of time to produce quality instruments and to carefully train individuals who can administer and interpret them in a sensitive manner (Adams, 1993; Hsueh, 2003; Krechevsky, 1998; McNamee, Chen, Masur, McCray, & Melendez, 2003; Shearer, 1996; Yoong, 2001).

The methods used to validate MI theory are not limited to the development of new psychological assessments. MI theory can also be validated by evaluating the results of applying the theory in a range of educational settings. Many articles in this volume indicate that both teachers and parents have consistently reported that MI theory has given them more accurate perceptions of children's intellectual potentials and more specific methods for supporting and developing these potentials. Kornhaber and her colleagues at Harvard University's Project Zero studied 41 elementary schools in the United States that had applied MI theory to school-based practices for at least 3 years. Among schools that reported improvements in standardized-test scores, student discipline, parent participation, or the performance of students with learning differences, the majority linked the improvements to MI-based interventions (Kornhaber, 1999; Kornhaber, Veenema, & Fierros, 2003). The effectiveness of these applications is an important source for the validation of MI theory.

What Is The Purpose Or Function Of A Theory?

Whether a theory has value to a specific field or society depends on the explanatory power and the generative power of the theory (Kuhn, 1962; Losee, 1980). A theory that has high explanatory power can account for a wide range of observations. It brings order and coherence to information, clarifying the relations of parts to whole, and describing underlying mechanisms. A theory that has high generative power orients investigators to the future by offering new frameworks for studying unknowns and contributing new knowledge to the field. It stimulates new ideas, provides new questions, and leads to new ways of understanding the world.

Both the explanatory and the generative power of MI theory are high. As described earlier, the amount and range of empirical evidence that Gardner (1993a) cites and synthesizes in making his case for MI theory is substantial. Further, MI theory makes sense to practitioners and fits their experience about individuals' intellectual strengths and weaknesses. That it makes sense is clear evidence of the explanatory power of MI theory.

Although not all psychologists agree with Gardner's theory of eight relatively independent intelligences, Gardner's claim that the nature of the human intelligences is emergent, responsive, and pluralistic is no longer a novel idea in the field of cognitive psychology. MI theory has contributed to changing our perception and understanding of human intelligences. Due to its high generative power, MI theory has stimulated countless new ideas and practices in the field of education (Campbell, Campbell, & Dickinson, 1996; Chen, 1993; Chen, Krechevsky, & Viens, 1998; Kornhaber, 1999; Kornhaber, Veenema, & Fierros, 2003; Lazear, 1994; New City School, 1994).

In the area of curriculum development, for example, MI-based curricula encompass a broad range of subject areas that include but go beyond skill development in reading, writing, and arithmetic. Because all intelligences are equally valuable, subjects such as visual arts and creative movement are also included in the curriculum. According to MI theory, the talented artist and the developing dancer are just as intelligent as the excellent reader, and each has an important place in society. Also, an authentic MI-based approach goes beyond learning factual knowledge. It also stresses the importance of promoting in-depth exploration and real understanding of the key concepts essential to a domain (Gardner, 2000).

Educators who work with at-risk children have been particularly drawn to the application of MI theory because it offers an approach to intervention that focuses on strengths instead of deficits. By the same token, MI theory extends the concept of the gifted child beyond those who excel in linguistic and logical pursuits to include children who achieve in a wide range of domains.

MI theory can be applied to the development of instructional techniques as well. For example, a teacher can provide multiple entry points to the study of a particular topic by using different media and encouraging students to express their understanding of the topic through diverse representational methods such as writing, three-dimensional models, or dramatizations. Such instructional approaches make it possible for students to find ways of learning that are attuned to their predispositions and therefore increase their motivation and engagement in the learning process. Use of these approaches also increases the likelihood that every student will attain some understanding of the topic at hand.

In summation, in discussions of whether MI theory is a scientific theory, two points warrant special attention. First, intelligence is not a tangible object that can be measured; it is a construct that psychologists define. As theoretical hypotheses differ, so does the methodology used to develop the theory and the evidence cited to validate the theory. Any attempt to apply a uniform standard for establishing the credibility and value of a theory at best fails to consider the possibility of alternative approaches, and at worst impedes the development of new ideas by constraining the use of new methodologies. Second, theories, particularly theories in the social sciences, are rarely proved or disapproved decisively, regardless of the methodology used to test the theoretical construct. A theory is not necessarily valuable because it is supported by the results of experimental tests. Rather, its value depends on the contributions it makes to understanding and to practice in the field. The value of MI theory has been clearly established by its many successful applications in the field.

References

Adams, M. (1993). *An empirical investigation of domain-specific theories of preschool children's cognitive abilities.* Unpublished doctoral dissertation, Tufts University, Medford, MA.

Campbell, L., Campbell, B., & Dickinson, D. (1996). *Teaching and learning through multiple intelligences.* Needham Heights, MA: Allyn & Bacon.

Chen, J. Q. (1993, April). *Working with at-risk children through the identification and nurturance of their strengths.* Paper presented at the biennial conference of the Society for Research of Child Development, New Orleans, LA.

Chen, J. Q., & Gardner, H. (1997). Alternative assessment from a multiple intelligences theoretical perspective. In D. P. Flanagan, J. L. Genshaft, & P. L. Harrison (Eds.), *Beyond traditional intellectual assessment: Contemporary and emerging theories, tests, and issues* (pp. 105–121). New York: Guilford.

Chen, J. Q., Krechevsky, M., & Viens, J. (1998). *Building on children's strengths: The experience of Project Spectrum.* New York: Teachers College Press.

Gardner, H. (1993a). *Frames of mind: The theory of multiple intelligences* (10th-anniversary ed.). New York: Basic Books.

Gardner, H. (1993b). *Multiple intelligences: The theory in practice.* New York: Basic Books.

Gardner, H. (1999). *Intelligence reframed: Multiple intelligences for the 21st century.* New York: Basic Books.

Gardner, H. (2000). *The disciplined mind: Beyond facts and standardized tests, the K–12 education that every child deserves.* New York: Penguin Books.

Hsueh, W. C. (2003, April). *The development of a MI assessment for young children in Taiwan.* Paper presented at the annual meeting of the American Educational Research Association, Chicago, IL.

Kornhaber, M. (1999). Multiple intelligences theory in practice (pp. 179–191). In J. Block, S. T. Everson, & T. R. Guskey (Eds.), *Comprehensive school reform: A program perspective.* Dubuque, IA: Kendall/Hunt Publishers.

Kornhaber, M., Veenema, S., & Fierros, E. (2003). *Multiple intelligences: Best ideas from research and practice.* Boston: Allyn and Bacon.

Krechevsky, M. (1998). *Project Spectrum preschool assessment handbook.* New York: Teachers College Press.

Kuhn, T. (1962). *The structure of scientific revolution.* Chicago: University of Chicago Press.

Lazear, D. (1994). *Seven pathways of learning: Teaching students and parents about multiple intelligences.* Tucson, AZ: Zephyr.

Losee, J. (1980). *A historical introduction to the philosophy of science* (2nd ed.). Oxford: University Press.

McNamee, G., Chen, J. Q., Masur, A., McCray, J., & Melendez, L. (2002). Assessing and teaching diverse learners. *Journal of Early Childhood Teacher Educators, 23*(3), 275–282.

New City School. (1994). *Multiple intelligences: Teaching for success.* St. Louis, MO: Author.

Popper, K. (1959). *The logic of scientific discovery.* London: Hutchison.

Shearer, B. (1996). *The MIDAS: professional manual.* Kent, OH: MI Research and Consulting.

Vygotsky, L. S. (1978). *Mind in society: The development of higher psychological processes* (M. Cole, V. John-Steiner, S. Scribner, & E. Souberman, Trans.). Cambridge, MA: Harvard University Press.

Yoong, S. (2001, November). *Multiple intelligences: A construct validation of the MIDAS Scale in Malaysia.* Paper presented at the International Conference on Measurement and Evaluation in Education, Penang, Malaysia.

JIE-QI CHEN is Associate Professor of Child Development and Early Education at Erikson Institute in Chicago. Her research interests involve the development of diverse cognitive abilities in young children, linking assessment to curriculum and instruction, and the use of computer technology in early childhood classroom. She currently holds a position of Fulbright senior specialist and is coauthor of *Building on Children's Strengths* (Teachers College Press) and *Effective Partnering for School Change: Improving Early Childhood Education in Urban Classrooms* (Teachers College Press), editor of *Early Learning Activities* (Teachers College Press), and contributor to the *Multiple Intelligences* entry for The Encyclopedia of Education (2nd ed, McMillan Reference).

UNIT 5
Cognitive Processes

Unit Selections

15. **Shouldn't There Be a Word...?**, Barbara Wallraff
16. **What Was I Thinking?**, Eric Jaffe
17. **Mysteries of the Mind**, Marianne Szegedy-Maszak

Key Points to Consider

- Why study cognition? Do you think the cognitive capacities of children match those of adults? What role do you think culture plays in cognitive development? What aspects of culture most influence how we process incoming information about our world? Besides culture and development, can you think of other factors that influence our cognitive activity? What role does education play in sharpening our cognitive abilities?

- Why study language? Is language related to intelligence? Is it related to cognition? Is thought central to our concept of being human and being separate from or better than other animals? How so?

- Why do we "coin" new words? Do new words added to a language tell us something about the individual who coined the word or about culture or a specific point in history? Can you provide some examples?

- How are our everyday cognitions flawed? Do experts make flawed judgments as well? What are some common reasons for flawed thinking? Can you provide examples of ways to overcome or prevent flawed thinking?

- How does science help us understand the human "mind"? How can our "mind" trick us into thinking something untrue is true? What was Freud's basic theory about the unconscious? Is there any evidence from today's research that supports the concept of the unconscious? Where else do you think research on the unconscious or on cognition will lead psychologists?

Student Website
www.mhcls.com/online

Internet References
Further information regarding these websites may be found in this book's preface or online.

American Association for Artificial Intelligence (AAAI)
   http://www.aaai.org/AITopics/index.html
Chess: Kasparov v. Deep Blue: The Rematch
   http://www.chess.ibm.com/home/html/b.html

As Rashad watches his four-month old, he is convinced that the baby possesses a degree of understanding of the world around her. In fact, Rashad is sure he has one of the smartest babies in the neighborhood. Although he is indeed a proud father, he keeps these thoughts to himself so as not to alienate his neighbors whom he perceives as having less intelligent babies.

Gustav lives in the same neighborhood as Rashad. However, Gustav doesn't have any children, but he does own two fox terriers. Despite Gustav's most concerted efforts, the dogs never come to him when he calls them. In fact, the dogs have been known to run in the opposite direction on occasion. Instead of being furious, Gustav accepts his dogs' disobedience because he is sure the dogs are just dumb beasts and don't know any better.

Both of these vignettes illustrate important and interesting ideas about cognition or thought processes. In the first vignette, Rashad ascribes cognitive abilities and high intelligence to his child; in fact, Rashad perhaps ascribes too much cognitive ability to his four-month old. On the other hand, Gustav assumes that his dogs are incapable of thought, more specifically incapable of premeditated disobedience, and therefore forgives the dogs.

Few adults would deny the existence of their cognitive abilities. Some adults, in fact, think about thinking, something which psychologists call metacognition. Cognition is critical to our survival as adults. But are there differences in mentation in adults? And what about other organisms? Can young children—infants for example—think? If they can, do they think like adults? And what about animals; can they think and solve problems? These and other questions are related to cognitive psychology and cognitive science, showcased in this unit.

Cognitive psychology has grown faster than most other specialties in psychology in the past 40 years. Much of this has occurred in response to new computer technology as well as to the growth of the field of cognitive science. Computer technology has prompted an interest in artificial intelligence, the mimicking of human intelligence by machines. Similarly the study of cognition has prompted the study of concept formation, problem solving, decision making, thinking, and language processing.

The first article in this unit offers the reader a look into the world of language. Writing for the prestigious *American Scholar*, Barbara Wallraff delves into the origin of words, not just any words but words new to a language. Each year thousands of words are coined in any given language, although not all of them can be found in the dictionary the following year. Such words, Wallraff claims, reveal something about the language and culture as well as something about the inner essence of humans.

A second article examines cognition in more depth. Nobel Laureate Daniel Kahneman shares his model of human thought as well as related flaws in thinking. Much of what Kahneman offers is based on his research about expert judgments in which he finds that even experts construct mistaken assumptions.

In "Mysteries of the Mind," author Marianne Szegedy-Maszak takes the reader on a journey into the unconscious. Freud was the first to suggest the existence of the unconscious, but early critics dismissed his ideas. Today, psychologists are more and more likely to accept the concept of unconscious thought because of modern neuroimaging studies as well as other research.

Shouldn't There Be a Word . . . ?

The holes in our language and the never-ending search for words to fill them

BARBARA WALLRAFF

I magine being the first person in the world ever to say anything. What fun it would be to fill a language with words: *tree, dog, wolf, fire, husband, wife, kiddies.* But putting names to things quickly gets complicated. For instance, if I call my husband *husband,* what should I call my friend's husband? Just for the sake of argument, let's say I name him *man.* So is my husband still only *husband,* or is he, too, man? Maybe he could go by both names. If we let him have more than one name, he can also be *father*—and *hunter-gatherer.* Let's make up words for actions as well as for things: The tree *grows* new leaves. The dog *runs*—he runs *away* from the wolf and *toward* the fire. You know what? This pastime has possibilities.

That isn't really how languages developed, of course. But in the beginning there weren't any words, and now, obviously, there are millions of them, in thousands of languages. Our own language, if we count all the terms in all the specialized jargons attached to English, has millions of words. Between prehistory and the present came a long period in which people who didn't know a word for something usually had no way of finding out whether any such word already existed. Suppose you wanted to know a plant's name—the name of a particular shrub that could be used medicinally as a sedative but could also be legal in high doses. If you asked around and nobody knew what it was called, you'd have little choice but to make up a name. Let's say *hemlock.* Why *hemlock* and not some other word? Nobody knows anymore. The *Oxford English Dictionary* says *hemlock* and its antecedents in Middle English and Old English are "of obscure origin: no cognate word is found in the other lang[uage]s."

William Shakespeare lived and wrote toward the end of that long period, during which English was taking shape but had not been gathered into dictionaries. His writing not only shows the richness the language had already achieved but also that Shakespeare was a prolific word coiner. *Besmirch, impede, rant,* and *wild-goose chase* are a few of the more than 1,000 words and phrases that he evidently added to our language. His coinages tend to be more a matter of tinkering or redefining than

of plucking words out of thin air (or *ayre,* as he spelled the word in the phrase "into thin ayre," in *The Tempest).* For instance, *smirch* was a verb before Shakespeare added the prefix *be-* to it. *Impediment,* derived from Latin, was in use in English for at least 200 years before Shakespeare came up with *impede.* But as scholars of Elizabethan English acknowledge, only a limited amount of writing survives from Shakespeare's time, apart from his own. Many of the words whose first recorded use appears in one of Shakespeare's plays may have been familiar to writers or conversationalists of his day. It's also possible that in conversation Shakespeare coined many more words than we know—but because he didn't write them down, they've been lost to history

The English language kept swallowing up, digesting, and drawing energy from other languages" words. As English grew, word lists of various kinds were compiled and circulated. Lists appeared in *The Egerton Manuscript,* from about 1450, and in *The Book of St. Albans,* printed in 1486. But the first comprehensive English dictionary, compiled by Nathan Bailey, was not published until 1730. Samuel Johnson did a bit of cribbing from Bailey to create his famous dictionary of 1755—even though the word *copyright* was by then in use. Still, it took about another half century for the word to make its way into Johnson's dictionary.

aquadextros (ak´ wa•dek´ strus), *adj.*
possessing the ability to turn the bathtub faucet on and off with one's toes

In 1783, a 25-year-old Noah Webster began publishing *The American Spelling Book,* which more than a million copies annually for years—an astonishing number considering that in 1790, according to the first United States Census, the nation's total population was less than four million. Far from resting on his laurels, Webster kept working away until he had finished his masterwork, the two-volume *American Dictionary of the English Language,* published in 1828. After that, Americans as well as Britons had fewer excuses to invent words.

Of course, coining words to meet real needs continued—and it continues today, particularly in specialized realms like medicine, technology, fashion, cooking, cartooning, and online games. Sometimes what constitutes a need for a term is subjective. Why do we need *myocardial infarction* when we already have *heart attack*? Physicians think we do. Why do we need *bling-bling* when we already *have flashy jewelry?* Movie stars and rap musicians think we do. New words coined to meet needs—objective or subjective, real or perceived—have been with us since the beginning.

From the usual point of view, a new word is successful if it catches on—with a subculture or with everyone—and eventually finds its way into dictionaries. But the impulse to coin words runs so deep that we coin many more words than we really need, most of which will never catch on. These words are not failures; they're pleasures. Coining words is like sex in that it's necessary to our species—but rarely do people engage in it for the sake of keeping humankind going. We do it because it's fun.

C redit for being the first to neologize publicly on purpose, for no serious purpose, is usually given to two Englishmen, Lewis Carroll and Edward Lear, for their nonsense verse. "Twas brillig, and the slithy toves / Did gyre and gimble in the wabe," Carroll wrote, in his poem "Jabberwocky," published in *Through the Looking Glass* in 1872. *Brillig? Slithy? Gyre? Gimble? Wabe?* Carroll (whose *non*-nom de plume *was* Charles Lutwidge Dodgson) coined them all.

In 1867, Lear wrote, "The Owl and the Pussy-cat went to sea / In a beautiful pea-green boat, / ... / They dined on mince, and slices of quince, / Which they ate with a runcible spoon." Behold the world's first use of *runcible spoon.* But what is such a thing? According to the *Oxford English Dictionary,* it is "a kind of fork used for pickles, etc., curved like a spoon and having three broad prongs of which one has a sharp edge." But, the OED notes, "the illustrations provided by Lear himself for his books of verse give no warrant for this later interpretation."

Though many nonsense words might seem arbitrary—can you guess from looking at *brillig* or *runcible* what it means?— a number of Lewis (Carroll's coinages have a special property. Humpty Dumpty explains this to Alice a bit further on in *Through the Looking Glass,* when she asks for his help with the unfamiliar words in "Jabberwocky":

> "'Brillig' means four o'clock in the afternoon—the time when you begin broiling things for dinner."
> "That'll do very well," said Alice; "and 'slithy'?"
> "Well, 'slithy' means 'lithe and slimy.' 'Lithe' is the same as 'active.' You see it's like a porunant-eau—there are two meanings packed up into one word."

Portmanteau words—eureka! With this idea, Carroll bestowed a versatile gift on the world of recreational neologizing. Because portmanteau words are derived from dictionary words,

they tend to be less opaque than other new coinages. In fact, *chortle,* another portmanteau word that Carroll coined in "Jabberwocky," became a dictionary word because people readily understood how to use it. The *Oxford English Dictionary* explains *chortle* roots like this: "app[arently] with some suggestion *of chuckle,* and of *snort.*" Unfortunately, the portmanteau itself ("a large leather suitcase that opens into two hinged compartments," as the *American Heritage Dictionary* defines it) is now found only in museums and antiques shops. It's probably time to hunt up a less anachronistic term to carry the meaning into the future. (Among the few suggestions I've heard for this, my favorite is *twone—two* portmanteaued with *one.)*

We owe a debt to Carroll and Lear, and what they did is delightful, but it is not exactly what I would call "recreational word coining." Carroll and Lear invented their words for literary purposes— much as Shakespeare did. Literary figures from James Joyce *(bababadalgharaghtakamminarronnkonnronnlonnerronntuonnthu nntrovarrhounailmskawntoohoohoordnenthumuk!)* and George Orwell *(Newspeak)* to J. R. R. Tolkien *(hobbit)* and J. K. Rowling *(quidditch)* have made up words the better to convey worlds largely of their invention. Recreational word coining, however, describes odd coining of the world we know.

Recreational redefining is a related field, which also describes the world we know. Therefore, before we get acquainted with the first true recreational word coiner, who came a bit later, let's meet the pioneer on this linguistic front—the American writer Ambrose Bierce. Bierce was a near contemporary of Carroll and Lear. In 1875 he finished a freelance manuscript that included 48 English words and his redefinitions of them. This, the first sulfurous spark of what would become *The Devils Dictionary,* failed to set the world on fire. Six years later, Bierce was named editor of *Wasp,* a new satirical journal, and he immediately began writing and publishing a feature that offered "twisty new definitions of shopworn old words," as Roy Morris Jr. explains in his introduction to the current Oxford edition of *The Devil's Dictionary.* Many of the words from *Wasp* also took their place among the 998 redefined words that ultimately made up Bierce's best-known book. An *admiral,* he wrote, is "that part of a war-ship which does the talking while the figure-head does the thinking." A *habit* is "a shackle for the free." *Zeal* is "a certain nervous disorder afflicting the young and inexperienced. A passion that goeth before a sprawl." In 1912, not long before Bierce lit out for Mexico and disappeared off the face of the earth, he published 12 volumes of his *Collected Works,* including *The Devils Dictionary.* Since then, the book has never been out of print.

The first true recreational word coiner was another American: Gelett Burgess. Like Carroll and Lear in England, Burgess published nonsense verse—one of his claims to fame is the poem "The Purple Cow." More to the point, in 1914 he published a spurious diclionan. *Burgess Unabridged: A New Dictionary of Words You Have Always Needed.* Among the words in it is *blurb*—another of Burgess's claims to fame, for this creation of his is still in use, with roughly the meaning he assigned it. Alas, few of his other words ever caught on—not without reason, as we shall see.

After a decades-long pause, a spate of books featuring recreational word coining began to appear. For instance, *An Exaltation of Larks,* which in 1968 began as a collection of venerable terms of venery ("a *pride* of lions," "a *murder* of crows," "a *gam* of whales"), has over several revisions incorporated more and more terms that the author, James Lipton (now better known as the host of *Inside the Actors Studio,* on the Bravo channel), either coined himself or found in the work of contemporary' writers: "a *phalanx* of flashers," Kurt Vonnegut; "a *mews* of cathouses," Neil Simon; "an *om* of Buddhists," George Plimpton.

The 1983 book *The Meaning of Liff and* its 1990 expanded edition *The Deeper Meaning of Liff* by the British writers Douglas Adams author of the 1979 best seller *The Hitchhiker's Guide to the Galaxy)* and John Lloyd, merrily misappropriated geographic names from *Aasleagh* ("a liqueur made only for drinking at the end of a revoltingly long bottle party when all the drinkable drink has been drunk") to *Zeal Monachorum* ("[Skiing term.] To ski with 'zeal monachorum' is to descend the top three-quarters of the mountain in a quivering blue funk, but on arriving at the gentle bit just in front of the restaurant to whizz to a stop like a victorious slalom-champion").

Between the publication of *Liff*'s first and second editions, sniglets gave *Liff* some stiff competition. Rich Hall, a writer and cast member on HBO's comedy show *Not Necessarily the News,* came up with the idea of a *sniglet* as "any word that doesn't appear in the dictionary, but should." Sniglets fans sent Hall words like *aquadextrous,* "possessing the ability to turn the bathtub faucet on and off with your toes," and *profanitype,* "the special symbols used by cartoonists to replace swear words

(points, asterisks, stars, and so on)." From 1984 to 1989 five books of sniglets were published.

Next came a more serious and high-minded variation on the theme. The writer Jack Hitt asked a number of writers and artists "if they had ever had the experience of running across a meaning for which there is no word," and he turned the words they proposed into a piece published in *Harper's Magazine* in 1990. This was so well received that Hitt expanded the article into a 1992 book. *In a Word.* Its contributors ranged from Katharine Hepburn to Cynthia Ozick, Lou Reed to Lionel Tiger.

Today there's *The Washington Post*'s Style Invitational contest, which has been running every week for nearly 13 years. Sometimes the week's contest has to do with neologizing or redefining existing words. For instance, readers are occasionally invited to "take any word, add, subtract or alter a single letter, and redefine the word." The published responses to this request include *diddleman,* "a person who adds nothing but time to an effort"; *nominatrix,* "a spike-heeled woman who controls the selection of candidates for party whip"; and *compenisate,* "to buy a red Porsche for reasons you don't quite understand."

There's my own "Word Fugitives" column, which appears in *The Atlantic Monthly.* Readers write in seeking words, other readers respond, I choose my favorite suggestions and publish them in the column, and we've all done our little bit to move civilization forward. But I've also accumulated a private stash of peoples questions that I've never, until now, gotten around to publishing.

What kinds of words do people want? Do the holes in our language tell us anything about our society? The requests I get for words easily sort themselves into six categories.

Words about our unruly inner lives.

In a sense, of course, all gaps in our language tell us something about our inner lives. Some linguists say that language organizes experience. But language itself is hideously disorganized, especially the English language. Sometimes we have plenty of synonyms or near synonyms to choose from: *idea, concept, thought, inspiration, notion, surmise, theory, impression, perception, observation, mental picture.* More specialized meanings get specialized words. If, say, you're looking for a word that can mean either "a phantom" or "an ideal"—why, *eidolon* stands ready to serve. And yet some fairly common things and phenomena remain nameless. For instance, what would you call the experience of hearing about something for the first time and then starting to notice it everywhere?

That particular hole in the language is worthy of note, because once you're aware of it, if you begin rooting around in coined words, you'll start noticing words intended to fill it. It was one of the first requests published in "Word Fugitives"; *déjà new* took top honors. As I discovered later, essentially the same question had been asked by the writer Lia Matera in *In a Word;* Matera suggested we call the experience *toujours vu.*

The 2001 book *Wanted Words 2*, edited by Jane Farrow, also asked the question and presented more than a dozen possible answers, including *newbiquitous* and *coincidently*.

Let's look at a couple of examples of inner-life-related questions. If you want answers, you'll have to supply your own, because, again, these haven't previously been published.

> *What would be a word for wanting to get someone's voice mail but getting the person instead? (submitted by C. Murphy, Medfield, Mass.)*

> *I would like a word for the opposite of déjà vu—a word that would describe the feeling of learning something a hundred times but never being able to remember it. (A. Felcher, Portland, Ore.)*

Words about *them*. Why is it that there never seem to be enough words in the dictionary to cover everyone we dislike? To make things worse, new kinds of dislikable people keep cropping up. For instance:

> *We need a word to describe a person who, owing to his life circumstances, clearly is not competent to provide advice but insists on doing so anyway. For example, an unemployed person who gives job-seeking advice to a person considering competing professional offers, or a receptionist who unabashedly offers medical advice to a roomful of doctors. (M. Kennet, Kibbutz Manara, Israel)*

> *I have a desperate need for a word that conveys the essential meaning of the phrase trailer trash with-*

out maligning innocent dwellings. *(K. Cox, Austin, Tex.)*

Words about the material world. A sizable majority of the words that lexicographers add our dictionaries are names for things. People just won't stop inventing things and perceiving old things in new ways. And things need names: *blogs, infinity pools, conflict diamonds.* A separate issue is commercial products, with their expensively, extensively negotiated and marketed names. Standard dictionaries exclude most product and brand names, but the proportion of "new" words that name things rises even higher if you count preexisting words and phrases that have been turned into brands: *Tiger* (computer operating system), *Magic Hat* (beer), *Juicy Couture* (sportswear), *BlackBerry* (portable communication device).

And yet it's relatively rare for one to get requests for coinages to name things. The obvious explanation would be that things already have names. Consider *aglets* (the tiny plastic wrappers at the ends of shoelaces) and *altocumulus undulatus* (the clouds in a herringbone sky) and *chads* (you remember: the little spots of paper that fall off punch cards). There is scarcely a thing so small or ethereal or insignificant or transient that someone somewhere has not named it. Nonetheless, here are two requests:

> *I seek a word or phrase to describe a cheap plastic thing that is better for a task than its expensive metal counterpart. (B. Gibson, Concrete, Wash.)*

> *We need a word for food that hasn't quite gone bad—the things you aren't sure whether you ought to throw them out. (A. Bernays and J. Kaplan, Cambridge, Mass.)*

Words about tribulations. This is a popular category. Granted, the annoyances that people write to me about tend to be petty—for instance, being terrible at transcribing numbers (if the problem is phone numbers, would that be *dialexia)* or finding oneself standing in the supermarket's slowest line (*misalinement?).* But just because they're petty is no reason to suffer them in silence. Somehow, putting a name to what happened—preferably a name no one else has ever heard—can be satisfying. The affliction is special, possibly unique. As in:

> *My name is Todd, but throughout my life, people—both close to me and mere acquaintances—have incorrectly called me Scott. The people who do this are unrelated to one another. I mentioned this during a luncheon gathering recently, and to my surprise another person at the table claimed a similar thing happens to his wife. I figure this phenomenon must occur with sufficient frequency to warrant a name of its own. Suggestions?" (S. Nichols [just kidding!—of course he's T. Nichols], Shorewood, Minn.)*

> *Is there a term for concentrating so hard on not saying the worst possible thing in a situation that it comes out? For instance, greeting a newly mal-coiffed friend: "Your hair!" (K. Lewin, Henderson, Nev.)*

Words about words. The words in this category are undeniably ethereal. Here many old words have fallen into disuse. We as a society would be better off if everyone knew what words like *pronoun, adjective,* and *preposition* mean. I believe this because I find it nearly impossible to talk about language and how it works its wonders without employing at least basic grammatical terms. If everyone bad these words down, we could move on to complaining that nowadays no one understands the likes of *meiosix* ("the use of understatement not to deceive, but to enhance the impression on the hearer," as H. W. Fowler explains in his *Modern English Usage)* and *tmesis* ("separation of the parts of a compound word by another word inserted between them"—for instance, *um-freaking-believable).* But let's not go there. Plenty of words about words remain to be coined. Here are two requests:

> *I am looking for a word to describe the deliberate misspelling of words and phrases for marketing purposes. For example, Citibank, Rite-Aid, Kool-Aid, and Krispy Kreme. It drives me crazy! (M. Harris, Brooklyn, N.Y.)*

> *Is there a term for those metaphorical insults like "She's one sandwich short of a picnic" and "He's not the sharpest knife in the drawer"? (J. Blum, San Francisco)*

Miscellany. Nouns, verbs, and a sprinkling of adjectives: these make up nearly all the words that show tip on our culture's "Most Wanted" poster. Years ago, on the Word Fugitives Web site, I asked for help in inventing a one-word preposition that would mean "in spite of or perhaps because of"; you'd be surprised how often that wordy locution comes up. But, nobody bit, as I recall, and now that Web page itself has gone missing.

Here are a couple of miscellaneous requests that remain:

> *There ought to be a word, parallel to "gossiping," for having social conversations about technological things: comparing kinds of new televisions or the merits of digital cameras or cell phones. (H. Shields, Hamilton, Mass.)*

> *I find it quite astonishing that in English there is no word for the sound produced by a camel. As you know, the camel is the most important animal in the Muslim world. In the midst of so much talk about the clash of civilizations, wouldn't coining such a word help, albeit in a small way, to create a discourse?" (M. A. Moftah, Cairo, Egypt)*

What are the characteristics of a great recreational coinage? It's complicated, because just about any syllable or series of syllables could mean just about anything in English. *Bumbershoot, gamp, ombrifuge, rundle*—these are venerable dictionary words, all of which happen to mean "umbrella." But are they any more plausible carriers of that meaning than the non-dictionary words *rainbrella* and *dunolly?* (*Rainbrella* was coined by a child, and *dunolly* was plucked from a map

and redefined as "an improvised umbrella" in *The Deeper Meaning of Liff.)* Furthermore, given that such seeming arbitrariness is more the rule than the exception in English, what are we doing when we rack our brains trying to come up with a brilliant coinage? What sets a keeper apart from a discard?

A number of shortcomings common to discards leap to mind. First is that the coinage is cryptic, opaque, impenetrable. For example, why should *culp*—a word coined by Gelett Burgess, in *Burgess Unabridged*—mean "a fond delusion; an imaginary attribute"? Why should *nulkin*—another of Burgess's words—mean "the core or inside history of any occurrence"? It's true that many dictionary words are of unknown origin and that many others reached their current meanings by circuitous, even bizarre, routes. In fact, Burgess's inventions often mimic dictionary words accurately. But most of them fail to satisfy. Pretend words are more fun when they illuminate the mental processes that brought them into being.

Portmanteau words tend to have this problem licked. It's not hard to figure out that *chortle* means "chuckle" and "snort"; that the 1923 word *guesstimate* is a combination of "guess" and "estimate"; that the more recent *Spanglish* mingles "Spanish" and "English." Sometimes, though, two old words in combination look as if they should be pronounced differently from the two words spoken separately—and then the portmanteau word becomes impenetrable. (Because I'll be finding fault with the words that follow, I'm going to be nice and not identify their coiners.) For instance, the useful modern coinage *eyelie,* meaning "to pretend not to see someone," wants to be pronounced "I-lee," doesn't it? Hyphenated—*eye-lie*—it looks inauthentic. But if you try to respell it *(eyelye)* so that readers will know how to pronounce it, the sense of its origin and what it means will be lost Discard.

---

diddleman (did´ 'l • man), *n.*
a person who adds nothing but time to an effort

Sometimes, too, a portmanteau word, like *arrowneous* ("the quality of one who drives against the arrow in a parking lot"), is pronounced so much like one of the words it comes from that it would be incomprehensible in speech. With rare exceptions, discard. Other portmanteaus fall short because they have associations they shouldn't. For instance, *hozone* is supposed to mean "the place where one sock in every laundry load disappears"—but unfortunately, nowadays the *ho* part of that word suggests prostitutes as readily as hosiery.

A similar potential flaw is the intentional irrelevant allusion, which naïve word coiners sometimes mistake for a pun. For instance, the responses I got to a request for a word to mean "going through the dirty-clothes hamper to find something clean enough to wear" included *cull-da-sack. Cull,* check: the word wanted has to do with culling, in the sense of selecting. *Sack,* check: the dirty clothes could just as well be in a laundry bag, or sack, as in a hamper. But what does the overall idea have to do with a cul-de-sac, or dead-end street? Uncheck. Discard. (What would be a better term for ransacking the hamper? How about *dry gleaning.)*

Some of the least appealing irrelevant allusions are naughty ones. For some reason, no matter what I ask for, I always get plays on *premature ejaculation* and *coitus interruptus.* Har-har-har! Similarly unappealing are irrelevant—or even relevant—allusions to Alzheimer's disease, schizophrenia, bipolar disorder, paraplegia, and so forth.

Another common flaw results from a failure to think the word through and craft it well. For instance, I like almost everything about *blabrynth* to fit the definition "the elaborate maze of voice-mail menus and prompts encountered when phoning businesses or government offices." But *labyrinth,* to which *blabrynth* is obviously meant to be related, has its *y* in the middle and an *i* in the last syllable. So shouldn't *blabrynth* be *blabberinth* or *blabyrinth*? Another example is "*petonic,* adj.: One who is embarrassed to undress in front of a household pet." We understand the *pet* part. But *onic*? Is that like in *catatonic*? But that's not "embarrassed"—that's immobilized. Furthermore, is *petonic* an adjective, or does it mean "one who . . . ," in which case it's a noun? Discard.

Two other flaws I often notice are nearly each other's opposites. On the one hand, there are supposed holes in the language that no one has ever stumbled into. Suppose the definition is "not wasteful of parsnips" or "a person who sticks up to plants." In these cases, who cares how cute the coinage is. *Parsnipmonions* and *photosycophant* aren't words that anyone could conceivably need; they don't describe the world we live in. On the other hand, there are supposed holes in the language for which perfectly good mainstream words already exist. For instance, *lexicaves* was coined to mean the indentations on the side of a dictionary, but in reality they are named *thumb indexes. Lobsterine* was coined to mean the green stuff that oozes from the center of a lobster, but the real name for this is *tomalley.*

If you avoid all those pitfalls and let inspiration strike, might your coinage eventually enter the mainstream to become a dictionary word? This is a fond hope that many people have for their brainchildren, but, alas, it is now my duty to dash it. The great majority of words coined for fun aren't real and never will be.

Allan Metcalf, the executive secretary of the American Dialect Society (ADS), has a lot of experience in delivering this particular bad news. Since 1990, Metcalf has overseen the society's annual selection of "Words of the Year." It used to bother him that even though the ADS's members are as well informed about English as anyone anywhere, the words they choose almost invariably lack staying power. Wanting to understand why, Metcalf undertook a study. The result was his 2002 book *Predicting New Words: The Secrets of Their Success.* "Successful new words," he wrote, "are alike in ways that promote their success, while unsuccessful new words are alike in ways that promote their failure."

dialexia (dī ´å • lek si • å), *n.*
being terrible at transcribing phone numbers

You might imagine that the main thing successful new words would have in common is that they fill conspicuous gaps in our language, but that's pretty much beside the point, according to Metcalf. I interviewed him by e-mail, and he wrote me: "To mix a few metaphors: If a newly minted word is bright and shiny, it is almost certain to crash, burn, go up in smoke, and vanish into thin air. Whole volumes of clever words proposed by the cleverest coiners have evaporated in this manner."

For instance, consider Rich Hall's five books of sniglets. Metcalf wrote, "These hugely popular books contained ingenious inventions like *flirr* 'a photograph that features the camera operator's finger in the corner,' and *tacangle,* 'the position of one's head while biting into a taco.' Of the hundreds of sniglets invented by Hall, his admirers, and his imitators, the only one that has made its way into a modicum of permanency is *sniglet* itself."

Misalinement (mis • á • līn • ment), *n.*
finding oneself standing in the supermarket's slowest line

Metcalf also brought up a collection of coinages intended seriously: the 2001 book *Dictionary of the Future: The Words, Terms and Trends That Define the Way We'll Live, Work and Talk,* by the futurologist Faith Popcorn and the consumer-marketing expert Adam Hanft. "It includes words like GENEology, 'the study of one's genetic history,' and *atmosFear,* to describe nervousness about pollution and attacks on our air, water, and food," Metcalf wrote. "Although Popcorn is famous as the inventor of *cocooning,* the name for a staying-at-home trend she discerned in 1986, since then all the labels she's affixed to her predictions (right or wrong) have peeled off."

Hall and Popcorn may be among the world's most famous word coiners, and yet they've had minimal success at getting their words into dictionaries. Metcalf wrote me:

> *What are we to make of so many failures? It is a sad story, documented in detail in my* Predicting New Words. *In that book I discuss five qualities that allow a new word to flourish. The most important of the five is "unobtrusiveness." To become part of our standard vocabulary, a new word has to look old. An example is heads-up—not the long-familiar exclamation of warning, "Heads up!," or the adjective heads-up meaning "alert" or "competent," but the noun that means something like "advance information." Americans have been giving each other this kind of heads-up since the late twentieth century, but only now are the dictionaries begin-*

ning to recognize it. It is perfectly camouflaged in the form of its predecessor.

So there you have the Catch-22 of word coining: If a word is clever enough that people will notice it and admire you for coining it, it's too clever to earn a place in our language for real. Is this bad news for us recreational neologizers? No doubt it will come as a blow to anyone who believes in elves and Tinkerbell. It may also upset the kind of person who, having won a game of Monopoly, is disappointed that the real estate and the money aren't real and his or hers to keep. (What would we call someone like that? Surely such a person is too rare to deserve a name.)

Not without reason did I say that my subject is coining words just for fun. Even if the lives of our young words are short, long live the pastime—game, diversion, entertainment, addiction—of coining words!

Barbara Wallraff is a contributing editor of *The Atlantic Monthly,* a syndicated newspaper columnist, and the author of *Word Court* and *Your Own Words.* This article is adapted from her new book, *Word Fugitives.*

What Was I Thinking?

Kahneman Explains How Intuition Leads Us Astray

ERIC JAFFE

This is a story without an ending. And that's not the only thing wrong with it.

In fact, there were a number of flaws in Nobel Laureate Daniel Kahneman's lecture "A Perspective of Flawed Thought," in March 2004 at the National Institutes of Health. Quite purposefully, the entire talk was full of them.

"I specialize in flaws," Kahneman said.

However appropriate that self-deprecating remark was to the topic, it hardly applied to the speaker's celebrated accomplishments. In addition to the 2002 Nobel Prize, which he received for his work applying psychologically realistic models to economic theory, APS Fellow Kahneman, Princeton University, has received most every award possible to a psychologist, including the 1990 APS William James Fellow Award.

Part of Kahneman's intent was to show that flawed thinking plays no favorites. Sure enough, despite his vast understanding of the subject, Kahneman himself claimed to be susceptible to misleading intuition, a realization he made while looking at the latest gallop poll, in which President George W. Bush's approval rating had shifted a statistically insignificant 2 percent from the previous week.

"I was influenced by this completely irrelevant data," he said. "I could not help myself from drawing inferences like, 'What happened this week?' or 'What's the explanation?' I was working on this intuitively and contrary to my better statistical judgment."

According to Kahneman, some human intuition is good, and some is erroneous. And like the incorrigible habit of the knuckle cracker, the bad ones are very difficult to correct.

One reason flawed intuition is allowed to permeate human thinking is its accessibility. For example, if the multiplication problem 17 times 24 is shown for only a moment before its answer, 408, is revealed, few solve it without a formal, lengthy act of computation. On the contrary, if the word "vomit" is displayed and immediately followed by the word "disgusting," it seems the accessible, almost instantaneous extension of the viewer's thinking.

"Intuitive impressions come to mind without explicit intention, and without any confrontation, and this is one of their distinctive aspects," he said.

To better understand the reasons for this accessibility, Kahneman has focused much of his research on expert intuitions. Expert intuitions are able to deal swiftly and decisively with a difficult matter—such as making a quick chess move or fighting a fire—that would seem to require extensive deliberation. Most of the time, a person with expert intuition is not really conscious of making a decision, but rather acts as though their instinctive choice is the only natural outcome of a circumstance.

"You can have a master chess player walking by a complicated chess position and, without slowing down, this player will say, 'White mates in three,' " Kahneman said. In the case of firefighters making perhaps life or death decisions, "something that is very close to the best solution came to mind, and nothing else."

APS Fellow Daniel Kahneman received the Nobel Prize in 2002 for his work applying psychologically realistic models to economic theory.

However, unless certain conditions of expertise—namely, prolonged practice and rapid, unequivocal feedback—are fulfilled, what develops is little more than the exigent knowledge of experience. This can lead to false impressions and overconfident experts, a subject explored by Kahneman and his long-time research partner, the late Amos Tversky.

"People jump to statistical conclusions on the basis of very weak evidence. We form powerful intuitions about trends and about the replicability of results on the basis of information that is truly inadequate," Kahneman said. For this reason, a person who is not an expert, even if thoroughly versed in a field of study, might make an intuitive mistake.

Kahneman leaned heavily on the closely related argument made by another, prominent psychologist, the late Paul Meehl. In the mid-1950s, Meehl gave clinicians personality information about individuals and asked that they predict behavioral outcomes. For example, the clinician might have been asked to decide whether a released prisoner would violate parole. The predictions were then compared to statistical models based on the subset of information available to the clinician.

In a study that still holds up over 50 years later, Meehl found that when the clinician competed with the statistical formula, the formula won almost every time. This finding has served as the basis for Kahneman's theory about overconfident experts.

"What you find is a great deal of confidence in the presence of very poor accuracy," Kahneman explained. "So the confidence people have is not a good indication of how accurate they are."

Overconfidence is accentuated by the failure of people to, in general, learn from their mistakes. "When something happens that a person has not anticipated, … they remain convinced that what they had predicted, although it didn't happen, almost happened," he said. The overconfidence is then propagated while the accuracy remains the same, and the cycle begins again.

In order to trace the roots of flawed intuition, Kahneman divided all thought into a two-system model, intuition and deliberate computation, whose particular attributes are almost completely opposite. Intuition is fast, uncontrolled, and, most importantly, effortless. Computation, on the other hand, is slow, governed by strict rules, and effortful.

"Most judgments in actions are governed by [intuitive thought]," he said. "Most of our mental life is relatively effortless." This is why effortful work, such as trying to remember a phone number of five years ago, is more susceptible to interference, and therefore less accessible.

> ## A bat and a ball together costs $1.10. The bat costs a dollar more than the ball. How much does the ball cost?
>
> Interference is often enabled by poor monitoring, a shortcoming that results from our normally unconditional acceptance of intuition. Not surprisingly, according to Kahneman, **50 percent of Princeton students** incorrectly answered 10 cents when given this problem. "What happens to Princeton students is they don't check," said Kahneman. It happens to MIT students too, though at a slightly lower rate," he joked (The answer for Princeton readers, is five cents.)

Interference is often enabled by poor monitoring, a shortcoming that results from our normally unconditional acceptance of intuition. In one study, Kahneman ran the following scenario past Princeton students: A bat and a ball together cost $1.10. The bat costs a dollar more than the ball. How much does the ball cost? Not surprisingly to Kahneman, 50 percent of Princeton students incorrectly answered 10 cents when given this problem in writing, because they unconditionally accepted their intuitions.

"What happens to Princeton students is they don't check," said Kahneman. "It happens to MIT students too, though at a slightly lower rate," he joked.

Take another common question eliciting intuitive flaw: When people were asked to guess how many murders there were in Michigan in a given year, and how many there were in Detroit, the median answers were 100 and 200, respectively.

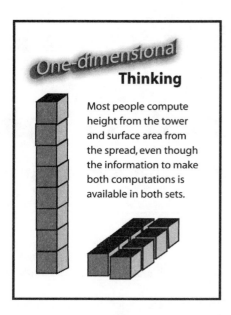

Most people compute height from the tower and surface area from the spread, even though the information to make both computations is available in both sets.

"A **fully rational** agent would find it possible to answer both questions equally easily, regardless of the display," Kahneman said. "We do not use all the information that is actually available."

"This by itself is not an error, but something is going on here that is not quite right," he said, referring to the presence of intuitive flaw. Occasionally someone asked about Michigan remembered Detroit is in Michigan, and their answer tended more toward 200, a meta-analytic process that reveals to Kahneman the ability of flawed thinking to mend itself if it recognizes all aspects of a situation.

"Accessibility, or the ease with which thoughts come to mind, has an influence not only on the operation of intuition—it almost defines intuition—but on the operations of computation," he said. "Our ability to avoid errors depends on what comes to mind, and whether the corrected thought comes to mind adequately."

But "what comes to mind" might actually be what does *not* come to mind. When looking at two sets of an equal number of cubes, one arranged vertically into a tower and the other spread flat, most people compute height from the tower and surface area from the spread, even though the information to make both computations is available in both sets.

"A fully rational agent would find it possible to answer both questions equally easily, regardless of the display," he said. "That's not what happens. We don't compute everything we could compute. We do not use all the information that is actually available."

For this reason, Kahneman argued that intuitive activities are very similar to perceptual activities, such as seeing and hearing. "These processes of perception are going to guide us in understanding intuition," he said. Take, for example, the following display sets, which are actually less defined than they appear:

Even though the B and the 13 are physically composed of the same elements, they are given context by association, and are rarely considered outside of this context. Though at the time this single-minded assessment doesn't seem wrong, it is in truth

```
┌─────────────────┐
│   ABC           │
│   12 13 14      │
└─────────────────┘
```

not become aware of. So consciousness is at the level of a choice that has already been made."

But despite all this understanding, Kahneman steered clear of offering a direct solution to flawed thinking—after all, he remained flummoxed by the gallop poll despite his 35 years studying flawed intuition. Besides, relying on computation instead of intuition would, according to Kahneman, create a slow, laborious, difficult, and costly world. What he did advocate is paying closer attention to the onset of faulty intuition.

about as rational as peeking through the keyhole of a glass door, and grossly limits our understanding of the world. Flawed intuition occurs with similar blinders.

"When people make decisions, they tend to suppress alternative interpretations," Kahneman said. "We become aware only of a single solution—this is a fundamental rule in perceptual processing. All the other solutions that might have been considered by the system—and sometimes we know that alternative solutions have been considered and rejected—we do

"The alternative to thinking intuitively is mental paralysis," he said. "Most of the time, we just have to go with our intuition, [but] we can recognize situations in which our intuition is likely to lead us astray. It's an unfinished story." He paused. "So, it's an unfinished story, so …" Kahneman hesitated for words. Something made a succinct peroration inaccessible, but the audience intuited the talk was over, and was correct—most likely.

Mysteries of the Mind

Your unconscious is making your everyday decisions

MARIANNE SZEGEDY-MASZAK

The snap judgment. The song that constantly runs through your head whenever you close your office door. The desire to drink Coke rather than Pepsi or to drive a Mustang rather than a Prius. The expression on your spouse's face that inexplicably makes you feel either amorous or enraged. Or how about the now incomprehensible reasons you married your spouse in the first place?

Welcome to evidence of your robust unconscious at work.

While these events are all superficially unrelated, each reveals an aspect of a rich inner life that is not a part of conscious, much less rational, thought. Today, long after Sigmund Freud introduced the world to the fact that much of what we do is determined by mysterious memories and emotional forces, the depths of the mind and the brain are being explored anew. "Most of what we do every minute of every day is unconscious," says University of Wisconsin neuroscientist Paul Whelan. "Life would be chaos if everything were on the forefront of our consciousness."

Fueled by powerful neuroimaging technology, questions about how we make snap decisions, why we feel uncomfortable without any obvious causes, what motivates us, and what satisfies us are being answered not through lying on a couch and exploring individual childhood miseries but by looking at neurons firing in particular parts of our brains. Hardly a week passes without the release of the results of a new study on these kinds of processes. And popular culture is so fascinated by neuroscience that *Blink*, journalist Malcolm Gladwell's exploration of "thinking without thinking," has remained on the bestseller lists for four weeks.

Most of us can appreciate the fact that we make up our minds about things based on thinking that takes place somewhere just out of our reach. But today, scientists are finding neural correlates to those processes, parts of the brain that we never gave their due, communicating with other parts, triggering neurotransmitters, and driving our actions. Says Clinton Kilts, a professor in the department of psychiatry and behavioral sciences at Emory, "There is nothing that you do, there is no thought that you have, there is no awareness, there is no lack of awareness, there is nothing that marks your daily existence that doesn't have a neural code. The greatest challenge for us is to figure out how to design the study that will reveal these codes."

Burgeoning understanding of our unconscious has deeply personal and also fascinating medical implications. The realization that our actions may not be the pristine results of our high-level reasoning can shake our faith in the strength of such cherished values as free will, a capacity to choose, and a sense of responsibility over those choices. We will never be able to control the rhythm of our heartbeats or the choreography of our limbic system. And yet, Gladwell writes that "our snap judgments and first impressions can be educated and controlled ... [and] the task of making sense of ourselves and our behavior requires that we acknowledge there can be as much value in the blink of an eye as in months of rational analysis."

Mental health. But unconscious processing is not just the stuff of compelling personal insight. For those with emotional disorders like anxiety, bipolar disorder, and schizophrenia, and others who suffer from traumatic brain injuries either from a stroke or an accident, peeling away the behavioral layers of their dysfunction has revealed fascinating activity out of conscious awareness that may eventually provide clues to more effective treatments. Recent research on minimally conscious patients, for example, shows language centers on fire when they hear personal stories recounted by a family member. Research on schizophrenia reveals that most who are afflicted have an impaired ability to smell, which researchers think may provide some clue to understanding why they have such difficulty perceiving social cues. Or consider the case of Sarah Scantlin, who was hit by a drunk driver and lay mute at the Golden Plains Health Care Center in Hutchinson, Kan., for 20 years. After the Sept. 22, 1984, crash, the doctor told her parents that it was a miracle she was even alive but that she would never talk or move again on her own. Last month she began to speak—a simple "OK" at first, then more words, even short sentences.

How does this happen? What was going on all that time? How do we get some access to this thing called the unconscious?

According to cognitive neuroscientists, we are conscious of only about 5 percent of our cognitive activity, so most of our decisions, actions, emotions, and behavior depends on the 95 percent of brain activity that goes beyond our conscious awareness. From the beating of our hearts to pushing the grocery cart and not smashing into the kitty litter, we rely on something that is called the adaptive unconscious, which is all the ways that our

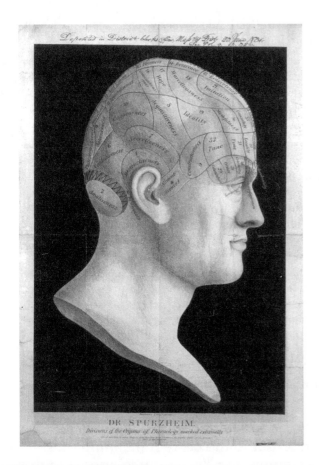

THE MIND IN THE BRAIN. Victorians were fascinated by phrenology, what they called "the only true science of the mind," which neatly partitioned the skull into different regions responsible for various emotions and traits. Photo courtesy Library of Congress.

brains understand the world that the mind and the body must negotiate. The adaptive unconscious makes it possible for us to, say, turn a corner in our car without having to go through elaborate calculations to determine the precise angle of the turn, the velocity of the automobile, the steering radius of the car. It is what can make us understand the correct meaning of statements like "prostitutes appeal to pope" or "children make nourishing snacks" without believing that they mean that the pope has an illicit life and cannibals are munching on children.

Consuming thoughts. Gerald Zaltman uses examples like these in many of his conversations. He may be an emeritus professor from the Harvard Business School, but he thinks about layers of consciousness like a neuroscientist. He is also a founding partner in Olson Zaltman Associates, a consulting firm that provides guidance to businesses seeking to better understand the minds—and in this case it is quite literally the minds—of consumers. As a professor of marketing, Zaltman obviously was very interested in figuring out what made people buy one thing and not the other. In the world of neuroscience, this goes to the heart of the profound questions of motivation. In the world of business, this goes to the bottom line.

When trying to probe the minds of consumers, Zaltman wondered if there was a way to move beyond the often-unreli-

"There is nothing that you do, there is no thought . . . nothing that marks your daily existence that doesn't have a neural code."

able focus group to get at the true desires of consumers, unencumbered by other noise, which would finally result in more effective sales and marketing.

His solution became U.S. Patent No. 5,436,830, also known as the Zaltman Metaphor Elicitation Technique, which is, according to the patent, "a technique for eliciting interconnected constructs that influence thought and behavior." From Hallmark cards to Broadway plays, from Nestlés Crunch bars to the design for the new Children's Hospital of Pittsburgh, ZMET has been used to figure out how to craft a message so that consumers will respond with the important 95 percent of their brains that motivates many of their choices. How? Through accessing the deep metaphors that people, even without knowing it, associate with a particular product or feeling or place.

Language is limited, Zaltman says, "and it can't be confused with the thought itself." Images, however, move a bit closer to capturing fragments of the rich and contradictory areas of unconscious feelings. Participants in his studies cut out pictures that represent their thoughts and feelings about a particular subject, even if they can't explain why. He discovered that when people do this, they often discover "a core, a deep metaphor simultaneously embedded in a unique setting." They are drawn to seasonal or heroic myths, for example, or images like blood and fire and mother. They are also drawn into deep concepts like journey and transformation. His work around the world has convinced him that the menu of these unconscious metaphors is limited and universal, in the manner of human emotions like hope and grief.

And Zaltman has found that even grand metaphors have their practical applications. The architectural firm Astorino and the design firm Fathom asked Zaltman for help in designing a new children's hospital that would make a difficult experience somehow easier for children, their parents, and the people who work there. With the classic ZMET technique, children, parents, and staff members cut out pictures they somehow associated with the hospital and were then interviewed for nearly two hours about these pictures, exploring the thoughts, feelings, and associations that they triggered. A stream of metaphors emerged in the conversation. A child brought in a picture of a mournful-looking pug, which she colored blue "because he's kind of sad, and that's the way I feel when I'm in the ICU or just can't get out of my room."

After each picture was thoroughly analyzed by the participants, the images were scanned, and another interviewer with a computer and a talent for the Photoshop program sat with the parent, child, or staff member and created a collage, a personal Rorschach test of the images. This snapshot of the participant's unconscious associations with the hospital was then enlarged to include personal narratives using the collage. The process is painstaking, but after the transcripts of these sessions are reviewed, even in all the enormous variety of human expression and emotion, core themes emerge. In the case of Children's Hospital, says Christine Astorino Del Sole of the Fathom firm, "the main metaphor was transformation, and the supporting metaphors were control, connection, and energy."

Brain scanning "shows that there is a life of the mind beyond what is apparent.... Does this mean that they are seeing words?"

So how does that translate into the physical space? When patients and their families walk into the new hospital, which will be completed in 2008, they will be surrounded by images of butterflies, the ultimate symbol of transformation. Patient rooms will be more like home, and children will be able to exercise some control over their personal space. A huge garden, embodying transformation as well as energy and connection, will be visible from all rooms and accessible to children and their families. "Before, design was a guessing game; it was hit or miss," says Del Sole. "But we know now that at the deepest level this hospital has to be about transformation." So when a sick child, or a worried parent, or a harassed nurse walks into this hospital, a deep and reassuring recognition of the potential beauties of transformation will resonate unconsciously.

Waves of cola. Zaltman, obviously, is not the only person peering into the mind of the consumer. In a neuroscientific take on the time-honored blind taste test, Coke and Pepsi once again squared off. In *Blink*, Gladwell describes how the Coca-Cola Co. made a costly mistake in using data from blind taste tests between Coke and Pepsi—in which Pepsi was emphatically preferred by most cola drinkers—to change the recipe and create the marketing debacle that was New Coke. Still, even with a less preferred taste, Coke remains No. 1 in the soft-drink world. More recent research that was published after Gladwell's book was finished may explain why.

Researchers at Baylor College of Medicine offered 67 committed Coke and Pepsi drinkers a choice, and in blind testing, they preferred Pepsi. When they were shown the company logos before they drank, however, 3 out of 4 preferred Coke. The researchers scanned the brains of the participants during the test and discovered that the Coke label created wild activity in the part of the brain associated with memories and self-image, while Pepsi, though tasting better to most, did little to these feel-good centers in the brain. P. Reed Montague, director of the Brown Foundation Human Neuroimaging laboratory at Baylor, explained when the study was released last October: "There's a huge effect of the Coke label on brain activity related to the control of actions, the dredging up of memories and self-image." The mere red-and-white image of Coke made the hippocampus, our brain's vault of memories, and the dorsolateral prefrontal cortex, which is responsible for many of our higher human brain functions like working memory and what is called executive function or control of behavior, light up. The point, says Montague, is that "there is a response in the brain which leads to a behavioral effect." And curiously, it has nothing to do with conscious preference.

The dog comes up and begins to sniff. If it remembers you, and you were a nice person, then instantly it wags its tail, perhaps even deigns to lick your wrist. It may avoid you. It may associate you with food or with a swift kick. And all those images, all those associations are evoked by one healthy whiff.

Aside from the basic inhibition against walking up to someone and sniffing, humans are no different. "An odor is not just a name—it is a whole context," says psychiatrist Dolores Malaspina of the New York State Psychiatric Institute and the Columbia University Medical Center. Olfactory information is "privileged," Malaspina explains, since it is the only one of our five senses that does not make a brief stop at the brain's relay station, the thalamus, before going to the ever so intellectual prefrontal cortex. Smell is unmediated, unfiltered, and it hits the prefrontal cortex with a wallop of intensity. Researchers have found that smell plays a strong role in our mating choices, even without our knowing it. And when female roommates synchronize their menstrual cycles, it is because the unconscious perception of odor sets off the endocrine system. Our brains, says Malaspina, "beginning with fetal development, are laid out to give precedence to olfactory perception."

The adaptive unconscious helps us to understand the correct meaning of a statement like "prostitutes appeal to the pope."

But what happens if olfactory perception doesn't work properly? Malaspina and other researchers are looking at the olfactory sense in emotional disorders and have found some intriguing results. While schizophrenia is seen as a disorder of hallucinations and delusions, a more compelling and disruptive element of the disorder is social impairment. Some people with schizophrenia can't seem to read social cues, or manage social relationships, or summon a social context for whatever encounter they are experiencing. And while hallucinations and delusions can be controlled often through medication, these basic social impairments cause far more difficulty in dealing with the daily demands of life.

Research has shown that many people with schizophrenia can also suffer from "clinically meaningful olfactory impairment," which includes dysfunction in higher brain centers such as the parietal lobes—the part of the brain that's responsible for integrating sensory output so as to understand something, like reading social cues or contextualizing those cues. Just as a smell can elicit an immediate image of a particular time and place, lacking that ability can deprive someone of a basic social and emotional anchor in life. "What we are learning is that smell is a good window into the unconscious basis for sociability and social interest," says Malaspina. "There is a tremendous explosion of interest in this forgotten sense. And it was under our noses all the time."

The scenario occurs in hospital rooms throughout the world, thousands of times every day. A brain-damaged father or mother or child lies in bed, not completely unconscious, not in a coma, but demonstrating only flickering consciousness, small behaviors that show there is some evidence of the person who once was there, some evidence that this person perhaps knows friends and family members are near by. Medically, these patients are categorized as existing in a minimally conscious state of awareness; it is estimated that there are 100,000 to 300,000 Americans in such a state right now. Sometimes these patients are able to actually utter the name of an object or to follow a very simple command. But for friends and family, they are no longer themselves. And because they find language so difficult, it is also assumed that they are unlikely to follow conversations.

The eye of the mind? But in a stunning study published this month in the journal *Neurology*, researchers used functional magnetic resonance imaging to study the brains of two minimally conscious patients and compared them with the brains of seven healthy men and woman. The scans revealed that the minimally conscious patients had less than half of the brain activity of the others. But then all the subjects were played a tape made by a family member or friend, recounting happy memories and shared experiences. One minimally conscious man listened to his sister reminiscing about her wedding and about the toast that he made. The result was astonishing: All those who were scanned, including the minimally conscious patients, shared similar brain activity, some with activation in the visual cortex. "This shows that there is a life of the mind beyond what is apparent," says Joseph Fins, chief of the medical ethics division of New York-Presbyterian Hospital-Weill Cornell Medical Center. But Fins, who was not involved in the study, points out that philosophical questions also emerge. "Does this mean that they are seeing words? Visualizing semantic concepts? Does this in some way conceptualize consciousness?" As Zaltman points out, language is only the narrowest determination of our thoughts. This study shows that our brains, even damaged brains, are exquisitely attuned to that fact.

For the brain damaged and for the healthy, despite the evidence of the prevalence of the unconscious in our daily lives, even as fervent a believer as Zaltman urges a bit of caution. "I don't think we know what the batting average is for purely rational reasons or reasons dressed up that way, or reasons dressed up as purely intuition. Both can get us into trouble—often do. And both serve us well." It is that great tension between the two, the intermingling of the known and the unknown, the conscious and the unconscious, the 5 percent and the 95 percent, that the pioneers exploring this vast and intricate universe of our minds will continue to probe. But there will most likely never be a complete understanding. After all, the enigmas of the mind, and the mechanics of the brain, will forever define the ultimate mystery of simply being human.

UNIT 6
Emotion and Motivation

Unit Selections

18. **Unconscious Emotion**, Piotr Winkielman and Kent C. Berridge
19. **Feeling Smart: The Science of Emotional Intelligence**, Daisy Grewal and Peter Salovey
20. **The Value of Positive Emotions**, Barbara L. Fredrickson
21. **Ambition: Why Some People Are Most Likely to Succeed**, Jeffrey Kluger
22. **Obesity—An Epidemic of the Twenty-First Century: An Update for Psychiatrists**, Richard I.G. Holt

Key Points to Consider

- What is motivation? What is an emotion? How are the two related to each other? Do you think they are inextricably related to one another?

- Are humans the only creatures that experience emotions, both positive and negative? Why did you answer as you did? Is your answer based on methodologically sound science or based on anecdote?

- From where do emotions originate? Why did you give the answer you did? Are various emotions controlled by different factors; for example, does the brain control some emotions while the situation controls other emotions? What role does the nervous system play in emotionality?

- Are we always aware of our emotions or are some emotions unconsciously stimulated and experienced? How? Why? What evidence can you provide that unconscious emotions exist?

- What are some positive emotions? What are some examples of negative emotions? Do you think there is an "appropriate" emotion for every situation? Why are some people unemotional and others expressive and animated? Why do you think psychologists are switching their emphasis from negative emotions, such as fear, to positive emotions, such as joy?

- What is emotional intelligence? Does everyone possess it? Is it a good trait to have? If an individual does not possess it, can he or she acquire it? How do people with high levels of emotional intelligence differ from people with low levels?

- Do you sometimes feel unmotivated or overwhelmed by too much to do? How can setting goals motivate you? Do you know how to prioritize goals such that the most important ones are attended to first? What are some of the more productive methods for setting goals?

- What is achievement motivation? How does it differ from general goal setting? Who seems to have lots of achievement motivation? From where does this motive come - nature or nurture?

- What is obesity? Why is obesity such a problem in modern American society? Why are psychologists and health care professionals concerned about the obesity epidemic? Why is the government concerned? What can each of us do to address the epidemic? Whose responsibility is the obesity epidemic anyway - the individual's or society's? Why did you come to the conclusion you did in answer to this last question?

Student Website

www.mhcls.com/online

Internet References

Further information regarding these websites may be found in this book's preface or online.

Emotional Intelligence Discovery
   http://www.cwrl.utexas.edu/~bump/Hu305/3/3/3/
John Suler's Teaching Clinical Psychology Site
   http://www.rider.edu/users/suler/tcp.html
Nature vs. Nurture: Gergen Dialogue with Winifred Gallagher
   http://www.pbs.org/newshour/gergen/gallagher_5-14.html

Jasmine's sister was a working mother and always reminded Jasmine about how exciting life on the road as a sales representative was. Jasmine stayed home because she loved her children, two-year old Min, four-year-old Chi'Ming, and newborn Yuan. On the day of the particular incident described below, Jasmine was having a difficult time with the children. The baby, Yuan, had been crying all day from colic. The other two children had been bickering over their toys. Jasmine, realizing that it was already 5:15 and her husband would be home any minute, frantically started preparing dinner. She wanted to fix a nice dinner so that she and her husband could eat after the children went to bed, then relax and enjoy each other.

This was not to be. Jasmine sat waiting for her no-show husband. When he finally walked in the door at 10:15, Jasmine was furious. His excuse that his boss had invited the whole office for dinner didn't reduce Jasmine's ire. Jasmine reasoned that her husband could have called to say that he wouldn't be home for dinner; he could have taken five minutes to do that. He said he did but the phone was busy. Jasmine berated her husband. Her face was taut and red with rage. Her voice wavered as she escalated her decibel level. Suddenly, bursting into tears, she ran into the living room. Her husband retreated to the safety of their bedroom and the respite that a deep sleep would bring.

Exhausted and disappointed, Jasmine sat alone and pondered why she was so angry with her husband. Was she just tired? Was she frustrated by negotiating with young children all day and simply wanted another adult around once in a while? Was she secretly worried and jealous that her husband was seeing another woman and had lied about his whereabouts? Was she combative because her husband's and her sister's lives seemed so much fuller than her own life? Jasmine was unsure just how she felt and why she exploded in such rage at her husband, someone she loved dearly.

This story, while sad and gender stereotypical, is not necessarily unrealistic when it comes to emotions. There are times when we are moved to deep emotion. On other occasions when we expect waterfalls of tears, we find that our eyes are dry or simply a little misty. What are these strange things we call emotions? What motivates us to rage at someone we love? And why do Americans seem to autopsy our every mood?

These questions and others have inspired psychologists to study emotions and motivation. The above episode about Jasmine, besides introducing these topics to you, also illustrates why these two topics are usually interrelated in psychology. Some emotions are pleasant, so pleasant that we are motivated to keep them going. Pleasant emotions are exemplified by love, pride, and joy. Other emotions are terribly draining and oppressive—so negative that we hope they will be over as soon as possible. Negative emotions are exemplified by anger, grief, and jealousy. Emotions and motivation and their relationship to each other are the focus of this unit.

Five articles round out this unit. The first three pertain to emotions while the last two are related to motivation. "Unconscious Emotion" is the first article; the author discusses whether or not emotions are volitional (voluntary). Psychologists traditionally have believed that we are aware of our emotions. Based on con-temporary research, the author claims this is not the case. Some emotions are unconscious such that we remain ignorant of them even though they exert influence over us.

The second article, "Feeling Smart: The Science of Emotional Intelligence," reveals information about a new but widely accepted concept in psychology—emotional intelligence. A person high in emotional intelligence is acutely aware of others' as well as his or her own emotional states. Moreover, the individual high in emotional intelligence manages emotional situations very well. Authors Daisy Grewal and Peter Salovey examine this concept in some detail.

The next selection in this unit examines a concept traditionally related to emotions—motivation. Various motives guide our behaviors and emotions, such as the need to stay safe, the need for food and water, the need to succeed, and so on. For example, when we experience a positive emotion (e.g. happiness) we are motivated to maintain that feeling but are just as motivated to short-circuit negative emotions, such as sadness.

Jeffrey Kluger, another author for *Time* magazine, reveals interesting information about ambition. Kluger connects ambition to what psychologists have conventionally called achievement motivation, the need to be successful. Who seeks achievement and why they do are the focus of this unit's penultimate article.

Finally, we consider one last article on motivation. The article is about a specific motive - hunger - and its related behavior, eating. In particular, the topic of this last article is overeating, a phenomenon becoming all too significant in America. Americans are growing larger and larger by the minute. We are surrounded by food advertisements and are encouraged to super size everything for only 99 cents more. The obesity epidemic is now so omnipresent that the government might step in. Psychologists are debating whether obesity is the individual's responsibility or the government's. In either regard, the individual's health is at risk.

Unconscious Emotion

Piotr Winkielman and Kent C. Berridge

ABSTRACT—Conscious feelings have traditionally been viewed as a central and necessary ingredient of emotion. Here we argue that emotion also can be genuinely unconscious. We describe evidence that positive and negative reactions can be elicited subliminally and remain inaccessible to introspection. Despite the absence of subjective feelings in such cases, subliminally induced affective reactions still influence people's preference judgments and even the amount of beverage they consume. This evidence is consistent with evolutionary considerations suggesting that systems underlying basic affective reactions originated prior to systems for conscious awareness. The idea of unconscious emotion is also supported by evidence from affective neuroscience indicating that subcortical brain systems underlie basic "liking" reactions. More research is needed to clarify the relations and differences between conscious and unconscious emotion, and their underlying mechanisms. However, even under the current state of knowledge, it appears that processes underlying conscious feelings can become decoupled from processes underlying emotional reactions, resulting in genuinely unconscious emotion.

To say that people are conscious of their own emotions sounds like a truism. After all, emotions are feelings, so how could one have feelings that are not felt? Of course, people sometimes may be mistaken about the cause of their emotion or may not know why they feel a particular emotion, as when they feel anxious for what seems no particular reason. On occasion, people may even incorrectly construe their own emotional state, as when they angrily deny that they are angry. But many psychologists presume that the emotion itself is intrinsically conscious, and that with proper motivation and attention, it can be brought into the full light of awareness. So, at least, goes the traditional view.

Our view goes a bit further. We suggest that under some conditions an emotional process may remain entirely unconscious, even when the person is attentive and motivated to describe his or her feelings correctly (Berridge & Winkielman, 2003; Winkielman, Berridge, & Wilbarger, in press). Such an emotional process may nevertheless drive the person's behavior and physiological reactions, even while remaining inaccessible to conscious awareness. In short, we propose the existence of genuinely unconscious emotions.

The Traditional View: Emotion as A Conscious Experience

The assumption that emotions are always conscious has been shared by some of the most influential psychologists in history. In his famous article "What Is an Emotion," James (1884) proposed that emotion is a perception of bodily changes. This perception forms a conscious feeling, which is a necessary ingredient of both simple affective states, such as pleasure and pain, and more complex emotions, such as love or pride. Con-

scious feeling is exactly what distinguishes emotion from other mental states. Without it, "we find that we have nothing left behind, no 'mind-stuff' out of which the emotion can be constituted …" (p. 193). For Freud (1950), too, emotions themselves were always conscious, even if their underlying causes sometimes were not: "It is surely of the essence of an emotion that we should feel it, i.e. that it should enter consciousness" (pp. 109–110).

The assumption that affective reactions are conscious is widely shared in the contemporary literature on emotion. Explaining how most researchers use the term "affect," Frijda (1999) said that the term "primarily refers to hedonic experience, the experience of pleasure and pain" (p. 194). Clore (1994) unequivocally titled one of his essays "Why Emotions Are Never Unconscious" and argued that subjective feeling is a necessary (although not a sufficient) condition for emotion. In short, psychologists past and present generally have agreed that a conscious feeling is a primary or even a necessary ingredient of affect and emotion.

Implicit Emotion and Unconscious Affect

By contrast, it is now widely accepted that cognitive processes and states can be unconscious (occurring below awareness) or implicit (occurring without attention or intention). So, it may not require much of a leap to consider the possibility of unconscious or implicit emotion. As Kihlstrom (1999) put it,

Paralleling the usage of these descriptors in the cognitive unconscious, "explicit emotion" refers to the person's conscious awareness of an emotion, feeling, or mood state; "implicit emotion", by contrast, refers to changes in experience, thought, or action that are attributable to one's emotional state, independent of his or her conscious awareness of that state. (p. 432)

Unconscious Elicitation of Conscious Affective Reactions

Research advances in the past few years challenge the traditional view by demonstrating "unconscious emotion," at least in a limited sense of unconscious causation. Several studies have shown that stimuli presented below awareness can elicit an affective reaction that is itself consciously felt. An example is subliminal induction of the mere-exposure effect, that is, a positive response to repeatedly presented items. In one study, some participants were first subliminally exposed to several repeated neutral stimuli consisting of random visual patterns. Later, those participants reported being in a better mood—a conscious feeling state—than participants who had been subliminally exposed to neutral stimuli that had not been repeatedly presented (Monahan, Murphy, & Zajonc, 2000). In other studies, changes in self-reported mood have been elicited by subliminal presentation of positive or negative images, such as pictures of snakes and spiders presented to phobic individuals (Öhman, Flykt, & Lundqvist, 2000).

But asserting that subliminal stimuli may cause emotion is different from asserting that emotional reactions themselves can ever be unconscious (Berridge & Winkielman, 2003; Kihlstrom, 1999). The research we just mentioned still fits into the conventional view that once emotions are caused, they are always conscious. In fact, these studies relied on introspective reports of conscious feelings to demonstrate the presence of emotion once it was unconsciously caused.

So the question remains: Can one be unconscious not only of the causes of emotion, but also of one's own emotional reaction itself—even if that emotional reaction is intense enough to alter one's behavior? Studies from our lab suggest that the answer is yes. Under some conditions, people can have subliminally triggered emotional reactions that drive judgment and behavior, even in the absence of any conscious feelings accompanying these reactions.

Uncorrected and Unremembered Emotional Reactions

In an initial attempt to demonstrate unconscious emotion, a series of studies examined participants' ratings of neutral stimuli, such as Chinese ideographs, preceded by subliminally presented happy or angry faces (Winkielman, Zajonc, & Schwarz, 1997). Some participants in those studies were asked to monitor changes in their conscious feelings, and told not to use their feelings as a source of their preference ratings. Specifically, experimental instructions informed those participants that their feelings might be "contaminated" by irrelevant factors, such as hidden pictures (Study 1) or music playing in the background (Study 2). Typically, such instructions eliminate the influence of conscious feelings on evaluative judgments (Clore, 1994). However, even for participants told to disregard their feelings, the subliminally presented happy faces increased and sublimi-

nally presented angry faces decreased preference ratings of the neutral stimuli. This failure to correct for invalid feelings indicates that participants might not have experienced any conscious reactions in the first place. Indeed, after the experiment, participants did not remember experiencing any mood changes when asked about what they had felt during the rating task. Still, memory is not infallible. A skeptic could argue that participants had conscious feelings immediately after subliminal exposure to emotional faces, but simply failed to remember the feelings later. Thus, it is open to debate whether these studies demonstrate unconscious emotion.

Unconscious Emotional Reactions Strong Enough to Change Behavior

We agreed that stronger evidence was needed. Proof of unconscious emotion requires showing that participants are unable to report a conscious feeling at the same time their behavior reveals the presence of an emotional reaction. Ideally, the emotional reaction should be strong enough to change behavior with some consequences for the individual. To obtain such evidence, we assessed participants' pouring and drinking of a novel beverage after they were subliminally exposed to several emotional facial expressions (Berridge & Winkielman, 2003; Winkielman et al., in press). Participants were first asked if they were thirsty. Next, they were subliminally exposed to several emotional expressions (happy, neutral, or angry) embedded in a cognitive task requiring participants to classify a clearly visible neutral face as male or female. Immediately afterward, some participants rated their feelings on scales assessing emotional experience and then were given a novel lemon-lime beverage to consume and evaluate. Other participants consumed and evaluated the beverage before rating their feelings. Specifically, in Study 1, participants were asked to pour themselves a cup of the beverage from a pitcher and then drink from the cup, whereas in Study 2, participants were asked to take a small sip of the beverage from a prepared cup and then rate it on various dimensions, including monetary value.

In both studies, conscious feelings were not influenced by subliminal presentation of emotional faces, regardless of whether participants rated their feelings on a simple scale from positive to negative mood or from high to low arousal, or on a multi-item scale asking about specific emotions, such as contentment or irritation. That is, participants did not feel more positive after subliminally presented happy expressions than after subliminally presented neutral expressions. Nor did they feel more negative after angry expressions than after neutral expressions. Yet participants' consumption and ratings of the drink were influenced by those subliminal stimuli—especially when participants were thirsty. Specifically, thirsty participants poured significantly more drink from the pitcher and drank more from their cup after happy faces than after angry faces (Study 1). Thirsty participants were also willing to pay about twice as much for the drink after happy than after angry expressions (Study 2). The modulating role of thirst indicates that unconscious emotional reactions acted through basic biopsychological mechanisms that determine reactions to incentives, such as a drink, rather than through cognitive mechanisms influencing interpretation of the stimulus (Berridge & Winkielman, 2003; Winkielman et al., 2002).

In summary, the studies just described show that subliminally presented emotional faces can cause affective reactions that alter consumption behavior, without eliciting conscious feelings at the moment the affective reactions are caused. Because the influence of emotional faces on consumption behavior was observed also for those participants who rated their feelings immediately after the subliminal presentation of the faces, these results cannot be explained by failures of memory. Thus, we propose that these results demonstrate unconscious affect in the strong sense of the term—affect that is powerful enough to alter behavior, but that people are simply not aware of, even when attending to their feelings.

Support From Evolution and Neuroscience

From the standpoint of evolution and neuroscience, there are good reasons to suppose that at least some forms of emotional reaction can exist independently of subjective correlates. Evolutionarily speaking, the ability to have conscious feelings is probably a late achievement compared with the ability to have behavioral affective reactions to emotional stimuli (LeDoux, 1996). Basic affective reactions are widely shared by animals, including reptiles and fish, and at least in some species may not involve conscious awareness comparable to that in humans. The original function of emotion was to allow the organism to react appropriately to positive or negative events, and conscious feelings might not always have been required.

The neurocircuitry needed for basic affective responses, such as a "liking' reaction[1] to a pleasant sensation or a fear reaction to a threatening stimulus, is largely contained in emotional brain structures that lie below the cortex, such as the nucleus accumbens, amygdala, hypothalamus, and even lower brain stem (Berridge, 2003; LeDoux, 1996). These subcortical structures evolved early and may carry out limited operations that are essentially preconscious, compared with the elaborate human cortex at the top of the brain, which is more involved in conscious emotional feelings. Yet even limited subcortical structures on their own are capable of some basic affective reactions. A dramatic demonstration of this point comes from affective neuroscience studies with anencephalic human infants. The brain of such infants is congenitally malformed, possessing only a brain stem, and lacking nearly all structures at the top or front of the brain, including the entire cortex. Yet sweet tastes of sugar still elicit positive facial expressions of liking from anencephalic infants, whereas bitter tastes elicit negative facial expressions of disgust (Steiner, 1973).

Even in normal brains, the most effective "brain tweaks" so far discovered for enhancing liking and related affective reactions all involve deep brain structures below the cortex. Thus, animal studies have shown that liking for sweetness increases after a drug that activates opioid receptors is injected into the nucleus accumbens (a reward-related structure at the base of the front of the brain). Liking reactions to sugar can even be en-

hanced by injecting a drug that activates other receptors into the brain stem, which is perhaps the most basic component of the brain. Such examples reflect the persisting importance of early-evolved neurocircuitry in generating behavioral emotional reactions in modern mammalian brains (Berridge, 2003; LeDoux, 1996). In short, evidence from affective neuroscience suggests that basic affective reactions are mediated largely by brain structures deep below the cortex, raising the possibility that these reactions might not be intrinsically accessible to conscious awareness.

Key Questions For Future Research

As we have argued, there are good theoretical reasons why some emotional reactions might be unconscious, and we suggest that our recent empirical evidence actually provides an example. However, several critical issues need to be addressed by future research.

The studies discussed here focused only on basic liking-disliking, so it is possible that the crucial property of unconscious emotion is simply positive-negative valence, rather than qualitative distinctions associated with categorical emotion (fear, anger, disgust, joy, etc.). However, evidence suggests that subcortical circuitry may be capable of some qualitative differentiation. For example, human neuroimaging studies reveal differential activation of the amygdala in response to consciously presented facial expressions of fear versus anger (Whalen, 1998). If future research shows that subliminally presented expressions of fear, anger, disgust, and sadness can create qualitatively different physiological and behavioral reactions, all without conscious experience, then there may indeed exist implicit affective processes deserving the label "unconscious emotion" in its strongest sense. Studies that simultaneously measure psychophysiology, behavior, and self-reports of emotion could be particularly useful to address such issues (Winkielman, Berntson, & Cacioppo, 2001).

The studies discussed here employed basic affective stimuli, such as subliminally presented facial expressions, to influence emotional behavior without eliciting conscious feelings. Future studies might address whether more complex stimuli that derive their positive or negative value from a person's cultural environment can also influence emotional behavior without eliciting any accompanying feelings. A related question concerns whether stimuli presented above the threshold of awareness can also change emotional behavior and physiology without influencing feelings.

The studies described here suggest that under some conditions emotional reactions are genuinely unconscious. But obviously many emotional states are conscious, even when elicited with subliminal stimuli (Monahan et al., 2000; Öhman et al., 2000). What determines when a basic emotional reaction is accompanied by conscious feelings? Is it possible for even a strong emotional reaction to be unconscious? What are the neural mechanisms by which emotion is made conscious?

How do behavioral consequences of conscious and unconscious reactions differ?

Finally, a question of practical importance to many emotion researchers, as well as clinicians, concerns the meaning of people's reports of their own emotions. The existence of verifiable but unconscious emotional reactions does not mean that subjective feelings are merely "icing on the emotional cake." At least, that is not our view. We believe that self-reports of feelings have a major place in emotion research and treatment. However, it is also clear that psychologists should not limit themselves to subjective experiences. A combination of approaches and techniques, from psychology and human and animal affective neuroscience, will best lead to understanding the relation between conscious and unconscious emotions.

Note

1. We use the term "liking" to indicate an unconscious reaction, not a conscious feeling of pleasure.

References

Berridge, K. C. (2003). Pleasures of the brain. *Brain and Cognition, 52,* 106–128.

Berridge, K. C., & Winkielman, P. (2003). What is an unconscious emotion: The case for unconscious 'liking.' *Cognition and Emotion, 17,* 181–211.

Clore, G. L. (1994). Why emotions are never unconscious. In P. Ekman & R.J. Davidson (Eds.), *The nature of emotion: Fundamental questions* (pp. 285–290). New York: Oxford University Press.

Freud, S. (1950). *Collected papers,* Vol. 4 (J. Riviere, Trans.). London: Hogarth Press and Institute of Psychoanalysis.

Frijda, N. H. (1999). Emotions and hedonic experience. In D. Kahneman, E. Diener, & N. Schwarz (Eds.), *Well-being: The foundations of hedonic psychology* (pp. 190–210). New York: Russell Sage Foundation.

James, W. (1884). What is an emotion. *Mind, 9,* 188–205.

Kihlstrom, J. F. (1999). The psychological unconscious. In L.A. Pervin & O. P. John (Eds.), *Handbook of personality: Theory and research* (2nd ed., pp. 424–442). New York: Guilford Press.

LeDoux, J. (1996). *The emotional brain: The mysterious underpinnings of emotional life.* New York: Simon & Schuster.

Monahan, J. L., Murphy, S. T., & Zajonc, R. B. (2000). Subliminal mere exposure: Specific, general, and diffuse effects. *Psychological Science, 11,* 462–466.

Öhman, A., Flykt, A., & Lundqvist, D. (2000). Unconscious emotion: Evolutionary perspectives, psychophysiological data and neuropsychological mechanisms. In R. D. Lane, L. Nadel, & G. Ahern (Eds.), *Cognitive neuroscience of emotion* (pp. 296–327). New York: Oxford University Press.

Steiner, J. E. (1973). The gustofacial response: Observation on normal and anencephalic newborn infants. *Symposium on Oral Sensation and Perception, 4,* 254–278.

Whalen, P. J. (1998). Fear, vigilance, and ambiguity: Initial neuroimaging studies of the human amygdala. *Current Directions in Psychological Science, 7,* 177–188.

Winkielman, P., Berntson, G. G., & Caccioppo, J. T. (2001). The psychophysiological perspective on the social mind. In A. Tesser & N. Schwarz (Eds.), *Blackwell handbook of social psychology: Intraindividual processes* (pp. 89–108). Oxford, England: Blackwell.

Winkielman, P., Berridge, K. C., & Wilbarger, J. (in press). Unconscious affective reactions to masked happy versus angry faces influence consumption behavior and judgments of value. *Personality and Social Psychology Bulletin.*

Winkielman, P., Zajonc, R. B., & Schwarz, N. (1997). Subliminal affective priming resists attributional interventions. *Cognition and Emotion, 11,* 433–465.

PIOTR WINKIELMAN, University of California, San Diego, and **KENT C. BERRIDGE,** University of Michigan.

Feeling Smart: The Science of Emotional Intelligence

A new idea in psychology has matured and shows promise of explaining how attending to emotions can help us in everyday life

DAISY GREWAL AND PETER SALOVEY

Over the past decade almost everyone tuned in to American popular culture has heard the term *emotional intelligence*. As a new concept, emotional intelligence has been a hit: It has been the subject of several books, including a best seller, and myriad talk-show discussions and seminars for schools and organizations. Today you can hire a coach to help you raise your "EQ," your emotional quotient—or your child's.

Despite (or perhaps because of) its high public profile, emotional intelligence has attracted considerable scientific criticism. Some of the controversy arises from the fact that popular and scientific definitions of emotional intelligence differ sharply. In addition, measuring emotional intelligence has not been easy. Despite these difficulties, research on emotional intelligence has managed to sustain itself and in fact shows considerable promise as a serious line of scientific inquiry. It turns out that emotional intelligence can indeed be measured, as a set of mental abilities, and that doing so is an informative exercise that can help individuals understand the role of emotions in their everyday lives.

Ten years after the appearance of that bestselling book and a *TIME* magazine cover that asked "What's your EQ?" it seems sensible to ask what is known, scientifically, about emotional intelligence. In the history of modern psychology, the concept represents a stage in the evolution of our thinking about the relation between passion and reason and represents an important outgrowth of new theories of intelligence. Work in this subfield has produced a four-factor model of emotional intelligence that serves as a guide for empirical research. In this article we will explain ways of assessing emotional intelligence using ability-based tests and some of the findings that have resulted from this method.

Before "Emotional Intelligence"

Philosophers have debated the relation between thought and emotions for at least two millennia. The Stoics of ancient Greece and Rome believed emotion far too heated and unpredictable to be of much use to rational thought. Emotion was also strongly associated with women, in their view, and therefore representative of the weak, inferior aspects of humanity. The stereotype of women as the more "emotional" sex is one that persists today. Even though various romantic movements embraced emotion over the centuries, the Stoic view of emotions as more or less irrational persisted in one form or another well into the 20th century.

But many notions were upended during the rapid development of modern psychology in the 20th century. Setting the stage for a new way of thinking about emotions and thought, psychologists articulated broader definitions of intelligence and also new perspectives on the relation between feeling and thinking. As early as the 1930s, psychometrician Robert Thorndike mentioned the possibility that people might have a "social intelligence"—an ability to perceive their own and others' internal states, motivations and behaviors, and act accordingly. In 1934 David Wechsler, the psychologist whose name today attaches to two well-known intelligence tests, wrote about the "nonintellective" aspects of a person that contribute to overall intelligence. Thorndike's and Wechsler's statements were, however, speculations. Even though social intelligence seemed a definite possibility, Thorndike admitted that there existed little scientific evidence of its presence. A similar conclusion was reached by psychometric expert Lee Cronbach, who in 1960 declared that, after half a century of speculation, social intelligence remained "undefined and unmeasured."

But the 1980s brought a surge of new interest in expanding the definition of intelligence. In 1983 Howard Gardner of Harvard University became famous overnight when, in the book *Frames of Mind*, he outlined seven distinct forms of intelligence. Gardner proposed an "intrapersonal intelligence" very similar to the current conceptualization of emotional intelligence. "The core capacity at work here," he wrote, "is access to one's own feeling life—one's range of affects or emotions: the capacity instantly to effect discriminations among these feelings and, eventually, to label them, to enmesh them in symbolic codes, to draw upon them as a means of understanding and guiding one's behavior."

Is "emotional intelligence," then, simply a new name for social intelligence and other already-defined "intelligences"? We hope to clear up this thorny question by explaining just what we attempt to measure when assessing emotional intelligence. Certainly it can be seen as a type of social intelligence. But we prefer to explicitly focus on the processing of emotions and knowledge about emotion-related information and suggest that this constitutes its own form of intelligence. Social intelligence is very broadly defined, and partly for this reason the pertinent skills involved have remained elusive to scientists.

Emotional intelligence is a more focused concept. Dealing with emotions certainly has important implications for social relationships, but emotions also contribute to other aspects of life. Each of us has a need to set priorities, orient positively toward future endeavors and repair negative moods before they spiral into anxiety and depression. The concept of emotional intelligence isolates a specific set of skills embedded within the abilities that are broadly encompassed by the notion of social intelligence.

Emotion and Thinking

New understandings of the relation between thought and emotion have strengthened the scientific foundation of the study of emotional intelligence. Using a simple decision-making task, neurologist Antonio R. Damasio and his colleagues at the University of Iowa have provided convincing evidence that emotion and reason are essentially inseparable. When making decisions, people often focus on the logical pros and cons of the choices they face. However, Damasio has shown that without feelings, the decisions we make may not be in our best interest.

In the early 1990s Damasio had people participate in a gambling task in which the goal is to maximize profit on a loan of play money. Participants were instructed to select 100 cards, one at a time, from four different decks. The experimenter arranged the cards such that two of the decks provided larger payoffs ($100 compared to only $50) but also doled out larger penalties at unpredictable intervals. Players who chose from the higher-reward, higher risk decks lost a net of $250 every 10 cards; those choosing the $50 decks gained a net of $250 every 10 cards.

One group of participants in this study had been identified as having lesions to the ventromedial prefrontal cortex of the brain. Patients with this type of brain damage have normal intellectual function but are unable to use emotion in making decisions. The other group was normal, meaning that their brains were fully intact. Because there was no way for any of the players to calculate precisely which decks were riskier, they had to rely on their "gut" feelings to avoid losing money.

Damasio's group demonstrated that the brain-lesion patients failed to pay attention to these feelings (which he deems "somatic markers") and subsequently lost significantly more money than the normal participants. Therefore, defects in the brain that impair emotion and feeling detection can subse-quently impair decision-making. Damasio concluded that "individuals make judgments not only by assessing the severity of outcomes, but also and primarily in terms of their emotional quality." This experiment demonstrates that emotions and thought processes are closely connected. Whatever notions we draw from our Stoic and Cartesian heritages, separating thinking and feeling is not necessarily more adaptive and may, in some cases, lead to disastrous consequences.

The Four-Branch Model

The term "emotional intelligence" was perhaps first used in an unpublished dissertation in 1986. One of us (Salovey), along with John D. Mayer of the University of New Hampshire, introduced it to scientific psychology in 1990, defining emotional intelligence as "the ability to monitor one's own and others' feelings, to discriminate among them, and to use this information to guide one's thinking and action."

Some critics have seen the concept of emotional intelligence as a mere outgrowth of the late-20th-century Zeitgeist—and indeed, as we reflect in the conclusion to this article, today the term has a vibrant pop-culture life of its own. But within psychology, the concept developed out of a growing emphasis on research on the interaction of emotion and thought. In the late 1970s psychologists conducted experiments that looked at a number of seemingly unrelated topics at the interface of feeling and thinking: the effect of depression on memory, the perception of emotion in facial expressions, the functional importance of regulating or expressing emotion.

Emotional intelligence is one of the concepts that emerged from this work. It integrates a number of the results into a related set of skills that can be measured and differentiated from personality and social skills; within psychology it can be defined as an intelligence because it is a quantifiable and indeed a measurable aspect of the individual's capacity to carry out abstract thought and to learn and adapt to the environment. Emotional intelligence can be shown to operate on emotional information in the same way that other types of intelligence might operate on a broken computer or what a photographer sees in her viewfinder.

Interested in helping the field of emotions develop a theory that would organize the numerous efforts to find individual difference in emotion-related processes, Salovey and Mayer proposed a four-branch model of emotional intelligence that emphasized four domains of related skills: (a) the ability to perceive emotions accurately; (b) the ability to use emotions to facilitate thinking and reasoning; (c) the ability to understand emotions, especially the language of emotions; and (d) the ability to manage emotions both in oneself and in others. This four-branch emotional intelligence model proposes that individuals differ in these skills and that these differences have consequences at home, school and work, and in social relations.

Perceiving and Using Emotions

The first domain of emotional intelligence, *perceiving emotions,* includes the abilities involved in identifying emotions in faces, voices, pictures, music and other stimuli. For example, the individual who excels at perceiving emotions can quickly tell when his friend is upset by accurately decoding his friend's facial expressions.

One might consider this the most basic skill involved in emotional intelligence because it makes all other processing of emotional information possible. In addition, our skill at reading faces is one of the attributes humans share across cultures. Paul Ekman of the University of California, San Francisco showed pictures of Americans expressing different emotions to a group of isolated New Guineans. He found that the New Guineans could recognize what emotions were being expressed in the photographs quite accurately, even though they had never encountered an American and had grown up in a completely different culture.

But emotion perception does vary across individuals. A study by Seth D. Pollak at the University of Wisconsin-Madison in 2000, for example, demonstrated that physical abuse might interfere with children's ability to adaptively perceive facial expressions.

Pollak asked abused and nonabused children, aged 8 to 10, to come into the laboratory to play "computer games." The children were shown digitally morphed faces that displayed emotional expressions that ranged from happy to fearful, happy to sad, angry to fearful, or angry to sad. In one of the games, the children were shown a single picture and asked to identify which emotion it expressed. Because all the faces expressed varying degrees of a certain emotion, the investigators were able to discover how the children perceived different facial expressions. They found that the abused children were more likely to categorize a face as angry, even when it showed only a slight amount of anger.

In addition, Pollak measured the brain activity of the children while completing this task using electrodes attached to their scalps. The abused children also exhibited more brain activity when viewing an angry face. This research shows that life experiences can strongly shape the recognition of facial expression. We can speculate that this difference in likelihood to perceive anger may have important consequences for the children's interactions with other people.

The second branch of emotional intelligence, *using emotions,* is the ability to harness emotional information to facilitate other cognitive activities. Certain moods may create mind-sets that are better suited for certain kinds of tasks.

In a clever experiment done during the 1980s, Alice Isen of Cornell University found that being in a happy mood helps people generate more creative solutions to problems. Isen brought undergraduates into the laboratory and induced either a positive mood (by showing them comedy clips) or a neutral mood (by showing them a short segment from a math film).

After watching one of the films, each student was seated at an individual table and given a book of matches, a box of tacks and a candle. Above the table was a corkboard. The students were given 10 minutes to provide a solution to the following challenge: how to affix the candle to the corkboard in such a way that it would burn without dripping wax onto the table. Those students who had watched the comedy films, and were therefore in a happier mood, were more likely to come up with an adequate solu-

tion to the problem: They realized that the task can be easily accomplished by emptying the box, tacking it to the wall and using it as a platform for the candle. It appears that emotional intelligence can facilitate certain tasks; the emotionally intelligent person can utilize pleasant feelings most effectively.

Understanding and Managing Emotion

Mayer and Salovey classified the third and fourth branches of the emotional intelligence model as "strategic" (rather than "experiential") intelligence. The third branch, *understanding emotions,* is the ability to comprehend information about relations between emotions, transitions from one emotion to another, and to label emotions using emotion words. A person who is good at understanding emotions would have the ability to see differences between related emotions, such as between pride and joy. The same individual would also be able to recognize, for instance, that irritation can lead to rage if left unattended.

Boston College psychologist Lisa Feldman Barrett has demonstrated that the ability to differentiate one's emotional states has important implications for well-being. Feldman Barrett and her colleagues asked a group of 53 undergraduates to keep a daily diary of their emotions for two weeks. Specifically, they assessed the most intense emotional experience they had each day by rating the intensity of their experience of nine emotions, represented by words, on a scale from 0, *not at all,* to 4, *very much.* Four of the emotion words related to positive emotion (happiness, joy, enthusiasm, amusement); five related to negative emotion (nervous, angry, sad, ashamed, guilty).

Feldman Barrett and her colleagues then calculated the correlations between reported experiences of positive emotions and also looked at how correlated were reported experiences of negative emotions. A subject whose reports of positive emotions are highly correlated is perceiving less differentiation between positive states. Similarly, larger correlations between the reports of each negative emotion indicate less differentiation between negative states.

At the end of the study, all participants completed a questionnaire assessing the extent to which they engaged in various emotion-regulation strategies during the previous two weeks (for example, "talking to others"). Greater differentiation between positive emotional states had no effect on regulation strategies. But differentiation of negative states clearly did. That is, participants who were able to more specifically pinpoint *what* negative emotion they were feeling each day also engaged in more strategies for managing their emotions. This shows that the ability to distinguish and label emotions may represent an important skill in learning how to handle emotions successfully.

The fourth branch of emotional intelligence is the ability to manage one's emotions as well as the emotions of others. This skill of *managing emotions* is perhaps the most commonly identified aspect of emotional intelligence. Emotional intelligence is far more than simply being able to regulate bad moods effectively. It can also be important to maintain negative emotions when needed. For example, a speaker trying to persuade her audience of some injustice should have the ability to use her own outrage to stir others to action.

An example of how using different strategies for managing emotions can have different consequences is found in the work of James S. Gross of Stanford University, in experiments during the mid-1990s. Gross showed undergraduates video clips from medical procedures, such as amputation, that elicit disgust. The students were divided into three different groups. In the suppression condition, the students were instructed to hide their emotions during the film as much as possible by limiting their facial expressions. In the reappraisal condition, students were instructed to view the film as objectively as possible and to remain emotionally detached from what they were seeing. The third group was given no special instructions before viewing the film. All of the students' reactions to the films were recorded by video camera, and their physiological reactions, such as heart rate and skin conductance, were also measured. In addition, participants were asked to make self-reports of their feelings before, during and after watching the film.

The students in the suppression and reappraisal conditions had strikingly different experiences from watching the film. In the suppression condition, participants were able to successfully reduce the outward experience of their emotions by reducing their facial expressions and other behavioral reactions to the film. However, they showed heightened physiological arousal and reported feeling as much disgust as controls. The participants in the reappraisal condition reported lower levels of disgust upon watching the film while not displaying any heightened physical arousal (compared to controls). Gross's work demonstrates that there might be important, and sometimes hidden, physical costs for those individuals who chronically suppress expression of their negative emotions; nevertheless, monitoring and evaluating one's emotions may be strategically useful.

Measuring Emotional Intelligence

Any attribute being suggested as a form of intelligence must meet the standards of psychometrics, the field of psychological measurement. Scientists must be able to show that tests do not merely capture personality traits or information about other abilities. Three approaches to measuring emotional intelligence have been used: self-report tests, reports made by others and ability-based tests. Self-report tests were developed first and continue to be widely used, owing to the ease with which they can be administered and scored. Test-takers agree or disagree with items that attempt to capture various aspects of perceived emotional intelligence. For example, the popular Self-Report Emotional Intelligence Test (SREIT), authored by Nicola Schutte, asks respondents to rate how much they agree with such items as "I have control over my emotions," and "(other people find it easy to confide in me.)"

Reports made by others are commonly collected using "360" instruments. People who frequently interact with one another (such as friends and colleagues) are asked to rate one another's apparent degree of emotional intelligence. These instruments commonly contain items similar to those used in self-report tests, such as the statement "This person has control over his or her emotions."

Unfortunately, self-report tests assess self-estimates of attributes that often extend beyond definitions of emotional intelligence. They tend to incorporate facets of personality and character traditionally measured by existing personality tests.

Assessing emotional intelligence through self-report measures also presents the same dilemma one would face in trying to assess standard analytic intelligence by asking people, "Do you think you're smart?" Of course most people want to appear smart. Also, individuals may not have a good idea of their own strengths and weaknesses, especially in the domain of emotions. Similarly, although reports made by others seem more promising in providing accurate information, they are also highly vulnerable to biased viewpoints and subjective interpretations of behavior.

In an attempt to overcome these problems, the first ability-based measure of emotional intelligence was introduced in 1998 in the form of the Multi-factor Emotional Intelligence Scale (MEIS). An improved and professionally published version of the MEIS, from which problematic items were eliminated, was released in 2002 in the form of the Mayer-Salovey-Caruso Emotional Intelligence Test (MSCEIT, named for Mayer, Salovey and collaborator David R. Caruso of the EI Skills Group).

The MSCEIT consists of eight different tasks—two tasks devoted to each of the four branches of emotional intelligence. For example, the first branch, perceiving emotions, is tested by presenting participants with a photograph of a person and then asking them to rate the amount of sadness, happiness, fear etc. that they detect in the person's facial expression. Skill in using emotions is tested by having people indicate how helpful certain moods, such as boredom or happiness, would be for performing certain activities, such as planning a birthday party. The understanding-emotions portion of the test includes questions that ask participants to complete sentences testing their knowledge of emotion vocabulary and how emotions can progress from one to another. The test section addressing the fourth branch, managing emotions, presents participants with real-life scenarios. Participants are asked to choose, from several options, the best strategy for handling the emotions brought up in each scenario. After completing the MSCEIT, scores are generated for each of the four branches as well as an overall total score.

How Good Is the Test?

Marc A. Brackett of Yale University and Mayer calculated the extensive overlap between self-report tests of emotional intelligence and commonly used tests of personality. Many studies of personality are organized around The Big Five model of personality; they ask participants to self-rate how much they exhibit the following traits; neuroticism, extraversion, openness, agreeableness and conscientiousness.

Brackett and Mayer administered scales assessing The Big Five to a group of college students along with the MSCEIT and the SREIT. They found that scores on Big Five personality traits were more highly correlated with participants' scores on the

SREIT than on the MSCEIT. The trait of "extraversion," for example, had a correlation of 0.37 with scores on the SREIT but only correlated 0.11 with scores on the MSCEIT. Therefore, it appears that self-report tests of emotional intelligence may offer limited information about a person above and beyond standard personality questionnaires.

The biggest problem one faces in trying to use an ability-based measure of emotional intelligence is how to determine correct answers. Unlike traditional intelligence tests, emotional intelligence tests can lack clear right or wrong solutions. There are dozens of ways one could handle many emotion-laden situations, so who should decide which is the emotionally intelligent way of doing things? Intrinsic to the four-branch model of emotional intelligence is the hypothesis that emotional skills cannot be separated from their social context. To use emotions in a useful way, one must be attuned to the social and cultural norms of the environment in which one interacts. Therefore, the model proposes that correct answers will depend highly upon agreement with others of one's own social group. Furthermore, experts on emotion research should also have the ability to identify correct answers, since scientific methods have provided us with good knowledge on correct alternatives to emotion-related problems.

Consequently, the MSCEIT is scored using two different methods: general consensus and expert scoring. In consensus scoring, an individual's answers are statistically compared with the answers that were provided by a diverse worldwide sample of 5,000 respondents aged 18 or older who completed the MSCEIT prior to May 2001. The sample is both educationally and ethnically diverse, with respondents from seven different countries including the United States.

In the consensus approach, greater statistical overlap with the sample's answers reflects higher emotional intelligence. In expert scoring, a person's answers are compared with those provided by a group of emotion experts, in this case 21 emotion investigators elected to the International Society for Research on Emotions (ISRE).

The amount of overlap between consensus and expert scoring has been carefully examined. Participants' responses have been scored first using the consensus method and then the expert method, and these results are then correlated with each other. The average correlation between the two sets of scores is greater than 0.90, indicating sizable overlap between the opinions of experts and the general consensus of test-takers. Laypeople and emotion experts, in other words, converge on the most "emotionally intelligent" answers. The scores of the experts tend to agree with one another more than do those of the consensus group, indicating that emotion experts are more likely to possess a shared social representation of what constitutes emotional intelligence.

The MSCEIT has demonstrated good reliability, meaning that scores tend to be consistent over time and that the test is internally consistent. In sum, given its modest overlap with commonly used tests of personality traits and analytic intelligence, the MSCEIT seems to test reliably for something that is distinct from both personality and IQ.

Putting Research to Work

Research on emotional intelligence has been put to practical use with unusual Speed. The reason may be simple: Experiments suggest that scores on ability-based measures of emotional intelligence are associated with a number of important real-world outcomes.

Emotional intelligence may help one get along with peers and supervisors at work. Paulo N. Lopes of the University of Surrey in the United Kingdom spearheaded a study conducted at a Fortune 500 insurance company where employees worked in teams. Each team was asked to fill out surveys that asked individuals to rate other team members on personal descriptors related to emotions such as, "This person handles stress without getting too tense," or "This person is aware of the feelings of others."

Supervisors in the company were also asked to rate their subordinates on similar items. Everyone who participated in the study also took the MSCEIT. Although the sample of participants was small, employees who scored higher on the MSCEIT received more positive ratings from both their peers and their supervisors. Their peers reported having fewer conflicts with them, and they were perceived as creating a positive atmosphere at work. Supervisors rated their emotionally intelligent employees as more interpersonally sensitive, sociable, tolerant of stress and possessing more leadership potential. Higher scores were also positively associated with rank and salary in the company.

Emotional intelligence may also be important for creating and sustaining good relationships with peers. A different study conducted by Lopes and his collaborators asked German college students to keep diaries that described their everyday interactions with others over a two-week period. For every social interaction that lasted at least 10 minutes, students were asked to record the gender of the person they interacted with, how they felt about the interaction, how much they had wanted to make a certain impression, and to what extent they thought they succeeded in making that impression.

Scores on the using-emotions branch of the MSCEIT were positively related to how enjoyable and interesting students found their interactions to be, as well as how important and safe they felt during them. Scores on the managing-emotions branch seemed most important in interactions with the opposite sex. For these interactions, students scoring high on managing emotions reported more enjoyment, intimacy, interest, importance and respect. In addition, managing emotions was positively related to the students' beliefs that they had made the desired impression on their opposite-sex partners (coming across as friendly, say, or competent).

Brackett also investigated how scores on the MSCEIT relate to the quality of social relationships among college students. American college students completed the MSCEIT along with questionnaires assessing the quality of their friendships and their interpersonal skills, In addition, these students were asked to recruit two of their friends to evaluate the quality of their friendship. Individuals scoring high in managing emotions were rated as more caring and emotionally supportive by their friends. Scores on managing emotions were also negatively related to friends' reports of conflict with them. In another recent study by Nicole Lemer and Brackett, Yale students who scored higher in emotional intelligence were evaluated more positively by their roommates; that is, their roommates reported experiencing less conflict with them.

Emotional intelligence may also help people more successfully navigate their relationships with spouses and romantic partners. Another study headed by Brackett recruited 180 young couples (mean age 25 years) from the London area. The couples completed the MSCEIT and then filled out a variety of questionnaires asking about aspects of the couples' relationships, such as the quality of the interactions with their partners and how happy they were with the relationship. Happiness was correlated with high scores for both partners, and where one partner had a high score and the other a low score, satisfaction ratings tended to fall in the intermediate range.

The Future of Emotional Intelligence

Context plays an important role in shaping how these skills are put into action. We can all name people—certain notable politicians come to mind—who seem extremely talented in using their emotions in their professional lives while their personal lives seem in shambles. People may be more adept at using the skills of emotional intelligence in some situations than others. A promising direction for future research is a focus on fluid skills rather than crystallized knowledge about emotions.

Although it has proved valuable so far as a test of general emotional intelligence, the MSCEIT requires refinement and improvement. We view the MEIS and the MSCEIT as the first in a potentially long line of improved ways of assessing emotional abilities.

We believe research on emotional intelligence will be especially valuable if focused on individual differences in emotional processes—a topic we hope will continue to generate more empirical interest. The science of emotion thus far has stressed principles of universality. Ekman's work on faces, mentioned above, and similar cross-cultural findings offer important insights into the nature of human emotional experience. However, in any given culture, people differ from one another in their abilities to interpret and use emotional information. Because individual deficits in emotional skills may lead to negative outcomes, anyone interested in improving emotional skills in various settings should focus on how and why some people, from childhood, are better at dealing with emotions than others. Such knowledge provides the hope of being able to successfully teach such skills to others.

The Popularization of "EQ"

Media interest in emotional intelligence was sparked by *New York Times* science writer Daniel Goleman's bestselling book *Emotional Intelligence* in 1995. In October of the same year came the *TIME* magazine cover and additional media coverage proclaiming emotional intelligence the new way to be smart and the best predictor of success in life.

The late 1990s provided the perfect cultural landscape for the appearance of emotional intelligence. The latest in a string of IQ controversies had broken out with the 1994 publication of *The Bell Curve,* which claimed that modern society has become increasingly stratified not by money, power or class, but by traditionally defined intelligence.

The Bell Curve was read as advocating a view that intelligence is the most important predictor of almost everything that seems to matter to most people: staying healthy, earning enough money, even having a successful marriage. Yet half the population, by definition, has below-average IQs; moreover, IQ is seen as difficult to change over one's lifespan. For many readers, *The Bell Curve* contained an extremely pessimistic message. As if to answer the growing fear that a relatively immutable IQ is the primary predictor of success in life, Goleman's book on emotional intelligence included the phrase, "Why it can matter more than IQ," right on the cover. The public responded favorably to this new promise, and the book soon became a staple on airport newsstands worldwide.

Skepticism over narrow definitions of the word "intelligence" resonated powerfully with a public that seemed to agree that something else—something more intangible—may more strongly determine the quality' of one's life. Evidence that the Scholastic Aptitude Test (SAT), which is highly correlated with IQ, fails to predict academic success especially well beyond the first year of college continued to fuel interest in how emotional skills, or something else beside traditional intelligence, may more significantly determine one's future accomplishments. Americans have always prided themselves on a strong work ethic; the motto that "slow and steady wins the race" represents an attitude that fits well with public conceptions of emotional intelligence as a mark of good character. Americans also have a strong collective self-image of equality, which popular views of emotional intelligence support by characterizing success as dependent on a set of skills that anyone can learn.

Goleman's book continues to be one of the most successful and influential of its genre, and other trade books concerned with emotional intelligence (or EQ, as it is referred to in the popular literature) have appeared in recent years. More than just a passing fad, or temporary backlash against standardized testing, emotional intelligence has captured the long-term interest of employers and educators. In just a few years, what started as a somewhat obscure area of science-driven research in psychology burgeoned into a multi-million-dollar industry marketing books, tapes, seminars and training programs aimed at increasing emotional intelligence.

Popularization has in some cases distorted the original scientific definition of emotional intelligence. Many people now equate emotional intelligence with almost everything desirable in a person's makeup that cannot be measured by an IQ test, such as character, motivation, confidence, mental stability, optimism and "people skills." Research has shown that emotional skills may contribute to some of these qualities, but most of them move far beyond skill-based emotional intelligence. We prefer to define emotional intelligence as a specific set of skills that can be used for either prosocial or antisocial purposes. The ability to accurately perceive how others are feeling may be used by a therapist to gauge how best to help her clients, whereas a con artist might use it to manipulate potential victims. Being emotionally intelligent does not necessarily make one an ethical person.

Although popular claims regarding emotional intelligence run far ahead of what research can reasonably support, the overall effects of the publicity have been more beneficial than harmful. The most positive aspect of this popularization is a new and much needed emphasis on emotion by employers, educators and others interested in promoting social welfare. The popularization of emotional intelligence has helped both the public and research psychology reevaluate the functionality of emotions and how they serve humans adaptively in everyday life. Although the continuing popular appeal of emotional intelligence is both warranted and desirable, we hope that such attention will stimulate a greater interest in the scientific and scholarly study of emotion. It is our hope that in coming decades, advances in cognitive and affective science will offer intertwining perspectives from which to study how people navigate their lives. Emotional intelligence, with its focus on both head and heart, may adequately serve to point us in the right direction.

Bibliography

Bechara, A., H. Damasio and A. R. Damasio. 2000. Emotion, decision making and the orbitofrontal cortex. *Cerebral Cortex* 10:295–307.

Brackett, M. A., and J. D. Mayer. 2003. Convergent, discriminant, and incremental validity of competing measures of emotional intelligence. *Personality and Social Psychology Bulletin* 29:1147–1158

Daniasio, A. R. 1994. *Descartes' Error, Emotion, Reason, and the Human Brain.* New York: Putnam.

Ekman, P. 1980. *The Face of Man: Expressions of Universal Emotions in a New Guinea Village.* New York: Garland STPM Press.

Feldman Barrett, L., J. Gross, T. Christensen and M. Benvenuto. 2001. Knowing what you're feeling and knowing what to do about it: Mapping the relation between emotion differentiation and emotion regulation. *Cognition and Emotion* 15:713–724.

Gardner, H. 1983. *Frames of Mind.* New York: Basic Books.

Goleman, D. 1995. *Emotional Intelligence.* New York: Bantam Books.

Gross, J. J. 1998. Antecedent and response focused emotion regulation: Divergent consequences for experience, expression, and physiology, *Journal of Personality and Social Psychology* 74:224–237,

Isen, A. M., K. A. Daubman and C. P. Nowicki. 1987. Positive affect facilitates creative problem solving, *Journal of Personality and Social Psychology* 52:1122–1131

Lopes, P. N., M. A. Brackett, J. Nezlck, A. Schutz, I. Sellin and P. Salovey. 2004. Emotional intelligence and social interaction. *Personality and Social Psychology Bulletin* 30:1018–1034.

Lopes, P. N., S. Côté, D. Grewal, J. Kadis, M. Gall and P. Salovey. Submitted. Evidence that emotional intelligence is related to job performance, interpersonal facilitation, affect and attitudes at work, and leadership potential.

Mayer, J. D., and P. Salovey. 1997. What is emotional intelligence? In *Emotional Development and Emotional Intelligence: Educational Implications,* ed. P. Salovey and D. Sluyter, pp. 3–31. New York: Basic Books.

Mayer, J. D., P. Salovey and D. Caruso. 2002. *The Mayer-Salovey-Caruso Emotional Intelligence Test (MSCEIT).* Toronto: Multi-Health Systems, Inc.

Mayer, J. D., P. Salovey, D. R. Caruso and G. Sitarenios. 2003. Measuring emotional intelligence with the MSCEIT V2.0. *Emotion* 3:97–105.

Pollak, S. D., and S. Tolley-Schell. 2003. Selective attention to facial emotion in physically abused children. *Journal of Abnormal Psychology* 22:323–338.

Salovey, P, and J. D. Mayer. 1990. Emotional intelligence. *Imagination, Cognition, and Personality* 9:185–211.

Salovey, P, J. D. Mayer and D. Caruso. 2002. The positive psychology of emotional intelligence. In *Handbook of Positive Psychology,* ed. C. R. Snyder and S. J. Lopez, pp. 159–171. New York: Oxford University Press.

Daisy Grewal is a doctoral student in the social psychology program at Yale University. She received her B.A. in psychology from the University of California, Los Angeles in 2002 and her M.S. in psychology from Yale in 2004. Her research focuses on gender stereotypes and prejudice, particularly in organizational contexts. **Peter Salovey,** who earned his Ph.D. from Yale in 1986, is Dean of Yale College and Chris Argyris Professor of Psychology at Yale, where he directs the Health, Emotion, and Behavior Laboratory and holds additional professorships in management, epidemiology and public health, and social and political studies. His research emphases are the psychological significance and function of mood and emotion, and the application of principles from social and personality psychology to promoting healthy behavior. Address for Salovey: Yale University, Department of Psychology, 2 Hillhouse Avenue, New Haven, CT 06520-8205. Internet for both: daisy.grewal@yale.edu.peter.salovey@yale.edu

The Value of Positive Emotions

The emerging science of positive psychology is coming to understand why it's good to feel good

Barbara L. Fredrickson

Back in the 1930s some young Catholic nuns were asked to write short, personal essays about their lives. They described edifying events in their childhood, the schools they attended, their religious experiences and the influences that led them to the convent. Although the essays may have been initially used to assess each nun's career path, the documents were eventually archived and largely forgotten. More than 60 years later the nuns' writings surfaced again when three psychologists at the University of Kentucky reviewed the essays as part of a larger study on aging and Alzheimer's disease. Deborah Danner, David Snowdon and Wallace Friesen read the nun's biographical sketches and scored them for positive emotional content, recording instances of happiness, interest, love and hope. What they found was remarkable: The nuns who expressed the most positive emotions lived up to 10 years longer than those who expressed the fewest. This gain in life expectancy is considerably larger than the gain achieved by those who quit smoking.

The nun study is not an isolated case. Several other scientists have found that people who feel good live longer. But why would this be so?

Some answers are emerging from the new field of positive psychology. This branch of psychological science surfaced about five years ago, as the brainchild of Martin E. P. Seligman, then president of the American Psychological Association (APA). Like many psychologists, Seligman had devoted much of his research career to studying mental illness. He coined the phrase *learned helplessness* to describe how hopelessness and other negative thoughts can spiral down into clinical depression.

At the start of his term as APA president, Seligman took stock of the field of psychology, noting its significant advances in curing ills. In 1947, none of the major mental illnesses were treatable, whereas today 16 are treatable by psychotherapy, psychopharmacology or both. Although psychology had become proficient at rescuing people from various mental illnesses, it had virtually no scientifically sound tools for helping people to reach their higher ground, to thrive and flourish. Seligman aimed to correct this imbalance when he called for a "positive psychology." With the help of psychologist Mihaly Csikszentmihalyi—who originated the concept of "flow" to describe peak motivational experiences—Seligman culled the field for scientists

whose work might be described as investigating "that which makes life worth living."

This is how many research psychologists, myself included, were drawn to positive psychology. My own background is in the study of emotions. For more than a dozen years, I've been studying the positive emotions—joy, contentment, gratitude and love—to shed light on their evolved adaptive significance. Among scientists who study emotions, this is a rare specialty. Far more emotion researchers have devoted their careers to studying negative emotions, such as anger, anxiety and sadness. The study of optimism and positive emotions was seen by some as a frivolous pursuit. But the positive psychology movement is changing that. Many psychologists have now begun to explore the largely uncharted terrain of human strengths and the sources of happiness.

The new discoveries generated by positive psychology hold the promise of improving individual and collective functioning, psychological well-being and physical health. But to harness the power of positive psychology, we need to understand how and why "goodness" matters. Although the discovery that people who think positively and feel good actually live longer is remarkable, it raises more questions than it answers. Exactly how do positive thinking and pleasant feelings help people live longer? Do pleasant thoughts and feelings help people live better as well? And why are positive emotions a universal part of human nature? My research traces the possible pathways for the life-enhancing effects of positive emotions and attempts to understand why human beings evolved to experience them.

Why So Negative?

There are probably a number of reasons why the positive emotions received little attention in the past. There is, of course, the natural tendency to study something that afflicts the well-being of humanity—and the expression and experience of negative emotions are responsible for much of what ails this world. But it may also be that the positive emotions are a little harder to study. They are comparatively few and relatively undifferentiated—joy, amusement and serenity are not easily distinguished from one another. Anger, fear and sadness, on the other hand, are distinctly different experiences.

This lack of differentiation is evident in how we think about the emotions. Consider that scientific taxonomies of basic emotions typically identify one positive emotion for every three or four negative emotions and that this imbalance is also reflected in the relative numbers of emotion words in the English language.

Various physical components of emotional expression similarly reveal a lack of differentiation for the positive emotions. The negative emotions have specific facial configurations that imbue them with universally recognized signal value. We can readily identify angry, sad or fearful faces. In contrast, facial expressions for positive emotions have no unique signal value: All share the *Duchenne smile*—in which the corners of the lips are raised and the muscles are contracted around the eyes, which raises the cheeks. A sim-

ilar distinction is evident in the response of the autonomic nervous system to the expression of emotions. About 20 years ago, psychologists Paul Ekman and Wallace Friesen at the University of California, San Francisco, and Robert Levenson at Indiana University showed that anger, fear and sadness each elicit distinct responses in the autonomic nervous system. In contrast, the positive emotions appeared to have no distinguishable autonomic responses.

The study of positive emotions has also been hindered because scientists attempted to understand them with models that worked best for negative emotions. Central to many theories of emotion is that they are, by definition, associated with urges to act in particular ways. Anger creates the urge to attack, fear the urge to escape and disgust the urge to expectorate. Of course, no theorist argues that people invariably act out these urges; rather, people's ideas about possible courses of action narrow in on these specific urges. And these urges are not simply thoughts existing in the mind. They embody specific physiological changes that enable the actions called forth. In the case of fear, for example, a greater amount of blood flows to the large muscle groups to facilitate running.

The models that emphasize the role of these specific action tendencies typically cast the emotions as evolved adaptations. The negative emotions have an intuitively obvious adaptive value: In an instant, they narrow our thought-action repertoires to those that best promoted our ancestors' survival in life-threatening situations. In this view, negative emotions are efficient solutions to recurrent problems that our ancestors faced.

Positive emotions, on the other hand, aren't so easily explained. From this evolutionary perspective, joy, serenity and gratitude don't seem as useful as fear, anger or disgust. The bodily changes, urges to act and the facial expressions produced by positive emotions aren't as

specific or as obviously relevant to survival as those sparked by negative emotions. If positive emotions didn't promote our ancestors' survival in life-threatening situations, then what good were they? Did they have any adaptive value at all? Perhaps they merely signaled the absence of threats.

The Broaden-and-Build Theory

We gain some insight into the adaptive role of positive emotions if we abandon the framework used to understand the negative emotions. Instead of solving problems of immediate survival, positive emotions solve problems concerning personal growth and development. Experiencing a positive emotion leads to states of mind and to modes of behavior that indirectly prepare an individual for later hard times. In my broaden-and-build theory, I propose that the positive emotions broaden an individual's momentary mindset, and by doing so help to build enduring personal resources. We can test these ideas by exploring the ways that positive emotions change how people think and how they behave.

My students and I conducted experiments in which we induced certain emotions in people by having them watch short, emotionally evocative film clips. We elicited joy by showing a herd of playful penguins waddling and sliding on the ice, we elicited serenity with clips of peaceful nature scenes, we elicited fear with films of people at precarious heights, and we elicited sadness with scenes of deaths and funerals. We also used a neutral "control" film of an old computer screen saver that elicited no emotion at all.

We then assessed the participant's ability to think broadly. Using global-local visual processing tasks, we measured whether they saw the "big picture" or focused on smaller details *(Figure 1, left)*. The participant's task is to judge which of two comparison figures is more similar to a "standard" figure. Neither choice is right or wrong, but one comparison figure

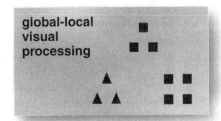 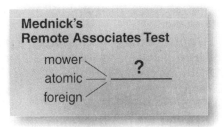

Figure 1. Psychological tests reveal that people tend to think broadly when they experience positive emotions. A global-local visual processing test *(left)* asks participants to judge which of two comparison figures *(bottom)* is most similar to a standard figure *(top)*. People experiencing positive emotions tend to choose the figure that resembles the standard configuration in global configuration *(the triangles)*. Similarly, people experiencing positive emotions score highly on tests of creativity such as Mednick's Remote Associates Test *(right)*, which asks people to think of a word that relates to each of three other words. (The answer is in the text below.) The positive emotions broaden people's mindsets, which allows them to solve problems like this more readily.

resembles the standard in global configuration, and the other in local, detailed elements. Using this and similar measures, we found that, compared to those in negative or neutral states, people who experience positive emotions (as assessed by self-report or electromyographic signals from the face) tend to choose the global configuration, suggesting a broadened pattern of thinking.

This tendency to promote a broader thought-action repertoire is linked to a variety of downstream effects of positive emotions on thinking. Two decades of experiments by Alice Isen of Cornell University and her colleagues have shown that people experiencing positive affect (feelings) think differently. One series of experiments tested creative thinking using such tests as Mednick's Remote Associates Test, which asks people to think of a word that relates to each of three other words. So, for example, given the words mower, atomic and foreign, the correct answer is power *(Figure 1, right)*. Although this test was originally designed to assess individual differences in the presumably stable trait of creativity, Isen and colleagues showed that people experiencing positive affect perform better on this test than people in neutral states.

In other experiments, Isen and colleagues tested the clinical reasoning of practicing physicians. They made some of the physicians feel good by giving them a small bag of candy, then asked all of them to think aloud while they solved a case of a patient with liver disease. Content analyses revealed that physicians who felt good were faster to integrate case information and less likely to become anchored on initial thoughts or come to premature closure in their diagnosis. In yet another experiment, Isen and colleagues showed that negotiators induced to feel good were more likely to discover integrative solutions in a complex bargaining task. Overall, 20 years of experiments by Isen and her colleagues show that when people feel good, their thinking becomes more creative, integrative, flexible and open to information.

Even though positive emotions and the broadened mindsets they create are themselves short-lived, they can have deep and enduring effects. By momentarily broadening attention and thinking, positive emotions can lead to the discovery of novel ideas, actions and social bonds. For example, joy and playfulness build a variety of resources. Consider children at play in the schoolyard or adults enjoying a game of basketball in the gym. Although their immediate motivations may be simply hedonistic—to enjoy the moment—they are at the same time building physical, intellectual, psychological and social resources. The physical activity leads to long-term improvements in health, the game-playing strategies develop problem-solving skills, and the camaraderie strengthens social bonds that may provide crucial support at some time in the future. Similar links between playfulness and later gains in physical, social and intellectual resources are also evident in nonhuman animals, such as monkeys, rats and squirrels. In human beings, other positive states of mind and positive actions work along similar lines: Savoring an experience solidifies life priorities; altruistic acts strengthen social ties and build skills for expressing love and care. These outcomes often endure long after the initial positive emotion has vanished.

My students and I recently tested these ideas by surveying a group of people to examine their resilience and optimism. The people were originally interviewed in the early months of 2001, and then again in the days after the September 11th terrorist attacks. We asked them to identify the emotions they were feeling, what they had learned from the attacks and how optimistic they were about the future. We learned that after September 11 nearly everyone felt sad, angry and somewhat afraid. And more than 70 percent were depressed. Yet the people who were originally identified as being resilient in the early part of 2001 felt positive emotions strongly as well. They were also half as likely to be depressed. Our statistical analyses showed that their tendency to feel more positive emotions buffered the resilient people against depression.

Gratitude was the most common positive emotion people felt after the

September 11th attacks. Feeling grateful was associated both with learning many good things from the crisis and with increased levels of optimism. Resilient people made statements such as, "I learned that most people in the world are inherently good." Put differently, feeling grateful broadened positive learning, which in turn built optimism, just as the broaden-and-build theory suggests.

My students and I have recently completed an experimental test of the building effect of positive emotions. Over the course of a month-long study of daily experiences, we induced one group of college students to feel more positive emotions by asking them to find the positive meaning and long-term benefit within their best, worst and seem-ingly ordinary experiences each day. At the end of the month, compared to others who did not make this daily effort to find positive meaning, those who did showed increases in psychological resilience.

So "feeling good" does far more than signal the absence of threats. It can transform people for the better, making them more optimistic, resilient and socially connected. Indeed, this insight might solve the evolutionary mystery of positive emotions: Simply by experiencing positive emotions, our ancestors would have naturally accrued more personal resources. And when later faced with threats to life or limb, these greater resources translated into greater odds of survival and greater odds of living long enough to reproduce.

The Undoing Hypothesis

We might also ask whether there are other immediate benefits to experiencing positive emotions, aside from the tautology that they make us "feel good." One effect relates to how people cope with their negative emotions. If negative emotions narrow people's mindsets and positive emotions broaden them, then perhaps positive emotions undo the lingering effects of negative emotions.

Such effects may extend to the physiological realm. The negative emotions have distinct physiological responses associated with them—autonomic activity (as mentioned earlier), including cardiovascular activity, which represents the body's preparation for specific action. A number of studies suggest that the

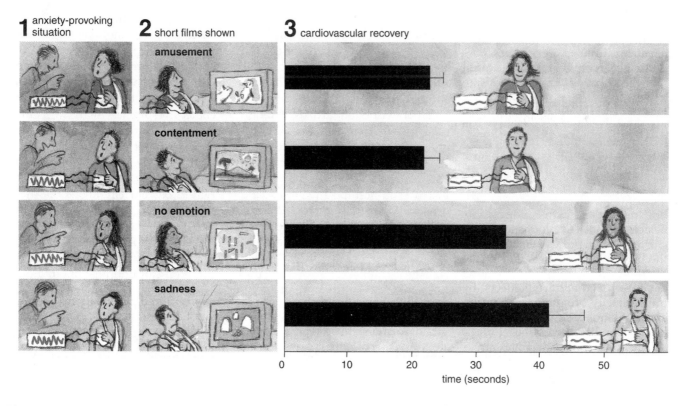

Figure 2. Undoing hypothesis suggests that positive emotions "undo" the lingering effects of negative emotions. This was examined by provoking anxiety in a group of participants by asking them to prepare a speech under time pressure. After learning that they did not have to deliver their speeches after all, the participants were shown one of four films, eliciting either amusement, contentment, no emotion or sadness. Measurements of the participants' heart rate, blood pressure and peripheral vasoconstriction revealed that feeling positive emotions leads to the quickest recovery to baseline measures obtained before they were placed in the anxiety-provoking situation. These undoing effects may partly explain the longevity of people who experience positive emotions more often.

cardiovascular activity associated with stress and negative emotions, especially if prolonged and recurrent, can promote or exacerbate heart disease. Experiments on non-human primates reveal that recurrent emotion-related cardiovascular activity also appears to injure the inner walls of arteries and initiate atherosclerosis. Because the positive emotions broaden people's thought-and-action repertoires, they may also loosen the hold that negative emotions gain on both mind and body, dismantle preparation for specific action and undo the physiological effects of negative emotions.

My colleagues and I tested this undoing hypothesis in a series of experiments. We began by inducing a negative emotion: We told participants that they had one minute to prepare a speech that would be videotaped and evaluated by their peers. The speech task induced the subjective feeling of anxiety as well as increases in heart rate, peripheral vasoconstriction and blood pressure. We then randomly assigned the participants to view one of four films: two films evoked mild positive emotions (amusement and contentment), a third served as a neutral control condition and a fourth elicited sadness.

We then measured the time elapsed from the beginning of the randomly assigned film until the cardiovascular reactions induced by the speech task returned to each participant's baseline levels. The results were consistent: Those individuals who watched the two positive-emotion films recovered to their baseline cardiovascular activity sooner than those who watched the neutral film. Those who watched the sad film showed the most delayed recovery (*Figure 2*). Positive emotions had a clear and consistent effect of undoing the cardiovascular repercussions of negative emotions.

At this point the cognitive and physiological mechanisms of the undoing effect are unknown. It may be that broadening one's cognitive perspective by feeling positive emotions

mediates the physiological undoing. Such ideas need further exploration.

Ending on a Positive Note

So how do the positive emotions promote longevity? Why did the happy nuns live so long? It seems that positive emotions do more than simply feel good in the present. The undoing effect suggests that positive emotions can reduce the physiological "damage" on the cardiovascular system sustained by feeling negative emotions. But some other research suggests that there's more to it than that. It appears that experiencing positive emotions increases the likelihood that one will feel good in the future.

My colleague Thomas Joiner and I sought to test whether positive affect and broadened thinking mutually enhance each other—so that experiencing one produces the other, which in turn encourages more of the first one, and so on in a mutually reinforcing ascent to greater well-being. We measured positive affect and broadened thinking strategies in 138 college students on two separate occasions, five weeks apart (times T1 and T2), with standard psychological tests. When we compared the students' responses on both occasions we found some very interesting results: Positive affect at T1 predicted increases in both positive affect and broadened thinking at T2; and broadened thinking at T1 predicted increases in both positive affect and broadened thinking at T2. Further statistical analyses revealed that there was indeed a mutually reinforcing effect between positive affect and broadened thinking. These results suggest that people who regularly feel positive emotions are in some respects lifted on an "upward spiral" of continued growth and thriving.

But positive emotions don't just transform individuals. I've argued that they may also transform groups of people, within communities and organizations. Community transformation becomes possible because

each person's positive emotion can resound through others. Take helpful, compassionate acts as an example. Isen demonstrated that people who experience positive emotions become more helpful to others. Yet being helpful not only springs from positive emotions, it also produces positive emotions. People who give help, for instance, can feel proud of their good deeds and so experience continued good feelings. Plus, people who receive help can feel grateful, and those who merely witness good deeds can feel elevated. Each of these positive emotions—pride, gratitude and elevation—can in turn broaden people's mindsets and inspire further compassionate acts. So, by creating chains of events that carry positive meaning for others, positive emotions can trigger upward spirals that transform communities into more cohesive, moral and harmonious social organizations.

All of this suggests that we need to develop methods to experience more positive emotions more often. Although the use of humor, laughter and other direct attempts to stimulate positive emotions are occasionally suitable, they often seem poor choices, especially in trying times. Based on our recent experiment with college students, my advice would be to cultivate positive emotions indirectly by finding positive meaning within current circumstances. Positive meaning can be obtained by finding benefits within adversity, by infusing ordinary events with meaning and by effective problem solving. You can find benefits in a grim world, for instance, by focusing on the newfound strengths and resolve within yourself and others. You can infuse ordinary events with meaning by expressing appreciation, love and gratitude, even for simple things. And you can find positive meaning through problem solving by supporting compassionate acts toward people in need. So although the active ingredient within growth and resilience may be positive emotions, the leverage point for accessing these benefits is finding positive meaning.

So, what good is it to think about the good in the world? The mind can be a powerful ally. As John Milton told us, "The mind is its own place, and in itself can make a heaven of hell, a hell of heaven." The new science of positive psychology is beginning to unravel how such transformations can take place. Think about the good in the world, or otherwise find positive meaning, and you seed your own positive emotions. A focus on goodness cannot only change your life and your community, but perhaps also the world, and in time create a heaven on earth.

Acknowledgments

The author would like to thank the University of Michigan, the National institute of Mental Health (MH59615) and the John Templeton Foundation for supporting some of the research described in this article.

Bibliography

Aspinwall, L. G., and U. M. Staudinger. 2003. *A Psychology of Human Strengths: Fundamental Questions and Future Directions for a Positive Psychology.* Washington, D.C.: American Psychological Association.

Danner, D. D., D. A. Snowdon and W. V. Friesen. 2001. Positive emotions in early life and longevity: Findings from the nun study. *Journal of Personality and Social Psychology* 80:804–813.

Fredrickson, B. L. 1998. What good are positive emotions? *Review of General Psychology* 2:300–319.

Fredrickson, B. L. 2000. Cultivating positive emotions to optimize health and well-being. *Prevention and Treatment* 3.http://journals.apa.org/prevention/volume3/toc-mar07-00.html

Fredrickson, B. L. 2001. The role of positive emotions in positive psychology: The broaden-and-build theory of positive emotions. *American Psychologist* 56:218–226.

Fredrickson, B. L., and T. Joiner. 2002. Positive emotions trigger upward spirals toward emotional well-being. *Psychological Science* 13:172–175.

Fredrickson, B. L., and R. W. Levenson. 1998. Positive emotions speed recovery from the cardiovascular sequelae of negative emotions. *Cognition and Emotion* 12:191–220.

Fredrickson, B. L., M. M. Tugade, C. E. Waugh and G. Larkin. 2003. What good are positive emotions in crises?: A prospective study of resilience and emotions following the terrorist attacks on the United States on September 11th, 2001. *Journal of Personality and Social Psychology* 84:365–376.

Isen, A. M. 1987. Positive affect, cognitive processes and social behavior. *Advances in Experimental Social Psychology* 20:203–253.

BARBARA L. FREDRICKSON is the director of the Positive Emotions and Psychophysiology Laboratory at the University of Michigan. In 2000 she won the Templeton Prize in Positive Psychology. Address: 3006 East Hall, 525 East University Avenue, University of Michigan, Ann Arbor, MI 48109–1109. Internet: blf@umich.edu

AMBITION:
Why Some People Are Most Likely to Succeed

A fire in the belly doesn't light itself. Does the spark of ambition lie in genes, family, culture—or even in your own hands? Science has answers

JEFFREY KLUGER

YOU DON'T GET AS SUCCESSFUL AS GREGG AND DREW shipp by accident. Shake hands with the 36-year-old fraternal twins who co-own the sprawling Hi Fi Personal Fitness club in Chicago, and it's clear you're in the presence of people who thrive on their drive. But that wasn't always the case. The twins' father founded the Jovan perfume company, a glamorous business that spun off the kinds of glamorous profits that made it possible for the Shipps to amble through high school, coast into college and never much worry about getting the rent paid or keeping the fridge filled. But before they graduated, their sense of drift began to trouble them. At about the same time, their father sold off the company, and with it went the cozy billets in adult life that had always served as an emotional backstop for the boys.

That did it. By the time they got out of school, both Shipps had entirely transformed themselves, changing from boys who might have grown up to live off the family's wealth to men consumed with going out and creating their own. "At this point," says Gregg, "I consider myself to be almost maniacally ambitious."

It shows. In 1998 the brothers went into the gym trade. They spotted a modest health club doing a modest business, bought out the owner and transformed the place into a luxury facility where private trainers could reserve space for top-dollar clients. In the years since, the company has outgrown one building, then another, and the brothers are about to move a third time. Gregg, a communications major at college, manages the club's clients, while Drew, a business major, oversees the more hardheaded chore of finance and expansion. "We're not sitting still," Drew says. "Even now that we're doing twice the business we did at our old place, there's a thirst that needs to be quenched."

Why is that? Why are some people born with a fire in the belly, while others—like the Shipps—need something to get their pilot light lit? And why do others never get the flame of ambition going? Is there a family anywhere that doesn't have its overachievers and underachievers—its Jimmy Carters and Billy Carters, its Jeb Bushes and Neil Bushes—and find itself wondering how they all could have come splashing out of exactly the same gene pool?

OF ALL THE IMPULSES IN humanity's behavioral portfolio, ambition—that need to grab an ever bigger piece of the resource pie before someone else gets it—ought to be one of the most democratically distributed. Nature is a zero-sum game, after all. Every buffalo you kill for your family is one less for somebody else's; every acre of land you occupy elbows out somebody else. Given that, the need to get ahead ought to be hard-wired into all of us equally.

And yet it's not. For every person consumed with the need to achieve, there's someone content to accept whatever life brings. For everyone who chooses the 80-hour workweek, there's someone punching out at 5. Men and women—so it's said—express ambition differently; so do Americans and Europeans, baby boomers and Gen Xers, the middle class and the well-to-do. Even among the manifestly motivated, there are degrees of ambition. Steve Wozniak co-founded Apple Computer and then left the company in 1985 as a 34-year-old multimillionaire. His partner, Steve Jobs, is still innovating at Apple and moonlighting at his second blockbuster company, Pixar Animation Studios.

"For me, ambition has become a dirty word. I prefer hunger."
—Johnny Depp

Not only do we struggle to understand why some people seem to have more ambition than others, but we can't even agree on just what ambition is. "Ambition is an evolutionary product," says anthropologist Edward Lowe at Soka University of America, in Aliso Viejo, Calif. "No matter how social status is defined, there are certain people in every community who aggressively pursue it and others who aren't so aggressive."

Dean Simonton, a psychologist at the University of California, Davis, who studies genius, creativity and eccentricity, believes it's more complicated than that. "Ambition is energy and determination," he says. "But it calls for goals too. People with goals but no energy are the ones who wind up sitting on the couch saying 'One day I'm going to build a better mousetrap.' People with energy but no clear goals just dissipate themselves in one desultory project after the next."

"Ambition is like love, impatient both of delays and rivals."
—Buddha

Assuming you've got drive, dreams and skill, is all ambition equal? Is the overworked lawyer on the partner track any more ambitious than the overworked parent on the mommy track? Is the successful musician to whom melody comes naturally more driven than the unsuccessful one who sweats out every note? We may listen to Mozart, but should we applaud Salieri?

Most troubling of all, what about when enough ambition becomes way too much? Grand dreams unmoored from morals are the stuff of tyrants—or at least of Enron. The 16-hour workday filled with high stress and at-the-desk meals is the stuff of burnout and heart attacks. Even among kids, too much ambition quickly starts to do real harm. In a just completed study, anthropologist Peter Demerath of Ohio State University surveyed 600 students at a high-achieving high school where most of the kids are triple-booked with advanced-placement courses, sports and after-school jobs. About 70% of them reported that they were starting to feel stress some or all of the time. "I asked one boy how his parents react to his workload,

and he answered, 'I don't really get home that often,'" says Demerath. "Then he handed me his business card from the video store where he works."

Anthropologists, psychologists and others have begun looking more closely at these issues, seeking the roots of ambition in family, culture, gender, genes and more. They have by no means thrown the curtain all the way back, but they have begun to part it. "It's fundamentally human to be prestige conscious," says Soka's Lowe. "It's not enough just to be fed and housed. People want more."

If humans are an ambitious species, it's clear we're not the only one. Many animals are known to signal their ambitious tendencies almost from birth. Even before wolf pups are weaned, they begin sorting themselves out into alphas and all the others. The alphas are quicker, more curious, greedier for space, milk, Mom—and they stay that way for life. Alpha wolves wander widely, breed annually and may live to a geriatric 10 or 11 years old. Lower-ranking wolves enjoy none of these benefits—staying close to home, breeding rarely and usually dying before they're 4.

Humans often report the same kind of temperamental determinism. Families are full of stories of the inexhaustible infant who grew up to be an entrepreneur, the phlegmatic child who never really showed much go. But if it's genes that run the show, what accounts for the Shipps, who didn't bestir themselves until the cusp of adulthood? And what, more tellingly, explains identical twins—precise genetic templates of each other who ought to be temperamentally identical but often exhibit profound differences in the octane of their ambition?

Ongoing studies of identical twins have measured achievement motivation—lab language for ambition—in identical siblings separated at birth, and found that each twin's profile overlaps 30% to 50% of the other's. In genetic terms, that's an awful lot—"a benchmark for heritability," says geneticist Dean Hamer of the National Cancer Institute. But that still leaves a great deal that can be determined by experiences in infancy, subsequent upbringing and countless other imponderables.

Some of those variables may be found by studying the function of the brain. At Washington University, researchers have been conducting brain imaging to investigate a trait they call persistence—the ability to stay focused on a task until it's completed just so—which they consider one of the critical engines driving ambition.

The researchers recruited a sample group of students and gave each a questionnaire designed to measure persistence level. Then they presented the students with a task—identifying sets of pictures as either pleasant or unpleasant and taken either indoors or outdoors—while conducting magnetic resonance imaging of their brains. The nature of the task was unimportant, but how strongly the subjects felt about performing it well—and where in the brain that feeling was processed—could say a lot. In general, the researchers found that students who scored highest in persistence had the greatest activity in the limbic region, the area of the brain related to emotions and habits. "The correlation was .8 [or 80%]," says professor of psychiatry Robert Cloninger, one of the investigators. "That's as good as you can get."

It's impossible to say whether innate differences in the brain were driving the ambitious behavior or whether learned behavior was causing the limbic to light up. But a number of researchers believe it's possible for the nonambitious to jump-start their drive, provided the right jolt comes along. "Energy level may be genetic," says psychologist Simonton, "but a lot of times it's just" Simonton and others often cite the case of Franklin D. Roosevelt, who might not have been the same President he became—or even become President at all—had his disabling polio not taught him valuable lessons about patience and tenacity.

IS SUCH AN EPIPHANY POSSIBLE FOR ALL of us, or are some people immune to this kind of lightning? Are there individuals or whole groups for whom the amplitude of ambition is simply lower than it is for others? It's a question—sometimes a charge—that hangs at the edges of all discussions about gender and work, about whether women really have the meat-eating temperament to survive in the professional world. Both research findings and everyday experience suggest that women's ambitions express themselves differently from men's. The meaning of that difference is the hinge on which the arguments turn.

"Ambition makes you look pretty ugly."
—Radiohead

Economists Lise Vesterlund of the University of Pittsburgh and Muriel Niederle of Stanford University conducted a study in which they assembled 40 men and 40 women, gave them five minutes to add up as many two-digit numbers as they could, and paid them 50¢ for each correct answer. The subjects were not competing against one another but simply playing against the house. Later, the game was changed to a tournament in which the subjects were divided into teams of two men or two women each. Winning teams got $2 per computation; losers got nothing. Men and women performed equally in both tests, but on the third round, when asked to choose which of the two ways they wanted to play, only 35% of the women opted for the tournament format; 75% of the men did.

"Men and women just differ in their appetite for competition," says Vesterlund. "There seems to be a dislike for it among women and a preference among men."

"Ambition, old mankind, the immemorial weakness of the strong."
—Vita Sackville-West

To old-line employers of the old-boy school, this sounds like just one more reason to keep the glass ceiling polished. But other behavioral experts think Vesterlund's conclusions go too far. They say it's not that women aren't ambitious enough to compete for what they want; it's that they're more selective about when they engage in competition; they're willing to get ahead at high cost but not at any cost. "Primate-wide, males are more directly competitive than females, and that makes sense," says Sarah Blaffer Hrdy, emeritus professor of anthropology at the University of California, Davis. "But that's not the same as saying women aren't innately competitive too."

As with so much viewed through the lens of anthropology, the roots of these differences lie in animal and human mating strategies. Males are built to go for quick, competitive reproductive hits and move on. Women are built for the it-takes-a-village life, in which they provide long-term care to a very few young and must sail them safely into an often hostile world. Among some of our evolutionary kin—baboons, macaques and other old-world monkeys—this can be especially tricky since young females inherit their mother's social rank. The mothers must thus operate the levers of society deftly so as to raise both their own position and, eventually, their daughters'. If you think that kind of ambition-by-proxy doesn't translate to humans, Hrdy argues, think again. "Just read an Edith Wharton novel about women in old New York competing for marriage potential for their daughters," she says.

Import such tendencies into the 21st century workplace, and you get women who are plenty able to compete ferociously but are inclined to do it in teams and to split the difference if they don't get everything they want. And mothers who appear to be unwilling to strive and quit the workplace altogether to go raise their kids? Hrdy believes they're competing for the most enduring stakes of all, putting aside their near-term goals to ensure the long-term success of their line. Robin Parker, 46, a campaign organizer who in 1980 was already on the presidential stump with Senator Edward Kennedy, was precisely the kind of lifetime pol who one day finds herself in the West Wing. But in 1992, at the very moment a President of her party was returning to the White House and she might have snagged a plum Washington job, she decamped from the capital, moved to Boston with her family and became a full-time mom to her two sons.

"Being out in the world became a lot less important to me," she says. "I used to worry about getting Presidents elected, and I'm still an incredibly ambitious person. But what I want to succeed at now is managing my family, raising my boys, helping my husband and the community. In 10 years, when the boys are launched, who knows what I'll be doing? But for now, I have my world."

But even if something as primal as the reproductive impulse wires you one way, it's possible for other things to rewire you completely. Two of the biggest influences on your level of ambition are the family that produced you and the culture that produced your family.

There are no hard rules for the kinds of families that turn out the highest achievers. Most psychologists agree that parents who set tough but realistic challenges, applaud successes and go easy on failures produce kids with the greatest self-confidence.

What's harder for parents to control but has perhaps as great an effect is the level of privilege into which their kids are born. Just how wealth or poverty influences drive is difficult to predict. Grow up in a rich family, and you can inherit either the tools to achieve (think both Presidents Bush) or the indolence of the aristocrat. Grow up poor, and you can come away with either the motivation to strive (think Bill Clinton) or the inertia of the hopeless. On the whole, studies suggest it's the upper middle class that produces the greatest proportion of ambitious people—mostly because it also produces the greatest proportion of anxious people.

When measuring ambition, anthropologists divide families into four categories: poor, struggling but getting by, upper middle class, and rich. For members of the first two groups, who are fighting just to keep the electricity on and the phone bill paid, ambition is often a luxury. For the rich, it's often unnecessary. It's members of the upper middle class, reasonably safe economically but not so safe that a bad break couldn't spell catastrophe, who are most driven to improve their lot. "It's called status anxiety," says anthropologist Lowe, "and whether you're born to be concerned about it or not, you do develop it."

> **"Ambition is so powerful a passion in the human breast that however high we reach, we are never satisfied."** —Niccolo Machiavelli

But some societies make you more anxious than others. The U.S. has always been a me-first culture, as befits a nation that grew from a scattering of people on a fat saddle of continent where land was often given away. That have-it-all ethos persists today, even though the resource freebies are long since gone. Other countries—where the acreage is smaller and the pickings are slimmer—came of age differently, with the need to cooperate getting etched into the cultural DNA. The American model has produced wealth, but it has come at a price—with ambition sometimes turning back on the ambitious and consuming them whole.

The study of high-achieving high school students conducted by Ohio State's Demerath was noteworthy for more than the stress he found the students were suffering. It also revealed the lengths to which the kids and their parents were willing to go to gain an advantage over other suffering students. Cheating was common, and most students shrugged it off as only a minor problem. A number of parents—some of whose children carried a 4.0 average—sought to have their kids classified as special-education students, which would entitle them to extra time on standardized tests. "Kids develop their own moral code," says Demerath. "They have a keen sense of competing with others and are developing identities geared to that."

Demerath got very different results when he conducted research in a very different place—Papua, New Guinea. In the mid-1990s, he spent a year in a small village there, observing how the children learned. Usually, he found, they saw school as a noncompetitive place where it was important to succeed collectively and then move on. Succeeding at the expense of others was seen as a form of vanity that the New Guineans call "acting extra." Says Demerath: "This is an odd thing for them."

That makes tactical sense. In a country based on farming and fishing, you need to know that if you get sick and can't work your field or cast your net, someone else will do it for you. Putting on airs in the classroom is not the way to ensure that will happen.

Of course, once a collectivist not always a collectivist. Marcelo Suárez-Orozco, a professor of globalization and education at New York University, has been following 400 families that immigrated to the U.S. from Asia, Latin America and the Caribbean. Many hailed from villages where the American culture of competition is alien, but once they got here, they changed fast.

As a group, the immigrant children in his study are outperforming their U.S.-born peers. What's more, the adults are dramatically outperforming the immigrant families that came before them. "One hundred years ago, it took people two to three generations to achieve a middle-class standard of living," says Suárez-Orozco. "Today they're getting there within a generation."

So this is a good thing, right? Striving people come here to succeed—and do. While there are plenty of benefits that undeniably come with learning the ways of ambition, there are plenty of perils too—many a lot uglier than high school students cheating on the trig final.

Human history has always been writ in the blood of broken alliances, palace purges and strong people or nations beating up on weak ones—all in the service of someone's hunger for power There's a point at which you find an interesting kind of nerve circuitry between optimism and hubris," says Warren Bennis, a professor of business administration at the University of Southern California and the author of three books on leadership. "It becomes an arrogance or conceit, an inability to live without power."

While most ambitious people keep their secret Caesar tucked safely away, it can emerge surprisingly, even suddenly. Says Frans de Waal, a primatologist at the Yerkes Primate Center in Atlanta and the author of a new book, Our Inner Ape: "You can have a male chimp that is the most laid-back character, but one day he sees the chance to overthrow the leader and becomes a totally different male. I would say 90% of people would behave this way too. On an island with three people, they might become a little dictator."

But a yearning for supremacy can create its own set of problems. Heart attacks, ulcers and other stress-related ills are more common among high achievers—and that includes nonhuman achievers. The blood of alpha wolves routinely shows elevated levels of cortisol, the same stress hormone that is found in anxious humans. Alpha chimps even suffer ulcers and occasional heart attacks.

For these reasons, people and animals who have an appetite for becoming an alpha often settle contentedly into life as a beta. "The desire to be in a high position is universal," says de Waal. "But that trait has co-evolved with another skill—the skill to make the best of lower positions."

Humans not only make peace with their beta roles but they also make money from them. Among corporations, an increasingly well-rewarded portion of the workforce is made up of B players, managers and professionals somewhere below the top tier. They don't do the power lunching and ribbon cutting but instead perform the highly skilled, everyday work of making the

DONALD TRUMP

Achievements

Before he ever uttered the words "You're fired," Trump developed more than 18 million sq. ft. of Manhattan real estate, naming most of it after himself.

Early Signs Of Ambition

While in college, Donald read federal foreclosure listings for fun. It paid off: he bought his first housing project before he graduated.

BILL CLINTON

Achievements

Former U.S. President, current global celebrity.

Early Signs Of Ambition

At 16, he beat out some 1,000 other boys to win a mock state senate seat and a trip to Washington, where he knew "the action was." Once in the capital, he got himself into position to shake hands with his idol, President John F. Kennedy.

OPRAH WINFREY

Achievements

Her $1 billion media empire includes movies, a magazine and her talk show, now in its 20th year.

Early Signs Of Ambition

She could read at 2, and although she was just 5 when she started school, she insisted on being put in first grade. Her teacher relented. The next year young Oprah was skipped to third grade.

TIGER WOODS

Achievements

At 21, he was the youngest golfer ever ranked No. 1 in the world. Now 29, he holds the record for most prize money won in a career—$56 million and counting.

Early Signs Of Ambition

At 6, he listened to motivational tapes—"I will make my own destiny"—while practicing his swing in the mirror.

MARTHA STEWART

Achievements

The lifestyle guru rules an empire that includes one magazine, two TV shows, a satellite-radio deal, a shelf full of best sellers and a home-furnishings line at Kmart.

Early Signs Of Ambition

As a grade-schooler, she organized and catered neighborhood birthday parties because, she says, the going rate of 50¢ an hr. for babysitting "wasn't quite enough money."

VERA WANG

Achievements

She turned one-of-a-kind wedding gowns into a $300 million fashion business.

Early Signs Of Ambition

Although from a wealthy family, she spent her high school summers working as a sales clerk in a Manhattan boutique. After college, she landed a job at *Vogue* magazine, where she put in seven-day workweeks, rose quickly and became a senior editor at 23.

CONDOLEEZZA RICE

Achievements

The current Secretary of State and former National Security Adviser was 38 when she became Stanford University's youngest, and first female, provost.

Early Signs Of Ambition

A gifted child pianist who began studying at the Birmingham Conservatory at 10, the straight-A student became a competitive ice skater, rising at 4:30 a.m. to spend two hours at the rink before school and piano lessons.

SEAN COMBS

Achievements

Diddy, as he's now known, is a Grammy-winning performer and producer and a millionaire businessman with a restaurant, a clothing line and a marketing and ad agency.

Early Signs Of Ambition

During his days at Howard University, he learned about business by doing: he sold term papers and tickets to dance parties he hosted.

JENNIFER LOPEZ

Achievements

The former Fly Girl dancer has sold 40 million records, is the highest-paid Latina actress in Hollywood and has launched fashion and perfume lines.

Early Signs Of Ambition

When she signed with Sony Music, she insisted on dealing with its chief, Tommy Mottola. She told him she wanted "the A treatment. I want everything top of the line."

BRITNEY SPEARS

Achievements

Her first single and first four albums made their debut at No. 1. Since then she has sold 76 million records and amassed a $150 million fortune.

Early Signs Of Ambition

Spears used to lock herself in the bathroom and sing to her dolls. After each number, she practiced smiling and blowing kisses to her toy audience.

TOM CRUISE

Achievements

He's a movie superstar who gets $25 million a film, an accomplished actor with three Oscar nods and a gossip staple who has sold a zillion magazines.

Early Signs Of Ambition

After his first role in a high school musical, he asked his family to give him 10 years to make it in show business. Within four, he was starring in the surprise hit film *Risky Business.*

company run. As skeptical shareholders look ever more askance at overpaid corporate A-listers, the B players are becoming more highly valued. It's an adaptation that serves the needs of both the corporation and the culture around it. "Everyone has ambition," says Lowe. "Societies have to provide alternative ways for people to achieve."

Ultimately, it's that very flexibility—that multiplicity of possible rewards—that makes dreaming big dreams and pursuing big goals worth all the bother. Ambition is an expensive impulse, one that requires an enormous investment of emotional capital. Like any investment, it can pay off in countless different kinds of coin. The trick, as any good speculator will tell you, is recognizing the riches when they come your way.

From *Time* Magazine, November 14, 2005, pp. 49-59. Copyright © 2005 by Time Inc. Reprinted by permission.

Obesity—An Epidemic of the Twenty-First Century: An Update for Psychiatrists

Abstract

Obesity is a chronic relapsing condition associated with significant morbidity and premature mortality. The prevalence of obesity has increased dramatically over the last 20 years and continues to do so, primarily as a result of changes in dietary intake and exercise patterns. There are considerable challenges associated with the management of the obesity epidemic involving both public health policies and individual treatment. Management of the obese individual involves lifelong lifestyle change for all, drugs for some, and surgery for a few. Appropriate selection of patients and the setting of realistic goals are crucial to the success of any weight-reducing programme. The aim of obesity management is to reduce associated morbidity and mortality, not necessarily to restore normal body weight. While the current trends in obesity are depressing, a better understanding of the pathophysiology and treatment of the condition should allow the clinician to be more optimistic for the future.

RICHARD I. G. HOLT

Developmental Origins of Health and Disease Division,
School of Medicine, University of Southampton, Southampton, UK.

Introduction

The prevalence of obesity has increased dramatically over the last two decades throughout the world (James *et al.*, 2001; James *et al.*, 2004), and obesity is now recognized as one of the most important public health problems of our time (Visscher and Seidell, 2001). The continuing trend towards increasing prevalence rates indicates that public health measures to prevent obesity are failing (Mokdad *et al.*, 2000).

Although there is a high degree of heritability for obesity (Allison *et al.*, 1996), the rapid rise in obesity prevalence suggests that environmental factors, such as altered diets and decreased energy expenditure, are responsible for the changing patterns of obesity within countries (Prentice and Jebb, 1995).

Body weight is tightly regulated such that even small mismatches of less than 100 kilocalories per day in energy intake and expenditure may result in massive obesity (Wynne *et al.*, 2004). This makes the management of the individual with obesity especially challenging. If we are to implement changes to reduce the health burden of obesity, it is important to understand the underlying causes, and to set realistic goals for weight management programmes. The purpose of this review is to examine the latest evidence from the obesity research field in order to help practising psychiatrists reduce the obesity burden among their patients.

What Is Obesity?

Obesity is defined as a body mass index (BMI) above 30 kg/m^2, while overweight is defined as a BMI above 25 kg/m^2 (World Health Organization, 1997). Morbid obesity occurs at a BMI above 40 kg/m^2. These definitions are based on the actuarial observation that mortality has a J-shaped relationship to BMI, with mortality being lowest within the BMI range of 20–25 kg/m^2, and increasing at BMIs above and below this range (Jarrett *et al.*, 1982; Lee *et al.*, 1993). The effect of a low BMI on mortality may have been overestimated in the past because of the effect of smoking and consequent illness, and clinical disorders causing weight loss (Figure 1) (Manson *et al.*, 1990). These data are based on white European subjects; for individuals of South Asian ethnicity, the upper limit of normal for BMI may need to be reduced (WHO Expert Consultation, 2004).

Why Worry About Weight Excess?

'Thou seest that I have more flesh than another man and therefore more frailty…'

King Henry IV Part 1 Act III, Scene III

It has been estimated that obesity reduces life expectancy by around 9 years and accounts for 30,000 deaths in the UK per annum. Obesity costs the National Health Service £480 million or 1.5% of total NHS expenditure (National Audit Office, 2001), and the indirect costs of obesity are probably around £2 billion.

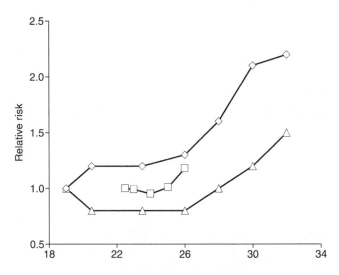

Figure 1 Relationship between BMI and relative risk of all-cause mortality in US men and women. ■ Men ▲ All women ◆ Non-smoking women with stable weight. Note how the J-shaped relationship disappears in women when only non-smoking women with stable weight are considered. Adapted from (Lee *et al.*, 1993; Manson *et al.*, 1990)

Overweight and obesity are associated with a number of metabolic and cardiovascular complications, musculoskeletal disease and several cancers (Table 1). Obesity increases the risk of diabetes, dyslipidaemia and insulin resistance by more than threefold, while increasing coronary heart disease and hypertension two- to threefold (Manson *et al.*, 1990; Meade *et al.*, 1993). Up to 80% of all new cases of diabetes can be attributed to obesity (Lean, 2000a). The risk of developing type 2 diabetes increases across the normal range, such that the risk of diabetes in a middle-aged woman whose BMI is greater than 35 kg/m^2 is 93.2 times greater than a woman whose BMI is below 22.5 kg/m^2 (Colditz *et al.*, 1995).

There is compelling evidence that our society discriminates against obese people (Wadden and Stunkard, 1985; Sonne-Holm and Sorensen, 1986). This can be damaging to the psychological well-being of obese individuals and may compound the effects of mental illness. Obese women are likely to leave school earlier, are less likely to be married and have higher rates of household poverty than women who are not overweight (Gortmaker *et al.*, 1993). These findings are independent of baseline socio-economic status and are not seen in people with other chronic conditions such as asthma or musculoskeletal abnormalities.

Limitations of BMI

In adult men of average weight, the percentage body fat is around 15–20%, while in women, this percentage is higher at 25–30%. As the health risks associated with obesity relate to an excess storage of body fat—and in particular visceral fat—certain individuals will be misclassified using BMI (Prentice and Jebb, 2001). For example, a lean young male bodybuilder may have an identical BMI to a middle-aged obese woman. Nevertheless,

across populations, BMI correlates well with percentage body fat, making this an easy measure of obesity.

Body fat may be preferentially located in the abdomen (central obesity) or surrounding the hips and thighs (peripheral obesity). Central obesity is associated with the metabolic syndrome and is a better predictor of health risk; at the same level of obesity, the more visceral fat, the greater the risk of developing cardiovascular and metabolic complications of obesity (Van Pelt *et al.*, 2001). Differences in the distribution of body fat explain why individuals from Asian backgrounds are at higher risk of the complications of obesity for any given BMI than white Europeans, as these individuals tend to have greater central fat distribution (McKeigue *et al.*, 1991). There are also gender differences in body fat distribution, with most women developing peripheral obesity, while men tend to develop central adiposity (Shimokata *et al.*, 1989).

Waist measurements can be used to identify individuals at high risk of developing the metabolic complications of obesity, particularly if combined with a fasting triglyceride concentration. Waist measurements of 100–102 cm in men and 88–90 cm in women alone provide useful reference values to identify obese individuals who may be at high risk for chronic metabolic diseases (Lean *et al.*, 1995; Lean *et al.*, 1998). If hypertriglyceridaemia (>2.0 mmol/L) is also present, over 80% of men with waist measurements greater than 90 cm will be at risk of developing the metabolic syndrome (Lemieux *et al.*, 2000).

Obesity Trends

The WHO MONICA project has been following obesity trends in 21 countries among randomly selected middle-aged participants from the early 1980s to the mid-1990s (Silventoinen *et al.*, 2004). The mean BMI, as well as the prevalence of overweight, has increased in virtually every Western European country, in Australia, the USA and China.

Within the UK, the prevalence of obesity in adults has almost trebled since 1980, such that in 2002, 23% of men and 25% of women were obese (Rennie and Jebb, 2005). The prevalence of obesity among children is lower, but increases in the prevalence of overweight are similar to the increases in obesity in adults. Obesity rates are higher in low social classes and in some ethnic minority groups, particularly in those from South Asia.

The CDC's Behavioral Risk Factor Surveillance System (BRFSS) provides dramatic evidence of the continuing rise in the prevalence of obesity within the United States (National Center for Chronic Disease Prevention and Health Promotion, 2005). Each year, state health departments use standard procedures to collect data through a series of monthly telephone interviews with US adults. In 1991, four states had obesity prevalence rates of 15–19% and no states had rates at or above 20%. In 2003, 15 states had obesity prevalence rates of 15–19%; 31 states had rates of 20–24%; and four states had rates more than 25%. As these data rely on self-reported height and weight, it is likely that they represent underestimates of the true prevalence of obesity.

Table 1   Health risks of obesity

Relative risk >3	Relative risk 2–3	Relative risk 1–2
Diabetes	Cardiovascular disease	Cancers post-menopausal breast, endometrial, colon
Gallbladder disease	Hypertension	Reproductive hormone abnormalities PCOS, impaired fertility, fetal defects
Dyslipidaemia	Osteoarthritis	Back pain
Insulin resistance	Hyperuricaemia	↑ Anaesthetic risk
Breathlessness	Gout	
Sleep apnoea		

Causes of Obesity

The causes of obesity are multifactorial, and range from purely genetic conditions such as leptin deficiency to entirely environmental conditions as seen in sumo wrestlers. Whatever the underlying cause, obesity will only occur when energy intake is greater than energy expenditure over a long period of time. If either energy intake increases or energy expenditure decreases, or both, the individual will gain weight. Both energy intake and expenditure are affected by internal homeostatic mechanisms as well as external environmental factors.

Given the diversity of factors affecting energy balance, it is remarkable how well body weight can be regulated. Most adults are able to maintain their body weight to within the few kilograms over 40 or more years in spite of having eaten in excess of 20 tonnes of food. Even in individuals who become obese, the mismatch between energy intake and energy expenditure is extremely small. Daniel Lamberts lived in Leicestershire, in the UK, during the eighteenth century, and he made a living exhibiting himself as a natural curiosity, having reached the weight of 700 pounds (320kg). When he died at the age of 39, it was estimated that he weighed 52 stone 11 pounds (336 kg), of which approximately 230 kg would have been fat, containing approximately two million kilocalories. Assuming that there was progressive weight gain throughout Mr Lamberts' life, his excess energy consumption would have been around 140 kilocalories per day—equivalent to just one apple!

Genetic Factors

The contribution of genetic factors to the development of obesity has been shown from twin, family and adoption studies, which suggest that up to 70% of the variance in BMI is accounted for by genetic variance (Allison *et al.*, 1996). Over the last decade, a number of human genes have been identified in which major missense or nonsense mutations have caused severe early-onset obesity, usually through the disruption of normal appetite control mechanisms (Table 2) (O'Rahilly *et al.*, 2003). Although these cases represent only a minority of all cases of obesity, genetic studies such as these will begin to identify the critical molecular components of the human energy balance regulatory systems, which should allow the targeting of more effective therapies in the future.

Table 2   Genetic syndromes and monogenic causes of obesity

Prader Willi
Bardet-Biedl
Laurence Moon
Biemond syndrome II
Alstrom
Schinzel
Stein Leventhal
Carbohydrate-deficient glycoprotein syndrome type 1
Cohen
Short stature obesity
Albright hereditary osteodystrophy
Borjeson-Forssman-Lehmann Syndrome
Fragile X Syndrome
Germinal cell aplasia
Sertoli cell only syndrome
Simpson dysmorphia
Leptin deficiency
Leptin receptor deficiency
Pro-opio-melanocortin deficiency
Melanocortin 4 receptor deficiency
Prohormone convertase 1 deficiency

Environmental Changes

Despite the strong contribution of genetics to the development of obesity, the current obesity epidemic cannot be explained by genetics alone. The change in obesity patterns have arisen as a result of an adverse environment interacting with a susceptible genotype.

Dietary Intake

The National Food Survey in the United Kingdom provides the longest running continuous survey of household consumption in the world (Prentice and Jebb, 1995). This survey has shown that, over the last 50 years, food consumption within the home has decreased. At first sight this appears to be paradoxical, but it must be remembered that as much as 50% of all food is consumed outside the home. Since the Second World War within

Table 3 Examples of light, moderate and vigorous physical activity

	Light EE <3.0 × BMR	Moderate EE: 3.0–6.0 × BMR	Vigorous EE: >6.0 × BMR
Walking	Slowly	Briskly	Fast or jogging
Cycling	Slowly	Steadily or up slopes	>10 mph or up hills
Swimming	Slowly	Moderate exertion	Fast or treading water
Gym work	Stretching exercises	Sit-ups	Stair ergometer, ski machine
Housework	Vacuum cleaning	Heavier cleaning	Moving furniture
Gardening	Weeding	Mowing the lawn with a power mower, sweeping, raking	Hand mowing or digging

EE = Energy expenditure; BMR = Basal metabolic rate

Europe, more food is produced than is required. This has led to intense competition and incentives to bulk buy; there can be few people who have never taken advantage of 'two for the price of one' offers or the better-value 'jumbo' pack.

The National Food Survey has also indicated that there are changes in the types of food we are eating, and that there has been a major shift from carbohydrate to fat consumption (Prentice and Jebb, 1995). This is important because most individuals regulate their meal size according to weight or volume, rather than caloric intake. Fat contains approximately 9 kilocalories per gram while carbohydrate and protein contain 4 kilocalories per gram. Short-term metabolic studies show that when the fat content of the diet is increased, the individual continues to eat the same quantity of food, and consequently moves into a positive energy balance (Stubbs *et al.*, 1995).

There is some evidence from cross-sectional and longitudinal studies that the proportion of energy consumed as fat is linked with an increase in the prevalence of obesity (Lissner and Heitmann, 1995). More recently, however, particularly in the UK and USA, there has been a decline in the proportion of energy consumed as fat, while the prevalence of obesity continues to rise (Heini and Weinsier, 1997). This may reflect the relatively long lag phase in the development of obesity, and it may be many years before this dietary change has an obvious impact on the prevalence of obesity.

Physical Activity

Mankind has evolved to undertake vigorous physical activity, and it should therefore be of little surprise that inactivity is associated with ill-health. Total energy expenditure is the sum of our basal metabolic rate, dietary-induced thermogenesis, adaptive thermogenesis (such as shivering) and physical activity. Of all of these, physical activity offers the greatest scope for an individual to increase their energy expenditure.

Physical activity can be defined as any bodily movement produced by skeletal muscle which results in energy expenditure, and can be subdivided into different components such as exercise or sport (Caspersen *et al.*, 1985). Activity can be also divided according to its intensity and duration (Table 3). Low-intensity activities may include walking or household work, while more intense activities may include running or cycling

faster than 10 miles an hour or up hills. Sedentary behaviour such as television viewing is also significant when considering weight gain, as it limits the opportunity to be active, and therefore reduces energy expenditure.

Physical inactivity is a major determinant of the current obesity epidemic (Prentice and Jebb, 1995). Several studies have shown that physically active people have lower levels of body fat and weight than inactive people (Schulz and Schoeller, 1994; Lahti-Koski *et al.*, 2002). Strong relationships between indicators of inactivity such as television viewing and car ownership with secular trends in obesity have also been reported (Prentice and Jebb, 1995).

Unfortunately, epidemiological studies have shown that we are becoming progressively less active. The Allied Dunbar National Fitness Survey, undertaken in 1995, indicated that 29% of men and 28% of women were classed as sedentary, while only 16% of men and 5% of women participated in regular vigorous activity (Fentem and Walker, 1995). Inactivity increases with age, but social class differences are not obvious because occupational activity is often balanced with leisure time activity. In the United States, 60% of adults are not regularly active and 25% reported no significant activity at all (US Department of Health and Human Services, 1996). Children are also becoming increasingly inactive (Fox, 2004).

Technological advances have reduced to our physical activity in many spheres. The increasing number of cars has reduced the amount of physical activity we undertake travelling to and from work. It is estimated that household appliances have reduced our energy expenditure by around 500 kilocalories per day within the home. We have endeavoured to compartmentalize our exercise into 30–40 minutes in the gym, two or three times a week, rather than focusing on increasing our energy expenditure throughout the day.

Psychological Factors

As well as eating because we need to eat, many of us also eat for pleasure. Much of the research into obesity has been concerned with the homeostatic control of eating rather than focusing on the hedonistic reasons why we eat. These two aspects of eating are complementary, and have two different CNS systems controlling them.

There is much to be learnt from studying the eating behaviours of people who gain weight (Blundell and Finlayson, 2004). Overweight individuals select more energy-dense foods, display enhanced hunger traits with less satiety, and they eat larger and more frequent meals (Blundell and Gillett, 2001). Their eating behaviour is also less inhibited. Individuals who tend to gain weight have a greater readiness to eat and will eat opportunistically. Differences in the timing of eating also exist: obese individuals tend to eat more in the afternoon and less in the morning. In contrast, enjoyment from food is seen as being less important in those who do not gain weight, and health, rather than taste, becomes a more important factor when choosing food.

Prevention of Obesity

Despite the apparent simplicity of the solution for preventing obesity, there is little evidence supporting the efficacy of health education programmes within the general population (Bouchard, 1996). Education alone is probably insufficient, and behaviour modification is also required (Jeffery et al., 1995). Healthcare professionals need to take obesity seriously, and must collectively support obesity prevention strategies in order to prevent the undermining of healthy lifestyle advice (Frank, 2004).

A public health and governmental response is also needed to reduce the obesity epidemic. This could include legislation or a more 'ecological' approach in which there is a coordinated strategy to influence the individual by education and behaviour change, and to minimize the impact of negative environment influences through economic, physical and socio-cultural pressures.

Management of the Individual with Obesity

The major aim of any weight management programme should be to improve health by reducing morbidity and mortality associated with obesity, rather than simply lowering weight and adiposity. A 10% weight loss is associated with a major reduction in death and the metabolic complications of obesity (Table 4) (Goldstein, 1992; Lean, 2000b).

Patient Selection

The scale of the problem means that we are unable to treat all patients with obesity, and therefore it is important to select patients who will gain most benefit from intervention (Teixeira et al., 2005). Several characteristics help to predict whether a patient will lose weight during a weight management programme, including high initial body mass, high central obesity, high energy intake and initial weight loss; the latter probably reflects the patient's ability to comply with the weight management programme. Patients need to be well motivated to undertake major lifestyle changes. High self-esteem and the acceptance of the need to change also predict weight loss. This is particularly challenging in the management of individuals with a mental illness, for whom obesity may well further complicate their mental health.

Table 4 Benefits associated with 10% weight loss

Survival	↓ 20–25% in premature mortality
Diabetes	↓ 50% in type 2 diabetes
	↓ 30–50% in blood glucose
Lipids	↓ 10% in total cholesterol
	↓ 30% in triglycerides
Blood pressure	↓ 10 mmHg in systolic BP
	↓ 20 mmHg in diastolic BP

Setting Realistic Goals

When managing the individual with obesity, it is important to set appropriate goals to prevent disappointment and frustration during the programme. A 10% weight loss is considered to be an appropriate initial goal because it is achievable, results in significant health benefits and can be maintained (Wadden et al., 1996). Unfortunately, most individuals want to achieve far greater weight loss than this. In one study in which patients are asked how much weight they would like to lose, only 1% said they would be happy with a weight loss of <10%, while 63% expected to lose more than 20% of their weight (Jeffery et al., 1998).

The natural history of body weight changes over time is a gradual increase in weight, so the first aim of a weight management programme is to prevent further weight gain (Figure 2) (Rossner, 1993). Congratulating patients on maintaining weight can improve self-esteem and lead to better long-term adherence to a weight loss programme.

Patients should be aware of the long-term challenge of weight loss. In the same way that weight gain usually occurs over many years, a lifelong change to a patient's lifestyle will be required in order to reduce weight. Patients should be encouraged not to think of 'short-term fixes'. The basal metabolic rate accounts for around 70% of our total energy expenditure. If energy intake falls below the basal metabolic rate, strong protective adaptations are initiated to try to maintain weight (Wilkin et al., 1983). An individual feels lethargic, tired and listless, and will be unable to maintain this situation for any length of time. Too great a calorie deficit will therefore lead to failure. In contrast, if a calorie reduction of around 500 kilocalories per day is advocated, the patient can lose around 1 kg of weight per week, and this is sustainable over the long term (Wadden et al., 1996; Poirier and Despres, 2001).

Dietary Strategies

There is a huge popular literature about diets that will aid weight loss. Most of these diets fail to appreciate that nutrition is a demand-led process and therefore any diet should meet the requirements of the body. There is an absolute need to include both fats and carbohydrates as energy sources, and any diet that excludes one or other of these components will create a mismatch between supply and demand. Diets need to be sustainable over the long-term and most diets that exclude different food types, such as the Atkins or Ornish diet, cannot be maintained for more than a few months (Dansinger et al., 2005).

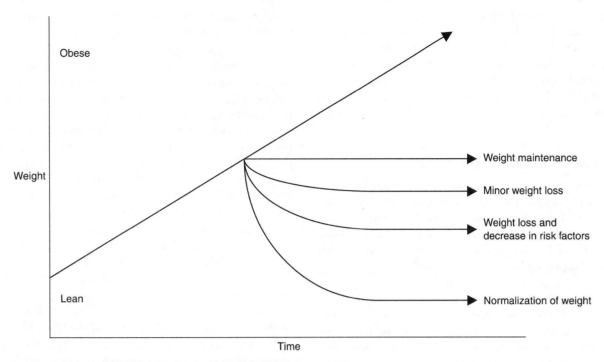

Figure 2 What is a successful outcome? Adapted from (Rossner, 1993)

The first aim of dietary advice must therefore be to ensure that the individual eats sufficient food to meet their metabolic needs. Patients should be advised to avoid extreme eating restraints and dieting. In order to reduce calorie consumption, two dietary changes should be considered: the types of food should be changed, and the portion sizes reduced. A systematic review of all dietary interventions lasting longer than 1 year found that there is little evidence to support the use of diets—apart from low fat diets—for weight reduction. Low fat diets for up to 36 months have resulted in modest weight losses of around 3.5 kg (Avenell *et al.*, 2004a). The consumption of low energy-dense foods and sweeteners may also reduce meal energy intake (Raben *et al.*, 2002; Rolls *et al.*, 2004a).

Portion size is extremely important. There is good evidence that energy intake is proportional to the amount of food available at mealtimes, and by reducing portion size, energy consumption falls (Diliberti *et al.*, 2004; Rolls *et al.*, 2004b). Over the last decade, the average size of a dinner plate in a US restaurant has increased from 9 inches to 12 inches, resulting in the same volume of food on a larger plate appearing smaller. This inevitably leads to an increase in portion size and the resultant over-consumption of food. Use of a smaller plate is a simple method by which individuals can reduce their portion size.

Re-establishing 'normal' eating behaviour and attitudes to food are also important (Brownell and Kramer, 1989). Many people eat for reasons that have nothing to do with hunger, such as being bored, coping with sadness or to be sociable. Encouraging healthy eating patterns can lead to a reduction in energy intake.

It is important that while food is being consumed, the individual's attention is focused on that food (Bellisle and Dalix, 2001). If attention becomes divided, such as when working at a computer, the reward gained from eating is reduced, and people tend to eat more. Food should not be associated with other activities, such as watching television, because this will lead to less healthy eating behaviours (Coon *et al.*, 2001). Individuals should be advised to eat only in a dining-room or at a kitchen table at mealtimes.

Cravings for food are often short lived and therefore a useful strategy can be to distract the patient with an alternative activity such as a five-minute walk when a craving occurs.

The value of commercial weight loss programmes has not been fully established, but they may lead to greater weight loss than an individual's own attempts to lose weight (Heshka *et al.*, 2003; Tsai and Wadden, 2005). Within a psychiatric setting, it is likely that group work, whereby individuals can gain support from other participants, will result in greater weight loss.

Exercise

Exercise can play a key role in a weight management programme (King and Tribble, 1991). High energy expenditure can readily outstrip energy intake and therefore promote weight loss in its own right; exercise is also important in the prevention of weight re-gain when combined with dietary interventions (Wadden *et al.*, 2004).

Individuals should be encouraged to decrease the amount of time they spend sitting or occupied in sedentary activities. Low intensity activity is of great importance for weight loss and weight loss maintenance; for example, an 80-year-old patient with agitated Alzheimer's disease will expend more calories per day than an Olympic athlete because the patient with Alzheimer's is walking for nearly 24 hours every day. The total time spent active is important, and exercise does not need to be taken in a single period. Patients need to think about ways of including physical activity in their everyday lives. This can be achieved in many areas; for example, a patient could be encouraged to use the stairs rather than a lift, to get off the bus one stop early, to park at the far end of the car park rather than right next to the door. Physical activity needs to fit in with daily life and the functional capabilities of the individual, and ideally should be pleasurable. The most appropriate type of exercise for any individual patient is one that will still be being pursued a decade later.

Pharmacological Interventions

Pharmacological treatment of obesity has a chequered history and many physicians still regard drug treatments with suspicion. Whilst it is true that the currently available drugs are relatively ineffective when used alone, when used in combination with lifestyle and behavioural modification programmes, they are a useful adjunct in the management of obesity.

The drugs that are currently available can be divided into two main categories: those acting on the gastrointestinal system, and centrally acting drugs that affect appetite. The two drugs that are currently available for the management of obesity are orlistat, which is a pancreatic lipase inhibitor, and sibutramine, which is a serotonin and noradrenaline reuptake inhibitor (Avenell *et al.*, 2004b). The latter is contraindicated in psychiatric disease and so the remainder of this section will concentrate on the use of orlistat.

Orlistat inhibits pancreatic and gastric lipases, thereby reducing ingested triglyceride hydrolysis. The treatment produces a dose-dependent reduction in dietary fat absorption that is near maximal at the currently available dose of 120 mg three times a day. In clinical trials lasting up to 4 years, orlistat led to modest weight loss of up to 10% (Torgerson *et al.*, 2004). This weight loss was associated with a reduction in other features of the metabolic syndrome including waist circumference, blood pressure, dyslipidaemia and hyperglycaemia (Torgerson *et al.*, 2004). In patients with impaired glucose tolerance, orlistat reduced the risk of incident diabetes by 37% over and above the effect of lifestyle intervention alone (Torgerson *et al.*, 2004). Some patients with pre-existing diabetes may be able to reduce or discontinue their oral hypoglycaemic medication when taking orlistat (Hanefeld and Sachse, 2002).

Case reports have also been published on the use of orlistat to treat the weight gain associated with antipsychotic drugs (Anghelescu *et al.*, 2000; Hilger *et al.*, 2002; Schwartz *et al.*, 2004). Orlistat led to a mean weight loss of between 6.1% and 35%, without any significant alteration in the plasma concentration of any of the antipsychotics.

The main limiting factor for the use of orlistat is the development of gastrointestinal side-effects secondary to fat malabsorption. These include liquid oily stools and faecal urgency and incontinence, and these can be associated with loss of fat soluble vitamins and malabsorption. As the consumption of a high fat diet will inevitably lead to severe gastrointestinal side-effects, it is important that the prescription of orlistat is accompanied by clear behavioural and dietary advice. Roche, who manufactures orlistat, has established a free telephone and on-line patient support programme, which has been shown to im-prove compliance with drug therapy and to achieve greater weight loss (Prentice *et al.*, 2004).

When orlistat was first introduced into the United Kingdom, its license limited its use to 2 years. However, as longer studies have been reported, and there is a greater appreciation of the chronic relapsing nature of obesity, this restriction has now been removed and patients can continue to use the drug as long as it remains effective (Torgerson *et al.*, 2004). The drug should not be considered ineffective because weight loss has stopped, provided the weight reduction is maintained. Discontinuation of the drug at this stage may well lead to weight re-gain. There is no published literature to suggest that orlistat is associated with the development of drug dependency.

Within the UK, orlistat is licensed for use in patients whose BMI is greater than 30 kg/m^2 or in patients with co-morbidity who have a BMI >28 kg/m^2. Initially, the drug should be used for a 3-month trial period and should only be continued if the patient loses more than 5% of their body weight. If the patient has not lost more than 10% of their weight within the first 6 months, continued use of orlistat should be reconsidered.

Several other drugs have been considered for use in the management of obesity, including pseudophedrine, ephedra, sertraline, yohimbine, amphetamine or its derivatives, bupropion, benzocaine, threachlorocitric acid and bromocriptine. There is currently a paucity of data supporting the effectiveness of these agents, and none of them were recommended in a recent Cochrane systematic database review (Norris *et al.*, 2005).

Of the drugs that are currently being developed for the management of obesity, rimonabant and topiramate deserve a special mention (Halford, 2004). Rimonabant is an endocannabinoid 1 (CB1) receptor antagonist, which has been shown to be effective in reducing body weight and in weight maintenance with up to 2 years of therapy in several phase III studies (Cleland *et al.*, 2004; Fernandez and Allison, 2004).

Endocannabinoids increase food intake through CB1 receptor activation and animal experiments show that antagonism of this receptor reduces sucrose and food intake. CB1 receptors are also found in peripheral tissues where activation of this receptor leads to increased insulin resistance, possibly through alteration in adipocytokine production, such as decreased adiponectin secretion. Antagonism of CB1 receptors leads to weight loss and a reduction in features of the metabolic syndrome, with only around half of the improvements in metabolic profile being explained by changes in weight. The main side-effects of rimonabant are depressed mood, anxiety and nausea, and therefore caution may be needed if this drug is to be used in patients with psychiatric illnesses. There have been small trials of CB1 antagonists in the treatment of schizophrenia, and while the results were inconclusive, no worsening of psychiatric symptoms was reported (Meltzer *et al.*, 2004).

Several case reports have suggested that topiramate may be useful in preventing the weight gain associated with antipsychotic drugs (Dursun and Devarajan, 2000; Lessig *et al.*, 2001; Levy *et al.*, 2002). As topiramate, which is a fairly new anticonvulsant, is increasingly being used as a mood stabilizer in bipolar and schizoaffective disorders, this additional benefit on weight is particularly desirable. Further studies are required before this treatment can be recommended for routine use.

Bariatric Surgery

Bariatric surgery is currently the only long-term cure for obesity. Two main types of surgical intervention are used in the management of obesity: malabsorption techniques bypass part of the stomach or small intestine, while restrictive surgery leads to reduced food intake by reducing the size of the stomach. The best evidence for the long-term effects of gastric surgery for obesity comes from the Swedish Obese Subjects study, where the weight loss after 2 years was typically between 30 and 40 kg. Quality of life improved dramatically following surgery and this was associated with major improvements in the metabolic side-effects of obesity (Sjostrom *et al.*, 2004). A review of bariatric surgery has also suggested that gastric bypass surgery is associated with a 99–100% prevention of diabetes in patients with impaired glucose tolerance and an 80–90% clinical resolution of diagnosed early type 2 diabetes (Ferchak and Meneghini, 2004).

At present, obesity surgery is only recommended for those with morbid obesity. Each patient requires an extensive preoperative assessment which includes psychological evaluations, as surgery will not treat an eating disorder, and may lead to worsening of the mental state if patients are dependent on food.

Conclusions

Obesity has become a major health problem throughout the world. While genetics can explain much of the variability of BMI within a given population, it is environmental changes over the last 50 years that have precipitated the obesity epidemic. A public health and governmental response is needed to reduce the unhealthy environment in which we now live. Managing the individual with obesity is challenging, but successful results can be obtained through lifestyle modification when combined with the setting of realistic goals and appropriate patient selection. Drug therapy is currently in its infancy, but the use of orlistat is a useful adjunct to other weight loss measures. Bariatric surgery is the only long-term solution for patients with morbid obesity. There can no longer be a place for therapeutic nihilism and we need to develop strategies within mental health settings to promote lifestyles that will both prevent and treat overweight and obesity.

Declaration of Interest

Dr Holt has received educational grants and fees for lecturing and consultancy work from Eli-Lilly & Company, Roche Pharmaceuticals and Abbott Laboratories.

References

Allison D. B., Kaprio J., Korkeila M., Koskenvuo M., Neale M. C., Hayakawa K (1996) The heritability of body mass index among an international sample of monozygotic twins reared apart. Int J Obes Relat Metab Disord 20: 501–506

Anghelescu I., Klawe C, Benkert O (2000) Orlistat in the treatment of psychopharmacologically induced weight gain. J Clin Psychopharmacol 20: 716–717

Avenell A., Brown T. J., McGee M. A., Campbell M. K., Grant A. M., Broom J, Jung R. T., Smith W. C. (2004a) What are the long-term benefits of weight reducing diets in adults? A systematic review of randomized controlled trials. J Hum Nutr Diet 17: 317–335

Avenell A., Brown T. J., McGee M. A., Campbell M. K., Grant A. M., Broom J, Jung R. T., Smith WC (2004b) What interventions should we add to weight reducing diets in adults with obesity? A systematic review of randomized controlled trials of adding drug therapy, exercise, behaviour therapy or combinations of these interventions. J Hum Nutr Diet 17: 293–316

Bellisle F., Dalix A. M. (2001) Cognitive restraint can be offset by distraction, leading to increased meal intake in women. Am J Clin Nutr 74: 197–200

Blundell J. E., Finlayson G. (2004) Is susceptibility to weight gain characterized by homeostatic or hedonic risk factors for overconsumption? Physiol Behav 82: 21–25

Blundell J. E., Gillett A (2001) Control of food intake in the obese. Obes Res 9 (Suppl 4): 263S–270S

Bouchard C (1996) Can obesity be prevented? Nutr Rev 54: S125–130.

Brownell K. D., Kramer F. M .(1989) Behavioral management of obesity. Med Clin North Am 73: 185–201

Caspersen C. J., Powell K. E., Christenson G. M. (1985) Physical activity, exercise, and physical fitness: definitions and distinctions for health-related research. Public Health Rep 100: 126–131

Cleland J. G., Ghosh J., Freemantle N., Kaye G. C., Nasir M., Clark A L., Coletta A P (2004) Clinical trials update and cumulative meta-analyses from the American College of Cardiology: WATCH, SCD-HeFT, DINAMIT, CASINO, INSPIRE, STRATUS-US, RIO-Lipids and cardiac resynchronisation therapy in heart failure. Eur J Heart Fail 6: 501–508

Colditz G. A., Willett W. C., Rotnitzky A., Manson J. E. (1995) Weight gain as a risk factor for clinical diabetes mellitus in women. Ann Int Med 122: 481–486

Coon K. A., Goldberg J., Rogers B. L., Tucker K. L. (2001) Relationships between use of television during meals and children's food consumption patterns. Pediatrics 107: E7

Dansinger M. L., Gleason J. A., Griffith J. L., Selker H. P., Schaefer E. J. (2005) Comparison of the Atkins, Ornish, Weight Watchers, and Zone diets for weight loss and heart disease risk reduction: a randomized trial. JAMA 293: 43–53

Diliberti N., Bordi P. L., Conklin M. T., Roe L. S., Rolls B. J. (2004) Increased portion size leads to increased energy intake in a restaurant meal. Obes Res 12: 562–568

Dursun S. M., Devarajan S (2000) Clozapine weight gain, plus topiramate weight loss. Can J Psychiatry 45: 198

Fentem P., Walker A (1995). Setting targets for England: challenging, measurable and achievable. In Killoran A. J., Fentem P., Caspersen C. J. (eds), Moving On: International Perspectives on Promoting Physical Activity. Health Education Authority, London

Ferchak C. V., Meneghini L. F. (2004) Obesity, bariatric surgery and type 2 diabetes—a systematic review. Diabetes Metab Res Rev 20: 438–445

Fernandez J. R., Allison D. B. (2004) Rimonabant Sanofi-Synthelabo. Curr Opin Investig Drugs 5: 430–435

Fox K. R .(2004) Childhood obesity and the role of physical activity. J. R. Soc Health *124*: 34–39

Frank E. (2004) Physician health and patient care. JAMA *291*: 637

Goldstein D. J. (1992) Beneficial health effects of modest weight loss. Int J Obes Relat Metab Disord 16: 397–415

Gortmaker S. L., Must A., Perrin J. M., Sobol A M, Dietz W. H. (1993) Social and economic consequences of overweight in adolescence and young adulthood. N Engl J Med *329*: 1008–1012

Halford J. C. (2004) Clinical pharmacotherapy for obesity: current drugs and those in advanced development. Curr Drug Targets 5: 637–646

Hanefeld M., Sachse G (2002) The effects of orlistat on body weight and glycaemic control in overweight patients with type 2 diabetes: a randomized, placebo-controlled trial. Diabetes Obes Metab *4*: 415–423

Heini A. F., Weinsier R. L. (1997) Divergent trends in obesity and fat intake patterns: the American paradox. Am J Med *102*: 259–264

Heshka S., Anderson J. W., Atkinson R. L., Greenway F. L., Hill J. O., Phinney S. D., Kolotkin R. L., Miller-Kovach K., Pi-Sunyer F. X. (2003) Weight loss with self-help compared with a structured commercial program: a randomized trial. JAMA *289*: 1792–1798

Hilger E., Quiner S., Ginzel I., Walter H., Saria L., Barnas C. (2002) The effect of orlistat on plasma levels of psychotropic drugs in patients with long-term psychopharmacotherapy. J Clin Psychopharmacol *22*: 68–70

James P. T., Rigby N., Leach R. (2004) The obesity epidemic, metabolic syndrome and future prevention strategies. Eur J Cardiovasc Prev Rehabil *11*: 3–8

James P. T., Leach R., Kalamara E., Shayeghi M. (2001) The worldwide obesity epidemic. Obes Res 9 Suppl 4: 228S-233S

Jarrett R. J., Shipley M. J., Rose G. (1982) Weight and mortality in the Whitehall Study. BMJ 285: 535–537

Jeffery R. W., Wing R. R., Mayer R. R. (1998) Are smaller weight losses or more achievable weight loss goals better in the long term for obese patients? J Consult Clin Psychol 66: 641–645

Jeffery R. W., Gray C. W., French S. A., Hellerstedt W. L., Murray D, Luepker R. V., Blackburn H. (1995) Evaluation of weight reduction in a community intervention for cardiovascular disease risk: changes in body mass index in the Minnesota Heart Health Program. Int J Obes Relat Metab Disord *19*: 30–39

King A. C., Tribble D. L. (1991) The role of exercise in weight regulation in nonathletes. Sports Med *11*: 331–349

Lahti-Koski M., Pietinen P., Heliovaara M., Vartiainen E. (2002) Associations of body mass index and obesity with physical activity, food choices, alcohol intake, and smoking in the 1982–1997 FINRISK Studies. Am J Clin Nutr *75:* 809–817

Lean M. E. (2000a) Obesity: Burdens of illness and strategies for prevention or management. Drugs Today (Barc) **36**: 773–784

Lean M. E. (2000b) Is long-term weight loss possible? Br J Nutr *83* (Suppl 1): S103–111

Lean M. E., Han T. S., Morrison C. E. (1995) Waist circumference as a measure for indicating need for weight management. BMJ 311: 158–161

Lean M. E., Han T. S., Seidell J. C. (1998) Impairment of health and quality of life in people with large waist circumference. Lancet *351*: 853–856

Lee I. M., Manson J. E., Hennekens C. H., Paffenbarger R. S., Jr (1993) Body weight and mortality. A 27-year follow-up of middle-aged men. JAMA *270*: 2823–2828

Lemieux I., Pascot A., Couillard C., Lamarche B., Tchernof A., Almeras N., Bergeron J., Gaudet D., Tremblay G., Prud'homme D., Nadeau A., Despres J. P. (2000) Hypertriglyceridemic waist: A marker of the atherogenic metabolic triad (hyperinsulinemia; hyperapolipoprotein B; small, dense LDL) in men? Circulation *102*: 179–184

Lessig M. C., Shapira N. A., Murphy T. K. (2001) Topiramate for reversing atypical antipsychotic weight gain. J Am Acad Child Adolesc Psychiatry *40*: 1364

Levy E., Margolese H. C., Chouinard G (2002) Topiramate produced weight loss following olanzapine-induced weight gain in schizophrenia. J Clin Psychiatry *63*: 1045

Lissner L., Heitmann B. L. (1995) Dietary fat and obesity: evidence from epidemiology. Eur J Clin Nutr *49*: 79–90

McKeigue P. M., Shah B., Marmot mg (1991) Relation of central obesity and insulin resistance with high diabetes prevalence and cardiovascular risk in South Asians. Lancet *337*: 382–386

Manson J. E., Colditz G. A., Stampfer M. J., Willett W. C., Rosner B., Monson R. R., Speizer F. E., Hennekens C H (1990) A prospective study of obesity and risk of coronary heart disease in women. N Engl J Med *322*: 882–889

Meade T. W., Ruddock V., Stirling Y., Chakrabarti R., Miller G. J. (1993) Fibrinolytic activity, clotting factors, and long-term incidence of ischaemic heart disease in the Northwick Park Heart Study. Lancet *342*: 1076–1079

Meltzer H. Y., Arvanitis L., Bauer D., Rein W. (2004) Placebo-controlled evaluation of four novel compounds for the treatment of schizophrenia and schizoaffective disorder. Am J Psychiatry *161*: 975–984

Mokdad A. H., Serdula M. K., Dietz W. H., Bowman B. A., Marks J. S., Koplan J. P. (2000) The continuing epidemic of obesity in the United States. JAMA *284*: 1650–1651

National Audit Office (2001) Tackling Obesity in England. The Stationery Office, London

National Center for Chronic Disease Prevention and Health Promotion (2005) US Obesity trends 1985–2003. **http://www.cdc.gov/ nccdphp/ dnpa/obesity/trend/maps/**

Norris S., Zhang X., Avenell A., Gregg E., Schmid C., Lau J. (2005) Pharmacotherapy for weight loss in adults with type 2 diabetes mellitus. Cochrane Database Syst Rev, CD004096

O'Rahilly S., Farooqi I. S., Yeo G. S., Challis B. G. (2003) Minireview: human obesity-lessons from monogenic disorders. Endocrinology *144*: 3757–3764

Poirier P., Despres J. P. (2001) Exercise in weight management of obesity. Cardiol Clin 19: 459–470 Prentice A. M., Jebb S. A. (1995) Obesity in Britain: gluttony or sloth? BMJ *311*: 437–439

Prentice A. M., Jebb S A (2001) Beyond body mass index. Obes Rev 2: 141–147

Prentice A., Jebb S., Blaskett A., Corner A (2004) A patient support programme for orlistat - analysis of adherence and weight loss. Int J Obes Rel Metab Disord 28 (Suppl 1)*:* S28

Raben A., Vasilaras T. H. Moller A. C., Astrup A (2002) Sucrose compared with artificial sweeteners: different effects on ad libitum food intake and body weight after 10 wk of supplementation in overweight subjects. Am J Clin Nutr 76: 721–729

Rennie K. L., Jebb S. A. (2005) Prevalence of obesity in Great Britain. Obes Rev 6: 11–12

Rolls B. J., Roe L. S., Meengs J. S. (2004a) Salad and satiety: energy density and portion size of a first-course salad affect energy intake at lunch. J Am Diet Assoc *104*: 1570–1576

Rolls B. J., Roe L. S., Kral T. V., Meengs J. S., Wall D. E. (2004b) Increasing the portion size of a packaged snack increases energy intake in men and women. Appetite *42*: 63–69

Rossner S. (1993). Is obesity incurable? In Ditschuneit H, Gries F.A., Hauner H. (eds), Obesity in Europe 1993. John Libbey & Co, London

Schulz L. O., Schoeller D. A. (1994) A compilation of total daily energy expenditures and body weights in healthy adults. Am J Clin Nutr 60: 676–681

Schwartz T. L., Jindal S., Simionescu M., Nihalani N., Azhar N., Tirmazi S., Hussein J. (2004) Effectiveness of orlistat versus diet and exercise for weight gain associated with antidepressant use: a pilot study. J Clin Psychopharmacol 24: 555–556

Shimokata H., Tobin J. D., Muller D. C., Elahi D., Coon P. J., Andres R. (1989) Studies in the distribution of body fat: I. Effects of age, sex, and obesity. J. Gerontol 44: M66–73

Silventoinen K., Sans S., Tolonen H., Monterde D., Kuulasmaa K., Kesteloot H., Tuomilehto J. (2004) Trends in obesity and energy supply in the WHO MONICA Project. Int J Obes Relat Metab Disord 28: 710–718

Sjostrom L., Lindroos A. K., Peltonen M., Torgerson J., Bouchard C., Carlsson B., Dahlgren S., Larsson B., Narbro K., Sjostrom C. D., Sullivan M., Wedel H. (2004) Lifestyle, diabetes, and cardiovascular risk factors 10 years after bariatric surgery. N Engl J Med 351: 2683–2693

Sonne-Holm S., Sorensen T. I. (1986) Prospective study of attainment of social class of severely obese subjects in relation to parental social class, intelligence, and education. BMJ 292: 586–589

Stubbs R. J., Harbron C. G., Murgatroyd P. R., Prentice A. M. (1995) Covert manipulation of dietary fat and energy density: effect on substrate flux and food intake in men eating ad libitum. Am J Clin Nutr 62: 316–329

Teixeira P. J., Going S. B., Sardinha L. B., Lohman T.G. (2005) A review of psychosocial pre-treatment predictors of weight control. Obes Rev 6: 43–65

Torgerson J. S., Hauptman J., Boldrin M. N., Sjostrom L. (2004) XENical in the prevention of diabetes in obese subjects (XENDOS) study: a randomized study of orlistat as an adjunct to lifestyle changes for the prevention of type 2 diabetes in obese patients. Diabetes Care 27: 155–161

Tsai A. G., Wadden T. A. (2005) Systematic review: an evaluation of major commercial weight loss programs in the United States. Ann Intern Med 142: 56–66

US Department of Health and Human Services (1996) Physical Activity and health. A report of the Surgeon General (Executive Summary). Superintendeny of Documents, Pittsburgh, PA

Van Pelt R. E., Evans E. M., Schechtman K. B., Ehsani A. A., Kohrt W. M. (2001) Waist circumference vs body mass index for prediction of disease risk in postmenopausal women. Int J Obes Relat Metab Disord 25: 1183–1188

Visscher T. L., Seidell J. C. (2001) The public health impact of obesity. Ann Rev Public Health 22: 355–375

Wadden T. A., Stunkard A. J. (1985) Social and psychological consequences of obesity. Ann Intern Med 103: 1062–1067

Wadden T. A., Butryn M. L., Byrne K. J. (2004) Efficacy of lifestyle modification for long-term weight control. Obes Res 12 (Suppl): 151S-162S

Wadden T. A., Steen S. N., Wingate B. J., Foster G D (1996) Psychosocial consequences of weight reduction: how much weight loss is enough? Am J Clin Nutr 63: 461S-465S

WHO Expert Consultation (2004) Appropriate body-mass index for Asian populations and its implications for policy and intervention strategies. Lancet 363: 157–163

Wilkin T. J., Choquet R. C., Schmouker Y., Rouquette N., Baldet L., Vannereau D. (1983) Maximum calorie (sub-threshold) dieting of the obese and its hormonal response. Acta Endocrinol 103: 184–187

World Health Organisation (1997) Obesity: preventing and managing the global epidemic. WHO, Geneva Wynne K., Stanley S., Bloom S. (2004) The gut and regulation of body weight. J Clin Endocrinol Metab 89: 2576–2582

UNIT 7
Development

Unit Selections

23. **Why Newborns Cause Acrimony and Alimony**, Dolores Puterbaugh
24. **The Methuselah Report**, Wayne Curtis
25. **A Peaceful Adolescence**, Barbara Kantrowitz and Karen Springen
26. **Ageless Aging: The Next Era of Retirement**, Ken Dychtwald
27. **The Borders of Healing**, Marianne Szegedy-Maszak

Key Points to Consider

- What are the various milestones or developmental landmarks that signal stages in human development? What purpose do various developmental events serve? Can you give examples of some of these events?

- Do parents matter or do you think genes mostly dictate child development? Do you think that both nature and nurture affect development?

- Why is embryonic and fetal life so important? How do the experiences of the fetus affect the child after birth? What factors deter the fetus from achieving its full potential? What would you say to a pregnant friend to help her understand how important prenatal life is?

- Do most parents look forward to the birth of their first child? What are the general expectations of new parents? What is the true reality of a new baby for first-time parents? How is marriage affected by the presence of a baby? What advice might you provide to a mother or father expecting the first child?

- Is it important for both parents to be present during their child's formative years? Do you think fathers and mothers differ in their interactions with their children? How so?

- How is adolescence defined? How are today's teens different from teens in the past, for example from their parents' generation? What roles do hormonal changes and brain development play in the maturation of adolescents? What societal factors influence teens' development? If you had to rank these factors, which would you choose as most influential and which as least significant? What can parents do to help guide their teens toward a healthy and positive adulthood? Need adolescence be a time of distress and conflict for families?

- Why do we age? Can we stay younger longer? What do you think Americans say is more important - a high quality but shorter life or a poorer quality and longer life? Why do you think they answer the way they do? How would you answer and why? Would you want to live to 100? What can you do to accomplish this? As adults extend their life expectancy, how does society have to adapt or change to accommodate them?

- Why is death a stigmatized topic in America? Do you think people should discuss it more often and more openly? Do you think they ever will? How do people in other cultures cope with the death of a loved one? Do you think that one style (Eastern or Western) of mourning is better than another?

Student Website
www.mhcls.com/online

Internet References
Further information regarding these websites may be found in this book's preface or online.

American Association for Child and Adolescent Psychiatry
http://www.aacap.org
Behavioral Genetics
http://www.ornl.gov/hgmis/elsi/behavior.html

The Garcias and the Szubas are parents of newborns. When the babies are not in their mothers' rooms, both sets of parents wander down to the hospital's neonatal nursery where pediatric nurses care for both babies—José Garcia and Kimberly Szuba. Kimberly is alert, active, and often crying and squirming when her parents watch her. On the other hand, José is quiet, often asleep, and less attentive to external commotion when his parents monitor him in the nursery.

Why are these babies so different? Are the differences gender related? Will these differences disappear as the children develop or will the differences become exaggerated? What does the future hold for each child? Will Kimberly excel at sports and José excel at art? Can Kimberly overcome her parents' poverty and succeed in a professional career? Will José become a doctor like his mother or a pharmacist as is his father? Will both of these children escape childhood disease, maltreatment, and the other misfortunes sometimes visited upon American children?

Developmental psychologists are concerned with all of the Kimberlys and Josés of our world. Developmental psychologists study age-related changes in language, motoric and social skills, cognition, and physical health. Developmental psychologists are interested in the common skills shared by all children as well as the differences between children and the events that create these differences.

In general, developmental psychologists are concerned with the forces that guide and direct development. Some developmental theorists argue that the forces that shape a child are found in the environment in such factors as social class, quality of available stimulation, parenting style, and so on. Other theorists insist that genetics and related physiological factors such as hormones underlie the development of humans. A third set of psychologists, in fact many psychologists, believe that some combination or interaction of all these factors, physiology and environment, or nature and nurture, are responsible for development.

In this unit, we are going to look at issues of development in a chronological fashion. In the first article, the author discusses with great candor how parenting a new baby negatively influences marriage. What many couples think will be a wonderful experience turns into a predictably difficult situation with marital happiness plunging greatly and sometimes resulting in divorce.

Adolescence is the topic of the third article, "A Peaceful Adolescence." Some parents and scientists predict that adolescence will be a time of trouble, including but not limited to adolescent-parent conflict, defiance, drug and alcohol use, or teen pregnancy. Barbara Kantrowitz and Karen Springen suggest that this is not the case; adolescence can be a time of peace and bonding between parents and teens.

The next article in this unit concerns aging. The way Americans age is changing and consequently sets the focus of the next article, titled "Ageless Aging." People can and do live longer than in the past. These changes herald further changes in the way our elderly citizens think, feel, and act as well as in the way society responds to them.

The final article in this series looks at the ultimate stage in development — death. Death is often stigmatized in America; few people openly discuss it or know much about it. The way we cope with grief in America differs significantly from the way members of other societies cope. "The Borders of Healing" explains various ways cultures and members mourn and deal with their dead.

Why Newborns Cause Acrimony and Alimony

"Differences in expectations of what parenting will bring to the marriage, and how to handle children, money, power, decisions, and chores all factor into the stresses that erode so many unions."

DOLORES PUTERBAUGH

Babies enter a couple's life through birth, adoption, or remarriage, creating new relationships, responsibilities, and joys. Whether a surprise, planned, or long sought, most babies are preceded with increased excitement, careful preparations, and growing hopes. Tiny clothing is bought; bedrooms are repainted; the best safety furniture and carriers obtained. Parents-in-waiting attend prenatal classes, scour books for information, and tolerate bushels of uninvited advice from family, friends, and strangers. Many couples seem overprepared, if such a thing is possible.

Yet, in the midst of this nearly obsessive planning and preparing, something often evades notice: about one in 10 couples divorce before their first child begins school. How can a baby generate such a series of emotional tidal waves that so often culminate in acrimony and alimony?

The changes in duties, income, and even the layout of the family home are anticipated; my experiences in the therapy room and with professional literature indicate that the true impact of these changes apparently strikes with little warning. If they are wise, aching new parents in hurting marriages will come for counseling before the damage is irreparable. At the beginning of counseling, Rebecca and Joshua (made-up characters) are angry, hurt, unappreciated, disappointed, and ashamed. "We always put the children first," they say proudly, but here they are, nearly dashed onto the rocks by an eight-pound tsunami.

The little tidal wave sweeps up both parents. Mom may be pulled up towards the crest, immersed in the profound relationship with the baby, while dad is swimming against the current under 20 feet of water. These roles will shift as the waves crest, break, and rise again. Changes of all sorts—from money to time to perceptions of power and responsibility—drive those waves of emotional change.

If one parent, often the mother, provides full-time care for the infant, the loss of income creates emotional tension as well as financial stress. Betty Carter, founder and director at the Family Institute of Westchester (N.Y.), discovered in her research that the primary wage earner gradually takes on more financial decisionmaking rather than sharing decisions as when both were employed. In marriages where couples maintain separate finances, the difficulties may be compounded: "my money" and "your money" become one person's money.

When Rebecca left her job to care for the baby, she felt like a child having to ask Joshua for money each week; to her, it was like he had a checkbook and she had an allowance. Their eventual solution was to budget an amount each partner can spend on personal activities and purchases, while setting up two individual checking accounts in addition to the family account. This way, each has "my money" and there is adequate "our money." Neither Joshua nor Rebecca will have to ask permission to have lunch with a friend or get angry about ATM transactions not entered into the family checkbook.

Reducing any feeling of dependency will have to include an effort to discuss finances in terms of "us" rather than "mine and yours." Feeling dependent can lead to feeling powerless, to resentment and a cutoff of communication; we only can resent those whom we feel have power over us. It may be that the working parent solicits input on decisions but that the nonworking parent seemingly is reluctant to act as a full partner—but each perceives it differently; one feels stuck with full responsibility while the other feels marginalized.

Who has power over whom? While the stay-at-home parent may feel dependent and helpless, the working parent certainly is not riding the wave. According to a study published in the *Journal of Marriage and the Family*, men who are the primary or sole wage earner for a growing family often define themselves as successful parents if they provide financially for the family, while their wives define successful parenting based on relationships with the children and their satisfaction with parenting. Dad is under pressure to work longer hours, earn more money, and increasingly be concerned about job security and benefits; a man who previously explored his options if his current position was not satisfactory may feel painted into a corner because others completely depend on him. Where his wife perceives power, he feels pressure. Separated by a wall of water, they are at odds, with fewer resources.

If they are typical, the couple has little time to discuss their differences. New parenthood correlates with less leisure time together, fewer positive interactions between the new parents, and a sense of reduced emotional availability for both spouses. Rebecca is preoccupied with managing the baby and household duties. Joshua is working longer hours and worrying about the bills and future expenses of childrearing. Like many couples, they may avoid addressing their problems—and tension will build between them. The financial freedom they had to go places has been reduced. Both are exhausted and stressed.

Angry that Joshua is "not helping," Rebecca turns more and more to her family and girlfriends for emotional support, discussing practical issues as well as her loneliness, need for adult companionship, and resentment towards her husband. Women, in particular, are likely to look for emotional support outside the marriage, from friends and family members. Turning primarily to outsiders for support, even extended family—rather than one another—can weaken the relationship, already challenged by financial stresses, interrupted sleep, and shifts in power and responsibility.

Differences in how men and women tend to define family roles, satisfactory parenting experiences, and their expectations for the marriage continue to foment trouble for many couples even after the first months of their child's infancy, when the parent on leave may have returned to work.

As introduced earlier, men often define themselves as successful parents based on how well they provide for their children. Society reinforces this perspective, from the marketing for the "best" infant equipment to the expectation that the parents of young adults should finance their offspring's education. Both men and women can fall victim to a societal message that children always must come first. Many men confess to resentment at the pressure to provide financially at the expense of getting to know and enjoy their kids, but, in line with cultural expectations, fathers often focus more on providing and less on hands-on parenting.

As published in the *Journal of Marriage and the Family*, William Marsiglio of the University of Florida found that over 10% of fathers never take their child (age four or under) anywhere on outings alone, while 15% never read to their young offspring. Men become more involved as their children mature. Fathers spend more time with sons and outgoing daughters; quiet daughters generally are more difficult for new dads. Mothers report consistent levels of interaction with their children regardless of temperament or parental satisfaction; indeed, the cultural pressure for mothers is to put the relationship with their children above everything else. However, the balance of the family and the relationship between spouses only can suffer when their primary commitment stops being to one another.

"For a woman ... children in the home tend to bring more work, restricted freedom and privilege, and less pleasurable time with her husband."

The differences between fathers' and mothers' involvement do not appear to be entirely explained by mothers being the at-home parent, as working moms spend much more time with their children than fathers do. Even the morning commute tends to include more parenting-related concerns for mothers than fathers. In many marriages, then, husbands tend to perceive, and act on, a greater range of options in their level of involvement with their children, with their wives carrying the greater part of the burden regardless of whether both parents are wage earners. In such a situation, the wife may grow to resent her husband. She perceives him as wielding more financial power and then acting on his apparent freedom to pick and choose how much to engage with his offspring. He, meanwhile, sees his previous best friend, lover, and companion putting him second, third, fourth—or lower-on the priority list despite his efforts to be a good husband and father.

Joshua, working longer hours and cutting back on his own activities, begins to shut down in the face of Rebecca's apparent anger towards him. From his perspective, he cannot understand why she seems to be turning against him when he is doing his best to be a good husband and father. She cannot see why he does not want to spend more time with the baby. Didn't they agree to start a family? She is returning to work and expects him to start doing his share.

The breakdown of household tasks is a common topic for general discussion, women's magazines, and the occasional serious researcher. While many women stereotypically may complain that their husband does "nothing" around the house, research indicates this may be only a slight exaggeration. In 2004, surveys in the *Journal of Marriage and the Family* revealed that, on average, a full-time working married woman with children spent over 80 minutes per workday on household tasks, while her employed spouse spent under 30. He, however, probably is working two-and-a-half to five hours more per week at a full-time job than she is, making up for some of those missed housework hours. On weekends, her total time went up to almost 140 minutes, while his was just over 50. As time passes, the presence of daughters brings relief not to mother, but to father: The "mother's helper" tends to take over chores previously done by dad, reducing his duties rather than mom's!

Despite generally perceived changes in the inequality of male-female responsibility to children, moms still are spending more time than dads on household chores and tending to the kids. Youngsters under five require constant supervision: even a baby-proofed house can be dangerous when—if only for a moment—an adult's back is turned. Somehow, working mothers are managing to spend well over twice as much time on chores, and perform those chores while keeping a watchful eye on children. It is arguable that those chores might take less time were she not simultaneously managing a toddler or two.

For a woman, then, children in the home tend to bring more work, restricted freedom and privilege, and less pleasurable time with her husband. Meanwhile, her husband tends to be working extra hours, worrying about finances, and looking forward to when the children are old enough for him to enjoy. While it is not a picnic for anyone, it is not surprising that mothers report greater distress during the new parenting period. It is a warning alarm for marriages that, for women, greater unhappiness with parenting is correlated to marital dissatisfaction. Essentially, for women, parenting, marriage, and self-image are part of the same package, while for men, dissatisfaction in one area can have nothing to do with another.

Interestingly, fathers often report less satisfaction with their role as parents than women, but compartmentalize this from their feelings about marriage. As women become resentful of men's decisions about finances, family time, and chores, they seek social and emotional support outside the marriage from family and friends. As fewer confidences are exchanged between the couple, emotional distance develops. As typified by Joshua and Rebecca, the gap may become a chasm if the husband feels criticized, unappreciated, or overwhelmed by his wife's disappointment and expectations, or if her attempts to make things better are not met with some compromise.

Marital researcher John Gottman, co-founder of the Seattle Marital and Family Institute and author of a number of books, including *Why Marriages Succeed or Fail*, has identified this turning away from one another—rather than towards one another—in times of trouble as one of the danger signs of impending marital failure. Turning away may be a case of seeming to ignore one another's efforts to mend fences or by investing emotionally outside of the marriage for needs previously met within the union. When couples stop talking about their differences, and no longer turn first to each other in times of joy and sadness, they become emotionally disengaged.

Happy marriages are correlated with low levels of distress over the challenges of parenting. Many marriage and family researchers have asserted that the quality of the marriage itself predicts the satisfaction with parenting. Healthy relationships more easily withstand the burdens of parenting. As we consider the evidence that so many new parents' marriages devolve into quagmires of power struggles over finances, parenting, and chores, it becomes clear that differences in expectations are best addressed before the baby arrives.

Besides a healthy, honest dialogue about expectations for parenting styles, couples should address how money will be handled, division of chores, who will take family medical leave to provide care for the infant, etc. Whether through family members, professional therapists, or secular or worship communities, classes and guided discussions can provide useful assistance for new parents and help short-circuit the patterns that lead to divorce preceding kindergarten for so many families. Couples preparing for parenthood would do themselves a great service by learning about one another's actual expectations of what family life will be like. In this era of smaller families, many premarital programs include discussions with long-married couples that can enlighten young people (who may have grown up with one or no siblings) about childcare, time demands of children, and some common pitfalls of early parenting. Those of us who have grown up in large families have few illusions about the time demands of parenting and are not shocked that a newborn can take control of a household or create emotional havoc. Inexperienced parents may have misconceptions about normal child development, leading to anger, frustration, and disappointment with the parenting role. How many of us have seen steely-eyed, clenched-jawed par-

ents striding through an amusement park pushing a stroller with an over-tired, crying child far too young to appreciate a $75 per person, 12-hour day in what is advertised as a family heaven? A one-hour visit to a petting zoo can challenge a young family; heavily invested days of mega-amusement parks are out of line with most young children's energy and attention spans. Experienced parents or older children in large families know this. New parents from small families may not.

A primary complaint of many mothers is their mate's lack of involvement with the kids: not just in sharing the burdens of the household, but in actual engagement. One of Rebecca's main contentions is that Joshua never seems to do anything with the baby: she feels everything is left to her by default. If she does get help, she added, it is with household chores rather than spending time with the baby. Many experts cite men's relative inexperience and lack of confidence in handling babies and small children. Added to this may be a solicitous new mother's tendency to hover and correct based on what she would do; daddy may be within the bounds of correct care, but if different from mommy, she is likely to correct him. Providing training to new fathers, and encouraging new mothers to withhold all but constructive criticism can improve inexperienced fathers' confidence and comfort in accepting more responsibility for direct child care.

"Many couples [are dissatisfied] with the marriage because the intimate emotional relationship has been subsumed into a parent-child-parent triangle."

Coaching both parents can help them handle various situations and ease fears, perhaps unspoken, that they will "lose it" and make a terrible mistake with their child. Discussing household tasks and division of duties sounds simple, but most therapists familiar with couples' work will assert that such discussions tend not to occur under ideal circumstances. Differences in standards are a good area to seek a workable truce. This requires real listening and work: if one parent believes toddlers need daily activities (play dates, gymnastic classes, etc.) and that the house must be vacuumed daily, it may be necessary to compromise with a mate who believes that weekly—or perhaps twice-a-week—vacuuming is sufficient and that babies do not need expensive daily activities.

Bullied by the popular media's obsession with telling parents how to build the perfect child, Rebecca scheduled exercise classes, music and reading groups, and other activities, besides holding herself up to an unrealistic expectation of household cleanliness. Joshua, meanwhile, was more concerned with having a happy, relaxed family. He could not see the purpose in being frantic about activities that were supposed to be fun or in "driving ourselves crazy" with daily cleaning routines. Simplistic as it sounds, switching tasks for a few days can be a real eye-opener for everyone. Coaching mothers in asking for the help they need directly from their spouse and in being proactive in arranging for breaks in childcare duties to pursue adult interests is another means to improving the situation. Mothers can take advantage of fathers' hands-on time by getting out of the house, having alone time in another room, or enjoying an uninterrupted phone call. In situations where the father is the full-time, at-home parent, the roles would reverse: he needs to spend time alone or with friends.

Many couples stop having couple time in exchange for family time, leading to dissatisfaction with the marriage because the intimate emotional relationship has been subsumed into a parent-child-parent triangle. This is unhealthy for the marriage and the children. Kids learn by observation. When they see parents putting one another last, they develop this as a template for their own future relationships. Children who later have difficulty maintaining truly intimate adult relationships should not be a surprise to parents who put family time far ahead of couple time.

I routinely "prescribe" a couple's night for every family I see, even if the problem is not the couple but a child's in-school behavior. The parents are urged to set aside one evening for themselves; they do not have to go anywhere or spend money. Couples with infants can schedule this around typical feeding times. If they have older kids, they are to send them to their rooms for an extra hour of reading before bedtime. This will provide a grown-ups' evening, as simple as a video and dinner, or a game of Scrabble, or pushing back the furniture for some dancing. Interestingly, my clients often report that their school-age children become enthusiastic about the parents' evening, for example, hearing a teenager explain to a friend, "No, we can't watch the game here.... It's my parents' date night. How about your house?" A kindergartner reminds the parents each Sunday, "Don't forget! It's your date night! We get to go to bed early and read." Children fear their parents divorcing. If Mom and Dad have a romantic night every week, it might be gross—but at least it's not a divorce, runs the child-logic. The youngster also is getting a powerful message about the importance of the marital relationship.

Differences in expectations of what parenting will bring to the marriage, and how to handle children, money, power, decisions, and chores all factor into the stresses that erode so many unions. A combination of education, support in seeking healthy ways to breach differences and strengthen the marital relationship, and, above all, turning towards one another to find solutions and support rather than turning separately to outsiders, serves to avoid and ameliorate the difficulties of early parenting that lead to so many fractured families before the first back-to-school night.

Dolores Puterbaugh, a psychotherapist in private practice in Largo, Fla., is a member of the Advisory Board of the International Center for the Study of Psychiatry and Psychology.

The Methuselah Report

Living to be 120 might be attainable, but is it desirable?

WAYNE CURTIS

❝**I** believe extraordinary longevity is absolutely inevitable," says Donald Louria, a professor at the New Jersey Medical School. "It's not a matter of if we'll have extraordinary longevity, but when."

How old is old? The average life span of an American born today is 77.2 years. It has stretched by about three months every year since the mid-19th century, says Louria, who organized a recent conference on longevity and its implications. Just by maintaining that pace the average American would expect to live more than 100 years by the end of this century. And that doesn't take into account revolutionary advances in health and medicine, which, Louria says, could very well boost the average life span to 110 or 120.

But will the future "buy us more life, or just more days alive?" wonders Vincent Mor, chair of the Department of Community Health at Brown University School of Medicine. Mor is optimistic that we'll be living not only longer but more fully as we age. Recent studies suggest older people are remaining more independent later in life, demonstrating an increase in what he calls "active life expectancy."

The larger unknown is what exactly this society of centenarians will look like and how well it will function in an era when some Americans may expect to spend nearly half their lives in retirement.

Advances in longevity come in two forms. The first is the prevention of diseases—including heart disease, cancer, stroke and diabetes—that tend to affect older people. Eliminating deaths from these causes would increase the average life span by 10 to 20 years, Louria predicts. "The first to fall will be heart disease and stroke," he says. "It's not going to happen tomorrow, but it is going to happen in this century."

The oldest documented human lived to be 122. To make that age commonplace, however, will require more than curing disease. "It's only going to occur by preventing aging and modifying the aging process itself," Louria says.

Secrets Of Aging

When Ponce de Leon thrashed around the swamps of Florida in search of the Fountain of Youth, it turns out, he was in the wrong place. The secrets of aging are actually kept in a sort of complex biologic bank vault outfitted with multiple doors. Safecrackers from various branches of medicine and science have been striving to get in, and the faint sound you hear is that of tumblers clicking into place.

Will the future 'buy us more life, or just more days alive?' wonders Vincent Mor, a gerontologist at Brown University.

Geneticists are fiddling with one door. Richard Miller, associate director of the University of Michigan's Geriatrics Center, says that genetic variations in mice can add as many as 173 days to their lives. That's not trivial. Producing a map of the genetic variations that lead to longer life would allow researchers to devise drugs that can manipulate the aging process, Miller says. We're closer to achieving this, he adds, than "we are to eliminating cancer or heart attacks."

At work on another vault door are nanotechnologists. Nanotechnology involves engineering matter at the molecular level, building miniature machines atom by atom. While regarded as among the most speculative of current sciences, it may well usher in a sweeping technological change.

"Living things are composed of molecular machines, and the tools for diagnosis are huge and imprecise," says Christopher Wiley of the Dartmouth-Hitchcock Medical Center. Nanobiotics would eliminate that disparity of scale, allowing the creation of biological robots that not only permit observation of the human body at the most refined level possible, but that can serve as sentinels to identify and prevent disease before symptoms even appear. In time, more sophisticated nanobots could be manufactured to enhance tissue or strengthen frail bones within the body, reversing more debilitating aspects of aging.

Nanobots might even be programmed to maintain homeostasis, that is, to keep our cells in a state of perfect equilibrium. "In theory, science could preserve a body at its peak physical state," Wiley says. "It's not that complicated," he insists. While this may sound like a futurist's fevered dream for the year 2500, Wiley points out that some nanotechnology companies are already on the brink of building tools to construct nanobots. Wiley predicts we'll see major advances in the nanotechnology of health care within the next decade or two.

Radical Calorie Cuts

Only slightly less bewildering is the study of caloric restriction—or the radical curbing of calorie intake to extend life. This may be the most immediately promising door to altering the aging process. The approach is based on a simple if curious fact: Cutting the intake of calories by 30 to 40 percent has consistently resulted in significantly lengthening the maximum life span of laboratory animals. It has proved more effective than exercise.

As the tools for longer living evolve, so must our patterns of housing, work, family relations and transportation.

Why? It's believed that a sharp drop in calories triggers a metabolic change that strengthens the immune system and increases our cells' capacity to produce new and healthy cells. Aging slows. One theory is that this mechanism evolved to help animals survive the lean winter months and thus ensure they pass on their genes by producing offspring in the more bountiful days of summer.

Even if similar effects are eventually proved in humans—and tests are just getting under way—few would choose to live a life of permanent hunger, admits George Roth, a senior scientist at the National Institute on Aging. But already in the works, Roth reports, is research to create drugs that would mimic the effects of a very low-calorie diet, providing the benefits of restricted calories without the hardships.

"We call it having your cake and eating it, too," he says.

What If It Works?

That your grandchildren will have children who could reasonably expect to live a century or more is the good news. And the bad news? Some experts fear we may also be engineering a world that might not be such a grand place to live.

The U.S. Census Bureau projects the population over the age of 85 to reach 21 million in the year 2050. Other demographers predict a number in the neighborhood of 53 million within a half century. With such a range of projections, it's hard to know where to start the planning. "Imagine the policy implications," says Kevin Kinsella of the Census Bureau.

"Quality of life is the big issue," says Louria, whose specialties are preventive medicine and community health. "Are we going to have large numbers of very old people who are vigorous, reasonably healthy, involved and productive? Or are we going to have a large percentage of people who are lonely, bored, not very healthy and depressed?"

Making procedures like hip replacement and cataract surgery routine are notable steps toward longer, fuller lives. Simple objects can bring welcome freedom for a great many older people, too. "The microwave oven is probably one of the most important things that has actually contributed to a reduction in dependence," Mor says, as have well-designed walkers that reduce the need for in-home assistance. "It's a very low-tech device but has a fairly substantial effect."

As the tools for longer living evolve, so too must the nation's patterns of housing, work, family relations and transportation. Having "lots of single-family homes and getting among them by SUV" may work well for people in their 40s and 50s, but it's "calamitous" for older people, says Bruce Vladeck, professor of health policies and geriatrics at the Mount Sinai School of Medicine in New York. "We have built a set of communities over the past few years to maximize social isolation."

Vladeck notes that informal care—that is, families tending elderly relatives at home—now accounts for between 66 and 85 percent of all care for those requiring assistance. But with the rise of what some call "the super senior," he wonders if 80-year-olds will be able to care for their 105-year-old parents, or if 50-year-old grandchildren will be willing to accept responsibility for the care of family elders. "No one has seen this phenomenon before," he says.

Work patterns will also alter sharply, with more people working longer. Retirement at 65 became institutionalized decades ago when younger workers flooded the job market. With labor shortages now forecast, Vladeck predicts that corporate and government policies will likewise change to discourage retirement, so more older Americans will find incentives to remain in the work force.

Then there's that elephant in the room: How will society pay for expanded health care, retirement benefits and the building of new communities to serve the very old? "When 30 to 40 percent of the population is over age 65, and 40 to 50 percent of adult life is spent in retirement," Louria points out, "Social Security and company pensions are not likely to be viable." Knight Steel, chief of the division of geriatrics at Hackensack University Medical Center, poses another question with no easy answer: "Who will pay for the heart transplant of a 100-year-old?"

The debate over these issues is just beginning. But before hand-wringing becomes too prevalent, maybe we should step back and take a longer view of the looming breakthrough in longevity. "In some basic ways, this is what society has sought since its inception," Vladeck says. "Rather than focus on the gloom and doom, maybe we ought to start out with the celebratory aspect of these changes."

Champagne, anyone?

Wayne Curtis, *who has written for the* Atlantic Monthly, Preservation *and other magazines, lives on Peaks Island, Maine.*

A Peaceful Adolescence

The teen years don't have to be a time of family storm and stress. Most kids do just fine and now psychologists are finding out why that is.

BARBARA KANTROWITZ AND KAREN SPRINGEN

At 17, Amanda Hund is a straight-A student who loves competing in horse shows. The high school junior from Willmar, Minn., belongs to her school's band, orchestra and choir. She regularly volunteers through her church and recently spent a week working in an orphanage in Jamaica. Usually, however, she's closer to home, where her family eats dinner together every night. She also has a weekly breakfast date with her father, a doctor, at a local coffee shop. Amanda credits her parents for her relatively easy ride through adolescence. "My parents didn't sweat the small stuff," she says. "They were always very open. You could ask any question."

Is the Hund family for real? Didn't they get the memo that says teens and their parents are supposed to be at odds until … well, until forever? Actually, they're very much for real, and according to scientists who study the transition to adulthood, they represent the average family's experience more accurately than all those scary TV movies about out-of-control teens. "Research shows that most young people go through adolescence having good relationships with their parents, adopting attitudes and values consistent with their parents' and end up getting out of the adolescent period and becoming good citizens," says Richard Lerner, Bergstrom chair of applied developmental science at Tufts University. This shouldn't be news—but it is, largely because of widespread misunderstanding of what happens during the teen years. It's a time of transition, just like the first year of parenthood or menopause. And although there are dramatic hormonal and physical changes during this period, catastrophe is certainly not preordained. A lot depends on youngsters' innate natures combined with the emotional and social support they get from the adults around them. In other words, parents do matter.

The roots of misconceptions about teenagers go back to the way psychologists framed the field of adolescent development a century ago. They were primarily looking for explanations of why things went wrong. Before long, the idea that this phase was a period of storm and stress made its way into the popular consciousness. But in the last 15 years, developmental scientists have begun to re-examine these assumptions. Instead of focusing on kids who battle their way through the teen years, they're studying the dynamics of success.

At the head of the pack are Lerner and his colleagues, who are in the midst of a major project that many other researchers are following closely. It's a six-year longitudinal study of exactly what it takes to turn out OK and what adults can do to nurture those behaviors. "Parents and sometimes kids themselves often talk about positive development as the absence of bad," says Lerner. "What we're trying to do is present a different vision and a different vocabulary for young people and parents."

The first conclusions from the 4-H Study of Positive Youth Development, published in the February issue of The Journal of Early Adolescence, show that there are quantifiable personality traits possessed by all adolescents who manage to get to adulthood without major problems. Psychologists have labeled these traits "the 5 Cs": competence, confidence, connection, character and caring. These characteristics theoretically lead to a sixth C, contribution (similar to civic engagement). The nomenclature grows out of observations in recent years by a number of clinicians, Lerner says, but his study is the first time researchers have measured how these characteristics influence successful growth.

The 5 Cs are interconnected, not isolated traits, Lerner says. For example, competence refers not just to academic ability but also to social and vocational skills. Confidence includes self-esteem as well as the belief that you can make a difference in the world. The value of the study, Lerner says, is that when it is completed next year, researchers will have a way to quantify these characteristics and eventually determine what specific social and educational programs foster them.

During these years, parents should stay involved as they help kids move on.

In the meantime, parents can learn a lot from this rethinking of the teen years. Don't automatically assume that your kids become alien beings when they leave middle school. They still care what their parents think and they still need love and guidance—although in a different form. Temple University psychology professor Laurence Steinberg, author of "The Ten Basic Principles of Good Parenting," compares raising kids to building a boat that you eventually launch. Parents have to build a strong underpinning so their kids are equipped to face whatever's ahead. In the teen years, that means staying involved as you slowly let go. "One of the things that's natural in adolescence is that kids are going to pull away from their parents as they become increasingly interested in peers," says Steinberg. "It's important for parents to hang in there, for them not to pull back in response to that."

Communication is critical. "Stay in touch with your kids and make sure they feel valued and appreciated," advises Suniya Luthar, professor of clinical and developmental psychology at Columbia University. Even if they roll their eyes when you try to hug them, they still need direct displays of affection, she says. They also need help figuring out goals and limits. Parents should monitor their kids' activities and get to know their friends. Luthar says parents should still be disciplinarians and set standards such as curfews. Then teens need to know that infractions will be met with consistent consequences.

Adolescents are often critical of their parents but they're also watching them closely for clues on how to function in the outside world. Daniel Perkins, associate professor of family and youth resiliency at Penn State, says he and his wife take their twins to the local Ronald McDonald House and serve dinner to say thank you for time the family spent there when the children had health problems after birth. "What we've done already is set up the notion that we were blessed and need to give back, even if it's in a small way." That kind of example sets a standard youngsters remember, even if it seems like they're not paying attention.

Parents should provide opportunities for kids to explore the world and even find a calling. Teens who have a passion for something are more likely to thrive. "They have a sense of purpose beyond day-to-day teenage life," says David Marcus, author of "What It Takes to Pull Me Through." Often, he says, kids who were enthusiastic about something in middle school lose enthusiasm in high school because the competition gets tougher and they're not as confident. Parents need to step in and help young people find other outlets. The best way to do that is to regularly spend uninterrupted time with teens (no cell phones). Kids also need to feel connected to other adults they trust and to their communities. Teens who get into trouble are "drifting," he says. "They don't have a web of people watching out for them."

Teens should build support webs of friends and adults.

At some point during these years, teen-agers should also be learning to build their own support networks—a skill that will be even more important when they're on their own. Connie Flanagan, a professor of youth civic development at Penn State, examines how kids look out for one another. "What we're interested in is how they help one another avoid harm," she says. In one of her focus groups, some teenage girls mentioned that they decided none would drink from an open can at a party because they wouldn't know for sure what they were drinking. "Even though you are experimenting, you're essentially doing it in a way that you protect one another," Flanagan says. Kids who don't make those kinds of connections are more likely to get in trouble because there's no one their own age or older to stop them from going too far. Like any other stage of life, adolescence can be tough. But teens and families can get through it— as long as they stick together.

With JULIE SCELFO

Ageless Aging:
The Next Era of Retirement

"Old age" and "retirement" must be rethought and redefined as the baby boomers surge through the later stages of life, according to a renowned authority on aging.

KEN DYCHTWALD

With the breakthroughs in medicine, public health, nutrition, and wellness in recent years, longevity has been steadily increasing. So what age should now be considered old?

Let's remember that the age selected to be the marker of old age was not sent from heaven or scripted in Moses' tablets. It was selected in the 1880s by Otto von Bismarck, who crafted Europe's first pension plan. Bismarck had to pick an age at which people would be considered too enfeebled to work and therefore eligible for state support and entitlement. He picked 65. At the time, the life expectancy in Europe and the United States was only 45 years. Now, life expectancy at birth for women has vaulted to nearly 80 and for men to about 74. In fact, if you were to craft a formula using a corresponding equation today, we would be retiring people at about 97. So to continue to use 65 as the marker of old age simply does not make any sense at all.

One misconception that people have about longevity is that it means more years added to the end of life. Few people would say, "If I could live longer, what I'd really like is to be old for twice as long." Rather, most people would say, "If I could live a little bit longer, I'd like to have a chance to reinvent myself. I'd like to have a chance to pursue some dreams that I might have put on the shelf when I was younger. I'd like to adjust the balance between work, leisure, and family, with the benefit of the kind of wisdom and experience that comes from having tried a few things out in the first half of my life." People don't want to be old longer. They want to be young and middle-aged longer. And many would prefer to live long, healthy lives without being any particular age at all, reflecting a new kind of ageless aging.

The Longevity Revolution: We've Only Just Begun

During the twentieth century, we did an excellent job of eliminating many of the diseases of youth, such as cholera, typhoid, smallpox, diphtheria, and pneumonia. Childbirth, once a major cause of premature death, has become safer for most women, and more children are born healthier. The effect of these improvements is that more of us are living longer and longer.

Extraordinary advances are still ahead. The maximum biological potential age of the human body is somewhere between 120 and 140 years, so with significant breakthroughs in the next quarter century—whether they be in pharmaceuticals, hormone therapy, therapeutic cloning, or stem-cell research—we could add another five, 10, or even 20 years to a person's life.

The downside, of course, is that chronic health problems will also increase. We're living longer but not necessarily staying healthy longer. Unfortunately, 59 million Americans have one form or another of heart disease. Two-thirds of the American population is overweight. Up to 50 million people struggle with chronic pain due to conditions like arthritis and bursitis. There are about 18 million people with either Type 1 or Type 2 diabetes. These lifestyle-related chronic diseases have become the modern plagues.

In an ancient Greek fable, Eos, the beautiful goddess of the dawn, falls in love with the warrior Tithonus. Distraught over his mortality, she goes to Zeus's chamber and begs Zeus to grant her lover immortality. "Are you certain that is what you want for him?" Zeus challenges. "Yes," Eos responds. As Eos leaves Zeus's chamber, she realizes in shock that she forgot to ask that Tithonus also remain eternally young and healthy. With each passing year, she looks on with horror as he grows older and sicker. His skin withers and becomes cancerous. His organs rot, and his brain grows feeble. Ultimately, the once-proud warrior is reduced to a collection of pained, foul, and broken bones—but he continues to live forever.

The story of Tithonus is a fitting allegory for what is occurring in the U.S. health-care system today. While we have eliminated many of the childhood diseases that took our ancestors' lives, the health-care system is woefully inept at preventing or treating the chronic health problems that arise in life's later years. Age-related chronic conditions such as Alzheimer's disease, arthritis, osteoporosis, diabetes, prostate and breast cancer, and heart disease are reaching pandemic proportions.

The most troublesome challenges ahead, however, could be due to the rising incidence of the diseases among the oldest of the old. Although some of today's over-85 population are fit and independent, 62.5% are so disabled that they are no longer able to manage the basic activities of daily living without help. Currently, 47% of people over age 85 suffer from some form of dementia—a condition that already afflicts 4 million Americans.

Impacts of the Wellness Movement

Having participated in promoting the wellness movement since its beginnings 30 years ago, I am convinced that we could all be doing a much better job of both lowering health-care costs and creating a much healthier, more vital, independent life by practicing better health habits. With each birthday, the body struggles with a wider range of problems. For example, I am 55. I am a relatively healthy and fit person, but I've got a right shoulder that's troubled with bone spurs and arthritis. And even though I haven't eaten meat for about 25 years, I have high cholesterol that I grapple with. I also find that it's a little easier to gain weight now than when I was younger, so I'm always trying to keep an eye out for my calorie consumption. So even though I am still a youthful, healthy person, each birthday brings on more challenges to work against on a day-to-day basis.

When we're young, we tend to take our health for granted. When we're in our 40s or 50s, we begin to notice that there are some changes going on and we start to take them much more seriously. And as we look at our own moms and dads, we can see both the positive and the negative outcomes of how well or how badly they have taken care of themselves. As we grow a little bit older, the desire to be healthy, attractive, and potent doesn't diminish, but it becomes harder to stay well and to look youthful. These are very powerful motivations. You wouldn't expect your car to function well if you didn't take care of it. You wouldn't expect your clothes to look good if you didn't take good care of them. You wouldn't expect your computer to work well if you didn't maintain it the way it needs to be maintained. More people now realize that, to be healthy, look healthy, feel healthy, and have wellness prevalent in their lives as they age, they need to take charge of their wellness and practice the kinds of behaviors that will get them there.

As they age, baby boomers are likely to continue setting new trends in the United States. In my new book, *The Power Years*, I argue that, instead of viewing life after 40 as a time of decline, retreat, and withdrawal, boomers are coming to see this as a terrific new opportunity to reevaluate their lives and consider their new options. They will be empowered by a great deal more experience and wisdom and will plot new courses. Instead of limitation, I believe they'll choose liberation—it's their nature.

Boomers are collectively reshaping the middle years of life into a new period for renewal and reinvention. "Middlescence"—an older and wiser version of adolescence—is emerging.

History provides us many role models for successful aging. Grandma Moses didn't start painting until she was almost 80. Galileo published his masterpiece, *Dialogue Concerning the Two New Sciences*, at 74. Frank Lloyd Wright designed the Guggenheim Museum in New York at 91. Mahatma Gandhi was 72 when he completed successful negotiations with Britain for India's independence. Society will be able to look forward to a multiplying pool of role models for this new, empowered maturity. Warren Buffett remains the world's most-respected investor at age 75. Film stars Sophia Loren and Sean Connery are still considered sexy in their seventh and eighth decades. And Federal Reserve Board Chairman Alan Greenspan remains capable and wise at 78.

Many people will reap the benefits of new freedoms as they grow older. As children leave home, parents' daily responsibilities are reduced. As busy schedules begin to let up, we'll have more free time than at any previous period of our lives. With these chunks of newfound leisure, we'll be free to pursue hidden passions and long-suppressed dreams: take a hike, write a novel, or sail the world.

As the boomer generation passes into maturity, now is the time for companies to adjust their thinking about men and women over age 50. When the leading edge of the baby boom first arrived, America and its institutions were totally unprepared. Waiting lists and long lines developed at hospitals across the country; facilities and staff were inadequate, and in some hospitals, hallways were used as labor rooms. Similarly, apartments and homes didn't have enough bedrooms for boomer kids, there was a shortage of baby food and diapers, and department stores couldn't keep enough toys in stock to meet the multiplying demand. When boomers took their first steps, the shoe, photo, and Band-Aid industries skyrocketed. Similarly, sales of tricycles, Slinkies, and Hula-Hoops exploded as the marketplace was flooded with products for kids.

When baby boomers reach any stage of life, the issues that concern them—whether financial, interpersonal, or even hormonal—become the dominant social, political, and marketplace themes of the time. Boomers don't just populate existing life stages or consumer trends—they transform them. On January 1, 1996, the first baby boomer turned 50. By the second decade of the twenty-first century, boomers will evolve into the largest elder generation in history. As the oldest members of the baby-boom cohort start turning 65 in 2011, they will swell the ranks of the "elderly" from approximately 40 million now to more than 70 million by 2030. But boomers will transform the look, meaning, experience, and purpose of maturity. As they reach age 65, it will not be viewed as "elderly."

Until recently, corporations, marketers, and entrepreneurs paid little attention to men and women over age 50. There was, after all, little to spark their interest in a group whose members tended to be financially disadvantaged, frugal, and perceived as set in their ways and uninterested in new products and ideas. But Americans in their 50s and older currently earn more than $2 trillion in annual income, own more than 70% of the nation's

New Opportunities for Aging Agelessly

In the years ahead, watch for growth in a wide variety of industries and services to meet the needs of a maturing marketplace, including:

- Specialty diagnosis and treatment centers for particular body parts, such as the eyes, ears, muscles, bones, or nervous system.
- Therapeutically cloned kidneys, livers, lungs, hearts, skin, blood, and bones for "tune-up" and replacement purposes.
- Nutraceuticals—foods and supplements engineered with macro- and micronutrients to fight aging.
- Cosmeceutical rejuvenation therapies for both men and women.
- Antiaging spas.
- High-tech exercise gear and equipment programmed to precisely "train" users to build stronger, healthier, and more youthful bodies.
- Smart acoustic systems in telephones, radios, and TVs that customize signals to accommodate the auditory range of each user's ears.
- Silver Seals—"for-hire" teams of elders with various problem-solving talents who are deployed to "fix" difficult community or business issues.
- Lifelong-learning programs at colleges, universities, churches, and community centers and on cable TV and the Internet.
- "Retirement Zone" stores featuring products and technologies appealing to older adults with free time.
- Adventure-travel services that send older adults to off-the-beaten-trail locations.

- Mature employment and career transition coordinators.
- Experience agents—similar to travel agents—that can be commissioned to orchestrate any type of request, whether it's a party, learning program, psychotherapy, sabbatical, travel adventure, spiritual retreat, introduction to new friends, or business partnerships.
- Mature dating services to help the tens of millions of single, mature women and men find new relationships.
- Longevity-oriented communities for health-minded elders.
- Intergenerational communes.
- Urban arts retirement communities that focus on cultural pursuits.
- University-based intergenerational housing for people who desire lifelong learning.
- Multinational time-share clubs for those who aren't interested in settling down in one location.
- Long-term care insurance financing to provide security against the possibility of late-life chronic health problems.
- Estate management and trust services to help families manage the $20 trillion inheritance cascade that is about to occur.
- Reverse mortgages to help people who are cash-poor but "brick-rich."

—Ken Dychtwald

Excepted from *The Power Years: A User's Guide to the Rest of Your Life* (Wiley, August 2005).

personal financial assets, and represent 50% of all discretionary spending power. In fact, their per capita discretionary spending is 2.5 times more than the average of younger households and is particularly strong in the financial services, health care, leisure, wellness, and beauty products categories.

The Challenge to Social Security

After studying aging issues for more than 30 years, I've concluded that the best way to guarantee a financially secure old age is to be a part of a very small generation and then give birth to a very large generation. That way, when you are in your 70s and they are in their 40s and 50s, they'll be paying enormous amounts of taxes for your support. That's exactly the situation for today's seniors.

In contrast, the baby boomers are part of a very large generation, who, relatively speaking, gave birth to a smaller number of kids to support them. Whereas the boomers' parents averaged four kids each, boomers themselves average around half that number. Because the boomers are also going to be living longer than anybody ever imagined, it's going to become increasingly difficult for government entitlements to support retirement at the age and level that we're seeing now. When Social Security was first created in the United States, the average life expect-

ancy was only 63 years, and there were 40 workers supporting each retiree. Now, there are only about 3.2 workers for each retiree. By the time I reach my middle 60s—about 10 years from now—there will only be about two workers supporting me, and I just don't think they're going to want to do that.

Many people are now choosing to continue working into their "retirement" years. We are on the verge of entering what I will call the "fourth era of retirement."

Four Eras of Retirement

The first era of retirement lasted for about 100,000 years and ended in the early twentieth century. During that era, you worked all of your life. That was not considered a bad thing, because work served a variety of purposes. In addition to providing a livelihood, work also offered a way of feeling worthwhile and productive. It was a great socialization activity, where you encountered people of all ages. You felt involved. If you had a very demanding job and your body was no longer able to conduct the work required to do that job, you would be transitioned to a more appropriate function. So if grandpa's job was to plow the fields and that became too hard, he might become involved with fixing the fences. But the idea that people were to retire was not a part of our consciousness. Working in maturity was viewed positively.

During the Industrial Revolution, all that abruptly changed. By the 1920s, the second era of retirement began and was well established with the crafting of Social Security in the 1930s. This wonderful program had two purposes: First, it was designed to create a thin safety net for older adults in a period of economic frailty. Second, with the unemployment levels skyrocketing to 25%, retirement provided an institutional process whereby older people would be removed from the workforce to make room for the young.

Then the third era of retirement emerged during the 1960s and 1970s, when we began to think of retirement as the "golden years" of life. In fact, the younger you retired, the more successful you were perceived to be. At the same time, longevity began to rise for adults, and so the post-work period became a stage lasting not two or three years, but 15 to 20 years or even longer. Ultimately, people began to think of retirement as a birthright—an entitlement. And that is the era in which we have been situated through the last quarter century. That era is fraying at the edges now, and I believe a fourth is now emerging.

The New Retirement Era: From Retirement to "Rehirement"

Recent research has shown that the modern retirement experiment is simply not working for most people. About half of all the retirees in the United States say they'd rather be working, though most don't want to work full time. Some might like to try doing something different and new, and most don't want all the pressure they had when they were young. Some even want to work for free as volunteers. A lot of people are now saying, "You know, this golden age thing is just not enough for me. While a few years of leisure is great—decades of nothing to do can be deadly!" So the new era of retirement will be "rehirement."

One reason for this growing interest in rehirement is that a lot of retirees are just plain bored: Last year, the average retiree watched 43 hours of television a week. Another reason is that most people simply cannot afford to live on a fixed income for 20 or more years. An increasing number of older adults are not interested in acting their age and retreating to the sidelines. Instead, they'd rather rebel against ageist stereotypes and are seeking to be productive and involved and even late-blooming in their maturity.

Again, we can look to a growing cadre of role models for the new style of aging. When you have John Glenn going up into space at 77, Sumner Redstone running Viacom at 80, and Lena Horne still on the concert circuit at 85, you are beginning to see the emergence of a new kind of lifestyle hero, an elder hero.

These forces are fueling the new, fourth era of retirement. People now do not really want to retire at all. Rather, they want a "turning point," a chance to step out of a full-time job or an exhausting career, take a break or sabbatical, and then reinvent themselves. Eventually, I believe, most people will want a better balance between work and leisure throughout their lives. As they mature, they would like to be able to work at what they want, perhaps working fewer hours with more recreation and leisure interspersed. They will want to stay in the game—not relegated to the sidelines.

Retirement is in the midst of a sweeping transformation. In the years to come, more older men and women will be starting up their engines and jumping back into the workforce, maybe even having the most-productive years of their lives.

Ageless Explorers vs. The Comfortably Content

Generalizing about retirees is proving increasingly wrongheaded. Already we are seeing lifestyle or attitudinal differences among different retiree groups today.

My firm, Age Wave, in collaboration with Harris Interactive and sponsored by AIG SunAmerica, recently interviewed 1,000 retiree households to find out how folks were doing and whether there were differences in their experience of retirement. From this research, we discovered that there were four distinct types of mature adults, each with its own experience of retirement.

We've named one of the segments the Ageless Explorers—a group that makes up 27% of the older adult U.S. population. These are people who are becoming the new role models for retirement. They feel youthful and active. They want to contribute to their community. They like to learn and make new friends. They're very much alive—all their pistons are firing, and they want to keep working. They view themselves as aging in an ageless way. When we asked these people when they thought they'd feel elderly inside, they said "Never."

Another group of retirees we call the Comfortably Contents, comprising 19% of the older adult population. These people are essentially living their golden years—which may turn out to be yesterday's retirement dream. Their primary desire in this stage of their lives is to simply relax and be free of worry, stress, and obligation. When we asked members of this segment when they thought they'd feel elderly inside, they said "Soon." This may well be a pleasant retirement for some, but for many people, this life of pure leisure is just not exciting or vibrant enough. My guess is that most boomers will become Ageless Explorers rather than Comfortably Contents.

The third segment, making up 22% of the older adult population, are the Live-for-Todays. These folks define themselves as fun and adventuresome. They're interesting and lively people, and they love the idea of continuing to grow as individuals. The problem is that they spent so much of their lives living for today that they now don't have enough money to feel comfortable. They have an enormous amount of worry and regret about how they're going to make it, and they feel anxious that they may not achieve the level of pleasure and joy that they had hoped for, due to their lack of financial preparedness.

The fourth and largest category—32%—are the Sick-and-Tireds. These are people who have been beaten down by life, and most are having a miserable time in retirement. They've got the least amount of money and have done the least to prepare for retirement. The effect of it is that their unfortunate state leaves them feeling hopeless and unwilling to do nearly anything with their lives. When we asked these people if they would like to go to the community college, they said "No." Would they like to volunteer in their local church programs? "No." Would they like to spend more time with their family? "No." Take a trip? "No." They've pretty much resigned themselves to the fact that their lives are winding down, and they are suffering their way to the end.

Our "Re-Visioning Retirement" study also revealed that about 80% of the next generation of "retirees," the boomers, expect to be working at least part time in their retirement. They apparently do not want to be as disconnected as many of today's retirees seem to be. Instead, they want a different balance in their lives: They want to enjoy extended amounts of leisure time, but they also want to be doing some work—maybe two or three days a week of regular work, or helping out from time to time on a community project, or running a small business from home. Our respondents also said that they want to continue learning and growing in their maturity. They want to be developing their human potential rather than just sitting in the rocking chair and watching TV.

The Transformation of Retirement

We're currently at the tipping point in which retirement is transforming into a new model. It is becoming a time for personal reinvention—new beginnings, lifelong learning, and a cyclic blend of work and leisure.

In addition to their desire to postpone old age, the boomers' propensity for personal growth and new lifestyle challenges will also render obsolete the traditional "linear life" paradigm, in which people migrate in lockstep first through education, then work, then leisure/retirement. In its place, a new "cyclic life" paradigm is emerging in which education, work, and leisure are interspersed repeatedly throughout the life span. It will become normal for 50-year-olds to go back to school and for

70-year-olds to reinvent themselves through new careers. Phased retirements, part-time and flex-time work, and "rehirements" will become common options for elder boomers who'll either need or want to continue working.

Most discussions about increasing longevity have been focused on how to live longer rather than on why. I worry that without envisioning a new purpose for old age, we could be creating a future in which the young are pitted against the old.

In youth, boomers were self-indulgent in their priorities. In their late teens and 20s, many shared an idealistic commitment to bettering society. During the past several decades of career building and child-rearing, these boomers had to put aside many of their early ideals. In the decades ahead, the boomers will complete America's transformation into a gerontocracy, as they take control of the nation's social and economic power.

If they can step outside their generational tendency toward self-centeredness and wield this power wisely and productively, they could rise to their greatest height and make a remarkable success of history's first multiethnic, multiracial, and multigenerational melting pot. But if they use their numbers and influence to bully younger generations and gobble up all of the available resources, political "age wars" could erupt in which the young lash out in anger and frustration at the weighty demands placed on their increasingly strained resources.

However, if they can learn to exemplify a new kind of wise, mature leadership, when the boomers' time on earth is over, perhaps they will be remembered as not just the largest generation in history, but also the finest.

KEN DYCHTWALD, founder of Age Wave, is a gerontologist, psychologist, public speaker, and best-selling author. His address is Age Wave, One Embarcadero Center, Suite 3810, San Francisco, California 94111. Web site www.AgeWave.com. His latest book, *The Power Years: A User's Guide to the Rest of Your Life,* will be published by Wiley in August.

Originally published in the July/August 2005 issue of *The Futurist*, pp. 16-21. Copyright © 2005 by World Future Society, 7910 Woodmont Avenue, Suite 450, Bethesda, MD 20814. Telephone: 301/656-8274; Fax: 301/951-0394; http://www.wfs.org. Used with permission from the World Future Society.

The Borders of Healing

Every culture has a different way of coping with the grief over the loss of loved ones

MARIANNE SZEGEDY-MASZAK

A disaster claims victims in many ways. The death and devastation from the post-Christmas tsunami killed thousands almost immediately. But as each day passes, many other lives are claimed by disease and untreated injuries. Then there are those who are physically all right but who struggle to cope with the shattering burden of grief, terror, and loss. One man from Sri Lanka says he has not slept for days because each time he closes his eyes he sees his wife and child swept out to their death. A 13-year-old boy from Banda Aceh remembers seeing the killer wave and hearing his father shout, "Run! Run!" He last saw his parents swept away in the roiling water.

Long after some semblance of order is restored to the afflicted countries, those who survived will have to contend with the emotional effects of the giant wave. And another huge public-health problem will face these countries—a problem that has nothing at all to do with germs. "What makes this so devastating to survivors is that the very things that they need to recover emotionally—the attachment to other people, the support of the community—have all been torn out from beneath them," says Jon Allen, a psychologist with Baylor College of Medicine and the author of *Coping With Trauma.*

The emotional consequences of trauma and disaster constitute a vast new field of professional inquiry. After the 9/11 terrorist attacks, a small mental health industry sprang up almost overnight, as post-traumatic stress disorder became as familiar a medical term as epilepsy. In the areas hardest hit by the tsunami, helping victims deal with the emotional effects of the breathtaking loss and devastation will be critical. "Most of what we know about psychological trauma is based on western models and research on western populations," says Gordon Nagayama Hall, professor of psychology at the University of Oregon and the editor of the journal *Cultural Diversity and Ethnic Minority Psychology.* "Very little research has been done on coping with trauma in Asian populations." The question is: Does it matter? Aren't there universal paths to healing that transcend national borders?

The answer to this is both yes and no. Experts in psychological and cultural issues point out that all human experience can be distilled through three major dimensions: the universal, the group, and the individual. These dimensions come into stark re-

lief during a disaster. "In the case of trauma," says Frederick Leong, professor of psychology at the University of Tennessee and the president of the Asian American Psychological Association, "the universal gets stimulated immediately. Everyone is together in their experience of the shock, of the need to survive, even in the first experience of grief." Universal human experience demands what virtually all experts in trauma recommend as an essential first response: immediate attention to the most basic human needs of food, water, shelter, sleep, and medical attention. An appreciation for the universality of human experience also means that normal responses to horrible events should not be seen as demanding the attention of a mental health expert. "If you have spent all day fishing floating bodies out of water, you will not sleep well," says David Ratnavale, a psychiatrist who has been advising the Sri Lankan government on disaster management for several years. "These are not psychiatric cases, and sleeplessness is not a medical problem."

But after the universal reactions, the cultural dimensions must come into play. "People are in a disaster zone in a culture that does not look at the diagnostic manual of the American Psychiatric Association," says Anthony Ng, chair of the APA's committee on disaster. "Anyone who comes to help must work within the confines of these cultures and see how mental health fits into it."

Less ego. Some experts say that Asian cultures tend to be more interdependent than western cultures. Manoj Shah, a psychiatrist at Schneider Children's Hospital on Long Island, went to Gujarat, India, after a devastating earthquake in 2001. In providing mental health care to the victims, he explained, Indian culture "fosters interdependency and is sociocentric rather than egocentric. Individuality and privacy are not encouraged. These characteristics lend themselves to group therapy." But there is a continuum for these relationships. "We are not like the Japanese, where everything is the company, or the society, or the community. And we are not as individualistic as western culture. We are somewhere in between."

While this model may be true in India, elsewhere in Asia this interdependence has another side. One of the few studies of Asian populations in stressful situations found that they tended not to seek support from others the way westerners tend to. Interdependence, in this cultural context, involves a concern for interpersonal harmony and concern over loss of face. "Loss of face involves fulfilling one's social role," says psychologist Hall. "Seeking the help of others might be perceived as burdensome and upsetting the harmony of these social relations."

"Some people will pray ... some will seek solace in burial rituals."

NEIL BOOTHY, *Columbia University School of Public Health*

The way people communicate further illustrates the importance of cultural sensitivity. Anthropologists and linguists point to two basic communication styles: high context and low context. Westerners tend to communicate in a low-context style, using words to explain nearly everything. Asian cultures, by contrast, are high-context cultures, valuing and emphasizing nonverbal communication. Eye contact, gestures, and facial expressions communicate even more than spoken language. "Not every culture is a talk-it-out type of culture," says psychologist Neil Boothby, a professor of public health at Columbia University who worked for Save the Children with the children of Banda Aceh for years before the tsunami, during the civil war. Now, he will return to cope with a more traumatic disaster. "Some people will pray, some will meditate, some will seek solace in burial rituals and things of that nature. At a minimum, a western approach to talking about things could be ineffective; at maximum it could be harmful."

For those providing relief, the challenge is to bolster existing local resources, like schools, religious groups, and civic associations, so they can provide the mental health support necessary for recovery. The essence of that support, as Baylor's Allen explains, can be found in the new attachments created out of the experience of loss and the chaos. Human relations, in the end, provide the security that can lead to a fragile sense of hope. "This is not a mental health thing," says Allen. "This is what people have been doing for tens of thousands of years."

UNIT 8
Personality Processes

Unit Selections

28. **Freud in Our Midst**, Jerry Adler
29. **Exploding the Self-Esteem Myth**, Roy F. Baumeister, Jennifer D. Campbell, Joachim I. Krueger, and Kathleen D. Vohs
30. **The Testing of America**, Caroline Hsu

Key Points to Consider

- What is the study of personality; what is the definition of personality? What are some of the general tenets of personality theories? Do you know any personality theories (e.g. psychoanalytic theory)? Can you differentiate one theory from another?

- What do you think contributes most to our unique personalities, biology or environment? If you answered biology, what does this imply about the possibility of personality change? If you answered environment, do you think that biology plays any role in personality? Is personality stable or ever changing across a lifetime? What are the advantages and disadvantages of a stable personality? What would be the advantages and disadvantages of an ever-changing personality?

- In a nutshell, describe the history of the study of personality. What early theories focused on human frailties and foibles? Do any theories focus on positive human experiences? What is psychoanalytic theory? Is Freudian theory dead? What contributions did Freud make to psychology? To our everyday life and our vocabularies?

- Why now the focus on more positive human qualities? Do you think psychology needs a better balance of the two (a focus on both positive and negative aspects) in its study of human personality?

- What is self-concept? What is self-esteem? Do you think these are the two most important concepts in the study of personality? How do people with high self-esteem differ from those with low self-esteem? Should teachers and parents endeavor to enhance children's self-esteem; that is, is high self-esteem necessarily and always good?

- How can personality be tested? What does a typical personality test look like; can you think of items that might appear on such a test? What personal qualities would be important to measure? Why and where are personality tests utilized? What are the criticisms of the use of personality assessment?

- Out of all the personality theories that you studied, which do you think is best and why? Was your answer based on science, anecdote, or something else?

Student Website
www.mhcls.com/online

Internet References
Further information regarding these websites may be found in this book's preface or online.

The Personality Project
   http://personality-project.org/personality.html

Sabrina and Sadie are identical twins. When the girls were young children, their parents tried very hard to treat them equally. The girls were dressed the same, fed the same meals and toys, and each had a kitten from the same litter. Whenever Sabrina received a present, Sadie received one. Both girls attended dance school and completed early classes in ballet and tap dance. In elementary school, the twins were both placed in the same class with the same teacher. The teacher also tried to treat them the same.

In junior high school, Sadie became a tomboy. She loved to play rough and tumble sports with the neighborhood boys. On the other hand, Sabrina remained indoors and practiced her piano. Sabrina was keenly interested in the domestic arts such as painting, needlepoint, and crochet. Sadie was more interested in reading novels, especially science fiction, and watching adventure programs on television.

As the twins matured, they decided it would be best to attend different colleges. Sabrina went to a small, quiet college in a rural setting, and Sadie matriculated at a large public university. Sabrina majored in English, with a specialty in poetry; Sadie switched majors several times and finally decided on a communications major.

Why, when these twins were exposed to the same early childhood environment, did their interests, personalities, and paths diverge later? What makes people, even identical twins at times, so unique, so different from one another?

The study of individual differences is the domain of personality. The psychological study of personality has included two major thrusts. The first has focused on the search for the commonalties of human life and development. Its major question is: How are humans, especially their personalities, affected by specific events or activities? Personality theories are based on the assumption that a given event, if it is important, will affect almost all people in a similar way, or that the personality processes that affect people are common across events and people. Most psychological research into personality variables has made this assumption. Failure to replicate a research project is often the first clue that differences in individual responses require further investigation.

While some psychologists have focused on personality-related effects that are presumed to be universal among humans, others have devoted their efforts to discovering the bases on which individuals differ in their responses to events. In the beginning, this specialty was called genetic psychology, because most people assumed that individual differences resulted from differences in genetic inheritance. By the 1950's the term genetic psychology had given way to the more current term: the psychology of individual differences.

Does this mean that genetic issues are no longer the key to understanding individual differences? Not at all. For a time, psychologists took up the philosophical debate over whether genetic or environmental factors were more important in determining behaviors. Even today, behavior geneticists compute the heritability coefficients for a number of personality and behavior traits, including intelligence. This is an expression of the degree to which differences in a given trait can be attributed to differences in inherited capacity or ability.

What is personality? Most researchers in the area define personality as patterns of thoughts, feelings, and behaviors that persist over time and over situations, are characteristic or typical of the individual, and usually distinguish one person from another.

We will examine several different concepts from the various theories of personality in this unit. In the first article, "Freud in Our Midst", author Jerry Adler writes about Freud and his landmark theory. Specifically, Adler explicates Freudian concepts such as the talking cure and the interpretation of everyday actions. Adler concludes that Freud indeed is not dead, even 150 years after his birth.

We next look at a second seminal idea in the area of the psychology of personality—self-esteem. Self-esteem is thought to be the most important element of the self-concept. High self-esteem, many psychologists believe, is that part of ourselves that keeps us centered and moving forward in our lives. It is a goal to be revered. "Not so," say the authors of the next article. They review the literature on high self-esteem and find that sometimes it does not produce the desired outcomes and, in some cases, might even be detrimental.

A final essay examines personality testing. It perhaps is in this domain that personality theorists and researchers have made their largest contribution to the field of psychology as well as have embroiled themselves in one of the greatest debates in the field. Personality tests are found everywhere—in schools, in places of employment, in research laboratories, and even in popular magazines—and sometimes misused or misinterpreted. The last article in this unit discloses the pros and cons of personality tests, especially in the world of work.

Freud in Our Midst

On his 150th birthday, the architect of therapeutic culture is an inescapable force. Why Freud—modern history's most debunked doctor—captivates us even now.

JERRY ADLER

We stand now at a critical moment in the history of our civilization, which is usually the case: beset by enemies who irrationally embrace their own destruction along with ours, our fate in the hands of leaders who make a virtue of avoiding reflection, our culture hijacked by charlatans who aren't nearly as depraved as they pretend in their best-selling memoirs. As we turn from the author sniveling on Oprah's couch, our gaze is caught by a familiar figure in the shadows, sardonic and grave, his brow furrowed in weariness. *So*, he seems to be saying, *you would like this to be easy. You want to stick your head in a machine, to swallow a pill, to confess on television and be cured before the last commercial. But you don't even know what your disease is.*

Yes, it's Sigmund Freud, still haunting us, a lifetime after he died in London in 1939, driven by the Nazis from his beloved Vienna. The theoretician who explored a vast new realm of the mind, the unconscious: a roiling dungeon of painful memories clamoring to be heard and now and then escaping into awareness by way of dreams, slips of the tongue and mental illness. The philosopher who identified childhood experience, not racial destiny or family fate, as the crucible of character. The therapist who invented a specific form of treatment, psychoanalysis, which advanced the revolutionary notion that actual diagnosable disease can be cured by a method that dates to the dawn of humanity: talk. Not by prayer, sacrifice or exorcism; not by drugs, surgery or change of diet, but by recollection and reflection in the presence of a sympathetic professional. It is an idea wholly at odds with our technological temperament, yet the mountains of Prozac prescribed every year have failed to bury it. Not many patients still seek a cure on a psychoanalyst's couch four days a week, but the vast proliferation of talk therapies—Jungian and Adlerian analyses, cognitive behavioral and psychodynamic therapy—testify to the enduring power of his idea.

And Freud: the great engine of an ongoing middlebrow bull session that has engaged our culture for a century. Without Freud, Woody Allen would be a schnook and Tony Soprano a thug; there would be an Oedipus but no Oedipus complex, and then how would people at dinner parties explain why the eldest son of George Bush was so intent on toppling Saddam? (This is a parlor game Freud himself pioneered in his analysis of Napoleon, who'd been dead for a century when Freud concluded that sibling rivalry with his eldest brother, Joseph, was the great drive in his life, accounting for both his infatuation with a woman named Josephine and his decision—following in the footsteps of the Biblical Joseph—to invade Egypt.) In America Freud is now more likely to be taken seriously as a literary figure than a scientific one, at least outside the 40 or so institutes that specifically train analysts. Just last year, in fact, NEWS-WEEK lumped Freud with Karl Marx as a philosopher whose century had come and gone, in contrast to the continuing intellectual relevance of Darwin. In an act of expiation, therefore, and to stake out the high ground before the tsunami of lectures, seminars and publications scheduled for his 150th birthday on May 6, we ask ourselves: Is Freud still dead? And if not, what is keeping him alive?

That he retains any life at all is remarkable. To innocently type his name into a search engine is to unleash a torrent of denunciation that began the moment he began publishing his work in the 19th century. Merely being wrong—as even his partisans admit he probably was about a lot of things—seems inadequate to explain the calumny he has engendered, so Freudians invoke a Freudian explanation. "The unconscious is terribly threatening," says Dr. Glen O. Gabbard, professor of psychiatry at Baylor College of Medicine. "It suggests we are moved by forces we cannot see or control, and this is a severe wound to our narcissism." Resistance came early from a bourgeoisie appalled by one of Freud's central tenets, that young children have a sexual fantasy life—a theory that American adults rejected by a margin of 76 to 13 in a NEWSWEEK Poll. And it's not just Western culture that Freud scandalized; as recently as last month, in an interview with David Remnick of The New Yorker, Sheik Nayef Rajoub of Hamas explained the necessity for Israel's destruction on the ground that "Freud, a Jew, was the one who destroyed morals."

And opposition came from feminists who would have you know that they don't envy any man his penis. It is now universally acknowledged that Freud's ideas about women's sexuality—in summary, that they were incomplete men—were so far wrong that, as his sympathetic biographer Peter Gay jokes, "If he were president of Harvard, he'd have to resign." The low point of Freud's reputation was probably the early 1990s, when women were filling the talk shows with accounts of childhood sexual abuse dredged from their unconscious. This was a no-win situation for Freud—who, admittedly, had staked out positions on both sides of this question, as he often did in his long career. Those who took the side of the accused parents and siblings blamed him for having planted the idea, in his early work, that the repressed memory of actual sexual abuse was a common cause of adult neurosis. Those who believed the accusers charged him with cravenly surrendering to community pressure when he ultimately decided that many of these recovered memories were actually childhood fantasies. "Sending a woman to a Freudian therapist," Gloria Steinem said at the time, "is not so far distant from sending a Jew to a Nazi."

His reputation has only barely begun to recover. In the wake of the repressed-memory wars, the vast Freud archive at the Library of Congress, much of which had been embargoed for decades into the future, has been opened to scholars. And Freud's debunkers are finding much to confirm what they've said all along, that his canonical "cures" were the product of wishful thinking and conscious fudging, and his theories founded on a sinkhole of circular logic. Efforts to validate Freudian psychology through rigorous testing or brain-imaging technology is still in its infancy. "I'm afraid he doesn't hold up very well at all," says Peter D. Kramer, a psychiatrist and author of "Listening to Prozac," who is working on a biography of Freud due to appear next year. "It almost feels like a personal betrayal to say that. But every particular is wrong: the universality of the Oedipus complex, penis envy, infantile sexuality."

How much debunking can Freud withstand? Jonathan Lear, a psychiatrist and philosopher at the University of Chicago, identifies a "core idea" on which Freud's reputation must rest, that human life is "essentially conflicted." And that the conflict is hidden from us, because it stems from wishes and instincts that are actively repressed—you don't have to believe that it involves a desire to have sex with one of your parents, if that idea strikes you as outlandish—because our conscious self cannot bear to acknowledge them. Identifying and resolving those conflicts as they emerge into awareness, deeply cloaked in symbolism, is the work of analysis.

Everything else is, ultimately, negotiable. Not even Freud's most orthodox adherents defend his entire body of work in all its details, but they do talk about the bigger picture. "He was wrong about so many things," says James Hansell, a University of Michigan psychologist. "But he was wrong in such interesting ways. He pioneered a whole new way of looking at things." Freud "helps us find deep meanings and motivations, and find meaning in love and work," says Dr. K. Lynne Moritz, a professor at St. Louis University School of Medicine and the incoming president of the American Psychoanalytic Association. Certainly he does, at least for some people, although that seems like a better recommendation for a poet than a scientist.

But then, deep meaning is just what some people want out of life, a fact that helps support the 3,400 members of Moritz's group (up, barely, from 3,200 in 1998) and 1,500 in a rival organization, the National Association for the Advancement of Psychoanalysis. That compares with 33,500 in the American Psychiatric Association. Psychiatrists are medical doctors trained to treat mental illness; they typically see patients referred to them specifically for drug therapy, or they work in hospitals or clinics with the seriously ill. The American Psychological Association, which represents psychotherapists without medical degrees, has 150,000 members. In the NEWSWEEK Poll, nearly 20 percent of American adults say they have had some form of therapy or counseling, and 4 percent are currently in therapy. The ability to tinker directly with the brain synapses, through drugs, holds the promise of making psychoanalysis redundant for some conditions. But patients respond differently, and for some a combination of drug and talk therapy seems to work best. Moritz maintains that for some conditions, such as adolescent borderline personality disorder, analysis remains the treatment of choice. As for Freud, he himself went through a brief phase in which he advocated drug therapy. Regrettably, the drug he advocated was cocaine. That remains the one salient fact that many Americans seem to have retained about him.

A major factor in the decline of psychoanalysis is the reluctance of insurance companies to foot the bill for an open-ended treatment at a cost of more than $2,000 a month. Back in the 1950s, analysis was a status symbol and a mark of sophistication, a role filled in society today by cosmetic surgery. But it is still a valued luxury good for those with the time and the means to live up to the Delphic injunction to "know thyself." "There are many people who don't respond to brief therapy or to medication," says Gabbard, "people who want the experience of being listened to and understood, to search for a truth about themselves that goes beyond symptom relief." Take one of Moritz's patients, a married woman in her 40s we'll call Doreen in honor of one of Freud's most famous cases, who was given the pseudonym Dora. Doreen is the model of many early Viennese patients, an educated upper-middle-class woman with an overtly tranquil and satisfying life. Like most patients today, her symptoms were vague and general. Neuroses no longer seem to manifest themselves in hysterical blindness or paralysis. "I decided I have a good life, but it could be better," she says. At work she was too eager to please, taking on more than she could handle; with her family she felt the need to stifle her playfulness and sense of humor. Probably many people wouldn't think it necessary to devote four hours a week for four years (and ongoing) to solving those problems, but to her it's been worth it, totally. "It makes you examine your life, retell your life, to understand where your attitudes, your beliefs and behaviors come from," she says. "I'm so much happier now. It's not something I could do alone. You have to confront the parts of yourself that are painful and shameful and difficult to face. Dr. Moritz asks the questions that cause me to dig deeper into myself."

That, of course, is the essence of Freud's technique. He was a man intoxicated with the voyage of inward discovery. You can see this clearly in his 1901 book "Psychopathology of Everyday Life." Here, Freud discusses an encounter with a young man who cannot recall the Latin word "aliquis" ("someone") in a passage from Virgil. To Freud, such moments are never without significance, and the very obscurity of the slip gave it added interest. Freud wouldn't waste couch time on a slip that was obvious to the person who uttered it. He employs his trademark technique of "free association" ("tell me the first thing that comes into your mind …") to uncover a link to "liquid," then to "blood," and through several other steps to the revelation that the young man was worried that a woman with whom he had been intimate had missed her period. What a tour de force for psychoanalysis!

Does it detract from our appreciation of his genius that the freelance historian Peter Swales has shown that there most probably was no such young man, that the memory lapse was probably committed by Freud himself and that the woman he was worried about was Minna Bernays, the sister of Freud's own wife?

Well, not to Lear. His reaction is, "I couldn't care less. I could imagine someone in Freud's position changing the story in that way. But it's just not very important [to our appreciation of his work]."

If Einstein had a romance with his sister-in-law, it wouldn't change what we thought about the speed of light. But this is Freud! His own thoughts and emotions were precisely the raw material from which he derived much of his theory. He is our postmodern Plato, our secular Saint Augustine. He fascinates us endlessly, even those who have made their reputations in part by denouncing him, like Frederick Crews, emeritus professor of English at UC Berkeley. Explaining Freud's enduring interest, he observes caustically, "Academic humanists find that by entering Freud's world of interlocking symbols and facile causal assertions they will never run out of shrewd-looking, counterintuitive things to say in their essays and books." As if that were a bad thing! Don't we all need an excuse now and then to sound smart by referring to interpretation as "hermeneutics"? Kramer finds echoes of Freud in T. S. Eliot's dreamlike symbolism, in the emotional transference (of boss to father to son) in Joyce's "Dubliners." ("Transference" refers to the displacement of emotion that a patient undergoes in therapy, making the therapist the object of feelings the patient has toward a parent. Mr. Soprano, take your hands off Dr. Melfi's throat, please.)

"We refer to Freud every day when we call someone 'passive-aggressive'," Kramer muses. "I don't know how people expressed that thought a hundred years ago." Not everyone is convinced by this argument, though: "Shakespeare managed to say an awful lot about human nature without the vocabulary provided by psychoanalysis," observes Patricia Churchland, of the University of California, San Diego, a leading philosopher of consciousness. She adds that in any case she finds that the language of analysis is being supplanted in popular culture by the jargon of neuroscience. People talk about getting their endorphins going. Someone acting rashly is said to be "frontal," referring to the part of the brain involved in impulse control.

Admittedly, hermeneutics isn't exactly where the action is in American society today. In the id-driven worlds of politics, athletics and business, Freud is the ultimate non-bottom-line guy; he pays off five years down the road in the non-negotiable cur-

rency of self-knowledge. When President George W. Bush told an interviewer in 2004 that he wouldn't "go on the couch" to rethink his decisions about the Iraq war, it so outraged Dr. Kerry J. Sulkowicz, a professor of psychiatry at NYU Medical School, that he wrote a letter to The New York Times pro-testing this slur on analysis, with the implication "that not understanding oneself is a matter of pride." Sulkowicz knows this attitude firsthand as a consultant to corporate CEOs and boards of directors, where he struggles daily to beat some introspection into his clients' heads. "There's so much emphasis on 'execution' and 'action' in the business world," he says. "I try to convey that action and reflection are not mutually exclusive." Freud's insights into the irrational and the unconscious find application in the corporation, where even high-level executives may bring transference issues into the office, seeking from their boss the approval they once craved from their parents. Freud's writings on group dynamics and sibling rivalry can serve the thoughtful CEO well, Sulkowicz adds. It helps, though, if the source is somewhat obscured. "I hardly ever talk about Freud by name," he says.

In the shadows, the tip of the cigar wiggles up and down in agitation. *Americans!* he seems to be thinking. *A money-grubbing mob; they made me fear for the future of civilization itself. I should have told them when I had the chance.*

Freud, rooted in the great civilizations of Europe, wrote little about America, which he visited briefly in 1909, but his attitude was clear from a few terse sentences in his dark classic, "Civilization and Its Discontents." Published in 1930, when Freud was already an old man, the book was a psychological meditation on the social contract: the surrender of mankind's natural instinct for aggression and sexual domination in exchange for the security and comfort of civilized society. But in Freud's view, that is not an easy bargain. Those instincts are powerful and their repression creates unconscious conflict—what Lear described as the "core idea" of Freudian thought. And that is the source of the disease that we cannot name, and that we can never really cure, because it is built into the human condition. It is no accident, says Lear, that Freud's reputation reached a low point in the early 1990s, which was not only the height of the recovered-memory hysteria, but also of the post-cold-war optimism that made a best seller of Francis Fukuyama's book "The End of History." Fukuyama predicted that the dissolution of the Soviet Union would pave the way for the triumph of liberal democracy around the world—an idea that came crashing to the ground one sunny morning in 2001. "We are always susceptible," Lear says, "to the illusion that these are not our problems. The end of history was a brave hope that the ongoing dynamic of human conflict was over." But what Freud has to say, which is worth hearing even if analysis never cures another patient, is that history will never end. Because it is made by human beings.

Exploding the Self-Esteem Myth

ROY F. BAUMEISTER, JENNIFER D. CAMPBELL, JOACHIM I. KRUEGER,
AND KATHLEEN D. VOHS

People intuitively recognize the importance of self-esteem to their psychological health, so it isn't particularly remarkable that most of us try to protect and enhance it in ourselves whenever possible. What *is* remarkable is that attention to self-esteem has become a communal concern, at least for Americans, who see a favorable opinion of oneself as the central psychological source from which all manner of positive outcomes spring. The corollary, that low self-esteem lies at the root of individual and thus societal problems and dysfunctions, has sustained an ambitious social agenda for decades. Indeed, campaigns to raise people's sense of self-worth abound.

Consider what transpired in California in the late 1980s. Prodded by State Assemblyman John Vasconcellos, Governor George Deukmejian set up a task force on self-esteem and personal and social responsibility. Vasconcellos argued that raising self-esteem in young people would reduce crime, teen pregnancy, drug abuse, school underachievement and pollution. At one point, he even expressed the hope that these efforts would one day help balance the state budget, a prospect predicated on the observation that people with high self-regard earn more than others and thus pay more in taxes. Along with its other activities, the task force assembled a team of scholars to survey the relevant literature. The results appeared in a 1989 volume entitled *The Social Importance of Self-Esteem* (University of California Press, 1989), which stated that "many, if not most, of the major problems plaguing society have roots in the low self-esteem of many of the people who make up society." In reality, the report contained little to support that assertion. The California task force disbanded in 1995, but a nonprofit organization called the National Association for Self-Esteem (NASE) has picked up its mantle. Vasconcellos, until recently a California state senator, is on the advisory board.

Was it reasonable for leaders in California to start fashioning therapies and social policies without supportive data? Perhaps, given that they had problems to address. But one can draw on many more studies now than was the case 15 years ago, enough to assess the value of self-esteem in several spheres. Regrettably, those who have been pursuing self-esteem-boosting programs, including the leaders of NASE, have not shown a desire to examine the new work, which is why the four of us recently came together under the aegis of the American Psychological Society to review the scientific literature.

In the Eye of the Beholder

Gauging the value of self-esteem requires, first of all, a sensible way to measure it. Most investigators just ask people what they think of themselves. Naturally enough, the answers are often colored by the common tendency to want to make oneself look good. Unfortunately, psychologists lack good methods to judge self-esteem.

Consider, for instance, research on the relation between self-esteem and physical attractiveness. Several studies have generally found clear positive links when people rate themselves on both properties. It seems plausible that physically attractive people would end up with high self-esteem because they are treated more favorably than unattractive ones—being more popular, more sought after, more valued by lovers and friends, and so forth. But it could just as well be that those who score highly on self-esteem scales by claiming to be wonderful people all around also boast of being physically attractive.

In 1995 Edward F. Diener and Brian Wolsic of the University of Illinois and Frank Fujita of Indiana University South Bend examined this possibility. They obtained self-esteem scores from a broad sample of the population and then photographed everybody, presenting these pictures to a panel of judges, who evaluated the subjects for attractiveness. Ratings based on full-length photographs showed no significant correlation with self-esteem. When the judges were shown pictures of just the participants' unadorned faces, the correlation between attractiveness and self-esteem was once again zero. In that same investigation, however, self-reported physical attractiveness was found to have a strong correlation with self-esteem. Clearly, those with high self-esteem are gorgeous in their own eyes but not necessarily to others.

This discrepancy should be sobering. What seemed at first to be a strong link between physical good looks and high self-esteem turned out to be nothing more than a pattern of consistency in how favorably people rate themselves. A parallel phenomenon affects those with low self-esteem, who are prone to floccinaucinihilipilification, a highfalutin word (among the longest in the Oxford English Dictionary) but one that we can't resist using here, it being defined as "the action or habit of estimating as worthless." That is, people with low self-esteem are not merely down on themselves; they are negative about everything.

This tendency has certainly distorted some assessments. For example, psychologists once thought that people with low self-esteem were especially prejudiced. But thoughtful scholars, such as Jennifer Crocker of the University of Michigan at Ann Arbor, questioned this conclusion. After all, if people rate themselves negatively, it is hard to label them as prejudiced for rating people not like themselves similarly. When one uses the difference between the subjects' assessments of their own group and their ratings of other groups as the yardstick for bias, the findings are reversed: people with *high* self-esteem appear to be more prejudiced. Floccinaucinihilipilification also raises the danger that those who describe themselves disparagingly may describe their lives similarly, thus furnishing the appearance that low self-esteem has unpleasant outcomes.

Given the often misleading nature of self-reports, we set up our review to emphasize objective measures wherever possible—a requirement that greatly reduced the number of relevant studies (from more than 15,000 to about 200). We were also mindful to avoid another fallacy: the assumption that a correlation between self-esteem and some desired behavior establishes causality. Indeed, the question of causality goes to the heart of the debate. If high self-esteem brings about certain positive outcomes, it may well be worth the effort and expense of trying to instill this feeling. But if the correlations mean simply that a positive self-image is a result of success or good behavior—which is certainly plausible—there is little to be gained by raising self-esteem alone. We began our two-year effort by reviewing studies relating self-esteem to academic performance.

School Daze

At the outset, we had every reason to hope that boosting self-esteem would be a potent tool for helping students. Logic suggests that having a good dollop of self-esteem would enhance striving and persistence in school, while making a student less likely to succumb to paralyzing feelings of incompetence or self-doubt. Modern studies have, however, cast doubt on the idea that higher self-esteem actually induces students to do better.

Such inferences about causality are possible when the subjects are examined at two different times, as was the case in 1986 when Sheila M. Pottebaum and her colleagues at the University of Iowa, tested more than 23,000 high school students, first in the 10th and again in the 12th grade. They found that self-esteem in 10th grade is only weakly predictive of academic achievement in 12th grade. Academic achievement in 10th grade correlates with self-esteem in 12th grade only trivially better. Such results, which are now available from multiple studies, certainly do not indicate that raising self-esteem offers students much benefit. Some findings even suggest that artificially boosting self-esteem may lower subsequent performance.

Even if raising self-esteem does not foster academic progress, might it serve some purpose later, say, on the job? Apparently not. Studies of possible links between workers' self-regard and job performance echo what has been found with schoolwork: the simple search for correlations yields some suggestive results, but these do not show whether a good self-image leads to occupational success, or vice versa. In any case, the link is not particularly strong.

The failure to contribute significantly at school or at the office would be easily offset if a heightened sense of self-worth helped someone to get along better with others. Having a good self-image might make someone more likable insofar as people prefer to associate with confident, positive individuals and generally avoid those who suffer from self-doubts and insecurities.

People who regard themselves highly generally state that they are popular and rate their friendships as being of superior quality to those described by people with low self-esteem, who report more negative interactions and less social support. But as Julia Bishop and Heidi M. Inderbitzen-Nolan of the University of Nebraska–Lincoln showed in 1995, these assertions do not reflect reality. The investigators asked 542 ninth-grade students to nominate their most-liked and least-liked peers, and the resulting rankings displayed no correlation whatsoever with self-esteem scores.

A few other methodologically sound studies have found that the same is true for adults. In one of these investigations, conducted in the late 1980s, Duane P. Buhrmester, now at the University of Texas at Dallas, and three colleagues reported that college students with high levels of self-regard claimed to be substantially better at initiating relationships, disclosing things about themselves, asserting themselves in response to objectionable behaviors by others, providing emotional support and even managing interpersonal conflicts. Their roommates' ratings, however, told a different story. For four of the five interpersonal skills surveyed, the correlation with self-esteem dropped to near zero. The only one that remained statistically significant was with the subjects' ability to initiate new social contacts and friendships. This does seem to be one sphere in which confidence indeed matters: people who think that they are desirable and attractive should be adept at striking up conversations with strangers, whereas those with low self-esteem presumably shy away from initiating such contacts, fearing rejection.

One can imagine that such differences might influence a person's love life, too. In 2002 Sandra L. Murray of the University at Buffalo found that people low in self-esteem tend to distrust their partners' expressions of love and support, acting as though they are constantly expecting rejection. Thus far, however, investigators have not produced evidence that such relationships are especially prone to dissolve. In fact, high self-esteem may be the bigger threat: as Caryl E. Rusbult of the University of Kentucky showed back in 1987, those who think highly of themselves are more likely than others to respond to problems by severing relations and seeking other partners.

Sex, Drugs, Rock 'n' Roll

How about teenagers? How does self-esteem, or the lack thereof, influence their love life, in particular their sexual activity? Investigators have examined this subject extensively. All in all, the results do not support the idea that low self-esteem predisposes young people to more or earlier sexual activity. If anything, those with high self-esteem are less inhibited, more willing to disregard risks and more prone to engage in sex. At the same time, bad sexual experiences and unwanted pregnancies appear to lower self-esteem.

If not sex, then how about alcohol or illicit drugs? Abuse of these substances is one of the most worrisome behaviors among young people, and many psychologists once believed that boosting self-esteem would prevent such problems. The thought was that people with low self-esteem turn to drinking or drugs for solace. The data, however, do not consistently show that low adolescent self-esteem causes or even correlates with the abuse of alcohol or other drugs. In particular, in a large-scale study in 2000, Rob McGee and Sheila M. Williams of the Dunedin School of Medicine at the University of Otago in New Zealand found no correlation between self-esteem measured between ages nine and 13 and drinking or drug use at age 15. Even when findings do show links between alcohol use and self-esteem, they are mixed and inconclusive. We did find, however, some evidence that low self-esteem contributes to illicit drug use. In particular, Judy A. Andrews and Susan C. Duncan of the Oregon Research Institute found in 1997 that declining levels of academic motivation (the main focus of their study) caused self-esteem to drop, which in turn led to marijuana use, although the connection was weak.

Interpretation of the findings on drinking and drug abuse is probably complicated by the fact that some people approach the experience out of curiosity or thrill seeking, whereas others may use it to cope with or escape from chronic unhappiness. The overall result is that no categorical statements can be made. The same is true for tobacco use, where our study-by-study review uncovered a preponderance of results that show no influence. The few positive findings we unearthed could conceivably reflect nothing more than self-report bias.

Another complication that also clouds these studies is that the category of people with high self-esteem contains individuals whose self-opinions differ in important ways. Yet in most analyses, people with a healthy sense of self-respect are, for example, lumped with those feigning higher self-esteem than they really feel or who are narcissistic. Not surprisingly, the results of such investigations may produce weak or contradictory findings.

Bully for You

For decades, psychologists believed that low self-esteem was an important cause of aggression. One of us (Baumeister) challenged that notion in 1996, when he reviewed assorted studies and concluded that perpetrators of aggression generally hold favorable and perhaps even inflated views of themselves.

Take the bullying that goes on among children, a common form of aggression. Dan Olweus of the University of Bergen was one of the first to dispute the notion that under their tough exteriors, bullies suffer from insecurities and self-doubts. Although Olweus did not measure self-esteem directly, he showed that bullies reported less anxiety and were more sure of themselves than other children. Apparently the same applies to violent adults.

After coming to the conclusion that high self-esteem does not lessen a tendency toward violence, that it does not deter adolescents from turning to alcohol, tobacco, drugs and sex, and that it fails to improve academic or job performance, we got a boost when

we looked into how self-esteem relates to happiness. The consistent finding is that people with high self-esteem are significantly happier than others. They are also less likely to be depressed.

One especially compelling study was published in 1995, after Diener and his daughter Marissa, now a psychologist at the University of Utah, surveyed more than 13,000 college students, and high self-esteem emerged as the strongest factor in overall life satisfaction. In 2004 Sonja Lyubomirsky, Christopher Tkach and M. Robin DiMatteo of the University of California, Riverside, reported data from more than 600 adults ranging in age from 51 to 95. Once again, happiness and self-esteem proved to be closely tied. Before it is safe to conclude that high self-esteem leads to happiness, however, further research must address the shortcomings of the work that has been done so far.

First, causation needs to be established. It seems possible that high self-esteem brings about happiness, but no research has shown this outcome. The strong correlation between self-esteem and happiness is just that—a correlation. It is plausible that occupational, academic or interpersonal successes cause both happiness and high self-esteem and that corresponding failures cause both unhappiness and low self-esteem. It is even possible that happiness, in the sense of a temperament or disposition to feel good, induces high self-esteem.

Second, it must be recognized that happiness (and its opposite, depression) has been studied mainly by means of self-report, and the tendency of some people toward negativity may produce both their low opinions of themselves and unfavorable evaluations of other aspects of life. Yet it is not clear what could replace such assessments. An investigator would indeed be hard-pressed to demonstrate convincingly that a person was less (or more) happy than he or she supposed. Clearly, objective measures of happiness and depression are going to be difficult if not impossible to obtain, but that does not mean self-reports should be accepted uncritically.

What then should we do? Should parents, teachers and therapists seek to boost self-esteem wherever possible? In the course of our literature review, we found some indications that self-esteem is a helpful attribute. It improves persistence in the face of failure. And individuals with high self-esteem sometimes perform better in groups than do those with low self-esteem. Also, a poor self-image is a risk factor for certain eating disorders, especially bulimia—a connection one of us (Vohs) and her colleagues documented in 1999. Other effects are harder to demonstrate with objective evidence, although we are inclined to accept the subjective evidence that self-esteem goes hand in hand with happiness.

So we can certainly understand how an injection of self-esteem might be valuable to the individual. But imagine if a heightened sense of self-worth prompted some people to demand preferential treatment or to exploit their fellows. Such tendencies would entail considerable social costs. And we have found little to indicate that indiscriminately promoting self-esteem in today's children or adults, just for being themselves, offers society any compensatory benefits beyond the seductive pleasure it brings to those engaged in the exercise.

The Testing of America

CAROLINE HSU

Are you an introvert or an extrovert? A confronter? An idealist? An analytical Enneagram type 5, or a free-spirited orange? Or are you, like most people, just a good old ESTJ? Whether you see the world through four-letter personality types, believe in ayurvedic *doshas*, or completed an online assessment before getting a job, chances are you've taken a personality test. If not, just wait: Personality tests are increasingly a part of American life, used to assess preschool applicants, match up college roommates, award promotions, and even match life partners. And they're big business: Personality testing companies make up a $400 million industry that's growing at an average of 10 percent a year. The tests are used in hiring, promotions, and professional development by a third of U.S. businesses. The Myers-Briggs Type Indicator, the most popular, is taken by an estimated 2.5 million people a year, and in the past three months alone, the online testing website *Tickle* administered 10 million personality tests.

Who are you? Yet despite some of the tests' scientific trappings, they may reveal less about "personality" than meets the eye. Within the field of psychology, there's not even a consensus on whether personality can be tested at all. While some psychologists regularly use tests to predict and understand behavior and guide individual change, others believe that personality is a moving target, determined by past experience and current environment. Some tests, like the Rorschach inkblots, are highly controversial yet still remain in use. And others, like the Myers-Briggs Type Indicator and its legions of imitators, have little academic support but are seen as largely harmless and sometimes very helpful in therapy and personal coaching.

"Personality tests are popular because they promise a shortcut," says writer Annie Murphy Paul, author of the forthcoming book *The Cult of Personality: How Personality Tests Are Leading Us to Miseducate Our Children, Mismanage Our Companies and Misunderstand Ourselves.* "There are now such large numbers of people in our schools, corporations, and legal system, we need a way to manage and screen them, and these tests ask what we're like as people and provide a neat, tidy label." While the SAT and IQ tests have been widely criticized and have adapted to meet those criticisms, personality tests have largely escaped serious examination. "The tests we use today reflect in large part the idiosyncratic and often eccentric personalities of their creators," says Murphy Paul. "Scientific proof of their effectiveness, however, is often lacking."

But John Putzier, a performance consultant and author of the new book *Weirdos in the Workplace,* argues that personality testing can be enormously valuable, precisely because often what is revealed as a weakness is actually a person's strength. "Someone who is analytical and likes to work by themselves all day might be a great engineer, planner, or accountant," says Putzier.

Ian Bilyj, 30, of Woodbridge, Va., first took the Myers-Briggs Type Indicator as part of a high school class. Students were assigned roles in a fictional company based on their four-letter type. Bilyj tested as a classic INTP, or an Introverted, Intuitive, Thinking Perceiver. In the world of Myers-Briggs, INTPs are often known as the Thinker, detached and analytical. Bilyj went on to become an engineer, a natural fit for his type, but also used college to work on his social skills. "I made a conscious effort to know people better, and when I took the test over after sophomore year of college, I had become an E," or Extrovert. Although personality type theory holds that core attributes such as introversion and extroversion don't change, in practice, as many as three quarters of Myers Briggs test takers have a different result upon retaking the test, according to a 1991 report by the National Research Council.

One of the newer uses of personality testing is electronic matchmaking. At the forefront is Neil Clark Warren, founder of the dating website *eHarmony.com.* Warren, a clinical psychologist, studied 2,000 married couples to devise his 436-question "compatibility index." *EHarmony* matches only couples who share similar levels in a minimum of 25 out of 29 areas of compatibility. Websites like *Tickle* and *Match.com* now have their own dating personality tests, too.

More controversial is the use of personality testing in high-stakes situations, like job interviews, parole hearings, and court cases. "One of the problems is there's no state or federal regulations on these tests," says Brad Seligman, a Berkeley, Calif., lawyer who has won clients million-dollar settlements for personality test questions that violated state law. In one particularly egregious case, welfare applicants in Contra Costa County were tested for substance abuse with queries like "True or False: I believe everything is turning out just the way the Bible said it would." Further investigation showed that the test incorrectly classified 44 percent of all applicants as addicts. The county paid $1.2 million to mislabeled test takers and stopped giving the test. In other cases, minorities have been able to show that tests were discriminatory.

Another controversy is brewing in the use of tests in custody disputes. The mmpi 2, a test designed to assess clinical mental disorders, is regularly administered in such cases. After taking the mmpi 2 as well as two other tests and undergoing a short interview, Tina Marie Camacho of Bay Shore, N.Y., was diagnosed with Munchausen syndrome by proxy, an illness where a parent seeking attention hurts or overmedicates a child. Despite the fact that Camacho's family pediatrician disagreed with the court-appointed psychologist's diagnosis, the personality test carried more weight, and Camacho lost custody of her two children.

"The worst test used well can be better than the best test used poorly."

Mo Therese Hannah was also forced to take the MMPI 2 as part of her court-ordered custody evaluation. Hannah, a psychology professor at Siena College in Loudonville, N.Y., knew the exact mechanics of the MMPI—she'd even taught classes about the test. She also knew that she was under a great deal of emotional stress from the trauma of the custody battle—stress that might make her appear an unstable mother. "I did try to take the test honestly," said Hannah, who was eventually awarded custody of her four children.

Bad behavior. But her situation also exemplifies the deep divide in psychology over just what personality is. "There's a tendency to think that everything a person does flows from his personality, but there are experiments that show what predicts behavior is not personality but situation," says John Darley, a social psychologist at Princeton University. A classic example is the infamous 1971 Stanford Prison Experiment, in which undergraduates chosen for their very "normalness" were randomly assigned roles as "prisoner" or "guard" and placed in a very realistic prison environment. In six days, the violence and cruelty had escalated to such levels that the study had to be called off.

"These tests are a snapshot, but life is a moving picture," says Ben Dattner, president of Dattner Consulting, a New York firm that administers personality tests. He cautions that tests can allow organizations to unfairly label an individual or allow an individual to rationalize faults that should be worked on. "To say that someone is an ENTP can be a stereotype that labels someone, 'You're a member of this group, and people like you are apt to have messy desks or be late for meetings,'" says Dattner. "Personality tests can offer one additional data point but shouldn't determine the outcome of decisions. The worst test used well can be better than the best test used poorly."

"Who am I? What should I do with my life? Why don't I get along with people who are different from me?"—these are all good questions, says Murphy Paul. As Americans live longer, change careers more often, and search for new ways to find life satisfaction, it's no surprise that they will continue to be drawn to such tests. "It gets the conversation going," concedes Murphy Paul. And yet the risk is that personality tests that purport to illuminate our true selves only create the illusion of insight.

From *U.S. News & World Report,* September 20, 2004, pp. 68-69. Copyright © 2004 by U.S. News & World Report, L.P. Reprinted by permission.

UNIT 9
Social Processes

Unit Selections

31. **To Err Is Human**, Bruce Bower
32. **Deception Detection**, Carrie Lock
33. **Mirror, Mirror: Seeing Yourself As Others See You**, Carlin Flora
34. **Young and Restless**, Afshin Molavi

Key Points to Consider

- Can you summarize some of the famous experiments in social psychology? Why were the studies conducted? What methods were used? Was deception an important part of each study? Are there techniques other than deception that could or should have been used? What were the results and the interpretations of each study? What does today's follow-up research indicate? Is newer research calling into question the older studies? How so?

- How do you catch a liar? Why are some people bad at deception detection? Are you fairly perceptive in this realm? Why do others fail at deceiving friends and family? What does science show about deception detection, (e.g. are there clues that liars give off)?

- Are there individuals who are masters of deception? Do you think lying is common? What motivates lying? When the recipient discovers the lie, what typically happens next?

- How does our sense of self develop? Is feedback from others the most important determinant of our self-concept? What types of feedback (and from whom) have the most impact? How is shyness and self-awareness related to seeing yourself as others see you? Do you think self-introspection plays any role in the development of self-concept?

- How does culture affect our social behavior? What are some of the essential differences between Muslim and Christian religions and cultures? Are there generational differences even within a culture? How and why do these differences develop? What do you think will be the outcome of the rampant social change taking part in Muslim areas of the world?

Student Website

www.mhcls.com/online

Internet References

Further information regarding these websites may be found in this book's preface or online.

National Clearinghouse for Alcohol and Drug Information
   http://www.health.org

Nonverbal Behavior and Nonverbal Communication
   http://www3.usal.es/~nonverbal/

Everywhere we look there are groups of people. Your introductory psychology class is a group. It is what social psychologists would call a secondary group, a group that comes together for a particular, somewhat contractual reason and then disbands after its goals have been met. Other secondary groups include athletic teams, church associations, juries, committees, and so forth.

There are other types of groups, too. One other type is a primary group. A primary group has much face-to-face contact, and there is often a sense of "we-ness" in the group (cohesiveness as social psychologists would call it.) Examples of primary groups include families, suite mates, sororities, and teenage cliques.

Collectives or very large groups are loosely knit, massive groups of people. A stadium full of football fans would be a collective. A long line of people waiting to get into a rock concert would also be a collective. A mob in a riot would be construed as a collective, too. As you might guess, collectives behave differently from primary and secondary groups.

Mainstream American society and any other large group that shares common rules and norms are also groups, albeit extremely large groups. While we might not always think about our society and how it shapes our behavior and our attitudes, society and culture nonetheless have a measureless influence on us. Psychologists, anthropologists, and sociologists alike are all interested in studying the effects of a culture on its group members.

In this unit we will look at both positive and negative forms of social interaction. We will move from focused forms of social interaction to broader forms of social interaction. In other words, we will move from interpersonal to societal processes.

Four articles comprise this section of the book. The first article provides a magnificent review of classic studies in social psychology, which basically is the study of how groups and individuals influence one another. Milgram's obedience to authority and Zimbardo's classic prison studies among others are detailed. For each classic study, subsequent research is reviewed. Newer studies are casting shadows over the classic studies' methods, results and interpretations.

The second article in this unit recounts research on deception or lying. Determining who is lying and who is telling us the truth is an important matter for human relationships. Social psychologists are making progress in their endeavor to learn the nonverbal clues for discerning deception from truth.

We next move to broader social behavior. In "Mirror, Mirror: Seeing Yourself as Others See You," Carlin Flora provides information about how others shape our self-concept. Feedback from others is thought to fashion what we think of ourselves. Our self-awareness and sociability, for example, are determined in whole or in part by what others reflect back to us.

Finally, in "Young and Restless," Afshin Molavi takes us on a voyage to Saudi Arabia, a rapidly changing Muslim society. Molavi reflects on the changes and their causes as well as on whether the sexes and the various generations are embracing such social transformations.

To Err Is Human

Influential research on our social shortcomings attracts a scathing critique

BRUCE BOWER

It's a story of fear, loathing, and crazed college boys trapped in perhaps the most notorious social psychology study of all time. In the 1971 Stanford Prison Experiment, psychologist Philip G. Zimbardo randomly assigned male college students to roles as either inmates or guards in a simulated prison. Within days, the young guards were stripping prisoners naked and denying them food. The mock prisoners were showing signs of withdrawal and depression. In light of the escalating guard brutality and apparent psychological damage to the prisoners, Zimbardo halted the study after 6 days instead of the planned 2 weeks.

Zimbardo and his colleagues concluded that anyone given a guard's uniform and power over prisoners succumbs to that situation's siren call to abuse underlings. In fact, this year, in a May 6 Boston Globe editorial, Zimbardo asserted that U.S. soldiers granted unrestricted power at Iraq's Abu Ghraib prison inevitably ended up mistreating detainees—just as the college boys did in the famous experiment.

Rot, says psychologist S. Alexander Haslam of the University of Exeter in England. No broad conclusions about the perils of belonging to a powerful group can be drawn from the Stanford study, in his view. Abuses by the college-age guards stemmed from explicit instructions and subtle cues given by the experimenters, Haslam asserts.

However one interprets the Stanford Prison Experiment, it falls squarely in the mainstream of social psychology. Over the past 50 years, researchers have described how flaws in study participants' behaviors and thinking create all sorts of mishaps in social situations.

This accounting of our monumental aptitude for ineptitude and cruelty has appealed both to social scientists and to the public; these experiments are among the most celebrated products of social science.

They're also profoundly misleading, say Joachim I. Krueger of Brown University in Providence, R.I., and David C. Funder of the University of California, Riverside. Mainstream social psychology emphasizes our errors at the expense of our accomplishments, the two psychologists contend. Also, because the work uses artificial settings, it doesn't explain how social behaviors and judgments work in natural situations, they believe.

In an upcoming *Behavioral and Brain Sciences*, Krueger and Funder compare much of current social psychology to vision research more than a century ago. At that time, visual illusions were considered reflections of arbitrary flaws in the visual system.

In 1896, a French psychologist proposed that visual illusions arise from processes that enable us to see well in natural contexts. For instance, during their years of visual experience, people come to achieve accurate depth perception by perceiving a line with outward-pointing tails as farther away than a line with inward-pointing tails. The result is the illusion that a line is longer when adorned with outward-facing tails than with inward-facing ones.

Subsequently, vision scientists unraveling illusions focused on elements of visual skill rather than on apparent shortcomings in the visual system. Krueger and Funder propose what they say is a similar shift—in which psychologists will consider how different behaviors and thought patterns might have practical advantages, even if they sometimes lead to errors.

Many social psychologists continue to search for what they regard as inherent flaws in people's behaviors and attitudes. In several responses published with Krueger and Funder's critique, these researchers describe their work as a necessary first step toward identifying ways to improve our social lives by learning to avoid errors in behavior and thought.

Krueger prefers an alternative approach. "A more balanced social psychology would seek to understand how people master difficult behavioral and cognitive challenges and why they sometimes lapse," he says.

Today, investigators interested in how evolution, culture, and the brain shape mental life are already on this track, Krueger says, as they probe the accuracy and practical impact of various social behaviors and beliefs.

Group Peril Social psychology's pioneers, with few exceptions, believed that individuals lose their moral compass in groups and turn into "irrational, suggestible, and emotional brutes," Krueger and Funder argue. Laboratory studies in the 1950s and 1960s laid the groundwork for the Stanford Prison Experiment by probing volunteers' conformity in the face of social pressure, chilling obedience to cruel authority figures, and unwillingness to aid needy strangers.

Yet the underlying complexity of such findings has often been ignored, Krueger and Funder say. In 1956, for instance, Solomon Asch placed individual volunteers in groups where everyone else had been instructed to claim that drawings of short lines were longer than drawings of long lines. Most of the time, volunteers acceded to the crowd's bizarre judgments.

Asch also studied conditions where volunteers simultaneously tended to resist conformity's pull. For example, when two volunteers entered a group, they often supported each other in a minority opinion. However, the story of individuals' submission to strange group beliefs received far more public attention than the other findings did.

Stanley Milgram upped the ante in 1974 by studying obedience to a malevolent authority figure. In his notorious work, an experimenter relentlessly ordered participants to deliver what they thought were ever-stronger electrical shocks to an unseen person whose moans and screams could be heard. As many as 65 percent of participants administered what they must have thought were highly painful, and perhaps even lethal, voltages (*SN: 6/20/98, p. 394*).

In further experiments, Milgram found that in certain conditions, obedience to the instruction to shock someone dropped sharply. These included situations in which two authorities gave contradicting orders or the experimenter gave instructions to shock himself. Yet these variations were overlooked, and Milgram's work achieved fame as a dramatic exposé of our obediently brutal natures.

A third set of studies demonstrated a seemingly uncaring side to human nature. This work grew out of the infamous 1964 murder of a New York City woman. Dozens of apartment dwellers did nothing as they heard the woman's screams and watched her being stabbed to death.

Bibb Latané of Florida Atlantic University in Boca Raton and John Darley of Princeton University set up simulated emergency situations in the late 1960s and demonstrated that the proportion of people attempting to aid a person in need declined as the number of bystanders increased. The presence of others depresses a person's sense of obligation to intervene in an emergency, as each bystander waits for someone else to act first, the researchers concluded. The nature of certain social situations encourages people to act in unseemly ways, Darley says.

Krueger and Funder don't draw that conclusion from these studies and others like them. They counter that there may be underlying factors, such as concerns for personal safety derived from real-life experiences, that make that behavior more sensible than it seems.

Our responses to real-life situations remain poorly understood, they contend. In their view, researchers have yet to probe thoroughly how behaviors emerge from the interplay between individuals' personalities and the situations in which they find themselves.

Guards Gone Wild The Stanford Prison Experiment offers a dramatic example of how scientists who agree with Krueger and Funder's critique can revise and draw new lessons from a classic social psychology investigation.

After noting the scarcity of research inspired by Zimbardo's report, Exeter's Haslam organized his own exploration of group power in December 2001. Because the 1971 Stanford experiment later attracted charges of ethical transgressions, an independent, five-person ethics committee monitored the new study.

Haslam built an institutional environment with three cells for 10 prisoners and quarters for five guards inside a London film studio, where cameras recorded all interactions. In May 2002, the British Broadcasting Corporation, which funded the project, aired four 1-hour documentaries on the "BBC Prison Study." Academic papers on the study are currently in preparation.

Haslam's interests differed significantly from those of Zimbardo. He wanted to draw conclusions about groups with hierarchies and, after setting up some ground rules, he removed himself from what went on.

Before the study got under way, guards were asked to come up with their own set of prison rules and punishments for violators. Haslam had stipulated that on the study's third day guards could promote any prisoners to guard status who showed "guardlike qualities" and that the prisoners would know about that provision.

In contrast, Zimbardo in the earlier experiment told guards that it was necessary to exert total control over prisoners' lives and to make them feel scared and powerless.

From the start, the guards in Haslam's experiment found it difficult to trust one another and work together. Moreover, unlike the guards in the earlier experiment, they were generally reluctant to impose their authority on prisoners.

On the third day, one prisoner received a promotion to guard. The remaining prisoners then began to identify strongly as a group and to challenge the legitimacy of the guards' rules and punishments.

A new prisoner entered the study on day 5 and began to question the guards' power and certain aspects of the study, such as what they regarded as excessive heating of the prison. From then on, in a rapidly shifting chain of events, prisoners broke out of their cells, and guards joined prisoners in what they called a commune.

However, two guards and two prisoners fomented a counterrevolution to set up strict authoritarian rule. Instead of opposing that group, the members of the commune became demoralized and depressed. As the situation deteriorated, Haslam's team stopped the experiment after 8 days, 2 days before its scheduled conclusion.

The BBC Prison Study indicates that tyranny doesn't arise simply from one group having power over another, Haslam says. Group members must share a definition of their social roles to identify with each other and promote group solidarity. In his study, volunteers assigned to be prison guards had trouble wielding power because they failed to develop common assumptions about their roles as guards.

"It is the breakdown of groups and resulting sense of powerlessness that creates the conditions under which tyranny can triumph," Haslam holds.

The Hot Hand Gets an Assist
An Irrational Belief Scores in Basketball

Professional basketball players and coaches rarely pay much attention to psychology experiments. Yet they scoffed in 1985 after psychologist Thomas Gilovich of Cornell University and two colleagues published a report that claimed to debunk the popular belief that hoopsters who hit several shots in a row have a "hot hand" and are likely to score on their next shot, as well.

Over an entire season, individual members of the Philadelphia 76ers exhibited constant probabilities of making and flubbing their shots, regardless of whether the immediately preceding shots had been hits or misses, Gilovich's team found. So, strings of successful shots don't reflect a shooter's hot hand.

Although belief in the hot hand is irrational, there may still be good reason to heed an illusory hot hand in a basketball game, says psychologist Bruce D. Burns of Michigan State University in East Lansing. Teams that preferentially distribute the ball to players on shooting streaks score more points than teams that don't, Burns asserted in the February *Cognitive Psychology*.

Gilovich's National Basketball Association (NBA) data show that scoring streaks occur more often among the best overall shooters, Burns notes. When players regard a string of scores by a teammate as a cue to set him up for more shots, they are favoring the strongest player.

Using a model of hot-hand behavior and computer simulations of basketball games based on the NBA data, Burns estimated that a professional team that follows the hot-hand rule scores one extra basket every seven or eight games. That's a small advantage, but enough to make a difference over a season.

Hot-hand beliefs probably boost team scoring to a greater extent in pick-up basketball games, where players know much less about their teammates' shooting abilities than NBA pros do, Burns says.—B.B.

Imperfect Minds During the past several decades, social psychology has moved from reveling in people's bad behavior to documenting faults in social thinking, according to Krueger and Funder. This shift reflects the influence of investigations, launched 30 years ago, by psychologists studying decision-making. That work showed that people don't use strict standards of rationality to decide what to buy or to make other personal choices.

Investigators have uncovered dozens of types of errors in social judgment. However, methodological problems and logical inconsistencies mar much of the evidence for these alleged mental flaws, Krueger and Funder assert.

For instance, volunteers who scored poorly on tests of logical thinking, grammatical writing, and getting jokes tended to believe that they had outscored most of their peers on those tests, according to a 1999 report by Cornell's Justin Kruger and David Dunning. In contrast, high scorers on these tests slightly underestimated how well they had done compared with others.

Kruger and Dunning concluded that people who are incompetent in a task can't recognize their own ineptitude, whereas expertise in a task leads people to assume that because they perform well, most of their peers must do the same.

Kruger, however, says, "This study exemplifies the rush to the conclusion that most people's social-reasoning abilities are deeply flawed."

Krueger and Funder hold that the results are undermined by a statistical effect known as regression to the mean. If participants take two tests, each person's score on the second test tends to revert toward the average score of all test takers. Thus, a person who had scored high on the first test is more likely to score lower on a second test. Similarly, low scorers from the first test will tend to come in higher on a second test than on the first. So, the Kruger and Dunning finding doesn't necessarily indicate that low scorers lack insight into the quality of their performance, Krueger adds.

In a published response, Dunning doesn't counter the statistical challenge but says that his results have been confirmed by further studies. He contends that, in general, social psychologists "would do well to point out people's imperfections so that they can improve upon them."

Krueger and Funder follow another scientific path. Instead of assuming that behavior and thinking are inherently flawed, they see errors as arising out of adaptive ways of interacting with the world.

"It is the breakdown of groups and resulting sense of powerlessness that creates the conditions under which tyranny can triumph."
—S. Alexander Haslam, University of Exeter

Krueger studies whether individuals see themselves in an unduly positive light and, if they do, whether such self-inflation contains benefits as well as costs.

Funder observes exchanges between pairs of volunteers to study how each individual assesses the other's personality. He determines which of the cues emitted by one person are detected by the other person and how they lead to an opinion about the first volunteer's personality.

While encouraging psychologists to look at positive aspects of social interactions, neither researcher harbors any illusions that what the two call the "reign of errors" in social psychology is about to end. They'd rather not add another mental mistake to the list.

Deception Detection

Psychologists try to learn how to spot a liar

CARRIE LOCK

"Is he lying?" Odds are, you'll never know. Although people have been communicating with one another for tens of thousands of years, more than 3 decades of psychological research have found that most individuals are abysmally poor lie detectors. In the only worldwide study of its kind, scientists asked more than 2,000 people from nearly 60 countries, "How can you tell when people are lying?" From Botswana to Belgium, the number-one answer was the same: Liars avert their gaze. "This is ... the most prevalent stereotype about deception in the world," says Charles Bond of Texas Christian University in Fort Worth, who led the research project. And yet gaze aversion, like other commonly held stereotypes about liars, isn't correlated with lying at all, studies have shown. Liars don't shift around or touch their noses or clear their throats any more than truth tellers do.

For decades, psychologists have done laboratory experiments in an attempt to describe differences between the behavior of liars and of people telling the truth. Some researchers, however, are now moving away from those controlled conditions and are inching closer to understanding liars in the real world. The researchers are examining whether several behaviors that have emerged as deception signals in lab tests are associated with real-life, high-stake lies. The psychologists are also testing how well professional sleuths, such as police and judges, can detect deceptions.

One thing, however, is certain: There is no unique telltale signal for a fib. Pinocchio's nose just doesn't exist, and that makes liars difficult to spot.

Lab Lies By studying large groups of participants, researchers have identified certain general behaviors that liars are more likely to exhibit than are people telling the truth. Fibbers tend to move their arms, hands, and fingers less and blink less than people telling the truth do, and liars' voices can become more tense or high-pitched. The extra effort needed to remember what they've already said and to keep their stories consistent may cause liars to restrain their movements and fill their speech with pauses. People shading the truth tend to make fewer speech errors than truth tellers do, and they rarely backtrack to fill in forgotten or incorrect details.

"Their stories are too good to be true," says Bella DePaulo of the University of California, Santa Barbara, who has written several reviews of the field of deception research.

Liars may also feel fear and guilt or delight at fooling people. Such emotions can trigger a change in facial expression so brief that most observers never notice. Paul Ekman, a retired psychologist from the University of California, San Francisco, terms these split-second phenomena "microexpressions." He says these emotional clues are as important as gestures, voice, and speech patterns in uncovering deceitfulness.

But not all liars display these signals, and one can't conclude people are lying because they don't move their arms or pause while telling their stories. These could be natural behaviors for them, not signs of lying. "They are statistically reliable indicators of deception," says Timothy Levine of Michigan State University in East Lansing, but that doesn't mean they're helpful in one-on-one encounters.

People don't seem to be very good at spotting deception signals. On average, over hundreds of laboratory studies, participants distinguish correctly between truths and lies only about 55 percent of the time. This success rate holds for groups as diverse as students and police officers. "Human accuracy is really just barely better than chance," says DePaulo.

Some researchers think, however, that the design of the laboratory studies is responsible for the poor rates of lie detection. "People are very good liars when nothing is at stake," says Aldert Vrij of the University of Portsmouth in England. "But a lab setting is not real life."

In most experiments, researchers tell the subjects whether or not to lie, and the lies have no effect on their lives. There's no significant reward for a liar who's believed or punishment for a judge who's duped. "There is definitely a lack of real-life stuff in this field of research," says Vrij.

True Liars Vrij has been looking at lies told not by participants in an experiment but by actual suspects in police-interrogation rooms. A major difficulty in using real-life lies is that the researchers themselves often don't know the truth. To overcome that obstacle, Vrij obtained police-recorded videotapes in which 16 suspects in the United Kingdom, charged with offenses such as arson and murder, told both lies and truths about their alleged involvement in the crimes. The police used forensic evidence, witness accounts, and the suspects' eventual confessions to determine the actual events.

Before learning the police conclusions, Vrij's team analyzed the videotapes for signs of the suspects' nonverbal reactions to questioning, such as gaze aversion, blinking, and hand-and-arm movements. They also looked at verbal cues, such as pauses in speech and speech disturbances, including "ahs," stutters, and incomplete sentences.

The differences between lying and truth telling were largely individual: Some suspects looked away more while lying than while telling the truth, and others increased their degree of eye contact, for example. The only general difference Vrij found between liars and truth tellers is that the liars blinked less frequently and paused longer while speaking.

In contrast to participants in the lab studies, the crime suspects didn't show any overall increase in speech disturbances or decrease in hand-and-arm movements. Because of the intense nature of a police interrogation, stressed truth tellers may display the same behaviors as liars do, Vrij speculates.

He is currently exploring lie detection from the side of the interviewer rather than the suspect. He showed 99 police officers tapes of real-life lies and truths and found that the officers were, at 65 percent accuracy, slightly better than lab-study participants at discerning the difference. But police are "still far away from perfect," Vrij points out.

He attributes the police officers' slightly better performance primarily to the nature of the lies they hear during an interrogation. "More is at stake, and that gives the lies away more," he says.

Most recently, Vrij has tested whether the police officers' accuracy rates are consistent in multiple tests. In this study, 35 police officers took four tests derived from interviews of either liars or truth tellers, and 70 percent of the professionals' calls were correct.

Although the officers again outperformed participants in lab studies, no individual officer stood out. "Our early findings indicate that none was consistently good or consistently bad," Vrij says. "Nobody is 80 percent overall."

Wizards Of Detection Other researchers, however, present evidence that highly skilled human lie detectors do exist. The scientists have been trying to identify such people and figure out how they recognize lies.

In a now-famous study from more than a decade ago, about 500 Secret Service agents, federal polygraphers, and judges watched 10 1-minute video clips of female nurses describing the pleasant nature films they were supposedly watching as they spoke. Half the women were instead watching what Ekman calls "terribly gruesome" medical films. The legal-system professionals were asked to determine the truth by reading the women's faces, speech, and voices.

Ekman and his coauthor Maureen O'Sullivan of the University of San Francisco motivated the women to lie by telling them that because nurses shouldn't be bothered by gory images, their believability related to their future career success.

Most of the observers uncovered lies at only about the level of chance. One group, however, outperformed the others. The

Secret Service group had a better-than-chance distribution, with nearly one-third of the agents getting 8 out of 10 determinations correct, the San Francisco psychologists reported in 1991.

O'Sullivan now says that her further studies of federal agents, forensic psychologists, and other groups of professionals indicate that a very small percentage of people are extremely good at spotting a phony. "We always found one or two people who were very good," she says.

Over the past decade, she has given a series of tests to more than 13,000 people from all walks of life, including therapists, police officers, law students, artists, and dispute mediators. In the first test, college students either lie or tell the truth about a strongly held opinion, such as their views on abortion or the death penalty. The researchers motivate the students by instituting a system of rewards and punishments, although for ethical reasons, the study participants know that they can withdraw at any time.

The subjects are told that if they are judged to be lying, even if they're not, they'll be locked in a dark room about the size of a telephone booth for 2 hours and subjected to intermittent blasts of noise. "We actually didn't do that, but that was the threat," says O'Sullivan.

If a student is believed, he or she earns $50 to $100. These rewards and punishments, Ekman says, "cross a certain threshold so that you generate similar behavior and emotional clues" in the experiment and in real life.

Observers who judge the students' opinions correctly 90 percent of the time or better move on to two more tests. The motivation for the students to lie remains the same.

In the first of these tests, students describe their participation in a mock crime scenario. The second test again uses nurses lying or not lying about watching nature films. Human lie detectors who get 80 percent correct on both the additional tests are "ultimate wizards" of lie detection, says O'Sullivan.

She has identified only 15 people as ultimate wizards, about 0.1 percent of the people who have taken the series of tests. "People who are extraordinarily good are extraordinarily good, no matter what the lie is," says Ekman. Another 16 people are "penultimate wizards," getting 80 percent on either the mock-crime test or the nature-film test, but not on both.

O'Sullivan has asked the wizards questions about their lie-detection processes. "All of them pay attention to nonverbal cues and the nuances of word usages and apply them differently to different people," she says. "They could tell you eight things about someone after watching a 2-second tape. It's scary, the things these people notice," she says.

O'Sullivan compares these skillful observers to Agatha Christie's fictional Miss Marple, who could instantly judge the veracity of someone by comparing him or her to people she'd already encountered.

Bond, however, doubts that O'Sullivan's experiments can be successfully applied to real-life liars. The system of rewards and punishment doesn't make the laboratory environment similar to a police-interrogation room. "A dark room and noise is not comparable to the threat of lethal injection," Bond says.

"Human accuracy is really just barely better than chance."—Bella Depaulo University of California, Santa Barbara

He also suggests that the supposed lie-detection wizards are just people who happen by chance to do well on all three of O'Sullivan's tests. O'Sullivan, however says that's unlikely.

Bond and DePaulo recently reviewed 217 studies going back 60 years that together include tens of thousands of subjects. The analysis found no evidence of significant differences between people in their ability to detect lies in various scenarios, Bond says.

Ekman and O'Sullivan speculate that if they could only study enough people, they might learn specific techniques that good lie detectors use. Then, it might be possible to deconstruct their skill and teach it to others, such as police officers, the researchers say.

Vrij, for instance, reports in the April *Applied Cognitive Psychology* that he has increased people's accuracy by a few percent by teaching them to make quick assessments of behaviors such as the frequency of hand movements. However, Levine speculates that even a bogus program can succeed by simply getting people to pay attention.

"Training may increase your hit rate a little bit in the long run, but you're still missing a lot," Levine says.

But because witnesses, hard facts, and physical evidence are often scarce, Ekman says, "it's worth training people to be as accurate as they can be."

From *Science News,* July 31, 2004, pp. 72-73. Copyright © 2004 by Science Services, Inc. Reprinted by permission via the Copyright Clearance Center.

Mirror Mirror: Seeing Yourself as Others See You

To navigate the social universe, you need to know what others think of you— although the clearest view depends on how you see yourself.

CARLIN FLORA

I gave a toast at my best friend's wedding last summer, a speech I carefully crafted and practiced delivering. And it went well: The bride and groom beamed; the guests paid attention and reacted in the right spots; a waiter gave me a thumbs-up. I was relieved and pleased with myself. Until months later—when I saw the cold, hard video documentation of the event. * As I watched myself getting ready to make the toast, a funny thing happened. I got butterflies in my stomach all over again. I was nervous for myself, even though I knew the outcome would be just fine. Except maybe the jitters were warranted. The triumph of that speech in my mind's eye morphed into the duller reality unfolding on the TV screen. My body language was awkward. My voice was grating. My facial expressions, odd. My timing, not quite right. Is this how people saw me? * It's a terrifying thought: What if I possess a glaring flaw that everyone notices but me? Or, fears aside, what if there are a few curious chasms between how I view myself and how others view me? What if I think I'm efficient but I'm seen as disorganized? Critical, but perceived as accepting?

While many profess not to care what others think, we are, in the end, creatures who want and need to fit into a social universe. Humans are psychologically suited to interdependence. Social anxiety is really just an innate response to the threat of exclusion; feeling that we're not accepted by a group leaves us agitated and depressed.

Others always rate you one point higher than you rate yourself on a scale of physical attractiveness.

The ability to intuit how people see us is what enables us to authentically connect to others and to reap the deep satisfaction that comes with those ties. We can never be a fly on the wall to our own personality dissections, watching as people pick us apart after meeting us. Hence we are left to rely on the accuracy of what psychologists call our "metaperceptions"—the ideas we have about *others'* ideas about us.

The Bottom Line: It Comes Down to What You Think About Yourself

Your ideas about what others think of you hinge on your self-concept—your own beliefs about who you are. "You filter the cues that you get from others through your self-concept," explains Mark Leary, professor of psychology at Wake Forest University in Winston-Salem, North Carolina.

Our self-concept is fundamentally shaped by one person in particular: Mama. How our mother (or primary caregiver) responded to our first cries and gestures heavily influences how we expect to be seen by others. "Children behave in ways that perpetuate what they have experienced," says Martha Farrell Erickson, senior fellow with the Children, Youth and Family Consortium at the University of Minnesota. "A child who had an unresponsive mother will act obnoxious or withdrawn so that people will want to keep their distance. Those with consistently responsive mothers are confident and connect well with their peers."

As an infant scans his mother's face he absorbs clues to who he is; as adults we continue to search for our reflections in others' eyes. While the parent-child bond is not necessarily destiny, it does take quite a bit to alter self-concepts forged in childhood, whether good or bad. People rely on others' impressions to nurture their views about themselves, says William Swann, professor of psychology at the University of Texas, Austin. His research shows that people with negative self-concepts goad others to evaluate them harshly, especially if they suspect the person likes them—they would rather be right than be admired.

The Top Line: You Probably Do Know What People Think of You

But it's likely you don't know any one person's assessment. "We have a fairly stable view of ourselves," says Bella DePaulo, visiting professor of psychology at the University of California at Santa Barbara. "We expect other people to see that same view immediately." And they do. On average there is consensus about how you come off. But you can't apply that knowledge to any one individual, for a variety of reasons.

For starters, each person has an idiosyncratic way of sizing up others that (like metaperceptions themselves) is governed by her own self-concept. A person you meet will assess you through her unique lens, which lends consistency to her views on others. Some people, for example, are "likers" who perceive nearly everyone as good-natured and smart.

Furthermore, if a particular person doesn't care for you, it won't always be apparent. "People are generally not direct in everyday interactions," says DePaulo. Classic work by psychologist Paul Ekman has shown that most people can't tell when others are faking expressions. Who knows how many interactions you've walked away from thinking you were a hit while your new friend was actually faking agreeability?

And there's just a whole lot going on when you meet someone. You're talking, listening and planning what you're going to say next, as well as adjusting your nonverbal behavior and unconsciously responding to the other person's. DePaulo calls it "cognitive busyness."

Because of all we have to contend with, she says, we are unable to effectively interpret someone else's reactions. "We take things at face value and don't really have the means to infer others' judgments." Until afterward, of course, when you mull over the interaction, mining your memory for clues.

Context is Key

While our personalities (and self-concepts) are fairly consistent across time and place, some situations, by their very structure, can change or even altogether wipe out your personality. You might feel like the same old you wherever you are, but the setting and role you happen to be playing affect what people think of you. Suppose you describe yourself as lighthearted and talkative. Well, no one could possibly agree if they meet you at your brother's funeral.

What Type of Person Can Handle Feedback …

Are you open to experience? Are you, say, perennially taking up new musical instruments or scouting out-of-the-way neighborhoods? If so, your curiosity will drive you to learn new things about the world and yourself. You'll be inclined to ask people how you're doing as you embark on new challenges, and you will gather a clearer idea of how you come off to others, says David Funder, professor of psychology at the University of California at Riverside.

How to Solicit a Character Critique (Yours!)

Muster your courage and set up an "exit interview" if you're left wondering why a relationship went south, in a spirit of fact-finding—that is, without hostility—contact your ex and ask for an honest and kind discussion of how things went awry. You're not looking to get your ex back (or get back at your ex) but to gather information to prevent lightning from striking twice. Ask questions ("What could I have done better?") and listen. Be sure you don't use the conversation to justify your old behavior.

People endowed with the trait of physical awareness have a keen sense of how they present themselves. If you are concerned with the observable parts of personality—voice, posture, clothes and walk—as an actor would be, says Funder, "you will control the impression you give, and your self-perception will be more accurate." If, for example, you slouch but don't know it, your droopy posture registers in the minds of those you meet and enters into how they see you—unbeknownst to you.

If you are someone who craves approval, you will tend to think you make a positive impression on other people. And generally, you will, says DePaulo.

People who have learned to regulate their emotions are in a much better position to know what others think of them, says Carroll Izard, professor of psychology at the University of Delaware: "They are able to detect emotions on others' faces and to feel empathy." If you are either overwhelmed with feelings or unable to express them at all, it becomes difficult to interpret someone else's response to you. Learning to give concrete expression to your feelings and to calm yourself in highly charged moments will give you a much better grip on your own and others' internal states.

Those with personalities that feed the accuracy of their metaperceptions are handsomely rewarded. "The more accurate you are about how others perceive you, the better you fare socially," says Leary. "Think of a person who thinks he's really funny but isn't. He interprets polite laughter as genuine laughter, but everyone is on to him and annoyed by him."

… And What Kind of Person Rejects Feedback

There are people who behave in ways that prevent them from getting direct feedback from others, which renders them less able to know how they come off. Maybe you're a boss who is prickly and hostile in the face of criticism. Or a student who bursts into tears over a bad evaluation. Either way, coworkers and teachers will start leaving you in the dark to fumble over your own missteps.

Such demeanor may even encourage others to lie to you, says DePaulo. You may project a fragility that makes others afraid they will break you by offering honest criticism.

> Too much concern about what others think of you can only constrict behavior and stifle the spirit.

Narcissism also blocks metaperception. Instead of wincing, as "normal" subjects do, when forced to see themselves on-screen, narcissists become even more self-biased, finds Oliver John, professor of psychology at the University of California at Berkeley. When he and his team videotaped people diagnosed as pathological narcissists, a group absorbed with themselves, their subjects loved watching the footage and uniformly thought they came off beautifully! The finding underscores how fiercely we defend our self-concepts, even if they reflect psychological instability.

Shyness: A Double Whammy

If you are socially anxious (otherwise known as shy), you likely fret that you don't come off well. Unfortunately, you're probably right. Shy people convey unflattering impressions of themselves, says DePaulo. But not for the reasons they think. People don't see them as lacking in smarts, wit or attractiveness but as haughty and detached. When you're anxious, you fail to ask others about themselves or put them at ease in any way, which can be seen as rude and self-centered.

In a way, many shy people are self-centered, points out Bernie Carducci, psychologist at Indiana University Southeast and author of Shyness: A Bold New Approach. They imagine that everyone is watching and evaluating their every move. They think they are the center of any social interaction, and because they can't stand that, they shut down (unlike an exhibitionist, who would relish it). Socially anxious people are so busy tracking what others think that they can't act spontaneously. Still, many people find them endearing, precisely because they don't hog attention.

The Powerful and the Beautiful

Neither group gets accurate feedback. "People are too dazzled or intimidated to react honestly to them," says Funder. Michael Levine, the head of a Hollywood public relations agency, has run up against many such people, who end up with a deluded sense of self thanks to a coterie of sycophants. If you are among the bold and the beautiful, he says, you must invite feedback by playing on the fact that people want desperately to be liked by you. "You must let them know that your approval is conditional upon their honesty with you."

Don't Worry—You're Not See-Through

The traits others judge us on fall roughly into two categories—visible and invisible. Funder has found that others notice our visible traits more than we ourselves do (the eye, after all, can't see its own lashes, as the Chinese proverb goes). You would rate yourself higher on the characteristic of "daydreams" than others would—simply because they cannot easily discern whether or not you're a daydreamer. They'll tend to assume you're not.

> There's always a trade-off between how good you want to feel—and what you want to know.

The good news, however, is that on a scale of physical attractiveness, others always rate you about one point higher than you rate yourself. This applies to "charm," too—another characteristic you can't easily convey to yourself, one that others naturally have a better window onto. "Imagine trying to be charming while alone on a desert island," Funder observes.

One common concern is that internal states are evident for all to see. In a study where subjects did some public speaking and then rated their own performances, the anxious ones in the group gave themselves a low rating, thinking that their inner churning was apparent to all. But audiences reported that they did just fine.

"Invisible" traits aren't entirely invisible—at least not to close friends. But an anxious friend would still rate herself higher on worry than we would.

The invisible/visible trait divide helps explain why people agree more on your positive attributes than your negative ones, says Eric Turkheimer, professor of psychology at the University of Virginia.

"First of all, people are less honest about their own negative traits," he says, "and many of these are 'stealth' traits. You'd have to know someone really well to have any thoughts on whether or not he 'feels empty inside,' for example."

Self-Awareness: A Blessing and a Curse

There is one sure way to see yourself from others' perspective—on videotape (as I did post-toast). But remember, the image is still filtered through your self-concept—it's still you watching you. Paul Silvia, assistant professor of psychology at the University of North Carolina at Greensboro, points to an experiment in which psychologically healthy adults watched tapes of themselves giving group presentations. They described it as quite sobering. They cued into their faults and judged themselves much more harshly than they would have had they relied on their own impressions of the experience. You evaluate yourself much more critically when you are self-aware, because you are focused on your failure to meet internal standards.

If I watch myself on tape, I'm not only viewing with my self-concept in mind, I'm comparing "me" to my "possible selves," the "me's" I wish to become. Here is where an unbridgeable gap opens up between people: I will never have a sense of anyone else's possible selves, nor they mine.

So, should we just rely on our memories of events, protective of self-esteem as they are, and eschew concrete documentation of ourselves? Not necessarily, says Silvia. But the dilemma reveals how self-awareness is a double-edged sword. Self-awareness furnishes a deep, rich self-concept—but it also can be paralyzing, warns Leary, author of *The Curse of the Self." Self-Awareness, Egotism and the Quality of Human Life*. "It leads you to overanalyze others' reactions to you and misinterpret them."

Many of the most unpleasant shades on our emotional palettes—embarrassment, shame, envy—exist solely in the interpersonal realm. We cannot feel them until we are self-aware enough to worry what others think about us. These emotions are supposed to motivate us to cut out potentially self-destructive behaviors. But, Leary points out, given the brain's natural bias toward false alarms, people feel overly embarrassed. Too much concern about what others think can only constrict behavior and stifle the spirit.

Do You Really Want to Know How You Come Off?

Report cards and annual reviews give you information on your performance in school and at work. But you'll rarely be treated to a straightforward critique of your character—unless someone blurts one out in a heated argument or you solicit it directly. "You could always ask a family member or someone else who knows you are stuck with them to tell you honestly what they think of you," says Funder. Publicist Levine took this approach a bit further when he asked several ex-girlfriends to each list three positive and three negative aspects of being in a relationship with him. "There was some consistency in their answers," he says. "It was challenging to take it in, but really helpful."

"There's always a trade-off between how you want to feel and what you want to know," says DePaulo. If ignorance is bliss, maybe it's best to trust someone's instinct to protect you. "But there are times when you really need accurate feedback," she says, "such as when you are trying to decide if you would be good in a certain career."

Perhaps the delicate balance between feeling good about yourself and knowing exactly how you come off is best maintained not by all those elusive "others." Maybe it's maintained by your most significant ones, the people who will keep you in line but appreciate you for who you are, not just for the impressions you leave behind.

Young and Restless

Saudi Arabia's baby boomers, born after the 1973 oil embargo, are redefining the kingdom's relationship with the modern world

AFSHIN MOLAVI

Scented smoke from dozens of water pipes mingled with Lebanese pop music at Al-Nakheel, a seaside restaurant in the Red Sea port of Jeddah. Saudi men in white robes and women in black *abayas*, their head scarves falling to their shoulders, leaned back on red cushions as they sipped tea and shared lamb kebab and hummus. Four young Saudi women, head scarves removed, trailed perfume as they walked past. Nearby, a teenage boy snapped photos of his friends with a cellphone. At an adjoining table, two young men with slicked-back hair swayed their heads to a hip-hop song echoing from the parking lot.

"Look around," said Khaled al-Maeena, editor in chief of the English-language daily *Arab News*. "You wouldn't have seen this even a few years ago."

Saudi Arabia, long bound by tradition and religious conservatism, is beginning to embrace change. You can see it in public places like Al-Nakheel. You hear it in conversations with ordinary Saudis. You read about it in an energetic local press and witness it in Saudi cyberspace. Slowly, tentatively, almost imperceptibly to outsiders, the kingdom is redefining its relationship with the modern world.

The accession of King Abdullah in August has something to do with it. Over the past several months he has freed several liberal reformers from jail, promised women greater rights and tolerated levels of press freedom unseen in Saudi history; he has reached out to marginalized minorities such as the Shiites, reined in the notorious religious "morals" police and taken steps to improve education and judicial systems long dominated by extremist teachers and judges. But a look around Al-Nakheel suggests another reason for change: demography

Saudi Arabia is one of the youngest countries in the world, with some 75 percent of the population under 30 and 60 percent under 21; more than one in three Saudis is under 14. Saudi Arabia's changes are coming not only from the authorities above, but also from below, driven by this young and increasingly urban generation. Even as some of them jealously guard parts of the status quo and display a zeal for their Islamic faith unseen in their parents' generation, others are recalibrating the balance between modernity and tradition, directing bursts of new energy at civil society and demanding new political and social rights. "We must face the facts," said al-Maeena, who is 54. "This huge youth population will determine our future. That's why we need to watch them carefully and train them well. They hold the keys to the kingdom."

Saudi Arabia, home to a quarter of the world's known oil reserves, is one of the United States' key allies in the Middle East. Yet its baby boom was launched by an act of defiance—the 1973 oil embargo, in which King Faisal suspended supplies to the United States to protest Washington's support for Israel in its war with Egypt and Syria. As oil prices rose, cash-rich Saudis began having families in record numbers. The kingdom's population grew about 5 percent annually from 6 million in 1970 to 16 million in 1989. (The current growth rate has slowed to about 2.5 percent, and the population is 24 million.)

Those baby boomers are now coming of age. And as Saudi analyst Mai Yamani writes in her book *Changed Identities: The Challenge of the New Generation in Saudi Arabia,* "Their numbers alone make them the crucial political constituency."

Their grandparents largely lived on subsistence farms in unconnected villages where tribe, clan and ethnicity trumped national identity. Their parents (at least the men) worked in the burgeoning state bureaucracy and trained with the foreign engineers and bankers who flocked to the kingdom; they lived in an era when television, foreign travel, multilane highways, national newspapers and mass education were novelties. But the boomers live in a mass culture fed by satellite TV and the Internet, consumerism, an intellectual glasnost and stirrings of Saudi nationalism. "I'm not sure young Saudis grasp the enormity of the changes in just three generations," al-Maeena told me. "It is like night and day."

The boomers, however, did not grow into fantastic wealth. In 1981, the kingdom's per capita income was $28,000, making it one of the richest countries on earth. But by 1993, when I first met al-Maeena in Jeddah during a year I spent there on a journalism exchange program, the kingdom was recovering from both a long recession (oil prices had dwindled) and a war on its border (the Persian Gulf war of 1991). Per capita income was declining rapidly; and boomers were straining the finances of a largely welfare-driven state. Government jobs and scholarships for foreign study grew scarce. (In 2001, per capita income was a quarter of what it had been in 1981.)

Arabic satellite television was in its infancy and state censorship was pervasive—in August 1990 the Saudi government prohibited the media from publishing news of Iraq's invasion of Kuwait for three days. But as the '90s progressed, technology forced change. Long-distance telephone service became affordable. The Internet began to shrink the world, Aljazeera became a boisterous news channel breaking social, political and religious taboos: Many young Saudis began to feel they were living in a country with outdated institutions: an education system that favored rote learning over critical thinking, a religious establishment that promoted an intolerant brand of Islam and a government that was falling behind its neighbors in economic development.

"I'm not sure young Saudis grasp the enormity of the changes in just three generations. It is like night and day."

"The 1990s were not a good decade for young people," said one young Saudi civil servant, who asked not to be named because he works for the government. "We didn't have the secure jobs of our parents' generation, and our government was basically incompetent and getting too corrupt." In the private sector, employers preferred skilled foreigners to newly minted Saudi college graduates. 'We were just sitting still while everyone else seemed to be moving forward," the civil servant added.

Then came September 11, 2001, and with it the revelation that 15 of the 19 men who launched the attacks on the United States were Saudis—acting under the auspices of another Saudi, Osama bin Laden. "That event and the [West's] anti-Saudi reaction made me feel more nationalist," said Khaled Salti, a 21-year-old student in Riyadh. "I wanted to go to America and defend Saudi Arabia in public forums, to tell them that we are not all terrorists. I wanted to do something for my country."

Ebtihal Mubarak, a 27-year-old reporter for the *Arab News,* said the attacks "forced us to face some ugly truths: that such terrible people exist in our society and that our education system failed us." She called May 12, 2003, another infamous date for many Saudis: Al Qaeda bombed an expatriate compound in Riyadh that day, killing 35, including 9 Americans and 7 Saudis. A series of attacks on Westerners, Saudi government sites and Arabs ensued, leaving hundreds dead. (In late February, Al Qaeda also took responsibility for a failed attempt to blow up a Saudi oil-processing complex.)

Most violent opposition to the ruling al-Saud family comes from boomers—jihadists in their 20s and 30s—but those extremists are hardly representative of their generation. "When we think of youth in this country, two incorrect stereotypes emerge," Hani Khoja, a 37-year-old business consultant and television producer, told me. "We think of the religious radical who wants to join jihadist movements, like the 9/11 guys, or we think of extremist fun-seekers who think only of listening to pop music and having a good time. But the reality is that most young Saudis are somewhere in the middle, looking for answers, curious about the world and uncertain of the path they should take."

In dozens of conversations with young Saudis in five cities and a village, it became obvious that there is no monolithic Saudi youth worldview. Opinions vary widely on everything from internal reform to foreign policy to the kingdom's relations with the United States and the rest of the West. Regional, ethnic and religious differences also remain. Young Saudi Shiites often feel alienated in a country whose religious establishment often refers to them as "unbelievers." Residents of Hijaz, a cosmopolitan region that encompasses Mecca, Jeddah and Medina, regularly complain about the religious conservatism and political domination of the Najd, the province from which most religious and political elites hail. Some Najdis scorn Hijazis as "impure Arabs," children fertilized over the centuries by the dozens of nationalities who overstayed a pilgrimage to Mecca. And loyalty to tribe or region may still trump loyalty to the state.

But despite these differences, the kingdom's baby boomers seem to agree that change is necessary. And collectively they are shaping a new national identity and a common Saudi narrative.

Ebtihal Mubarak is one of several talented female reporters and editors on the *Arab News* staff. That in itself is a change from my days at the paper more than a decade ago. In recent years the *News* has doubled its full-time Saudi female staff and put more female reporters out in the field. Mubarak reports on the small but growing movement for greater political and social rights for Saudis. Persecution by extremists is a common theme in her work. As she surfed Saudi Internet forums one day last fall, she came across a posting describing an attack on a liberal journalist in the northern city of Hail. "A journalist's car had been attacked while he was sleeping," she said. "A note on his car read: 'This time it s your car, next time it will be you.'"

"The *hijab* is such an overexamined issue in the West. I like wearing it. We as women face more serious issues."

A few years ago, such an episode would probably have ended with the Hail journalist intimidated into silence. But now, Mubarak worked the phones, speaking with the journalist, the police and outside experts, and put together a story for the next day's paper, quoting the journalist: "What happened to me is not just a threat to one individual but to the whole of society." Thanks to the Internet, the episode became a national story, and the subject of vigorous debate.

And yet: after Mubarak exercised the power of the press, she faced the limited power of Saudi women. Once she filed her story, she hung around the newsroom, glancing at her watch—waiting for a driver, because under a patriarchal legal system Saudi women may not drive. "I feel like I'm always waiting for someone to pick me up," she said. "Imagine a reporter who cannot drive. How will we beat the competition when we are always waiting to be picked up by someone?"

Mubarak reflects how much Saudi society has changed, and how much it hasn't. Like her generational peers, she comes from the urban middle class. Yet as a working woman, she represents a minority: only 5 percent of Saudi women work outside the home. Most are stifled by a patriarchal society and a legal system that treats them like children.

Beyond matters of mobility and employment opportunity is the issue of spousal abuse, which, according to Saudi newspapers, remains prevalent. In one high-profile case, the husband of Rania al-Baz, the country's first female broadcaster, beat her nearly to death in 2004. Saudi media covered the case with the zeal of British tabloids, creating widespread sympathy for the victim and sparking a national debate on abuse. The case even made it to "Oprah," where al-Baz was hailed as a woman of courage. Once the spotlight dimmed, however, the broadcaster succumbed to pressure from an Islamic judge and from her own family to forgive her husband.

Tensions between the old and the new aren't always so consequential, but they persist. Hani Khoja, the TV producer, told me that he "wanted to show that it is possible to be religious and modern at the same time" on the popular youth-oriented show "Yallah Shabab" ("Let's Go Youth"). Another program that promotes a more modern view of Islam is "Kalam Nouam" ("Speaking Softly"). One of its hostesses, Muna Abu Sulayman, embodies that blend. Born in 1973, Abu Sulayman followed her father, a liberal Islamic scholar, around the globe, including nine years in the United States, where she studied English literature. (Saudi universities opened their doors to women in 1964.) Today, in addition to her television work, she advises billionaire businessman Prince Al-Waleed bin Talal on philanthropic activities that seek to build links between the Islamic world and the West.

The prince's company, Kingdom Holdings, has the only known Saudi workplace that allows Muslim women to choose whether to wear the *hijab* (the Islamic veil and other modest apparel) or Western dress. (The prince also employs the only female Saudi pilot.) Kingdom Holdings' quarters look more Beirut than Riyadh, with fashionable women in corporate attire shuffling between offices. Abu Sulayman, however, chooses to wear the hijab—on the day I met her, a striking green head scarf and shirt ensemble. "The hijab is such an over-examined issue in the West," she told me. "I like wearing it. We as women face more serious issues."

And even as she acknowledges that "the opportunities available to me today were unavailable a generation ago," she says, "We are hopeful to achieve more. I expect my daughter to be living in an entirely different world."

"I want to get things done.... I will try to do it quietly and not just to score political points against the extremists."

"I am from Burayda, that famous city you Western journalists are curious about," Adel Toraifi said when we met at a Holiday Inn in Riyadh. He was smiling—Burayda is the heartland of Wahhabi Islam. Toraifi, now 27, came of age in one of the most conservative regions of the kingdom.

More than two centuries ago, Sheikh ibn Abd al Wahhab emerged from the desert there with a puritanical vision of Islam focused on the concept of *tawhid*, or the oneness of God. At the time, he made a key alliance with the local al-Saud ruler, who pledged to support the passionate preacher in return for support from the religious establishment. Eventually, Wahhabism spread across central Arabia, even when the al-Sauds lost power twice in the 19th cen-

tury (to regain it again in the early 20th). When King Abdulaziz ibn Saud, the founder of modern Saudi Arabia, began his march across the Arabian Peninsula in the early 20th century to reclaim his tribal lands, he revived the bargain with the descendants of Sheikh ibn Abd al Wahhab, known today as the al-Alsheikh family.

The essential outlines of that relationship remain intact. Wahhabi preachers hold the highest positions of religious authority while the al-Sauds hold political authority. Today's Saudi Wahhabist is quick to condemn those who belong to other schools of religious thought as impure or, worse, kufr, unbelievers. That explains part of the political radicalism of young Saudi jihadists—but only part.

Another explanation might lie in the evolution of Saudi Arabia's education system. In the 1960s and '70s, the kingdom fought a rear-guard battle with Egypt for regional hearts and minds. To counter Gamal Abdel Nasser's secular pan-Arab nationalism, the Saudis promoted a conservative pan-Islamism. While Egypt, Syria and Jordan were expelling Islamist radicals, many of whom were college graduates, Saudi Arabia welcomed them as teachers.

When Toraifi was 13, he decided to become a religious scholar in the Wahhabi tradition. For five years, he led an ascetic life, studying the Koran and the sayings of the Prophet Muhammad several hours a day "I was not a radical," he said, "but my mind was not open, either. I dreamed of becoming a respected scholar, but I had never read a Western book or anything by an Islamic modernist or Arab liberal."

As he walked home from evening prayer one day, he was hit by a car. After three months in a coma, he spent more than a year recuperating in a hospital, thinking and reading. "I thought to myself: I did everything right. I prayed. I fasted. I learned the Koran by heart, and yet I got hit by a car. It was troubling to me."

Once recovered, Toraifi took to reading Western philosophy and Arab liberals with a seminarian's zeal. He studied engineering, but political philosophy was his passion. After taking a job as a development executive with a German technology company; he began writing articles critical of Wahhabism—including one published shortly after the May 12, 2003, attacks warning that a "Saudi Manhattan" was coming unless religious extremism was checked. He was excoriated in some religious Internet forums, but the government largely let it pass.

Then Toraifi repeated his views on Aljazeera, whose coverage had often been critical of the royal family. That, apparently, crossed a line: afterward, Toraifi said, Saudi intelligence detained him for several days before letting him go with a warning. Then an establishment newspaper offered him a column—writing about foreign, but not domestic, affairs. The gesture was seen as an attempt to bring a critic into the mainstream. But he dismisses concerns that he might have been co-opted. "I will continue speaking about the importance of democracy;" he told me. (In December, he accepted a fellowship at a British think tank, where he is writing a paper on Saudi Arabia's reform movement.)

The Al-Sauds number some 7,000 princes and princesses. The most senior princes are sons of the late Ibn Saud, who died in 1953, and most are in their 60s, 70s and 80s. Their sons include Prince Bandar bin Sultan, the former Saudi ambassador to the United States, and Prince Turki al-Faisal, the former director of

Saudi intelligence and the current ambassador to the United States. Third- and fourth-generation princes have just begun to make their marks, and while the occasional rumor about corruption or a wild night in a European disco makes the rounds, several third-generation princes are becoming important drivers of modernization.

"I was not radical but my mind wasn't open, either.... I had never read a Western book or anything by an Islamic modernist."

Mohammed Khaled al-Faisal, 38, is one of them. The Harvard MBA runs a conglomerate of diverse businesses, including a world-class industrialized dairy farm. When I visited his Riyadh office, he proudly described an initiative that his company had taken to hire village widows and unmarried women to work at the dairy.

"In order to circumvent protest from local religious authorities, we reached out to them and asked them to consult with us on the proper uniforms the women should wear on the job," he said. "We didn't ask them if we could employ women; we simply brought them into the discussion, so they could play a role in how we do it. I am a businessman. I want to get things done. If my aim is to employ more women, I will try to do it quietly and not just to score political points against the extremists."

Economic reform, he went on, is "the chariot that will drive all other reforms." What Saudi Arabia needs, in his judgment, is more small and medium-sized businesses and the jobs they would provide.

"I see my older brother unemployed," said Hassan, a dimpled 14-year-old. "I'm afraid that will happen to me too." The four other students in the room, who ranged in age from 13 to 16, nodded their heads in agreement.

They and their teacher met me in an office in Qatif, in the oil-rich Eastern Province—home to most of Saudi Arabia's Shiite Muslims. Some of the most vitriolic abuse from Saudi religious authorities and ordinary citizens is directed at Shiites, who make up only 15 percent of the population. Though they share job anxiety with their Sunni peers, they feel that upward mobility belongs primarily to Sunnis.

Two of the youths attend a village school several miles away; while the other three go to the local public high school. The lack of a college in Qatif, many Shiites say, is an example of the discrimination they feel.

I asked if teaching had improved since 9/11. "The new teachers are good," said Ali, a smiling 15-year-old, "but the old ones are still around and still bad." The students said their teachers praised bin Laden, ridiculed the United States or described Shiites as unbelievers.

Recently, Ali said, he had brought sweets to school to celebrate the birthday of a prominent Shiite religious figure, and his teacher reprimanded him with anti-Shiite slurs.

I asked if they ever thought of leaving Saudi Arabia.

"No, Qatif is my home," said Hassan. "I am proud to be from Qatif."

Are they proud to be from Saudi Arabia?

Mohammad, who had spoken very little, answered: "If the government doesn't make us feel included, why should we be proud to be from Saudi Arabia? If they did include us more, then I think we would all be proud."

"I see my older brother unemployed," says one of the students in the room. "I'm afraid that will happen to me too."

Public pop concerts are banned in the kingdom, so musically inclined young Saudis gather at underground events or in small groups. Hasan Hatrash, an *Arab News* reporter and musician, took me to a heavy-metal jam session in Jeddah.

Hatrash, who abstains from drink and covers the hajj, the annual Islamic pilgrimage, for local papers, had spent the past two years in Malaysia, waiting tables and playing guitar in bars. When I asked about his eclectic tastes, he said, "I am a Hijazi. We have DNA from everywhere in the world!"

At a walled villa in Jeddah, young men were tuning guitars and tapping drums. Ahmad, who is half-Lebanese and half-Saudi, is the lead singer of a band known as Grieving Age. He introduced me around. A few of the musicians, including Ahmad, had long hair and beards, but most did not. One wore a Starbucks shirt—for his job, afterward. Another worked as an attendant on Saudia, the national airline, and a third worked in insurance. All seemed exceedingly polite.

They played songs from the genre heavy-metal fans call "melodic death." It had a haunting appeal, though the lyrics were, predictably unintelligible amid the heavy bass. On the wails, a poster of the British band Iron Maiden competed for space with one of Mariam Fares, a sultry Lebanese pop star.

When Hatrash took the stage, he played a series of guitar favorites, such as Jimi Hendrix's Purple Haze and softer rock, to the seeming delight of the heavy-metal aficionados. Throughout the evening, more young men arrived—but no women. Some took turns playing; others just watched. By midnight, the jam session had wound down. "This is a tame event, as you can see," Hatrash said. "There is no drinking or drugs. We are just enjoying the music."

I asked if he could envision a day when he could play in public, instead of behind closed doors.

He just smiled and launched into another song. Someone jumped up to accompany him on the bass, and Ahmad mouthed the lyrics. The guy in the Starbucks shirt rushed out the door, late for his shift.

AFSHIN MOLAVI, a fellow at the New America Foundation, has covered the Middle East for many publications.

UNIT 10
Psychological Disorders

Unit Selections

35. **The Age of Depression**, Allan V. Horwitz and Jerome C. Wakefield
36. **Soldier Support**, Christopher Munsey

Key Points to Consider

- Do you know anyone with a mental illness? If yes, can you describe the symptoms experienced by the individual? How did this individual get diagnosed? Is the individual on medication or in therapy? Is the treatment working?

- Do you think that mental disorders are biologically or psychologically caused or do both contribute? If we discover that mental disorders are instigated by something physiological, do you think mental disorders will remain the purview of psychology? Why? What other professionals will need to be involved in diagnosis, treatment, and research?

- If mental disorders are biological, do you think they might be "contagious" (caused by disease and passed from person to person)? Do you think that most mental disorders are brain disorders? Why did you answer this way?

- What do you think of the way mental health professionals diagnose mental disorder? Do you really believe that each disorder has a distinct symptoms pattern? How would you diagnose someone who shows symptoms of multiple disorders? Do you think it is possible for someone to have more than one disorder at a time?

- What is depression? Can you provide a brief history of the study of depression? Do you agree that we have promoted simple sadness to a diagnosable disorder? Is clinical depression more severe than sadness? Is depression more common in today's society or has the definition and emphasis simply changed?

- What specifically is post-traumatic stress disorder? Can people other than soldiers suffer from it? Why is the war in Iraq more likely to cause PTSD than other wars? What other situations can cause PTSD (hint: motor vehicle accidents)? Are there viable treatments for PTSD?

- What are some other common disorders, e.g. schizophrenia? What are their causes and symptoms? What role does the nervous system play in these other disorders? What role does the environment play?

Student Website

www.mhcls.com/online

Internet References

Further information regarding these websites may be found in this book's preface or online.

American Association of Suicidology
http://www.suicidology.org

Anxiety Disorders
http://www.adaa.org/mediaroom/index.cfm

Ask NOAH About: Mental Health
http://www.noah-health.org/en/mental/

Mental Health Net Disorders and Treatments
http://www.mentalhelp.net/

Mental Health Net: Eating Disorder Resources
http://www.mentalhelp.net/poc/center_index.php/id/46

National Women's Health Resource Center (NWHRC)
http://www.healthywomen.org

Jay and Harry were two brothers who owned a service station. They were the middle children of four. The other two children were sisters, the oldest of who had married and moved out of the family home. Their father retired and turned the station over to his sons.

Harry and Jay had a good working relationship. Harry was the "up-front" man. Taking customer orders, accepting payments, and working with parts distributors, Harry was the individual who dealt most directly with the public, delivery personnel, and other people accessing the station. Jay worked behind the scenes. While Harry made the mechanical diagnoses, Jay was the mastermind who did the corrective work. Some of his friends thought Jay was a veritable mechanical genius; he could fix anything.

Preferring to spend time by himself, Jay had always been a little odd and a bit of a loner. Jay's friends thought his emotions had been more inappropriate and intense than other people's emotional states, but they passed it off as part of his eccentric talent. On the other hand, Harry was the stalwart in the family. He was the acknowledged leader and decision-maker when it came to family finances.

One day Jay did not show up for work on time. When he did, he was dressed in the most garish outfit and was laughing hysterically and talking to himself. Harry at first suspected that his brother had taken some illegal drugs. However, Jay's condition persisted and, in fact, worsened. Out of concern, his family took him to their physician who immediately sent Jay and his family to a psychiatrist. After several visits, the diagnosis was schizophrenia. Jay's maternal uncle had also been schizophrenic. The family somberly left the psychiatrist's office and traveled to the local pharmacy to fill a prescription for anti-psychotic medications. They knew they would make many such trips to retrieve the medicine that Jay would likely take the rest of his life.

What caused Jay's drastic and rather sudden change in mental health? Was Jay destined to be schizophrenic because of his family tree? Did competitiveness with his brother and the feeling that he was less revered than Harry cause Jay's descent into mental disorder? How can psychiatrists and clinical psychologists make accurate diagnoses? Once a diagnosis of mental disorder is made, can the individual ever completely recover?

These and other questions are the emphasis in this unit. Mental disorder has fascinated and, on the other hand, haunted us for centuries. At various times in our history those who suffered from these disorders were persecuted as witches, tortured to drive out demons, punished as sinners, jailed as a danger to society, confined to insane asylums, or at best hospitalized for simply being too ill to care for themselves.

Today, psychologists propose that the notion of mental disorders as "illnesses" has outlived its usefulness. We should think of mental disorders as either biochemical disturbances, brain malfunctions, or disorders of learning in which the person develops a maladaptive pattern of behavior that is then maintained by the environment. At the same time, we need to recognize that these reactions to stressors in the environment or to the inappropriate learning situations may be genetically preordained; some people may be more susceptible to disorders than others. The propensity for mental disorder lies within all of us, stronger or weaker depending on the individual, and then the environment triggers the disorder.

Mental disorders are serious problems and not just for the individual who is the patient or client. The impact of mental disorder on the family (just as for Jay's family) and friends deserves our full attention, too. Diagnosis, symptoms, and the implications of the disorders are covered in some of the articles in unit ten. The following unit, eleven, will explore further the concept of treatment of mental disorders.

Depression is one of the commonest forms of mental disorder. No scientist or diagnostician knows for sure from where depression comes—biochemistry, genes, or environment. All professionals, however, are deeply concerned because depression in its severe form can lead to suicide. In "The Age of Depression," the author looks at the history of the study of depression and concludes that our treatment of sadness has stepped up over the last few decades. The consequences to the individual and to society are elaborated in this article.

Another common mental affliction is anxiety and fear. Anxiety disorders take several forms—such as post-traumatic stress disorder, which is addressed in the next article. Post-traumatic stress disorder is increasingly common, especially given recent wars. Some individuals are able to recover from wars, terrorist attacks, and other traumatic events; other individuals are not so fortunate. In specific, how soldiers and the army are attempting to prevent or treat what is commonly known as combat fatigue is highlighted in this timely article.

The Age of Depression

ALLAN V. HORWITZ AND JEROME C. WAKEFIELD

As the *New York Times* tells the story, Sherri Souza's husband is a National Guardsman posted in Iraq whose long-anticipated return home was canceled after the Pentagon unexpectedly extended his tour of duty. Like most spouses in this situation, Mrs. Souza is acutely disappointed. She misses her husband, worries about his safety, and is anxious for her family's future should he be killed or injured. When his scheduled e-mails are late, she becomes distressed and sometimes crawls into bed to await word of his safety. In the past, she might have described herself as very "sad," "lonely," or "worried." Now, however, she characterizes herself as "depressed." She is taking medication for her symptoms.

The characterization of our emotional reactions to life's challenges as "depression" is more than just a change in colloquial expression. It represents a transformation in psychiatric thinking. Psychiatrists are diagnosing more and more of the population as "depressed," by which they primarily mean the medical condition of *major depressive disorder*. Psychiatric epidemiological studies indicate that depression now afflicts about 10 percent of adults in the United States each year and about a quarter of the population at some point in their lives. This number has been steadily growing, they say: For the past several decades, each successive generation has reported more depressive disorders than the previous one. These enormous numbers have mobilized psychiatry, general medical practice, and the psychopharmacology industry to mount a coordinated (and profitable) offensive. Today, better recognition of unreported, hidden, or "sub-clinical" depression (that is, depression exhibiting fewer than the number of symptoms usually required for diagnosis) pushes prevalence numbers ever higher.

Not only the number of people said to be depressed but also the number actually treated has increased greatly in recent years. The percentage of the overall population in mental-health treatment for "mood disorders," the category of psychiatric disorder that includes major depression and related conditions, has nearly doubled since the early 1980s. Moreover, in 1997, fully 40 percent of all psychotherapy patients were diagnosed with some mood disorder, compared to 20 percent in 1987. Three times more people were treated for depression in primary medical care in 1997 than ten years earlier. The consumption of antidepressant medications both in absolute numbers and in percentage of diagnosed patients receiving medication has also dramatically expanded; persons treated for depression were four and one-half times more likely to receive psychotropic medication in 1997 than in 1987. At present, three of the seven highest-selling prescription drugs (Prozac, Paxil, and Zoloft) of any sort are antidepressants. W.H. Auden's "Age of Anxiety" appears to have been succeeded by our own "Age of Depressive Disorder."

No plausible theory of depressive disorder, whether genetic, psychological, or social, can explain why rates of depression would have increased so much in such a short period of time. Instead, the explanation appears to lie in changes in the ways that physicians, mental-health professionals, and people themselves characterize and diagnose their mental states. There are, and always have been, true depressive disorders, in which the response to loss goes awry and takes on a debilitating life of its own. But in the past, such disorders were distinguished from normal sadness that arises in response to life's vicissitudes. That traditional, common-sense distinction has broken down in contemporary psychiatry, resulting in the conflation of depressive disorders with normal sadness. The sources and social implications of this breakdown are as yet largely unappreciated.

A History of Depression

How did this transformation of sadness into depression occur? To grasp the answer, the current approach to diagnosis must be placed in the historical context of 2,500 years of contrary medical and psychiatric practice. To follow this story to the present, one must also confront the esoterica of modern psychiatric classification as represented by successive editions of the American Psychiatric Association's *Diagnostic and Statistical Manual of Mental Disorder* (*DSM-I* through *DSM-IV*). Often called the "Bible of Psychiatry," the four incarnations of the *DSM* have offered official diagnostic definitions for all mental disorders.

As long as written records have been kept, Western cultures have recognized that depression can be a mental disorder. Hippocrates, writing in the fifth century B.C., provided the first known definition of the phenomenon as a distinct disorder: "If fear or distress last for a long time it is melancholia." While theories of depressive disorder have changed, the symptoms that indicate the disorder have not. For Hippocrates, its symptoms could include prolonged despondency, blue moods, detachment, nameless fears, irritability, restlessness, sleeplessness, aversion to food, and suicidal impulses, much like today's criteria. But Hippocrates's definition indicates not that such symptoms alone indicate disorder but that such symptoms over an abnormally long duration do.

A century later, Aristotle elaborated the distinction between normal and pathological mood states. He separated melancholic states that arose from the conditions of everyday life from disorders that involved "groundless" despondency of lengthy duration and thus stemmed from internal factors:

> We are often in the condition of feeling grief without being able to ascribe any cause to it; such feelings occur to a slight degree in everyone, but those who are thoroughly possessed by them acquire them as a permanent part of their nature.

As in Aristotle's passage, the key distinction in ancient definitions of melancholia was between states of sadness "without cause" and those that had similar symptoms arising from actual losses; only the former were mental disorders. "Without cause" does not mean uncaused, for throughout history depression has been attributed to postulated physical or psychological causes such as excessive black bile, disturbances in the circulation of blood, or depletion of energy. Rather, "without cause" means that the symptoms of depression were not associated with the sorts of environmental events that would appropriately lead to sadness, such as bereavement, rejection in love, economic failure, and the like. Conversely, ancient Greek and Roman physicians would not consider symptoms of depression that occur "with cause" as signs of a mental disorder. Such normal reactions express, in the words of the second-century Roman Physician Aretaeus, "mere anger and grief, and sad dejection of mind." The symptoms could be identical in the two conditions; the distinction lay in the relation of the symptoms to the context in which they appeared. Symptoms that arose in contexts that could be expected to produce them, and that abated in a reasonable period of time after the triggering events ended, indicated normal functioning. Comparable symptoms that arose without appropriate triggering events, or had greater duration or intensity than was appropriate to the triggering events, potentially indicated disorder.

The same distinction can be found in Robert Burton's classic work *The Anatomy of Melancholy*, published in 1621. Burton defined melancholic disorder as "a kind of dotage without a fever, having for his ordinary companions fear and sadness, *without any apparent occasion*" (emphasis added). Burton considered such states "contrary to nature," and thus disordered. He considered the propensity to self-limiting melancholic feelings in response to loss and disappointment to be a normal part of human nature. He describes

> that transitory melancholy which goes and comes upon every small occasion of sorrow, need, sickness, trouble, fear, grief, passion, or perturbation of the mind, any manner of care, discontent, or thought, which causeth anguish, dullness, heaviness, and vexation of spirit.... And from these melancholy dispositions, no man living is free, no Stoic, none so wise, none so happy ... [none] so well composed, but more or less, some time or other,

he feels the smart of it. Melancholy, in this sense is the character of mortality.

The traditional distinction between abnormal depression "without cause" and normal depression "with cause" persisted into the twentieth century. In psychoanalytic discussions of depression, the former was called "melancholy" and the latter "mourning." In Freud's central article on depression, "Mourning and Melancholia," he asserted that symptoms associated with mourning, although intense, were a normal and self-healing condition that did not require medical treatment:

> Although grief involves grave departures from the normal attitude to life, it never occurs to us to regard it as a morbid condition and hand the mourner over to medical treatment. We rest assured that after a lapse of time it will be overcome, and we look upon any interference with it as inadvisable or even harmful.

Freud added an epicycle to the tradition. He observed that, although the symptoms of mourning and melancholia both include profound dejection, loss of interest in the outside world, inability to feel pleasure, and inhibition of activity, melancholia also frequently includes an extreme and inexplicable ("without cause") decline in self-esteem beyond the normal self-recriminations after a loss.

American psychiatry developed successive versions of its own classification system starting early in the twentieth century. Until quite recently, psychiatric definitions of depressive disorder continued to reflect the historical distinction between depression "with" and "without" cause. The first standardized classification system in the United States, the 1918 *Statistical Manual for the Use of Hospitals for Mental Diseases*, defines "reactive depression" much as Hippocrates did, to contrast it with normal sadness that arises in response to a great variety of losses:

> Here are to be classified those cases which show depression in reaction to obvious external causes which might naturally produce sadness, such as bereavement, sickness and financial and other worries. The reaction, of a more marked degree and of longer duration than normal sadness, may be looked upon as pathological.

The *DSM-I* (1952) and *DSM-II* (1968) that succeeded the *Statistical Manual* emphasized psychoanalytic concepts. The *DSM-II* defined "depressive neurosis" as follows: "This disorder is manifested by an excessive reaction of depression due to an internal conflict or to an identifiable event such as the loss of a love object or cherished possession." In defining depressive disorders as "excessive" reactions, the *DSM-II* recognized that they are either disproportionate to actual loss or they involve no loss at all and result from internal causes (assumed to consist of internal conflict). Here, as in the 1918 hospital manual's definition, normal triggers beyond loss of a loved one were recognized, such as loss of a cherished possession.

For two and one-half millennia, psychiatry has held that normal human nature includes a propensity toward potentially intense sadness after certain kinds of losses. Disorder can be judged to exist, it has widely been agreed, only when explanations in terms of triggering events fail to establish a normal cause for the intensity or duration of symptoms.

The Revolution in Psychiatric Diagnosis

The tradition of systematically distinguishing intense normal sadness from depressive disorder was largely abandoned with the publication of the *DSM-III* in 1980. This neglect has continued through various revisions to the current *DSM-IV* (1994). This shift occurred as part of a broader revolutionary transformation of psychiatric classification guided by Robert Spitzer, the *DSM-III*'s editor-in-chief and head of the *DSM-III* Task Force.

The great weakness of the *DSM-I* and *DSM-II* was that their vague definitions were not capable of generating standardized methods of classifying and studying mental disorders. Because psychiatrists had to use considerable personal judgment in fitting a patient to a diagnosis, psychiatric diagnosis was notoriously unreliable. Given the same information about the same patient, different doctors were likely to arrive at different diagnoses.

In addition, the psychoanalytic dominance in psychiatry was waning, and there was a sharp reaction against the psychoanalytic assumptions of the *DSM-II*. Psychiatric practice and research had split into rival theoretical fiefdoms ranging from behavioral and cognitive theories to the increasingly influential biological approach, each of which had its own idiosyncratic theory-based definitions of mental disorders. This made communication among practitioners difficult. It meant that research within different theoretical schools was based on incommensurable definitions, was not cumulative, and could not be usefully compared. It also put many practitioners and researchers in the uncomfortable position of being unable to accept psychiatry's standard definitions of disorders because of the theoretical assumptions built into them.

On top of all of this, psychiatric diagnosis was under attack from a variety of sources. Behaviorists claimed that all behavior is the result of normal learning processes and that no mental disorders in the medical sense really exist. The "anti-psychiatry" movement, inspired by, among others, the psychiatrist Thomas Szasz and the sociologist Thomas Scheff, portrayed psychiatric diagnosis as a matter of labeling socially undesirable, but not truly medically disordered, behavior with medical terminology to justify using psychiatric intervention to control the behavior. Between psychiatry's theoretical fragmentation, its diagnostic unreliability, and the anti-psychiatry critique, psychiatry's claim to scientific status and even its legitimacy as a medical field seemed in jeopardy.

The *DSM-III* inaugurated basic changes in psychiatric diagnosis to address these challenges. Explicit diagnostic criteria based on lists of observable symptoms were provided as definitions for each of the disorders, allowing improved reliability. Symptom lists provided criteria on which virtually all clinicians of opposed theoretical schools could agree. References to postulated psychodynamic causes of a disorder (for example, inter-

nal conflict, defense against anxiety) were consequently purged. The *DSM-III*'s diagnostic criteria were theory-neutral in the sense that they did not presuppose any particular theory of the cause of psychopathology, psychoanalytic or otherwise; the criteria were descriptive rather than etiological. Competing theories could henceforth try to prove their claims without begging the question by defining disorders in their own terms, and research became cumulative and comparable across theories. The psychoanalytic dominance of psychiatric diagnosis, unwarranted by the state of the evidence, was effectively ended. Rival approaches were allowed to compete on a flat conceptual playing field.

However, a major drawback of symptom-based criteria was that they eliminated the consideration of the context in which symptoms arose. One reason for the abandonment of context was the quest for reliability. Most depressions occur after some triggering event, so requiring that reactions be disproportionate to context would mean that clinicians would be frequently judging proportionality, substantially reducing reliability. (Never mind that increased reliability at the cost of validity and diagnostic logic is of no real value.) A second reason for leaving out context is that the *DSM-III* was supposed to be theory-neutral, which was interpreted to mean that it had to be neutral as to how the disorder was caused, although one could argue that distinguishing normal responses to events from disorders is not really a theory-laden distinction. Moreover, there was an impression that psychotropic medication worked on all depressions irrespective of the relation to triggering events, so that the "with versus without cause" distinction was considered irrelevant to treatment decisions. (However, even if medication sometimes works with normal reactions, the normality-versus-disorder distinction could have prognostic implications and thus could be an important consideration in whether or how aggressively to treat a condition.) Finally, there was a fear of misdiagnosing the truly disordered as normal, especially given that depressed patients are subject to suicide risk.

Granting some validity to these rationales, there does not seem to have been an organized attempt to balance potential harms from underdiagnosis and overdiagnosis, as is done with many medical tests. The problem remained that, as the previous 2,500 years of psychiatric diagnostic practice had attested, without an exploration of context and meaning, one simply cannot tell whether someone is likely suffering from intense normal sadness or a depressive disorder.

From Sadness to Depression

This brings us to how, in the case of depression, the *DSM-III* criteria went conceptually awry. (For brevity, we focus on "major depressive disorder" and ignore related diagnoses.) The *DSM-III* replaced *DSM-II*'s vague criteria with specific symptomatic criteria. These criteria have remained more or less the same through the current *DSM-IV*, on which we focus.

Nearly all recent studies of depressive disorder are based on the *DSM-IV*'s definition. Different specialists use this definition for different purposes: clinicians for diagnosing persons who have sought their help; epidemiologists for determining the number of people in the general population who are depressed; researchers for finding the causes of depression and for evaluating the effectiveness of treatments; economists for estimating the costs associated with depression; pharmaceutical companies for marketing their products; reimbursers for establishing medical necessity and determining quality-of-care standards; and mental-health advocates for quantifying how widespread this condition is. The *DSM-IV* definition is used not only in the United States but has also come to be the standard definition worldwide. The logic of *DSM-IV*'s definition of depressive disorder is key to understanding depression as a social fact.

The definition requires that five symptoms out of the following nine must be present during a two-week period (the five must include either depressed mood or loss of interest and pleasure): (1) depressed mood; (2) diminished interest or pleasure in activities; (3) weight gain or loss or change in appetite; (4) insomnia or hypersomnia (excessive sleep); (5) psychomotor agitation or retardation (slowing down); (6) fatigue or loss of energy; (7) feelings of worthlessness or excessive or inappropriate guilt; (8) diminished ability to think or concentrate or indecisiveness; and (9) recurrent thoughts of death or suicidal ideation or suicide attempt. In addition, to eliminate rare cases where symptoms are so mild as to be insignificant, symptoms must cause clinically significant distress or impairment in social, occupational, or other important areas of functioning.

Any person satisfying these criteria is today considered to have a depressive disorder, with three exceptions to be considered shortly. Yet, symptoms such as depressed mood, loss of interest in usual activities, insomnia, lessened appetite, and inability to concentrate might naturally occur for two weeks if a major loss or humiliation is experienced. Such reactions, even when quite intense due to the severity of the trigger, are surely part of normal human experience.

Two exceptions to the *DSM-IV* depression criteria simply shift the diagnosis to other categories of mood disorder—bipolar (manic-depressive) illness, or depression caused by a medication or a general medical condition. The third exception is the only acknowledgment of the existence of normal sadness—bereavement after the death of a loved one. Depression is diagnosed only when

> The symptoms are not better accounted for by Bereavement, i.e., after the loss of a loved one, the symptoms persist for longer than 2 months or are characterized by marked functional impairment, morbid preoccupation with worthlessness, suicidal ideation, psychotic symptoms, or psychomotor retardation.

The bereavement exclusion thus allows that reactions of intense grief are not truly depressive disorders, unless the reaction lasts more than two months or it includes one out of a list of five especially serious symptoms.

The bereavement exclusion is notable for the limited range of normal grief reactions it allows. Surely grief reactions lasting more than two months are not necessarily disordered. And surely the five specified symptoms do not each necessarily indicate disorder: A normally bereaved individual may for two weeks experience "marked functional impairment" (such as not

feeling up to usual work or social activities), may think that a lost partner was his or her "better half" and feel worthless or inadequate to life's tasks without him or her, or may entertain the notion that he or she might be better off "joining" the deceased partner, all without necessarily indicating disorder.

The most important thing, however, about the bereavement exclusion is that it offers exclusions only for reactions to the death of a loved one. Yet normal sadness reactions that are symptomatically similar to depressive disorders are not limited to bereavement. They encompass reactions to a wide range of negative events such as betrayal by romantic partners, being passed over for an anticipated promotion, failure to achieve long-anticipated goals, or discovering a life-threatening illness in oneself or a loved one. Of course, to qualify as normal responses that satisfy *DSM-IV* criteria, such reactions must involve a serious loss, and coping mechanisms must enable the individual to adapt to the new circumstances and get over the symptoms within a reasonable time after the precipitating event ends. If such a trajectory of adaptation does not occur, then one might infer that the original reaction had somehow caused an internal psychological dysfunction that now maintains a reaction that is no longer normal. But there are many intense reactions to loss that, just like normal bereavement responses, might satisfy *DSM-IV* symptom criteria but are not disorders.

The basic flaw, then, is that the *DSM-IV* fails to exclude from the disorder category sadness reactions to events other than death of a loved one that are intense enough to meet the *DSM-IV*'s criteria but are still normal reactions. The age of depressive disorder in which we find ourselves today is partly an artifact of a logical error.

Community Studies of Depression

In a clinical assessment, the clinician can in principle override the *DSM-IV* diagnostic criteria for depression and judge that an individual satisfying the criteria nonetheless is having a normal reaction. But no such back-up validation procedure exists when questionnaires about symptoms are administered to community members to measure how much disorder exists in the general population. Thus invalid criteria have particular scope for mischief in such studies.

A vast extension of the application of the symptom-based concept of mental disorder occurred when *DSM* criteria became the basis for large epidemiological studies attempting to measure the extent of mental disorder among people in the community who are not undergoing mental-health treatment. Because from *DSM-III* onward diagnoses were based entirely upon symptoms, epidemiologists could easily construct lists of questions that could be used to determine whether a respondent met *DSM* criteria for disorder, including depressive disorders. Lay interviewers could administer such questionnaires, allowing researchers to obtain psychiatric diagnoses comparable to those a psychiatrist would obtain, without the prohibitive expense of psychiatric interviewers. The results would presumably provide good estimates of how much untreated mental disorder existed in the community. These estimates were intended to guide policy makers in allocating resources by establishing how much unmet need existed for psychiatric services. The decision to use objective measures of symptoms in community studies largely stems from considerations of practicality and cost, and an uncritical acceptance of the *DSM*'s symptom-based criteria, not from independent tests showing these methods are accurate in identifying disorder.

Findings from two major national studies, the Epidemiological Catchment Area Study (ECA) conducted in the early 1980s and the National Co-Morbidity Study (NCS) conducted in the early 1990s are the basis for the estimates regarding the prevalence of mental disorder that are now widely cited in the scientific, policy, and popular literatures. The NCS estimates that about 5 percent of subjects had a current (30-day) episode of major depression, about 10 percent had this diagnosis in the past year, about 17 percent had an episode over their lifetime, and about 24 percent reported enough symptoms for a lifetime diagnosis of either major depression or a related disorder, dysthymia.

Are the many cases of putative major depression uncovered in community studies equivalent to treated clinical cases? The odds are against it. These studies follow the *DSM* in ignoring the context of symptoms, thus confounding ordinary sadness with genuine disorder without recourse to clinical judgment to correct the error. For example, in the ECA study the most common symptoms among those reporting symptoms are "trouble falling asleep, staying asleep, or waking up early" (33.7 percent), being "tired out all the time" (22.8 percent), and "thought a lot about death" (22.6 percent). College students during exam periods (particularly those studying existential philosophy), people who must work overtime, or those worrying about an important upcoming event could all experience these symptoms naturally. Thus conditions that neither respondents nor clinicians would consider reasons for entering treatment can nonetheless indicate disorder in community surveys. Moreover, the symptoms are required to last for only two weeks, allowing many transient and self-correcting symptoms to become the basis for diagnosis. While most studies do not report the context of symptoms, in one study of adolescent depression that did, the single greatest trigger for presumed depression was the breakup of a romantic relationship, suggesting that a potentially large proportion of "disorders" were actually misclassifications of normal responses.

The sorts of experiences that produce normal sadness responses—breakups of romantic relationships and marriages, job losses, disappointed career goals, and the like—are certainly not uncommon in community populations. A survey respondent might recall symptoms such as sad mood, insomnia, overeating, tiredness, and lessened pleasure in usual activities, that lasted for at least two weeks after such an event. Although these symptoms might have dissipated as soon as a new relationship developed, another job was found, or the goal was finally achieved, this individual might satisfy *DSM* criteria and join the 20 million people who are said to suffer from the presumed disorder of depression each year. In all likelihood, community studies did not so much uncover high rates of depressive disorders as they demonstrated that the natural results of stressful social experiences could meet *DSM*'s symptom criteria for depression. Ironically, reporting such overwhelmingly high rates backfired. It ended up encouraging skepticism and dismissal by policy makers. It also promoted fears of the financial consequences of insurance parity.

The Constituencies for Depression

Many factors, some legitimate and some less defensible, drove psychiatry and epidemiology to use symptom-based, context-free criteria for disorder. Once this conceptually flawed diagnostic system was generally accepted, it became inadvertently advantageous to various constituencies in the pursuit of their agendas. The medicalization of sadness achieved a social impact far beyond the narrow domain of clinical psychiatric diagnosis. That this approach works against the basic psychiatric goal of validly distinguishing disorder from nondisorder has simply been ignored.

The National Institute of Mental Health (NIMH), the major American sponsor of research on mental illness, became a key beneficiary of the new approach. The conflation of mental disorder and ordinary sadness legitimized a broad interpretation of the NIMH's mandated domain and allowed it to argue persuasively for increased funding on the basis that mental disorder is rampant in the population. Allowing some painful but normal psychological reactions to be considered disorders also effectively depoliticized the NIMH's previous concern with the problematic psychological consequences of social problems such as poverty, racism, and discrimination.

This transformation has some benefits. American society is now more compassionate about psychological disorder than previously. Nor is it necessarily unhelpful for nondisordered but disadvantaged people to receive supportive mental-health treatment addressing some of the psychological challenges they face. However, doing so via unreasonably broad definitions of psychological disorder has the potential cost of stigmatizing the disadvantaged as mentally ill, replacing social policy with unwarranted medical treatment, and creating a one-dimensional public discourse that can undermine our capacity for making moral and political distinctions.

Mental-health researchers have also adapted to current criteria and have much to lose if traditional measures of depression should return. Symptom-based criteria are relatively easy to use. They reduce the cost and complexity of research studies, and allow for higher research productivity. Enhanced reliability confers the appearance of a more scientific approach, although in fact considerations of validity should trump reliability. Moreover, the *DSM*'s criteria are used in virtually all of the thousands of studies done in recent years on depression, and many researchers' careers are built around these studies. Consequently, any major reconceptualization of diagnostic criteria would throw all that into doubt. Adequately distinguishing normal sadness from depressive disorder could also possibly narrow opportunities for research funding, especially if the NIMH followed suit by focusing its efforts on true disorder. Nevertheless, as researchers certainly appreciate, reaching the goal of understanding the etiology and appropriate treatment of depressive disorder ultimately depends on using a valid definition of disorder as the basis for sample selection.

For mental-health clinicians, symptom-based measures of depression justify reimbursement from third-party insurers for the treatment of a broader range of patients than might otherwise qualify, because insurers generally will pay to treat disorders but not mere problems of living. Individual clinicians are faced every day with patients seeking help who are suffering from conditions that appear to be intense normal sadness, but that satisfy the *DSM*'s criteria for disorder. Many private-practice clinicians will readily admit that a sizable proportion of their "depression" caseload consists of individuals who are psychiatrically normal but experiencing stressful life events. To obtain reimbursement for the treatment of such patients, the clinician must classify the individual within a *DSM* category of disorder, and depression is one of the more commonly used and easier ones to justify given the ubiquity of its symptoms. The result is a strange case of two "wrongs" seemingly making a "right": The *DSM* provides flawed criteria that do not adequately distinguish disorder from nondisorder; the clinicians, knowingly or unknowingly, incorrectly classifies a normal individual as disordered (Why should the clinician question a diagnosis officially sanctioned by the *DSM*?); and the patient receives desired treatment for which the therapist is reimbursed.

Such conceptually questionable diagnosis and consequent reimbursement are easily rationalized when the alternative seems insensitive and when rigid reimbursers may refuse desired treatment to people who are suffering. There are complex policy issues lurking here that would benefit from public discussion, however. In other areas of medicine, treatment of the nondisordered is openly debated: Should growth hormones be given to normal but short children? Should post-menopausal women be reimbursed for fertility treatment? When does the use of Viagra represent a medical necessity? In psychiatry, faulty criteria camouflage such treatment and allow the issue to be avoided.

One cost of this avoidance is that some critics use the expansiveness of the *DSM* criteria to argue against reimbursement parity for mental-health care. When the issue of parity arises, the first objection sure to be heard is that such parity would break the health-care bank because it would allow every instance of normal unhappiness to qualify for treatment. Such objections are buttressed by the ridicule frequently heaped on *DSM* criteria in the popular media. A more honest discussion of normal versus abnormal conditions and their appropriate rights to reimbursement might help to address some of these objections.

Family advocacy organizations, such as the National Alliance for the Mentally Ill (NAMI), which became an influential political force during the 1980s, have at the top of their political agenda the achievement of insurance reimbursement parity for mental disorder. Their major argument is that certain mental disorders as currently defined, including depression, are biological disorders, just like physical disorders, and deserve to be treated equally with respect to reimbursement. Admitting that current *DSM* criteria fail to distinguish true depressive disorders

from normal sadness reactions would certainly muddy this argument, and appears to go against these groups' agendas. In the long run, however, the case for better treatment might be strengthened if such a distinction was carefully made and the conceptual flaws in current criteria eliminated, so that the criteria did indeed pick out only plausible cases of disorder. The truly disordered would then become the more exclusive focus of treatment and resource allocation.

Pharmaceutical companies are perhaps the most visible beneficiaries of symptom-based diagnoses. Although there is little evidence that these companies influenced the development of the *DSM-III*, its symptom-based approach created a broader market of disorder for their products to treat. In addition, they are now major sponsors of the activities and research of psychiatrists and advocacy groups. While some concern has arisen about problems with side effects, suicide risk, and dependency, in general, the transformation of sadness into depression has been enormously profitable for these companies. Ubiquitous drug ads now warn the public that common symptoms such as sadness, anxiety, sleep problems, or overeating may be signs of mental disorder. Like clinicians, the drug companies can legitimately explain that they are only using the criteria officially sanctioned by the psychiatric profession, even as they further confuse the public about the boundary between normality and disorder.

Perhaps the most successful effort of pharmaceutical companies has been to increase the diagnosis of depressive disorder and prescribing of medication by general physicians. The inadequate supply of psychiatrists and other trained mental-health professionals to deal with the enormous numbers of presumably depressed people uncovered by epidemiological studies has served as the rationale for an urgent push to have non-mental-health personnel diagnose and treat depression. To aid busy physicians who have no time to perform psychiatric assessments, pharmaceutical companies have supported the development of easy-to-use symptom checklists based on *DSM* criteria. These lists can be routinely administered to patients, whatever the reason for their visit to the doctor. By catching some cases of disorder, such screening can be beneficial. But, obviously, even a patient who is psychiatrically normal may have recently felt intense sadness, for example, in response to a life crisis. The screening instruments physicians use to detect depression follow the *DSM* in intentionally ignoring all such contextual considerations in reaching a diagnosis.

The result is both unsurprising and shocking: In some studies, levels of mood disorders in general medical practices approach or exceed 25 percent. This includes subclinical diagnoses with fewer than the *DSM*-required number of symptoms, which are included as potentially treatable depressions in the most widely used physician scale. Because physicians are not trained in psychotherapeutic intervention, medication is the most likely treatment.

Whether medicating normally sad individuals that meet *DSM* criteria is usually helpful or harmful is unknown and is a topic that has received virtually no study. The reason is simple: The *DSM* criteria used by researchers do not allow the distinction to be made. Freud's speculation that medical "interference" in normal sadness can be "inadvisable or even harmful" may have some truth; research by the psychologist James Coyne suggests that medical interventions designed to prevent depression may have little effect or can sometimes even worsen depression by disrupting normal coping processes and heightening patient focus on negative experiences. Whatever the answer, surely we ought to be studying this question. That would require making important distinctions between normal and disordered sadness responses. And that would in turn require honestly confronting the conceptual invalidities that now afflict the diagnosis of depressive disorder.

Psychiatry and Society

For thousands of years, symptoms of sadness that were "with cause" were separated from those that were "without cause." Only the latter were viewed as mental disorders. The framers of the *DSM-III* did not explicitly try to expand the domain of disorder and in some ways its definition of depression is more stringent than in previous manuals. The *DSM-III*'s decontextualized symptom-based criteria for depressive disorder had the unintended consequence, however, of classifying some instances of intense normal sadness as disordered. This greatly expanded the domain of pathological depression, especially when applied to untreated community samples. Reported prevalence rates of depressive disorders have correspondingly increased, triggering attempts to detect and treat depression in new ways, such as in the offices of general medical practitioners.

The medicalization of sadness in psychiatric diagnoses has had broader cultural consequences. When people are constantly exposed to pharmaceutical advertisements, public service messages, and news stories that conflate depression with normal sadness, and are assured that no stigma attaches to such diagnoses, they may naturally tend to monitor themselves for such symptoms, reframe their own experiences of sadness as signs of a mental disorder, and seek professional help for their problems.

The result has been skyrocketing rates of treatment for depression that give the possibly mistaken impression that actual rates of depression have increased.

While the medicalization of sadness undoubtedly has a number of beneficial aspects both in relieving suffering and occasionally in preventing disorder, it also has many costs that should not be accepted uncritically. Most sadness diminishes with the passage of time, even in the absence of therapeutic interventions. To the extent that sadness results from ordinary human misery, changing or accepting the situations that led to the sadness might be as effective, or more effective, than medication or psychotherapy. Encouraging general physicians and mental-health professionals to diagnose and treat mild depression can thus be an inefficient use of their time. The dangers of overintervention with normal conditions are real and need to be balanced against those of undertreatment. One element in deliberatively reaching such a balance is the formulation of a conceptually valid approach to the distinction between disorder and nondisorder.

Depression can be a serious and sometimes life-threatening condition, and depressive disorders must be taken seriously. In addition, one might argue that in many cases there is no good reason why people suffering from normal sadness should be prevented from taking antidepressant medication, if it proves effective and safe to do so. Freud was surely incorrect, at least in relation to our contemporary medical practices, to assert that "it never occurs to us" to treat such painful normal conditions medically. Whether public policy ought to encourage such treatment broadly, and whether such treatment if widely adopted might somehow reduce the depth of human experience of loss and thus indirectly of caring, are further questions in need of exploration. Offering skilled help to those who are suffering and capable of benefiting from such help, whether disordered or nondisordered, is a moral imperative. But it is not clear that relabeling normal forms of misery as depressive disorder is beneficial or yields wise public policy.

Soldier Support

Psychologists help troops handle the stresses of combat in Iraq and the anxieties of coming home.

CHRISTOPHER MUNSEY
Monitor Staff

Last fall near the city of Ar Ramadi in Iraq, the strain of combat was beginning to overwhelm a platoon from an Army unit supporting infantry pursuing insurgents, says Lt. Col. Kathy Platoni, PsyD, an Army psychologist. The soldiers were worn down by a constant toll of attacks from insurgents, pushed close to the edge of panic by fear.

"They were afraid to die, because so many of them had," Platoni says.

The insurgents' most frequent method of attack came via improvised explosive devices (IEDs), bombs planted by insurgents on roads and highways used by U.S. forces, but other soldiers had been killed or wounded by small arms fire, rocket-propelled grenades and sniper bullets. "They watched their beloved fellow soldiers being blown up all the time, burning to death right in front of them," she says.

Concerned about the soldiers' ability to continue functioning given their level of fear and sheer physical exhaustion, Platoni worked with the unit's leadership to give many of them a 48-hour reprieve from operations.

During the break, the soldiers got a chance to sleep, take a shower, eat a hot meal and talk to mental health professionals about their experiences, if they wanted to talk. Following the brief respite, the soldiers returned to their duties, still facing constant danger, but better able to manage their fears and concentrate on the job at hand.

Platoni, a mobilized Army reservist and private practitioner in Beavercreek, Ohio, organized the reprieve project with fellow soldier and mental health specialist Sgt. George McQuade during a 10-month stint working at forward operating bases in Iraq last year. Nicknamed FOBs in military lingo and scattered across Iraq, the bases are where U.S. servicemen and -women live and operate from while serving in the country.

The need for psychological services, she says, is evident in the sobering statistics: As of mid-March, 2,302 service members had been killed in action in Iraq and more than 17,124 had been wounded. Every day in Iraq, psychologists like Platoni are helping soldiers, Marines, sailors and airmen cope with the traumatic effects of combat and the stresses of living and working far from home and family in austere, dangerous conditions. They're also helping service members adjust to life after Iraq when they return home.

How Therapy Is Delivered

In fact, the Army has redoubled its mental health efforts, making psychologists and combat stress-control teams more accessible to deployed soldiers, instituting more stress-control training for deploying soldiers and surveying individual units for problems.

For example, working with the Marines, Navy medicine has adopted a new approach called OSCAR, for Operational Stress Control and Readiness. Instead of assigning a Navy psychologist from outside the unit's existing medical support staff, the program matches psychologists with Marine regiments in the months before a deployment, continuing during a rotation in Iraq, then back home, so that closer relationships can be built between psychologists and a unit's leadership.

Psychologists across military branches say their goal is keeping service members mentally focused during deployment and fostering resilience that encourages service members to rely on both their individual and unit strengths. Keeping soldiers or Marines focused can help them stay sharp in a hazardous environment requiring constant vigilance, psychologists say.

Often, doing that requires psychologists to get out from behind a desk in the larger, relatively more secure FOBs and experience firsthand what some service members see patrolling the roads and neighborhoods of Iraqi cities and towns every day.

"Just living in this environment can be overwhelming."

Bret Moore
U.S. Army

Different Types of Stress

Psychologists say service members encounter two broad kinds of stress in Iraq. The first is combat stress, created by directly experiencing roadside bomb explosions, suicide vehicle bomber attacks and combat operations. Besides the threat of IEDs, service members also have to deal with the unnerving threat of lethal mortar and rocket attacks targeting service members where they work and sleep.

The second is operational or deployment stress, created by being deployed overseas and working in harsh conditions. Service members live with very little privacy and typically sleep jammed together in tents, trailers and bunkers, all while enduring an outside environment with temperatures topping 130 degrees in the summer and cold rain and mud in the winter.

And while the immediacy of e-mail makes it much easier for family members to stay in touch, it sometimes exacerbates stress when spouses relay bad news and expect help with financial problems and kids in trouble back home.

Psychologists say they help service members cope with the different types of stress in a number of ways. Working from a FOB in northern Iraq, Army Capt. Bret Moore, PsyD, is the officer-in-charge of a three-person preventive team from the 85th Medical Detachment, making care available to about 5,000 soldiers. "Just living in this environment can be overwhelming," Moore says.

The Army deals with soldiers experiencing combat stress using a set of precepts, BICEPS. The acronym stands for:

- *Brevity.* Treatment will be short, addressing the problem at hand.
- *Immediacy.* An intervention will take place quickly, before symptoms worsen.
- *Centrality.* Treatment will be set apart from medical facilities, as a way to reduce the stigma soldiers might feel about seeking mental health services.
- *Expectancy.* A soldier experiencing problems with combat stress is expected to return to duty.
- *Proximity.* Soldiers are treated as close to their units as possible and are not evacuated from the area of operations.
- *Simplicity.* Besides therapy, the basics of a good meal, hot shower and a comfortable place to sleep ensure a soldier's basic physical needs are met.

All told, Moore says about 98 percent of soldiers sent to restoration areas come back to their units.

If a soldier isn't sent to a restoration area for 48- to 72-hour respite, Moore says he's only got enough time for between five and six therapy sessions with each soldier. The therapy's goal is keeping the soldier with his or her unit and functioning, he says. Moore uses a variety of techniques, ranging from cognitive-behavioral therapy to handing out CDs explaining deep breathing and other relaxation practices. To strengthen resiliency, he advises soldiers to exercise every day—preferably through a team sport—to eat balanced meals and to sleep when they can, he says.

It's not just Army psychologists helping care for soldiers. Another psychologist, Air Force Capt. Michael Detweiler, PhD, runs a life skills support center at an overseas base in Southwest Asia.

Detweiler describes himself as the only mental health provider for about 10,000 service members, mostly Army and Air Force personnel. Besides assisting soldiers in dealing with trauma, he often helps service members get along better.

"We live with the same people we work with...so the same people who drive you crazy at work are the same people you live with," Detweiler says.

Other important roles for psychologists in Iraq are helping leaders understand morale problems or handle interpersonal difficulties within units. Navy psychologist Lt. Cmdr. Gary Hoyt, PsyD, served with two Marine regimental combat teams in 2004 in Iraq, during which he regularly went out on patrols. Being present and exposed to the same dangers helped him earn the trust of junior enlisted Marines.

If the tempo of operations was too high, if they weren't getting enough sleep or if they were struggling with the big-picture "whys" of their mission in Iraq, Hoyt says he heard about it. With his access to leaders, Hoyt served as a conduit for those concerns, letting battalion-level officers know what was bothering junior Marines.

"There's no way they're going to hear this input directly from the junior ranks," he says. Besides talking to senior leadership, Hoyt says he stressed education and training of small-unit leaders about combat stress so Marines could spot problems themselves and help each other tackle them before the problems worsened.

Follow-up Care Strengthened

Besides offering mental health treatment for deployed soldiers, the Army also seeks to detect symptoms of post-traumatic stress disorder or other combat-related psychological problems when they return home, says Col. Bruce Crow, PsyD, the Army's chief psychologist. Currently, the best estimates are that about 15 percent of soldiers returning from Iraq will show symptoms of post-traumatic stress, Crow says.

As part of a militarywide initiative, all service members receive a health screening about 90 days after they return home. In addition, all soldiers and their families can tap into counseling through the Deployment Cycle Support Program.

Aiding in this effort is Lt. Col. Platoni, who works with returning combat soldiers on adjusting to life in the civilian world.

UNIT 11

Psychological Treatments

Unit Selections

37. **The Quandary Over Mental Illness**, Richard E. Vatz
38. **The Discover Interview: Nobel Laureate Eric Kandel**, Susan Kruglinski
39. **Offering Hope to the Emotionally Depressed**, Norbert R. Myslinski
40. **Computer- and Internet-Based Psychotherapy Interventions**, C. Barr Taylor and Kristine H. Luce

Key Points to Consider

- Do you know what interventions for mental disorders are commonly available today? Why do Americans appear to be in love with psychotherapy? Or are they? Are Americans more in love with quick fixes such as medications?

- Do you think that supportive laypersons can be as effective as psychotherapists? Is professional assistance for psychological problems always necessary? Can people successfully change themselves without benefit of therapy?

- In general, what is psychotherapy? Why would doing research on psychotherapy be difficult? Besides the process itself and how it works (e.g. therapist empathy), what other measures would be important to include in research on therapy? Do psychotherapists need to know anything about biology? If yes, what?

- What are some of the common medications used to treat mental disorders? Which specific medications are used to treat which disorders? What are the disadvantages and advantages of medication over the talking cure?

- Why are more and more people turning to cybertherapy or the Internet for help with mental disorders and other psychological problems? How can we research whether cybertherapy is effective? Why is this an important research topic? Do you think, in general, the Internet is a safe place to seek advice? How would you know a reliable website on mental disorder from a flawed one? How could you discern a good therapist from a charlatan on the Internet?

Student Website

www.mhcls.com/online

Internet References

Further information regarding these websites may be found in this book's preface or online.

The C.G. Jung Page
http://www.cgjungpage.org
Knowledge Exchange Network (KEN)
http://www.mentalhealth.org
NetPsychology
http://netpsych.com/index.htm
Sigmund Freud and the Freud Archives
http://plaza.interport.net/nypsan/freudarc.html

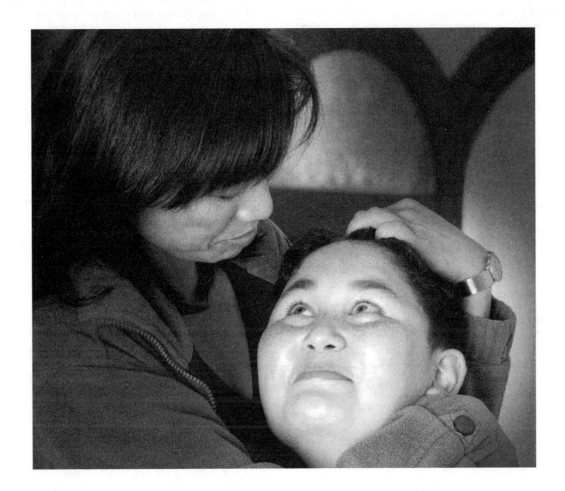

Have you ever had the nightmare that you are trapped in a dark, dismal place? No one will let you out. Your pleas for freedom go unanswered and, in fact, are suppressed or ignored by domineering authority figures around you. You keep begging for mercy but to no avail. What a nightmare! You are fortunate to awake to your normal bedroom and to the realities of your daily life. For the mentally ill, the nightmare of institutionalization, where individuals can be held against their will in what are sometimes terribly dreary, restrictive surroundings, is a reality. Have you ever wondered what would happen if we took perfectly normal individuals and institutionalized them in such a place? In one well-known and remarkable study, that is exactly what happened.

In 1973, eight people, including a pediatrician, a psychiatrist and some psychologists, presented themselves to psychiatric hospitals. Each claimed that he or she was hearing voices. The voices, they reported, seemed unclear but appeared to be saying "empty" or "thud." Each of these individuals was admitted to a mental hospital, and most were diagnosed as being schizophrenic. Upon admission, the "pseudopatients" or fake patients gave truthful information and thereafter acted like their usual, normal selves.

Their hospital stays lasted anywhere from 7 to 52 days. The nurses, doctors, psychologists, and other staff members treated them as if they were schizophrenic and never saw through their trickery. Some of the real patients in the hospital, however, did recognize that the pseudopatients were perfectly normal. Upon discharge almost all of the pseudopatients received the diagnosis of "schizophrenic in remission," meaning that they were still clearly defined as schizophrenic; they just weren't exhibiting any of the symptoms at the time of release.

What does this study demonstrate about mental illness? Is true mental illness readily detectable? If we can't always pinpoint mental disorders (the more professionally accepted term for mental illness), how can we treat them? What treatments are available and which treatments work better for various diagnoses? The treatment of mental disorders is a challenge. The array of available treatments is ever increasing and can be downright bewildering—and not just to the patient or client! In order to demystify and simplify your understanding of various treatments, we will look at them in this unit.

We commence with a general article about mental disorders and treatments, "The Quandary Over Mental Illness." There are as many forms of treatment as there are mental disorders. The heated debates about what constitutes a mental disorder, which treatments are appropriate or effective, whether medication outperforms the talking cure as well as other issues are deliberated in the first article.

In the second article, a Nobel Prize winner is interviewed. Eric Kandel has successfully combined psychology and biology to uncover much about mental life and psychotherapy. The interview also reveals his related research on memory and consciousness. Kandel indeed believes the two sciences make good partners and that all psychologists, especially psychotherapists, should be conversant with biological concepts.

People are turning more and more to the Internet to search for help with mental health issues. Researchers are just now examining whether this trend bodes well for the future. As you will read in the last article of this anthology, much more research is needed on the efficacy and safety of cyber-therapy.

The Quandary Over Mental Illness

RICHARD E. VATZ

IN 2001, there was an important event concerning the decades-old struggle between critics of psychiatry and worldwide institutional psychiatry. The Fifth International Russell Tribunal on Human Rights in Psychiatry—of which the author was a member of the jury—a concept based on the Vietnam War Crimes Tribunal of the 1960s, heard accusations regarding the historical, legal, and rhetorical abuses of human rights committed in the name of psychiatry, particularly in the mid 20th century.

Individuals who believed they were victimized by psychiatric coercion provided testimony relevant to their experiences, which consisted of events regarding forced drugging, electroshock, involuntary hospitalization, etc. The accused (international psychiatry), which could be construed as establishmentarian institutional psychiatry, was not represented at the hearings.

The findings of the Tribunal's jury concluded with the statement, "We find psychiatry guilty of the combination of force and unaccountability, a classic definition of totalitarian systems. Compensation should be made for harms … done. Public funds should be made available for humane and dignified alternatives to coercive psychiatry."

Some of the hearings would have been protested as an anachronism by representatives of American psychiatry. Indeed, the verdict represented a compromise worked out by the disparate members of the jury.

In the present-day U.S., there are millions who have engaged in talk therapy, as well as 20,000,000 or so who are using—or have used—Prozac, other selective serotonin reuptake inhibitors, and various psychoactive drags through prescription. This widespread usage constitutes the normalization of pharmacological mood enhancers; normalization marked by the extensive prescribing of these drags, often by nonpsychiatric physicians, arguably, in some cases, merely for the enhanced happiness of their users. This is called cosmetic psychopharmacology, a term coined by psychiatrist Peter Kramer in his landmark work, *Listening to Prozac*.

This brave new world hardly puts to rest the tension among those who dispute the concept, if not the experience, of mental illness. Even some traditional psychiatrists deplore the casual use of pharmacological measures to solve the problems in living that are an inescapable part of life. The battles between mental health advocates and critics generally seem not only to be endless, but completely irresolvable.

We wish to stipulate that, by the following attempt at a partial meeting of the minds, if not a rapprochement, between psychiatry and its critics, we do not include many in the latter group often referred to as "anti-psychiatry." Although, at times, the amorphous anti-psychiatric movement is depicted by some as including almost anyone critical of psychiatry, the term is more accurately associated specifically with the late R.D. Laing and, to a lesser degree, with David Cooper (who invented the term) as well as Gregory Bateson.

Szasz Steps Up

Thomas Szasz, who often is erroneously labeled as personifying anti-psychiatry, promotes views that are, in fact, antithetical to some of the seminal views held by authentic anti-psychiatry scholars. Szasz's positions correctly are distinguished from those of the anti-psychiatry movement by his conservatism and belief in individual responsibility and control, and it is that perspective of psychiatric criticism for which we are trying to create a limited reconciliation. The views of Szasz, Peter Breggin, Ron Leifer, Jeffrey Schaler, and others are not all, we maintain, completely irreconcilable with each and every view of modern-day psychiatry.

[Before we procede further, however, let us be clear: Szasz is a personal friend and subject of a book of ours, but he was not consulted regarding this piece, nor has he approved any of the text which follows.]

The major tenets of Szasz's approach are the following, with apologies for our somewhat oversimplifying his arguments: mental illness is a myth because the mind is not an organ; the mind is a construct, and a construct cannot be diseased, except metaphorically. Further, there are no pathological correlates specific to any given mental illness. As he has argued in several of his works, texts in pathology make no reference to mental illness; therefore, mental illness is a bogus disease.

Many psychiatrists—even those with some sympathy for the argument that much of what is called mental illness reflects no more than common difficulties in living—insist, as does eminent psychiatrist E. Fuller Torrey, that there can be no brooking the fact that schizophrenia, which Szasz calls psychiatry's sacred symbol, is a disease. To this argument, Szasz no longer responds—he does not like the word "concedes"—that schizophrenia is not a disease. Instead, using the pathological criterion of demonstrable lesion as disease, Szasz puts forth that, if schizophrenia validly could be attributed to a brain lesion—as Parkinsonism, for example, can be—then it would be an authentic illness. His point is that some schizophrenia—only that which is linked to a brain lesion—then would be a neurological illness, not a psychiatric disorder.

Thus, although Szasz does consider some cases of schizophrenia to be authentic diseases, his concern is that any concession of this point would lead to the rampant definition of virtually all those whom psychiatrists wish to label as "mentally ill" as "schizophrenic," especially for the purpose of qualifying for third-party payments for insurance.

Indeed, some of the diseases that the American Psychiatric Association calls "severe mental illness" may be seen by psychiatrists and their critics as "illness." Again, it is Szasz's contention that, what is called mental illness never is authentic mental disease, since the mind is not an organ, but may, in some cases, be authentic brain disease when it meets certain objective and scientific criteria.

For the vast majority of untoward behaviors labeled as mental illness, Szasz contends that they are freely chosen behaviors for which the agent must take responsibility; psychiatry tends to ascribe responsibility for only socially-approved actions. In Pharmacracy, Szasz deplores "the seemingly unappeasable thirst to medicalize, pathologize, and therapeutize all manner of behaviors manifesting as personal or social problems." Moreover, while behavior may be the cause or consequence of a disease—a possible area of some limited agreement between psychiatrists and critics—"behavior, per se, cannot, as a matter of definition, be a disease." Practically speaking, no responsible critic of psychiatry denies that unwanted behaviors are "treatable" in the nonmedical sense that persuasion can influence behavior, but that does not make the feeling or behavior a "disease."

Historically, the rhetoric of mental illness has conflated the most dubious of alleged psychiatric illnesses (e.g., adjustment, dysthymic, social anxiety, and body dysmorphic disorders), with the most compelling the "severe mental illnesses," such as schizophrenia. Parenthetically, the use of the term "disorder" surely will remain a sticking point between psychiatry and its critics—Szasz considers it a "weasel term" which allows psychiatry to assert and deny that it is treating "illnesses" simultaneously. To some extent, it is the inclusion of minor mental illnesses (critics would say "problems in living") with outrageously large estimates of incidence of mental illnesses which has created such widespread incredulity at psychiatric pretensions.

One of the reasons that an objective observer must be pessimistic regarding hopes for reconciliation between psychiatry and its critics are the estimates of the number of mentally ill people in the U.S., a number which has increased precipitously over the years. In a brochure on its web page, the American Psychiatric Association states: "During any one-year period, up to 50 million Americans—more than 22 percent—suffer from a clearly diagnosable mental disorder." Moreover, the National

Institute of Mental Health approximates that 52,000,000 adults have a diagnosable mental illness. The APA and NIMH both claim that over 50% of all Americans will be mentally ill at some time in their lives. There is no way to disconfirm any of these statistics. Rex Cowdry, former head of the National Institute of Mental Health, notes that such high estimates of the incidence of mental illness simply do not "pass the laugh test." Perhaps, but there is little public dissent against the psychiatric profession concerning this data.

Simultaneous with the concerns regarding promiscuous diagnosis of mental illness is the proliferation in the use of psychiatric drags. Not only is there long-term concern regarding the effects of such medication, as in the use of Ritalin in children, there is the rising conviction that chemicals are no better than placebos in many cases. The Washington Post reports that, "After thousands of studies, hundreds of millions of prescriptions and tens of billions of dollars in sales, two things are certain about pills that treat depression: Antidepressants like Prozac, Paxil and Zoloft work. And so do sugar pills.… In the majority of trials conducted by drug companies in recent decades, [placebos] have done as well as—or better than—antidepressants. Psychiatrist Arif Kahn, in trials for the Food and Drag Administration, found that in a majority of trials that 'the effect of antidepressants could not be distinguished from that of the placebo.'"

Surely, there must be some common ground here among psychiatrists, primary care physicians (who provide most of the antidepressant drug prescriptions to patients), and critics of psychiatry. If there is a current prototype of what Szasz calls "the manufacturing of mental illness" and the attending pharmacological issues, including their costs, it could well be with respect to "social anxiety disorder" (also known as "social phobia"), although it is not the only one that we suspect even some psychiatrists disbelieve. (A few years ago, a psychiatrist confided to us that whenever he had a patient who was troubled, he just wrote down "adjustment disorder" as a catch-all psychiatric diagnosis to facilitate third-party payments.)

We first criticized social anxiety disorder years ago in an op-ed piece in the Baltimore Sun. Often criticized as a medicalized version of "shyness," it rapidly was normalized into the psychiatric-pharmaceutical complex. The Washington Post detailed in an exposé of the selling of this alleged disorder that the significant consequence of false disorders is what even conventional mental health sources claim is "blurring the line between normal personality variation and real psychiatric conditions [which] can trivialize serious mental illness."

What's more, the conflation of personality differences with alleged brain disorders creates a broad market not only for talk therapy, but pharmacological prolificacy. The Post documents social anxiety disorder proponents' covering and promoting the condition as part and parcel of a public relations campaign. There were "pitches to newspapers, radio and TV, satellite and Internet communications, and testimonials from advocates and doctors who said social anxiety was America's third most common mental disorder with more than 10 million sufferers." As the Post pointed out, the campaign was so successful that "media accounts of social anxiety rose from just 50 stories in 1997 and 1998 to more than 1 billion references in 1999 alone." All of this publicity was to promote the selling of Paxil, with sales rising 18%.

It should be pointed out that the selling of social anxiety disorder transpired at the behest of the makers of Paxil, Glaxo SmithKline, not physicians.

Psychiatrist Paul McHugh's work could provide some grist for a partial meeting of the minds between the psychiatric establishment and Szasz. McHugh maintains that, too often, psychiatry proceeds on a disease by disease basis; an alleged mental disorder becomes what often is derided as the "mental illness du jour"—such as, again, body dysmorphic disorder a few years ago or multiple personality disorder, which McHugh abjures. Many critics judge such disorders to be false, but atypical.

The point probably is best made in McHugh's trenchant December, 1999, *Commentary* article, "How Psychiatry Lost Its Way." This piece—its brilliance somewhat lessened due to its insufficient citing of Szasz—opines that "Proposals for new psychiatric disorders have multiplied so feverishly that the DSM [Diagnostic and Statistical Manual of Mental Disorders] itself has grown from a mere 119 pages in 1968 to 886 pages in the latest edition."

This prolific creation of new mental disorders is due to the emphasis on "appearances." In response to McHugh's article, we penned a correspondence reply, saying that McHugh was "right on the mark in ... many areas ..." but that "many of the points argued by [him] have been articulated by Dr. Szasz over the years." Some of these include McHugh's contentions that, as stated above, there is a substantial increase in "new, nonorganic, bogus" mental illnesses; psychiatry utilizes a criterion of reliability rather than validity; there is collusion between some pharmaceutical companies and some psychiatric diagnosticians; there is a significant role in self-fulfilling prophesy in the evidence put forth for the public's "suffering" from mental illness (a point often made by Jeffrey Schaler, author of *Addiction's a Choice*); and the changing of behaviors by psychotropic drugs ("Everyone is more attentive when on Ritalin") affects anyone who takes them, and therefore, said changes cannot be validly used as indicative of the existing psychiatric disorders.

Prescription Pressure

Regardless, the gravamen of the piece—that there is a proliferation of new, scientifically unverified psychiatric disorders and a "thoughtless prescription of medication for them"—is one of the bases for building some understanding, if not wholesale agreement, between psychiatry and its detractors.

None of this gainsays the differences—and some might claim they are unbridgeable—between Szasz and McHugh, as well as psychiatry and Szasz, such as the overriding importance Szasz attributes to free will, which only is partially recognized by McHugh. He, for example, speaks of some drugs as being "addictive," whereas Szasz argues that, while a person can become reliant on them, individuals always maintain the ability to refuse to continue to take substances.

So, where would Szasz have to yield if we are forging a compromise? He insists that no psychiatric diagnosis can be

"pathology-driven" since all psychiatric illnesses are human creations. To the extent that schizophrenia and other now so-called major psychiatric illnesses have consistent pathological correlates, he would say that they may be illnesses. Where would psychiatry have to yield on the same issues? The American Psychiatric Association would have to revamp its diagnostic manual to include only those mental disorders which, when medically analyzed, are brain diseases that have consistent pathological definitions. Psychiatry would be the study and practice of the attention—pharmacological and counseling—given those with behaviorally-affected neurological disorders.

One of Szasz's central concerns always has been the involuntariness of psychiatric clients. This is a critically important aspect of his views because if it were well-understood, people would not lump him in with anti-psychiatry, which, again, he considers an irresponsible movement since he does not oppose, as he calls it, "psychiatric practice between consenting adults."

One of the most irreconcilable areas of disagreement between psychiatry and its critics is the question of legal responsibility for one's actions; most strikingly, the insanity plea. In an article several years ago in Liberty, "The Trouble with Szasz," Ralph Slovenko, a respected writer on psychiatry and the law, notes that psychiatry gets a bad rap insofar as its interaction with the criminal justice system is concerned. Slovenko points out that, it is the court which rules, not the psychiatrist. This is a profoundly disingenuous argument, for it merely asserts without proof a hierarchically inferior role of the psychiatrist. One easily could argue that it is repeatedly psychiatric expertise to which courts typically turn to make final dispositions in the "law-psychiatry axis."

Speaking of which, Slovenko unquestioningly parrots the new received wisdom that "Not Guilty by Reason of Insanity" represents the "rare" case, ignoring the deep involvement that psychiatry wields in the criminal justice system in alternative sentencing, mitigation of sentences, plea bargains, and the like. Moreover, the "low" percentage of successful NGRI cases, generally accepted to be one-quarter of one percent, masquerades the fact that, over the years, this translates into thousands of cases.

There are areas of psychiatry that simply are irreconcilable due to intervening institutional issues. A major tenet of Szasz's views is his opposition to the threat of the "Therapeutic State," the use of psychiatry through the misleading rhetoric of therapy to deprive people of their life, liberty, and property rights. Szasz would argue against any extra-legal interference in depriving people of their freedom, while many psychiatrists want the power, among other things, to declare people incompetent or dangerous to themselves and others. While we may side with Szasz on the issue of people's freedom to pose a not illegal danger to others, the weakness of the criminal justice system in protecting such people, say, for example, wherein stalking is not illegal, often leaves people at the mercy of predators. We might—although Szasz would not—concede that psychiatry might be useful in depriving dangerous people of their freedom, but only as a method of last resort.

The foregoing attempt at some agreement between psychiatry and its critics is consistent with a rhetorician's persuasive duty to find "common ground" between those who profoundly disagree with one another. Admittedly, though, there will be those who say that the disagreements between responsible psychiatrists and responsible critics of psychiatry are irreconcilable.

RICHARD E. VATZ, Associate Psychology Editor of *USA Today*, is professor of rhetoric and communication, Towson (Md.) University and 2004 winner of the "President's Award for Distinguished Service to the University."

The Discover Interview: Nobel Laureate Eric Kandel

Does psychotherapy work? We'd be a lot more certain if we slapped a little science on it

SUSAN KRUGLINSKI

Neurobiologist Eric Kandel's early fascination with how the mind works led him into training as a psychiatrist interested in psychoanalysis. But in the 1960s he traded a therapist's sport jacket for a lab coat and began studying one of the slimiest creatures on Earth. At a time when brain researchers thought nothing could be learned from invertebrates, Kandel stunned the fledgling world of neuroscience by uncovering the mechanisms of memory in sea slugs, which earned him a Nobel Prize in 2000. He also coedited *Principles of Neural Science,* the book every medical student in America is required to read—all 1,414 pages of it.

In his new book, *In Search of Memory: The Emergence of a New Science of Mind,* Kandel examines the convergence of four critical fields—behaviorist psychology, cognitive psychology, neuroscience, and molecular biology. Still busy trying to coax more information out of sea slugs, Kandel also serves as a professor of biochemistry, physiology, and psychiatry at Columbia University, where his laboratory is located.

Your most recent lab work involves the potent emotion of fear. What have you learned?
We have identified some of the genes in the mouse that are important for both learned fear and instinctive fear. We've shown that by knocking out the stathmin gene, we can produce a mouse that is relatively fearless.

How does a fearless mouse behave?
Normally, when you put a mouse into an open field, it walks along the edge of the field, where the walls are—the mouse is in an enclosed chamber with walls around it—because it's afraid of being attacked by an intruder, and it makes occasional dashes into the center to make sure it's not missing some food or an interesting sexual partner. If you frighten a mouse, it stays in one corner and doesn't move at all. If you knock out this gene that is important for fear, the animal spends a lot of time in the center. It is no longer afraid.

Does the knockout shut down instinctual fear?
Yes, but it works on learned fear too.

Can you imagine using this research to benefit humans?
This gene could become a new target for antianxiety agents. We've also opened up the biology of happiness, showing that you can produce an animal that is more relaxed than normal, and this recruits activity in the pathways that are involved in positive reinforcement. That might open up a biology of security and comfort.

How do you study happiness?
In order to produce learned fear, you take a neutral stimulus like a tone, and you pair it with an electrical shock. Tone, shock. Tone, shock. So the animal learns that the tone is bad news. But you can also do the opposite—shock it at other times, but never when the tone comes on. Under those circumstances the tone indicates security and safety. We find that the animal acts as if it is content and secure, even more than it does without any shocks whatsoever. When we looked in the brain, we found that not only were the pathways that mediated fear turned off but also that happiness pathways were activated. The caudate nucleus, a part of the brain that mediates the effects of drugs that make you feel good, is lit up by this procedure.

So fear and happiness are part of the same system?
That's right, but I want to be clear that the knockout mice and the happiness procedure are not identical. They are different experiments. We showed that fear comes to a certain neural circuit and that there are genes that control that neural circuit, and you can turn that circuit on and off with specific genes. Period, end of paragraph. In a separate set of studies, we looked to see whether we can behaviorally—without manipulating genes—produce the opposite, and that is happiness. And that is how we got onto this paradigm. They may be related—it may be the same genes that shut off fear and turn on happiness, but we don't know that yet.

How is your research in memory related to fear and happiness?
Let's assume that you have a traumatic experience in childhood. Let's say you were sexually abused. You may or may not remember the cognitive components of it—the molester bothering you. But there are associated with the experience a series of autonomic and emotional changes that are implicit. And that component is learned fear. Seeing a strange person may therefore elicit in you a response that may be completely inappropriate—that strange person may have nothing to do with the molestation event, but somehow there are similarities that you recognize that bring this back. You learn emotional experiences as much as you learn cognitive experiences, except that they are more unconscious. Sometimes one represses the cognitive component of it, but it's often more difficult to repress the emotional component.

'I was disappointed that psychoanalysis was not more scientific'

You have written that your training in psychotherapy influences your neurobiological work. Isn't there a split between psychotherapists and neurobiologists?
Yes, but I think it's a temporary one and perhaps an unnecessary one. I'm on an advisory board for the Ellison Medical Foundation, which is exploring whether one can use MRI brain imaging to evaluate the outcome of psychotherapy.

Haven't you questioned the value of psychoanalysis?
Early in my career, I was disappointed that psychoanalysis was not becoming more empirical, was not becoming more scientific. It was primarily concerned with individual patients. It wasn't trying to collect data from large groups of people who have been analyzed.

Will the Ellison project address this kind of problem?
What our study group is discussing is whether or not the time is ripe to use brain imaging to evaluate the outcome of psychotherapy. There are now two forms of psychotherapy that have been medically proven to be effective. One is cognitive behavioral therapy, developed by Aaron Beck at the University of Pennsylvania. The other is interpersonal therapy, which was developed by Myrna Weissman here at Columbia. Those are two scientifically validated forms of short-term therapy. In 20 sessions you can see improvements in mildly and moderately depressed patients. And there have been some preliminary studies with obsessive-compulsive neurosis where you can see a metabolic abnormality in the caudate nucleus in imaging. If you treat people with psychotherapy and they get better, that metabolic abnormality is reversed, which is the same thing that happens if you give them pharmacological treatment, like Prozac. So that's encouraging. We want to see whether there is a science here, whether or not the foundation should get interested in it. And people like Tom Insel, head of the National Institute of Mental Health, are going to participate as evaluators.

No one has ever conducted studies like this?
It has never been done systematically. We would like to consider doing it on a larger scale, maybe having several universities studying patients with different diagnostic categories to see how a controlled psychotherapy trial produces physical brain changes as a result of treatment.

Why has no one used imaging techniques to study psychotherapy before?
The field is very young. It's only recently that people got confident that psychotherapy under these circumstances works. The imaging methodology is relatively new, and the resolution is not that great yet. We need biological markers for each mental illness in order to see whether or not they can be reversed. So there are lots of technical problems. You know, our understanding of the mind is at a very early stage. These are the most difficult problems in all of biology.

Which illnesses might be considered for study?
Primarily obsessive-compulsive neurosis and anxiety disorders, such as post-traumatic stress disorders.

When did you first begin questioning psychotherapy?
I guess when I was at the National Institutes of Health, and when I came back into my psychiatric residency, which was in the 1960s. I was 30 years old. I was training as a psychiatrist. I had a personal analysis as part of my training. But it was not my personal analysis that caused me to question it. I actually benefited greatly from it. It was the fact that psychoanalysis as a discipline was not becoming scientific.

What do you think of psychotherapy these days?
Well, it is a little chaotic because there are lots of competing therapies out there. We might want to compare modes of therapy. I mean, who knows which is best? It's possible that you might benefit from one, and I might benefit from another. The different kinds of patients, different kinds of disorders, might be selectively treated by one kind of psychotherapy versus another. But that, I think, requires an independent standard for evaluation. And I think imaging might be one of the tools that provides that.

Do you think that some of the therapies are problematic?
I have no way of knowing that. I think it's problematic that people have not gone to the trouble to study this.

Has the psychology-neurobiology split hurt patients?
I think that psychopharmacological treatments have revolutionized psychiatry. On the other hand, I think anyone practicing psychiatry realizes that drug therapy is very effective but not perfect, that there are some patients who don't benefit from it, that there are some patients who benefit from drugs together with psychotherapy, and that in some cases psychotherapy by itself works. There was a time when psychoanalysts wanted nothing to do with biology, and biologists didn't want to touch psychoanalysis. That's changing. Now we need to have a systematic approach to the psychotherapeutic component of treatment, just as we have to the psychopharmacological aspects of treatment. That has not been done. What the Ellison Foundation and I are hoping to encourage is a more holistic approach to psy-

chiatry, in which psychotherapy is put on as rigorous a level as psychopharmacology.

What does a psychotherapist need to know?

First, I think that people working in psychiatry should have a background in neuroscience, because psychiatry is in fact a form of clinical neuroscience. Second, that insofar as there are psychotherapies that are made available to patients, they should be shown to be effective. I am proposing a demanding criterion: that you be able to detect abnormalities in patients beforehand by such brain-imaging techniques as functional MRI [which measures blood flow in the brain], and then use imaging to see whether or not there is a change in those markers for the disease as the therapy progresses. Therapists need not necessarily use the insights of biology in their therapy, but they should be aware of what the indices are, have their patients imaged, and be able to follow the outcome.

Has any recent research in neuroscience surprised you?

Oh, my gosh, there are lots of things. For example, the study of decision making in the brain by people like Paul Glimcher is very interesting. William Newsome's work on the importance of value in decision making. Giacomo Rizzolatti's work on empathy, on how monkeys copy one another, is of profound significance. The work on smell by Richard Axel and Linda Buck is extremely interesting. I think the work on the molecular basis of sociological phenomena by Tom Insel and Cori Bargmann is very interesting. And Tom Jessell's work with neuronal networks is extraordinarily important. Sten Grillner's work on the workings of complex neurocircuitry is also of extreme importance. I would say the progress in understanding motor systems, the cognitive role in motor systems, is a brilliant advance and has revolutionized our understanding of how the nervous system is wired.

Does the research trickle down to therapists?

Yes. I would think that residents in psychiatry should be trained in neuroscience, like residents in neurology are. And this is happening. In fact, I see them as being sort of interrelated disciplines. I mean, the modes of therapy are different, and the character structure of the practitioners is different. But they are both treating the brain as an organ that is the target of disease.

But that isn't really happening, is it?

I don't think that's fair to say. Fields move slowly. It's happening. Nothing happens as fast as I would like it to. Even *Discover* magazine doesn't publish things as rapidly as I would like it to! [laughs]

What are the big unanswered questions in neuroscience?

I think we need to understand how sensory information is translated into action. We need to understand how unconscious mental processes develop. Where do they occur? What are the processing steps? What is the nature of decision making? Of free will? Can we get a vantage point on consciousness?

How close are we to understanding consciousness?

I think we have not made much empirical progress. But I think we have made a fair amount of conceptual progress. The work of Gerald Edelman and Antonio Damasio and of Christof Koch and Francis Crick has been influential in getting people to think about these problems in a useful way.

What do you think researchers will find consciousness to be?

Oh, my gosh. I have no guesses. I think it's a very deep problem, and I don't really have any original ideas about that.

Offering Hope to the Emotionally Depressed

Based on advances in our understanding of the brain and its response to stress, promising new therapies for depressive disorders are on the horizon.

Norbert R. Myslinski

L ife is an adventure, with many ups and downs. At times, we accomplish our objectives and gain various benefits and comforts; at other times, we stumble and fall, or the course of events puts us in difficult situations. Accordingly, our mood oscillates between joy and sorrow, elation and dejection.

Many people, however, find themselves stuck in a prolonged state of depression. Unable to shake off their gloomy feelings, they lose interest in activities they once enjoyed, and they no longer function normally. Moreover, their physical health declines, and their relationships with family and friends are adversely affected. They are suffering from clinical depression—a serious mood disorder, not a passing phase of feeling "blue."

Clinical depression can occur in several forms. The three main types are known as *major depression* (or *unipolar depression*), *dysthymia*, and *bipolar disorder (or manic depression)*. Taken together, they appear to be the most common group of mental health problems in the world, affecting people of every race, culture, and ethnicity. While a small percentage of children are affected, the elderly are much more vulnerable.

It has been estimated that more than 20 million people in the United States suffer from depressive mood disorders. The cost in terms of lost productivity and medical care runs into tens of billions of dollars per year.

Symptoms and Causes

Major depression is a disabling condition that severely hampers the patient's abilities of working, eating, sleeping, and relating to others. Each episode lasts two or more weeks, and most patients go through cycles of remissions and relapses.

Symptoms of major depression include feelings of sadness, despair, and anxiety, as well as problems of fatigue, forgetfulness, and loss of concentration. The affected person may gain or lose a significant amount of weight, sleep too much or too little, and lose his ability to experience pleasure. This type of depression is also associated with suicides and increased risk of death. Different patients suffer from different combinations of these symptoms, and the level of severity varies from patient to patient and one episode to the next.

Long periods of depression adversely affect a person's health, social relationships, and day-to-day functioning. He may gain or lose weight, sleep too much or too little, and have difficulty remembering things and concentrating on tasks.

Dysthymia is a milder form of depression that does not disable the affected individual, but the symptoms are chronic and persist for two or more years. A patient with dysthymia may occasionally suffer from episodes of major depression as well.

Bipolar disorder is an illness in which the patient alternates between mania and depression. A manic episode is characterized by a number of symptoms, including feelings of elation and high energy, increased talkativeness, and a heightened sexual drive. In some cases, the affected individual is unusually irritable and behaves inappropriately in social settings. Here again, the symptoms and their severity vary from patient to patient.

Some cases of major depression and bipolar disorder appear to be inherited, as the disease can be traced from one generation to the next. Most patients, however, do not have a family history of depression. The illness may be brought on by various stressful situations, such as difficulties with social relationships or personal finances, leading to low self-esteem and a pessimistic view of one's life. Additional risk factors include medical conditions such as stroke, heart disease, immune dysfunction, and Parkinson's disease. In one study, Professor Charles Nemeroff of Emory University found that 45 percent of adults who reported being depressed for two or more years had experienced abuse or parental loss during childhood.

The National Institute of Mental Health (NIMH) notes that although depression is not a normal part of aging, more than 2 million of the 34 million Americans in the age-group 65 and above suffer from it. Moreover, 20 percent of all suicides are committed by people in this age-group, even though they constitute only 13 percent of the U.S. population.

In the past, many patients were confined to mental institutions, while others lived as social outcasts on the streets of major cities. In the 1950s, a few seriously depressed patients had stimulating electrodes implanted in their brain's pleasure centers.

During the last 50 years or so, three main strategies have been employed for the treatment of depression. They are (1) psychotherapy, which relies on psychological methods; (2) pharmacotherapy, which involves the use of medications; and (3) electro-convulsive therapy, which shocks the patient's brain with electrical stimuli. These strategies are still used today, with a number of modifications introduced over the years. As our understanding of depression and methods of treatment have advanced, promising new approaches are on the horizon.

How Do Neurons Communicate?

The brain and other parts of the nervous system contain neurons (nerve cells) that form an intricate communications network. The main body of each neuron has many short branches called dendrites and a long projection called an axon. When two neurons form a connection with each other, the axon of one cell almost touches a dendrite of another, leaving a tiny space called a synaptic gap or synaptic cleft.

The process of sending a signal from one neuron to the next involves the activation of a chemical messenger called a neurotransmitter, which is stored in vesicles (sacs) in the axon terminal. An electrical impulse generated from the main body of the first neuron flows down the axon and triggers the release of neurotransmitter molecules into the synaptic gap. A number of these molecules attach to sites called receptors on the dendrite of the second neuron, and if the dendrite is sufficiently activated, it sends an electrical impulse to the main body of that cell. The process may then be repeated to transmit the signal to the next neuron in the network. Excess neurotransmitter molecules in the synaptic gap are broken down by enzymes or are re-absorbed by the neuron that released them.

—*The Editor*

Psychotherapy

Many psychotherapeutic approaches have been used in treating depression, but the most productive ones seem to be (a) interpersonal therapy, which helps the patient develop his social relationships, and (b) cognitive-behavioral therapy, which gets the individual to critically examine and test erroneous assumptions derived from the depressed condition. Both approaches reduce the risk of relapse, as long as the patient continues with the therapy.

In most cases, psychotherapy works best when it involves the patient's spouse and family. They therefore need to learn more about the illness and how they can offer emotional support and assist with interpersonal issues.

Researchers are currently looking into new applications for existing psychotherapeutic techniques. For instance, they are investigating problem-solving approaches that can be used by the primary care provider, and they are testing a modified form of behavior therapy (called dialectic behavior therapy) for depressed elderly with personality disorders. More research is needed to establish optimal conditions for using the new approaches.

It should be noted that not all individuals respond to psychotherapy, and only a minority achieve full remission. A combination of psychotherapy and antidepressant medication is more effective than either used alone.

Pharmacotherapy

Current pharmacotherapy is based on the monoamine hypothesis, which holds that depression is the result of depressed levels of certain substances—classified as monoamines—in the brain. The three main monoamines are serotonin, dopamine, and norepinephrine, which function as neurotransmitters (chemical messengers) that carry messages from one neuron (nerve cell) to the next [see the sidebar "How Do Neurons Communicate?" above].

Today's antidepressant drugs enhance the levels of monoamines in the brain (particularly in the synaptic gaps between neurons), by either preventing their degradation by enzymes or blocking their re-absorption into the neurons that released them. There are three categories of these drugs: (1) TCAs (tricyclic antidepressants), which include imipramine (Tofranil) and amitriptyline (Elavil); (2) MAOIs (monoamine oxidase inhibitors), such as phenelzine (Nardil) and isocarboxazid (Marplan); and (3) SSRIs (selective serotonin reuptake inhibitors), such as fluoxetine (Prozac), sertraline (Zoloft), and paroxetine (Paxil).

These medications have several limitations. It may take as long as six weeks of treatment before an initial therapeutic effect is felt, and longer for maximum relief. Moreover, the drugs relieve depression in less than 70 percent of patients who take them. After two months of treatment, only 35–45 percent of patients taking standard doses of the most common antidepressants return to premorbid levels of functioning.

The drugs also produce a number of side effects, some of which are serious. They should therefore be taken with caution and only as advised by a qualified physician. When taking MAOIs, the patient must follow a strict diet to avoid harmful effects.

In searching for better medications, researchers are now basing their work on the stress hypothesis, which states that depression is due to long-term stress, raising the level of stress hormones—such as cortisol—and causing our body's homeostatic mechanisms (which maintain equilibrium of various substances in the body) to malfunction.

Many types of stress enhance the secretion of corticotropin-releasing factor (CRF) from the hypothalamus in the brain, setting off a cascade of events. CRF stimulates the secretion of corticotropin (adrenocorticotropic hormone, ACTH) from the pituitary gland, and ACTH in turn stimulates the release of cortisol from the adrenal glands.

Several lines of evidence suggest a connection between depression and elevated levels of CRF and cortisol. For example, when CRF has been directly administered into the brains of experimental animals, the animals have shown symptoms of depression, including difficulty in sleeping, changes of eating habits, and lack of interest in copulation.

Cortisol belongs to a group of steroids known as glucocorticoids. People suffering from rheumatoid arthritis are often treated with glucocorticoids, which have anti-inflammatory properties, but one possible side effect is the onset of depression.

In light of the stress hypothesis and the above observations, a number of research teams are looking for drugs that can inhibit or reverse the action of CRF or cortisol. For instance, the NIMH and several pharmaceutical companies are studying CRF antagonists—that is, substances that prevent CRF from exerting its effects. These drugs seem promising in the treatment of both depression and anxiety disorders.

Zoloft and Paxil are antidepressants that exert their effect by enhancing the level of the mood-regulating chemical messenger serotonin in the gap junctions between neurons in the brain.

Long-term elevations of cortisol levels in the blood can also inhibit the action of brain-derived neurotrophic factor (BDNF), a substance that is important in maintaining healthy cells and creating new ones. Inhibition of BDNF leads to the suppression of neurogenesis (neuron growth) and causes degeneration of parts of the brain, particularly the hippocampus and prefrontal cortex. Autopsy studies have shown that the hippocampus is 10-20 percent smaller in depressed individuals. This shrinkage can lead to difficulties in learning and remembering.

Some researchers are therefore looking for drugs that stimulate neurogenesis. Professor Rene Hen of Columbia University has shown that neurogenesis is necessary for traditional antidepressants to work. It now appears that a class of drugs known as PDE (phosphodiesterase) inhibitors, as well as BDNF and classical antidepressants, can alter not only the function of the brain but also its structure by stimulating the growth of new neurons.

When a person is under stress, his body undergoes certain hormonal changes, including elevation of the level of cortisol in the blood. Excess cortisol over a prolonged period triggers a mechanism that leads to degeneration of parts of the brain such as the hippocampus and prefrontal cortex.

Substance P, a neuropeptide known for its involvement in the sensation of pain, is another chemical released in response to stress. It is found in the prefrontal cortex, the hippocampus, and other regions of the brain associated with regulating emotion. While studying the substance P antagonist named MK-869, researchers at Merck discovered that it was effective against depression. Several companies are now working on substance P inhibitors, which may be the next class of medications marketed for depression.

In addition to these approaches, there is interest in the antidepressant effects of inhibiting glutamate—the brain's main excitatory neurotransmitter—or stimulating dopamine, a neurotransmitter for feelings of pleasure. Glutamate, however, is so ubiquitous that nonspecific inhibition would lead to serious side effects. A drug that specifically inhibits some glutamate receptors but not others is needed. One such drug under investigation is memantine.

In the case of dopamine, any drug that enhances its effects may have a high abuse potential. Most pharmaceutical companies are therefore reluctant to invest in such medications. Even so, NIMH is working on pramipexole, a drug of this type, which is currently used to treat Parkinson's disease.

Electric and Magnetic Therapies

Electroconvulsive therapy (ECT) involves a procedure in which electrodes are attached to the patient's head, and an electric current is passed briefly through his brain, inducing a seizure. Just before the treatment, the patient is given anesthetics and muscle relaxants to prevent his body from thrashing about violently. His brain, however, undergoes intense electrical disruption.

We still do not know how this treatment works or if it causes permanent damage. It is usually reserved for severely depressed patients who are not helped by drugs and those who are suicidal and need immediate help, until other forms of therapy can take effect.

In the early 1990s, an American Psychiatric Association task force concluded that 80-90 percent of those treated show improvement. The relief, however, lasts for only a few weeks or months. To extend the duration of relief, some clinicians treat their patients with ECT every three to six months, but there is no good evidence of the safety of this approach.

Patient acceptance of ECT varies widely. Some greatly appreciate their improvement, but others hate it, especially when it is accompanied by memory loss. As many as 30-40 percent of patients report lasting memory loss. This can be very dehumanizing, considering that all our life experiences are stored as a collection of memories.

A safe, painless, noninvasive alternative now being investigated is transcranial magnetic stimulation (TMS). Clinical trials are currently underway in the United States, but this treatment is already available in Canada. It is one of the most promising nonpharmaceutical methods that can be used to switch areas of the brain on and off.

In the TMS procedure, a short pulse of electric current is passed through a wire coil (or pair of coils) placed over the patient's scalp. The flow of electricity through the coil generates a magnetic field that enters the brain. The field strength has been estimated to reach tens of thousands of times the strength of the earth's magnetic field, but each pulse is shorter than a millisecond. The magnetic field in turn induces small electric currents in the brain's neurons.

Unlike ECT, TMS does not require the patient to be anesthetized, and it does not result in memory loss. In addition, TMS can be focused on certain regions of the brain, while ECT cannot. One limitation of TMS is that the magnetic field can penetrate only a few centimeters into the brain's outer cortex. A single TMS session has virtually no side effects, except for a minor headache occasionally.

In the 1990s, psychiatrist Mark George was one of the first to study the treatment of depression with daily sessions of a modified form of TMS known as repetitive TMS (rTMS). In this procedure, the magnetic field is activated in several successive pulses. George found that repeat ed stimulation of the prefrontal cortex produced a significant (albeit small) antidepressant effect. Some patients who did not respond to other treatments benefited sufficiently from this procedure so they could be sent home from the hospital.

To date, the antidepressant effects of rTMS have been modest. In addition, rTMS can induce seizures, unless certain guidelines are followed. Research in this area continues to improve this technology.

A related treatment that creates beneficial seizures in depressed individuals is known as magnetic seizure therapy (MST). Described as a "supercharged" version of TMS, MST is performed on patients after they have been anesthetized. This method is being refined so that the patient does not suffer from memory loss.

Two additional methods, involving electrical stimulation of' the brain, are currently being investigated for the treatment of depression. In one case, known as deep brain stimulation, a small electrode is implanted in the brain and connected to a pacemaker in the chest. The pacemaker sends high-frequency electrical impulses to the electrode, thereby activating that part of the brain. In the second method, named vagus nerve stimulation, a stimulator implanted in the chest is connected to an electrode attached to the left vagus nerve—a nerve that runs through the neck and connects parts of the body to the brain. In this case, the brain is stimulated indirectly via the vagus nerve.

Future Outlook

Clinical depression involves not only environmental factors, such as stress, but genetic factors as well. One would expect, for instance, the involvement of genes coding for such substances as the monoamines, CRF, cortisol, BDNF, and their receptors. It is therefore thought that gene therapy will be a future approach to controlling depression. A critical challenge will be to deliver appropriate genes to the intended neurons.

To date, no specific genes causing depression have been definitively identified, but numerous suggestions have been made. For example, some familial types of depression are thought to be related to a gene for a protein that transports serotonin across membranes. With a disorder as complex as depression, however, the risk of developing it seems associated with the products of many genes interacting with one another and with nongenetic factors.

Additional treatments that have been contemplated include the use of pacemakers or emotional gene chips implanted in patients' brains. Yet, until the new treatment modalities are perfected, most cases of depression will continue to be treated with established therapies.

However that may be, any treatment is effective only if it is used. Most people who have clinical depression are not treated. Almost half of those who are depressed do not ask for help, and only one person in five who need treatment ends up receiving it. The longer a depressed individual goes without treatment, the more resistant to treatment he becomes.

An immediate task is to educate the public to recognize serious depression in themselves and others, and to understand that it is a treatable medical disorder. Researchers, clinicians, and policymakers should be involved in finding ways to deliver effective therapies to those who need them, regardless of the patients' social or economic status. Unless a concerted effort is made to do so, our search for more effective treatments will carry little weight.

NORBERT R. MYSLINSKI is associate professor of neuroscience at the University of Maryland. He is also director of the International Brain Bee and Maryland Brain Awareness Week.

Computer- and Internet-Based Psychotherapy Interventions

ABSTRACT: Computers and Internet-based programs have great potential to make psychological assessment and treatment more cost-effective. Computer-assisted therapy appears to be as effective as face-to-face treatment for treating anxiety disorders and depression. Internet support groups also may be effective and have advantages over face-to-face therapy. However, research on this approach remains meager.

C. BARR TAYLOR[1] AND KRISTINE H. LUCE
Department of Psychiatry, Stanford University Medical Center, Stanford, California

In recent years, the increasing number of users of computer and Internet technology has greatly expanded the potential of computer- and Internet-based therapy programs. Computer- and Internet-assisted assessment methods and therapy programs have the potential to increase the cost-effectiveness of standardized psychotherapeutic treatments by reducing contact time with the therapist, increasing clients' participation in therapeutic activities outside the standard clinical hour, and streamlining input and processing of clients' data related to their participation in therapeutic activities. Unfortunately, the scientific study of these programs has seriously lagged behind their purported potential, and these interventions pose important ethical and professional questions.

Computer-Based Programs

Information

A number of studies have demonstrated that computers can provide information effectively and economically. An analysis of a large number of studies of computer-assisted instruction (CAI) found that CAI is consistently effective in improving knowledge (Fletcher-Flinn & Gravatt, 1995). Surprisingly, few studies evaluating the use of CAI for providing information related to mental health or psychotherapy have been conducted.

Assessment

Traditional paper-based self-report instruments are easily adapted to the computer format and offer a number of advantages that include ensuring data completeness and standardization. Research has found that computer-administered assessment instruments work as well as other kinds of self-report instruments and as well as therapist-administered ones.

Clients may feel less embarrassed about reporting sensitive or potentially stigmatizing information (e.g., about sexual behavior or illegal drug use) during a computer-assisted assessment than during a face-to-face assessment, allowing for more accurate estimates of mental health behaviors. Studies show that more symptoms, including suicidal thoughts, are reported during computer-assisted interviews than face-to-face interviews. Overall, the evidence suggests that computers can make assessments more efficient, more accurate, and less expensive. Yet computer-based assessment interviews do not allow for clinical intuition and nuance, assessment of behavior, and nonverbal emotional expression, nor do they foster a therapeutic alliance between client and therapist as information is collected.

Recently, handheld computers or personal digital assistants (PDAs) have been used to collect real-time, naturalistic data on a variety of variables. For example, clients can record their thoughts, behaviors, mood, and other variables at the same time and when directed to do so by an alarm or through instructions from the program. The assessment of events as they occur avoids retrospective recall biases. PDAs can be programmed to beep to cue a response and also to check data to determine, for instance, if responses are in the right range. The data are easily downloaded into computer databases for further analysis. PDAs with interactive transmission capabilities further expand the potential for real-time data collection. Although PDAs have been demonstrated to be useful for research, they have not been incorporated into clinical practice.

Computer-Assisted Psychotherapy

Much research on computer-based programs has focused on anxiety disorders (Newman, Consoli, & Taylor, 1997). Researchers have developed computer programs that direct participants through exercises in relaxation and restfulness; changes in breathing frequency, regularity, and pattern; gradual and progressive exposure to aspects of the situation, sensation, or objects they are afraid of; and changes in thinking patterns. Although the majority of studies report symptom reduction, most are uncontrolled trials or case studies and have additional methodological weaknesses (e.g., small sample sizes, no follow-up to assess whether treatment gains are maintained, focus on individuals who do not have clinical diagnoses).

Computer programs have been developed to reduce symptoms of simple phobias, panic disorder, obsessive-compulsive disorder (OCD), generalized anxiety disorder, and social phobia. In a multi-center, international treatment trial (Kenardy et al., 2002), study participants who received a primary diagnosis of panic disorder were randomly assigned to one of four groups: (a) a group that received 12 sessions of therapist-delivered cognitive behavior therapy (CBT), (b) a group that received 6 sessions of therapist-delivered CBT augmented by use of a handheld computer, (c) a group that received 6 sessions of therapist-delivered CBT augmented with a manual, or (d) a control group that was assigned to a wait list. Assessments at the end of treatment and 6 months later showed that the 12-session CBT and the 6-session CBT with the computer were equally effective. The results suggested that use of a handheld computer can reduce therapist contact time without compromising outcomes and may speed the rate of improvement.

An interactive computer program was developed to help clients with OCD, which is considered one type of anxiety disorder. The computer provided three weekly 45-min sessions of therapy involving vicarious exposure to their obsessive thoughts and response prevention (a technique by which clients with OCD are taught and encouraged not to engage in their customary rituals when they have an urge to do so). Compared with a control group, the clients who received the intervention had significantly greater improvement in symptoms. In a follow-up study with clients diagnosed with OCD, computer guided telephone behavior therapy was effective; however, clinician-guided behavior therapy was even more effective. Thus, computer-guided behavior therapy can be a helpful first step in treating patients with OCD, particularly when clinician-guided behavior therapy is unavailable. Computers have also been used to help treat individuals with other anxiety disorders, including social phobia and generalized anxiety disorder, a condition characterized by excessive worry and constant anxiety without specific fears or avoidances.

CBT also has been adapted for the computer-delivered treatment of depressive disorders. Selmi, Klein, Greist, Sorrell, and Erdman (1990) conducted the only randomized, controlled treatment trial comparing computer- and therapist-administered CBT for depression. Participants who met the study's criteria for major, minor, or intermittent depressive disorder were randomly assigned to computer-administered CBT, therapist-administered CBT, or a wait-list control. Compared with the control group, both treatment groups reported significant improvements on depression indices. The treatment groups did not differ from each other, and treatment gains were maintained at a 2-month follow-up.

Little information exists on the use of computer-assisted therapy for treating patients with complicated anxiety disorders or other mental health problems. Thus, further study is needed.

The Internet

Internet-based programs have several advantages over stand-alone computer-delivered programs. The Internet makes health care information and programs accessible to individuals who may have economic, transportation, or other restrictions that limit access to face-to-face services. The Internet is constantly available and accessible from a variety of locations. Because text and other information on the Internet can be presented in a variety of formats, languages, and styles, and at various educational levels, it is possible to tailor messages to the learning preferences and strengths of the user. The Internet can facilitate the collection, coordination, dissemination, and interpretation of data. These features allow for interactivity among the various individuals (e.g., physicians, clients, family members, caregivers) who may participate in a comprehensive treatment plan. As guidelines, information, and other aspects of programs change, it is possible to rapidly update information on Web pages. The medium also allows for personalization of information. Users may select features and information most relevant to them, and, conversely, programs can automatically determine a user's needs and strengths and display content accordingly.

Information

Patients widely search the Internet for mental health information. For example, the National Institute of Mental Health (NIMH) public information Web site receives more than 7 million "hits" each month. However, the mental health information on commercial Web sites is often inaccurate, misleading, or related to commercial interests. Sites sponsored by nonprofit organizations provide better and more balanced information, but search engines often list for-profit sites before they generate nonprofit sites. Furthermore, education Web sites rarely follow solid pedagogical principles.

Screening and Assessment

Many mental health Web sites have implemented screening programs that assess individuals for signs or symptoms of various psychiatric disorders. These programs generally recommend that participants who score above a predetermined cutoff contact a mental health provider for further assessment. The NIMH and many other professional organizations provide high-quality, easily accessible information combined with screening instruments. Houston and colleagues (2001) evaluated the use of a Web site that offered a computerized version of the Center for Epidemiological Studies' depression scale (CES-D; Ogles, France, Lunnen, Bell, & Goldfarb, 1998). The scale was completed 24,479 times during the 8-month study period. Fifty-eight percent of participants screened positive for depression, and fewer than half of those had previously been treated for depression. The Internet can incorporate interactive screening, which already has been extensively developed for desktop computers. Screening can then be linked to strategies that are designed to increase the likelihood that a participant will accept a referral and initiate further assessment or treatment.

On-Line Support Groups

Because Internet-delivered group interventions can be accessed constantly from any location that has Internet access, they offer distinct advantages over their face-to-face counterparts. Face-to-face support groups often are difficult to schedule, meet at limited times and locations, and must accommodate inconsistent attendance patterns because of variations in participants' health status and schedules. On-line groups have the potential to help rural residents and individuals who are chronically ill or physically or psychiatrically disabled increase their access to psychological interventions.

A wide array of social support groups is available to consumers in synchronous (i.e., participants on-line at the same time) or asynchronous formats. The Pew Internet and American Life Project (www.pewinternet.org) estimated that 28% of Internet users have attended an on-line support group for a medical condition or personal problem on at least one occasion. After a morning television show featured Edward M. Kennedy, Jr., promoting free on-line support groups sponsored by the Wellness Community (www.wellness-community.org), the organization received more than 440,000 inquiries during the following week! The majority of published studies on Internet-based support groups suggest that the groups are beneficial; however, scientific understanding of how and when is limited. Studies that examine the patterns of discourse that occur in these groups indicate that members' communication is similar to that found in face-to-face support groups (e.g., high levels of mutual support, acceptance, positive feelings).

Only a few controlled studies have examined the effects of Internet-based support programs. One such study investigated the effects of a program named Bosom Buddies on reducing psychosocial distress in women with breast cancer (Winzelberg et al., in press). Compared with a wait-list control group, the intervention group reported significantly reduced depression, cancer-related trauma, and perceived stress.

On-Line Consultation

On-line consultation with "experts" is readily available on the Internet. There are organizations for on-line therapists (e.g., the International Society for Mental Health Online, www.ismho.org) and sites that verify the credentials of on-line providers. However, little is known about the efficacy, reach, utility, or other aspects of on-line consultation.

Advocacy

The Internet has become an important medium for advocacy and political issues. Many organizations use the Internet to facilitate communication among members and to encourage members to support public policy (e.g., the National Alliance for the Mentally Ill, www.nami.org).

Internet-Based Psychotherapy

The Internet facilitates the creation of treatment programs that combine a variety of interactive components. The basic components that can be combined include psychoeducation; social support; chat groups; monitoring of symptoms, progress, and use of the program; feedback; and interactions with providers. Although many psychotherapy programs developed for desktop computers and manuals are readily translatable to the Internet format, surprisingly few have been adapted in this way, and almost none have been evaluated. Studies show that Internet-based treatments are effective for reducing symptoms of panic disorder. Compared with patients in a wait-list control group, those who participated in an Internet-based posttraumatic stress group reported significantly greater improvements on trauma-related symptoms. During the initial 6-month period of operation, an Australian CBT program for depression, MoodGYM, had more than 800,000 hits (Christensen, Griffiths, & Korten, 2002). In an uncontrolled study of a small subsample of participants who registered on this site, program use was associated with significant decreases in anxiety and depression. Internet-based programs also have been shown to reduce symptoms of eating disorders and associated behaviors. Users consistently report high satisfaction with these programs.

Treatment programs for depression, mood swings, and other mental health disorders are being designed to blend computer-assisted psychotherapy and psychoeducation with case management (in which a therapist helps to manage a client's problems by following treatment and therapy guidelines) and telephone-based care. These programs might also include limited face-to-face interventions, medication, and support groups. The effectiveness of these programs remains to be demonstrated.

Eventually, the most important use of the Internet might be to deliver integrated, home-based, case-managed, psychoeducational programs that are combined with some face-to-face contact and support groups. Unfortunately, although a number of such programs are "under development," none have been evaluated in controlled trials.

Ethical and Professional Issues

Web-based interventions present a number of ethical and professional issues (Hsiung, 2001). Privacy is perhaps the most significant concern. The Internet creates an environment where information about patients can be easily accessed and disseminated. Patients may purposely or inadvertently disclose private information about themselves and, in on-line support groups, about their peers. Although programs can be password-protected, and electronic records must follow federal privacy guidelines, participants must be clearly informed that confidentiality of records cannot be guaranteed.

Internet interventions create the potential that services will be provided to patients who have not been seen by a professional or who live in other states or countries where the professionals providing the services are not licensed to provide therapy. Professional organizations are struggling to develop guidelines to address these concerns (e.g., Hsiung, 2001; Kane & Sands, 1998).

Because of its accessibility and relative anonymity, patients may use the Internet during crises and report suicidal and homicidal thoughts. Although providers who use Internet support groups develop statements to clearly inform patients that the medium is not to be used for psychiatric emergencies, patients may ignore these instructions. Thus, providers need to identify ancillary procedures to reduce and manage potential crises.

Given the continuing advances in technology and the demonstrated effectiveness and advantages of computer- and Internet-based interventions, one might expect that providers would readily integrate these programs into their standard care practice. Yet few do, in part because programs that are easy to install and use are not available, there is no professional or market demand for the use of computer-assisted therapy, and practitioners may have ethical and professional concerns about applying this technology in their clinical practice. Thus, in the near future this technology may primarily be used for situations in which the cost-effectiveness advantages are particularly great.

Conclusion

Computers have the potential to make psychological assessments more efficient, more accurate, and less expensive. Computer-assisted therapy appears to be as effective as face-to-face therapy for treating anxiety disorders and depression and can be delivered at lower cost. However, applications of this technology are in the early stages.

A high priority is to clearly demonstrate the efficacy of this approach, particularly compared with standard face-to-face, "manualized" treatments that have been shown to be effective for common mental health disorders. Studies that compare two potentially efficacious treatments require large samples for us to safely conclude that the therapies are comparable if no statistically significant differences are found. Kenardy et al. (2002) demonstrated that multi-site, international studies sampling large populations could be conducted relatively inexpensively, in part because the intervention they examined was standardized. If a treatment's efficacy is demonstrated, the next step would be to determine if the therapy, provided by a range of mental health professionals, is useful in large, diverse populations. Examination of combinations of therapies (e.g., CBT plus medication) and treatment modalities (Taylor, Cameron, Newman, & Junge, 2002) should follow. As the empirical study of this technology advances, research might examine the utility and cost-effectiveness of adapting these approaches to treating everyone in a community who wants therapy.

Continued use of the Internet to provide psychosocial support and group therapy is another promising avenue. As in the case of individual therapy, research is needed to compare the advantages and disadvantages between Internet and face-to-face groups, determine which patients benefit from which modality, compare the effectiveness of professionally moderated groups and self- or peer-directed groups, and compare the effectiveness of synchronous and asynchronous groups.

As research progresses, new and exciting applications can be explored. Because on-line text is stored, word content can be examined. This information may teach us more about the therapeutic process or may automatically alert providers to patients who are depressed, dangerous, or deteriorating.

Although research in many aspects of computer-assisted therapy is needed, and the professional and ethical concerns are substantial, computers and the Internet are likely to play a progressively important role in providing mental health assessment and interventions to clients. Thus, mental health professionals will need to decide how they will incorporate such programs into their practices.

Recommended Reading

Taylor, C. B., Winzelberg, A. J., & Celio, A. A. (2001). The use of interactive media to prevent eating disorders. In R. H. Striegal-Moore & L. Smolak (Eds., *Eating disorders: Innovative directions in research and practice* (pp. 255–269). Washington, DC: American Psychological Association.

Yellowlees, P. (2001). *Your guide to e-health: Third millennium medicine on the Internet.* Brisbane, Australia: University of Queensland Press.

References

Christensen, H., Griffiths, K. M., & Korten, A. (2002). Web-based cognitive behavior therapy: Analysis of site usage and changes in depression and anxiety scores. *Journal of Medical Internet Research, 4*(1), Article e3. Retrieved July 16, 2002, from http://www.jmir.org/2002/1/e3

Fletcher-Flinn, C. M., & Gravatt, B. (1995). The efficacy of computer assisted instruction (CAI): A meta-analysis. *Journal of Educational Computing Research, 3,* 219–241.

Houston, T. K., Cooper, L. A., Vu, H. T., Kahn, J., Toser, J., & Ford, D. E. (2001). Screening the public for depression through the Internet. *Psychiatric Services, 52,* 362–367.

Hsiung, R. C. (2001). Suggested principles of professional ethics for the online provision of mental health services. *Medinfo, 10,* 296–300.

Kane, B., & Sands, D. Z. (1998). Guidelines for the clinical use of electronic mail with patients: The AMIA Internet Working Group, Task Force on Guidelines for the Use of Clinic-Patient Electronic Mail. *Journal of the American Medical Informatics Association, 5,* 104–111.

Kenardy, J. A., Dow, M. G. T., Johnston, D. W., Newman, M. G., Thompson, A., & Taylor, C. B. (2002). *A comparison of delivery methods of cognitive behavioural therapy for panic disorder: An international multicentre trial.* Manuscript submitted for publication.

Newman, M. G., Consoli, A., & Taylor, C. B. (1997). Computers in assessment and cognitive behavioral treatment of clinical disorders: Anxiety as a case in point. *Behavior Therapy, 28,* 211–235.

Ogles, B. M., France, C. R., Lunnen, K. M., Bell, M. T., & Goldfarb, M. (1998). Computerized depression screening and awareness. *Community Mental Health Journal, 34* (1), 27–38.

Selmi, P. M., Klein, M. H., Greist, J. H., Sorrell, S. P., & Erdman, H. P. (1990). Computer-administered cognitive-behavioral therapy for depression. *American Journal of Psychiatry, 147,* 51–56.

Taylor, C. B., Cameron, R., Newman, M., & Junge, J. (2002). Issues related to combining risk factor reduction and clinical treatment for eating disorders in defined populations. *The Journal of Behavioral Health Services and Research, 29,* 81–90.

Winzelberg, A. J., Classen, C., Alpers, G., Roberts, H., Koopman, C., Adams, R., Ernst, H., Dev, P., & Taylor, C. B. (in press). An evaluation of an Internet support group for women with primary breast cancer. *Cancer.*

Note

1. Address correspondence to C. Barr Taylor, Department of Psychiatry, Stanford University Medical Center, Stanford, CA 94305-5722; e-mail: btaylor@stanford.edu.

Index

A

abnormal pathology, 53
abuse: physical, 101; repressed, 149
academic studies, of psychology, 3–5
accountability, societal, 7
adolescence. *See* teenagers
affection reaction, 95–96
Age-Related Eye Disease Study (AREDS), 46, 47, 48
aggression, self-esteem and, 153
aging, 43–44, 46, 47, 48, 106, 134–136, 139–143
alcoholism, 31
Allied Dunbar National Fitness Survey, 121
Allport, Gordon, 10
Alzheimer's disease, 35, 38, 70, 71, 106, 123
ambition, 112–117
American Dialect Society (ADS), 83
American Dictionary of the English Language, 79
Anatomy of Melancholy, The (Burton), 176
anger, 67, 107
antidepressant drugs, 188, 195
"antipsychiatry" movement, 177, 187
anxiety disorder, 8, 31, 88, 164, 199
Armed Services Vocational Aptitude Battery, 8
Asia, coping with trauma in, 144, 145
attention-deficit hyperactivity disorder (ADHD), 63, 64, 65
attitudes, inherent flaws in, 158
authority figure, obedience to, 159
autism, 38
automakers, group dynamics and, 10
autonomic nervous system responses, conditioning, 7

B

baby boomers: aging and, 139–143; in Saudi Arabia, 168, 169
Bandura, Albert, 11, 14
bariatric surgery, 125
basal metabolic rate, 121
BBC Prison Study, 159
behavior(s), 99, 188; emotional, 96; genetics and, 31; inappropriate, 8; individual, 7; flaws in, 158; modification, 8; prejudice and, 9–10; shaping, 14
"behavioral economics," 15
Behavioral Risk Factor Surveillance System (BRFSS), 119
Bell Curve, The, 104
BICEPS, combat stress and, 183
Binet, Alfred, 8
bipolar disorder, 88, 178, 194
birth control, 13–14
blind obedience studies, 12
blindess, 45; age-related, 43
Blink (Gladwell), 88, 90
body mass index, 118, 119, 120, 124, 125
brain: damage, 100; electric stimulation of, 195, 196–197; injury, 70; neuroscience and, 28–29; stress and, 194; structure of, 35–39; study, 90, 91
BrainCogs software, 61
brain-derived neurotrophic factor (BDNF), cortisol and, 196, 197
Brief Tour of Human Consciousness (Ramachandran), 28–29

Brown v. Board of Education of Topeka, KS, 9–10
Burgess Unabridged (Burgess), 82

C

Carroll, Lewis, 79
CAT scanning, 35
cataracts, 45–49
Catholic nuns, study of, 106
causality: concept of, 24–25; understanding of, 24
CB1 receptors, 124
cerebrospinal fluid (CSF), 35
Changed Identities: The Challenge of the New Generation in Saudi Arabia (Yamani), 168
character: critiquing, 165; Freud on, 148
children, 9; amnesia and, 68; character development and, 148; emotions and, 101; immigrant, 115; mothers and, 164; parenting and, 10, 130–133; self-esteem and, 152
Clare, Linda, 70
classical conditioning, 8
Classroom Performance System, 60
clinical depression, 8, 194, 197
Clinton, Bill, 116
coercive psychiatry, 187
cognitive management skills, 61
cognitive neuroscience, 88
cognitive psychology, 11, 72
cognitive science, 4–5
combat stress, 182–183
Combs, Sean, 116
Comfortably Contents, retirees as, 142
communication, 161; adolescents and, 138; study of, 6
compassion, 110
competition, 114
computed tomography (CT), 35
computer programs: psychotherapy and, 198–202; simulations, 61; software, for learning, 59–62
concept mapping tools, 60
consciousness, 53, 95, 96
consultation, online, 200
Core Concepts in Psychology (Zimbardo, Weber, & Johnson), 6
correlations, concept of, 24–25
corticotrophin-releasing factor (CRF), stress and, 196, 197
cortisol, 115, 196
criminal justice, 11–12, 189
critical thinking skills, developing, 19
Cronbach, Lee, 99
Cruise, Tom, 116
Csikszentmihalyi, Mihaly, 106
CTOOLS software, 60
culture, ambition and, 114
Curse of the Self: Self-Awareness, Egotism and the Quality of Human Life, The (Leary), 167
cynicism, 20–21

D

Damasio, Antonio R., 100
dating service, 141, 154
deception, detection of, 161–163
decision making, 85, 100
Deeper Meaning of Liff, The,

dementia, 70
DePaulo, Bella, 161, 164, 165, 166
depression, 31, 175–181, 194–197, 199; clinical, 8 community studies of, 178–179; constituencies for, 179–181; diagnosing, 177; history of, 175–177; from sadness to, 177–178
developmental psychologists, 3–4, 9
Devils Dictionary, The, 80
diabetes, 139; obesity and, 119, 124; type 2, 119, 125, 139
Diagnostic and Statistical Manual of Mental Disorder 175, 176, 177, 178, 179, 180, 181, 189
dictionary, 78–84
Dictionary of the Future: The Words, Terms and Trends That Define the Way We'll Live, Work and Talk (Popcorn and Hanft), 83
diet: high-fat, 124; low-fat, 123; strategies, 122
disaster, emotional consequences of, 144
Discovering Psychology, 6
discrimination, 9–10; obesity and, 119
dream, as precognition, 24
dyslexia, video games and, 13
dyslipidaemia, obesity and, 119
dysthymia, 179, 194

E

education: desegregation in, 9–10, 12; multiple intelligences theory and, 73, 74; psychology and, 12, 30; in Saudi Arabia, 170; teaching for understanding in, 59–62
Educational Testing Service (ETS), 60
Ekman, Paul, 161, 165
elderly, 9, 13, 43–44, 106, 134–136, 139–143
emotion(s), 68, 99–105, 107, 109, 110; four-branch model of, 100; negative, 101; perceiving and using, 100–101; positive, 95–98, 101, 106–111; racial prejudice and, 9–10; thinking and, 100; unconscious, 95–98; understanding and managing, 101–102
emotional intelligence, 99–105
Emotional Intelligence (Goldman), 104
emotional quotient (EQ), 99
environment, factors of, 37, 120
Epidemiological Catchment Area Study (ECA), 179
ethics, Internet and, 200–201
exercise, weight loss and, 123–124
eye sight, 45–49
eyewitness testimony, 11–12

F

facial expression, 101, 107
fascinoma, 53
"Fast ForWard," 13
fear, 107, 191–192
feedback: accurate, 166; direct, 165–166
floccinaucinihilipilification, 151, 152
"free association," 149–150
Freud, Sigmund, 8, 9, 65–68, 88, 148–150, 176, 180–181
friendship, social relationships and, 103
Funker, David C., 158, 159, 160, 165, 166

Index

G

Gardner, Howard, 72, 99
gene(s): brain and, 36; environment and, 37; influence of, 30–34; obesity and, 120, 125
g-force, unconsciousness and, 53
Gizmos software, 61
G-LOC, 53, 54
gratitude, 108–109
gray:white ratio, of brain, 38
GRE standardized testing, 8
Greyson scale, 53
grief, coping with, 144
group(s): dynamics, 10; influence of, 158–159

H

halothane, 53
happiness, 191
healing, 144–145
health-management programs, 13
hearing, sense of, 38, 43–44
heart disease, obesity and, 119
heritability, psychological traits and, 30–34
Heschl's gyrus (HG), 38
Hippocrates, 175–176
HIV infection, 14
hominid evolution, brain studies and, 36
hominid fossils, 37
human rights, psychiatry and, 187–190
hypertension, obesity and, 119

I

In a Word, 80
Industrial Revolution, retirement and, 142
Inspiration software, 60
intelligence(s): 30, 99, 103; intellectual, 8; multiple, 72–75
internal states, 99
International Society for Research on Emotions (ISRE), 103
Internet-based psychotherapy, 198–202
interpersonal cognitive problem solving skills (ICPS), 12
intuition, flawed, 85–87
Iraq, 182, 183
Islam, 169

J

Jacques, Paul, 46
"jigsaw classrooms," 12
Jung, Carl, 9

K

Kahneman, Daniel, 85
Kandel, Eric, 191–193
ketamine, 53
King Abdulaziz ibn Saud, 170
King Abdullah, 168
Kirsch, Ned, 71
Krueger, Joachim I., 158, 159, 160

L

language, developing, 78–84
Lear, Edward, 79
learning: disabilities, 63; psychology and, 59; teaching for understanding in, 59–62
Leary, Mark, 164, 165, 167
Leichtman, Michelle, 68, 69
lepin deficiency, 120
lie(s), detecting, 161–163

life expectancy, obesity and, 118
lobal expansion, 36, 37
Logal Science Explore Series, 61
longevity, 134, 139–140
Lopez, Jennifer, 116
lutein, 43, 46, 47, 48

M

macula degeneration, 45, 47–49
magnetic resonance imaging (MRI), 13, 35, 36, 38, 39, 71, 91
manic depression, 194; criteria of, 178
marketplace: imaging and, 89; mature, 141
marriage, stress and, 130–133
matchmaking, electronic, 154
Mayer-Salovey-Caruso Emotional Intelligence Test (MSCEIT), 102, 103, 104
McHugh, Paul, 189
Meaning of Liff, The, 80
media: communicating with, 7; motivation and, 13, 14
Mednick's Remote Associates Test, 108
melancholia, 176
memory, 191; emotions and, 67–68; enhancers, 70–71; flexibility of, 63–71; recall, 65, 68; rehabilitation, 70; repression, 65, 66, 149; research, 69; technologies, 71; training, 64; tunnel, 67
mental ability, genetic influence on, 31
mental health, 188; human rights and, 187–190; Internet and, 198–202; unconscious processing and, 88
messages, positive, 14–15
metabolic diseases, chronic, 119
metacognitiion, understanding and, 59–62
Metalunan aliens, 36
"metaperceptions," 164, 165, 166
metaphor, unconscious association and, 89
metaphysic(s): pseudoscience and, 22; religious claims and, 22
Milgram, Stanley, 12, 159
military, combat stress and, 182–183
Mill, John Stuart, 24
Miller, George, 7, 63
mind, mysteries of, 88–91
MindMapper software, 60
misconceptions, of students, 59–62
mmpi 2, clinical mental disorders testing and, 155
Modern English Usage (Fowler), 82
mood(s): enhancer, 187; states, normal and pathological, 176
Morse, Melvin, 53, 54
mothers, 164. parenting
motivation, 89, 99; ambition and, 115; intrinsic, 13; research in learning and conditioning and, 7; unconscious, 9
MRI, 35, 36, 38, 39, 193
Mullen, Mary, 68
Multi-factor Emotional Intelligence Scale (MEIS), 102, 104
multiple intelligences, theory of, 72–75
Muslim, 170
Myers-Briggs Indicator, 154
mystics, 52
myths, psychology and, 20

N

nanobiotics, 135
narcissism, 166
National Alliance for the Mentally Ill (NAMI), 180
National Association for Self-Esteem, 151

National Co-Morbidity Study (NCS), 179
National Food Survey, 120–121
National Institute of Mental Health (NIMH), 179
Native Americans, 69
near-death experiences, 52–55
neural code, 88
neuroanatomy, 35
neuroimaging technology, 88
neurological diseases, study of, 35
neurological syndrome, 28
neuroscience, 28–29, 35, 89, 97, 193
neurotic disorders, 8
Niederle, Muriel, 114
Not Necessarily the News, 80
nutraceuticals, 141

O

obesity, 118–127; causes of, 120; macula degeneration and, 49; management of, 122–125; pharmacological interventions for, 124; prevention of, 122; psychological factors affecting, 121–122
obsessive-compulsive disorder, 199
Office of Public Opinion Research, 10
operant conditioning principles, 7
Our Inner Ape (de Waal), 115
out-of-body experience, 52–55
Oxford English Dictionary, 78, 79

P

panic disorder, 8, 31, 199
paranormal claims, 20, 21
parcellation, 36
parenting, 8, 9, 69; child bonding and, 164; stress and, 130–133
pathological depression, 181
Paxil, 175, 196
PDE (phosphodiesterase) inhibitor, 196
Penfield, Wilder, 54, 55
perception: emotions and, 100–101; process of, 86
personal digital assistants (PDAs), 71
personality, 30, 31; Big Five model of, 102; testing, 154–155; traits, 102
persuasion, study of, 6
PET, 35
pharmaceutical companies, 180
pharmacotherapy, 192, 195–196
phobia, 8, 199
phrenology, 35–39, 89
physical activity, obesity and, 121, 123–124
planum temporale, 38
politics, polling and, 10
"pop psych," 9, 72
Population Communications International (PCI), 14
population control, 13–14
"Positive Psychology," 14
positron emission tomography (PET), 35
posttraumatic stress disorder (PTSD), 12, 54, 65
preconception, influence of, on learning, 59–62
Predicting New Words: The Secrets of Their Success (Metcalf), 83
prejudice, 9–10
prescription drugs, 189
problem-solving, 59
Procustes analysis, 37
Prozac, 175
pseudoscience, science and, 19–23
psychoanalysis, 148, 149

psychology: academic studies of, 3–5; applied, 8; contributions of, 8; research of, 6–18
Psychology and Life (Ruch & Zimbardo), 6
psychopathology, 177
psychopharmacology, 106, 187
psychotherapy, 8, 106, 191–193, 195; computer programs and, 198–202

Q

"Quiet Rage: The Sanford Prison Experiment," 12

R

racial prejudice, 9–10
reactive depression, 176
reading disabilities, 63
reason, emotions and, 100
regions of interest (ROIs), on brain surface, 36
"rehirement," 142
reinforcement, positive, 8
religion, 22; heritability of, 33
repressed memories, 149
researchers, psychology, 3–5
retirement, 135, 142–143; baby boomers and, 139–143
"Re-Visioning Retirement" study, 143
reward, in learning and conditioning, 7
Rice, Condoleezza, 116
robots, biological, 135

S

sadness, 107, 179, 180; depression and, 177–178
safety, behavior-based (BBS), 11
Sanford Prison Experiment, 12
SAT testing, 8
Saudi Arabia, 168–171
Scheff, Thomas, 177
schizophrenia, 31, 38, 88, 90, 188, 189
Scholastic Aptitude Test (SAT), 104
school(s). *See* education
science, pseudoscience and, 19–23
Seattle study, 53
SEAR program, of Navy, 12
segregation, 12
self-awareness, 166–167
self-directed change, 9
self-esteem, 151–153, 176
self-image, 152, 164–167
Self-Report Emotional Intelligence Test (SREIT), 102, 103
Seligman, Martin, 14, 106
senses: hearing, 38, 43–44; smell, 44, 88, 90; taste, 44, 50–51; vision, 43
September 11, 2001, 12, 68, 108, 169, 171
serotonin, 124, 175, 187
sex, 37–38
Shakespeare, William, 78
shyness, 166
Shyness: A Bold New Approach (Carducci), 166
Sick-and-Tireds, elderly as, 142–143

SimCity software, 60
Simonton, Dean, 113, 114
single photon emission computed tomography (SPECT) scans, 55
6-*n*-propylthiouracil, 50
"sixth" sense, 44
skepticism, 20–21
Skinner, B. F., 7, 8
smell, sense of, 44, 88, 90
social anxiety, 164, 166, 188
social shortcomings, 158–160
Social Importance of Self-Esteem, The, 151
"social intelligence," 99–100
social modeling, theory of, 11
social phobia, 188, 199
social psychology, 11, 158–160
social relationships, 103
social thinking, 160
socioeconomic status, children and, 30
spatial cognition, principles of, 11
Spears, Britney, 116
SPECT (single photon emission computed tomography) scans, 55
Sri Lana, disaster management in, 144
Stanford Prison Experiment, 158, 159
Statistical Manual for the Use of Hospitals for Mental Diseases, 176
status anxiety, 115
stereotyping, 9, 10
Stewart, Martha, 116
stimuli: affective, 97; subliminal, 96, 97
storytelling, power of, 14
stress, 54; combat, 182–183; depressive disorders and, 194, 196; high achievers and, 115; negative emotion and, 110; trauma and, 65; psychological, 9; violence and trauma, 12, 144–145
students, techniques for learning and, 59–62
subliminal stimuli, 96, 97
success, ambition and, 112–117
suicide, thoughts of, 178
supertaste, 50
support group, Internet, 200
Swedish Obese Subjects study, 125
Szasz, Thomas, 177, 187–189

T

taste, sense of, 44, 50–51
teaching, for understanding, 59–62
technology, as learning tools, 59–62
teenagers, 137–138; self-esteem and, 152–153
theory methodology, 72
therapy, 149; cognitive behavior, 8, 199; depressive disorder, 194–197; drug, 125, 149, 189; electroconvulsive, 195, 196–197; group, 144; magnetic seizure, 197; talk, 8, 149; touch, 12–13
thinking, 19, 60, 85–87
This Island Earth 36
Thorndike, Robert, 99
"360" instruments, 102
topiramate, 124
transcranial magnetic stimulation (TMS), 197

trauma, 12, 65, 144
Trump, Donald, 116
twin studies, 33; genes and, 36

U

understanding, teaching for, 59–62
untreated mental disorder, 178–179
urban legends, psychology and, 20

V

vagus nerve stimulation, 197
Vesterlund, Lise, 114
violence prevention, 12
vision, sense of, 11, 38, 43, 45–49, 107–108
visual processing tasks, 107–108
visually impaired, aids for, 11
visual-spatial tests, 38
vitamins, antioxidant, 46, 48
vocational testing, 8
volumetrics, 35
von Bismarck, Otto, 139
Vygotsky, Lev, 73

W

Walden Two (Skinner), 7
Wang, Qi, 69
Want, Vera, 116
Wanted Words 2 (Farrow), 81
WebLearn software, 60
Webster, Noah, 78–79
Wechsler, David, 99
weight, 118–127; management programs, 122–125; over-, 47; *See also* obesity
wellness movement, 140–141
WHO MONICA project, 119
Why God Won't Go Away (Newberg and D'Aquili), 55
Winfrey, Oprah, 116
Wolpe, Joseph, 8
women: brain and, 37–38; competition and, 114; cosmetic therapies and, 141; education of, 14; emotions of, 99; employers and, 140; family planning and, 13–14; Muslim, 170; parenting and, 130–133; psychology and, 13; in Saudi Arabia, 169, 170; vitamins and, 46
Woods, Tiger, 116
word coinage, recreational, 78–84
Wozniak, Steve, 113

Y

Yale Communication and Attitude Change Program, 6

Z

Zagon aliens, 36
Zaltman, Gerald, 89, 91
Zimbardo, Philip G., 158
Zoombinis software, 61

Test Your Knowledge Form

We encourage you to photocopy and use this page as a tool to assess how the articles in *Annual Editions* expand on the information in your textbook. By reflecting on the articles you will gain enhanced text information. You can also access this useful form on a product's book support Web site at *http://www.mhcls.com/online/*.

NAME: DATE:
_____

TITLE AND NUMBER OF ARTICLE:
_____

BRIEFLY STATE THE MAIN IDEA OF THIS ARTICLE:

_____

LIST THREE IMPORTANT FACTS THAT THE AUTHOR USES TO SUPPORT THE MAIN IDEA:

_____

WHAT INFORMATION OR IDEAS DISCUSSED IN THIS ARTICLE ARE ALSO DISCUSSED IN YOUR TEXTBOOK OR OTHER READINGS THAT YOU HAVE DONE? LIST THE TEXTBOOK CHAPTERS AND PAGE NUMBERS:

_____

LIST ANY EXAMPLES OF BIAS OR FAULTY REASONING THAT YOU FOUND IN THE ARTICLE:

_____

LIST ANY NEW TERMS/CONCEPTS THAT WERE DISCUSSED IN THE ARTICLE, AND WRITE A SHORT DEFINITION:

We Want Your Advice

ANNUAL EDITIONS revisions depend on two major opinion sources: one is our Advisory Board, listed in the front of this volume, which works with us in scanning the thousands of articles published in the public press each year; the other is you—the person actually using the book. Please help us and the users of the next edition by completing the prepaid article rating form on this page and returning it to us. Thank you for your help!

ANNUAL EDITIONS: Psychology 07/08

ARTICLE RATING FORM

Here is an opportunity for you to have direct input into the next revision of this volume.
We would like you to rate each of the articles listed below, using the following scale:

1. **Excellent: should definitely be retained**
2. **Above average: should probably be retained**
3. **Below average: should probably be deleted**
4. **Poor: should definitely be deleted**

Your ratings will play a vital part in the next revision.
Please mail this prepaid form to us as soon as possible.
Thanks for your help!

RATING	ARTICLE	RATING	ARTICLE
	1. Why Study Psychology?		32. Deception Detection
	2. Does Psychology Make a Significant Difference in Our Lives?		33. Mirror, Mirror: Seeing Yourself As Others See You
	3. The 10 Commandments of Helping Students Distinguish Science from Pseudoscience in Psychology		34. Young and Restless
			35. The Age of Depression
	4. Causes and Correlations		36. Soldier Support
	5. The Amazing Brain: Is Neuroscience the Key to What Makes Us Human?		37. The Quandary Over Mental Illness
			38. The Discover Interview: Nobel Laureate Eric Kandel
	6. Genetic Influence on Human Psychological Traits		39. Offering Hope to the Emotionally Depressed
	7. The Structure of the Human Brain		40. Computer- and Internet-Based Psychotherapy Interventions
	8. Sensational Tune-ups		
	9. Eye Wise: Seeing Into the Future		
	10. A Matter of Taste		
	11. Extreme States		
	12. Teaching for Understanding		
	13. Memory Flexibility		
	14. Theory of Multiple Intelligences: Is It a Scientific Theory?		
	15. Shouldn't There Be a Word...?		
	16. What Was I Thinking?		
	17. Mysteries of the Mind		
	18. Unconscious Emotion		
	19. Feeling Smart: The Science of Emotional Intelligence		
	20. The Value of Positive Emotions		
	21. Ambition: Why Some People Are Most Likely to Succeed		
	22. Obesity—An Epidemic of the Twenty-First Century: An Update for Psychiatrists		
	23. Why Newborns Cause Acrimony and Alimony		
	24. The Methuselah Report		
	25. A Peaceful Adolescence		
	26. Ageless Aging: The Next Era of Retirement		
	27. The Borders of Healing		
	28. Freud in Our Midst		
	29. Exploding the Self-Esteem Myth		
	30. The Testing of America		
	31. To Err Is Human		

(Continued on next page)

BUSINESS REPLY MAIL
FIRST CLASS MAIL PERMIT NO. 551 DUBUQUE IA

POSTAGE WILL BE PAID BY ADDRESEE

McGraw-Hill Contemporary Learning Series
2460 KERPER BLVD
DUBUQUE, IA 52001-9902

IhIhuIiIIIhuIIhuuIIhIuIuIuIIhuuIuIuII

ABOUT YOU

Name   Date

Are you a teacher? ❑   A student? ❑
Your school's name

Department

Address   City   State   Zip

School telephone #

YOUR COMMENTS ARE IMPORTANT TO US!

Please fill in the following information:
For which course did you use this book?

Did you use a text with this ANNUAL EDITION?   ❑   yes   ❑   no
What was the title of the text?

What are your general reactions to the *Annual Editions* concept?

Have you read any pertinent articles recently that you think should be included in the next edition? Explain.

Are there any articles that you feel should be replaced in the next edition? Why?

Are there any World Wide Web sites that you feel should be included in the next edition? Please annotate.

May we contact you for editorial input?   ❑   yes   ❑   no
May we quote your comments?   ❑   yes   ❑   no